# EFFECTIVE EXECUTIVE'S

**The Seven Core Skills Required to Turn Outlook into a Business Power Tool**

# GUIDE TO OUTLOOK 2002

# EFFECTIVE EXECUTIVE'S

**The Seven Core Skills Required to Turn Outlook into a Business Power Tool**

# GUIDE TO OUTLOOK 2002

Jason Gerend
Charles Bermant

REDMOND TECHNOLOGY PRESS

Effective Executive's Guide to Outlook 2002:
The Seven Core Skills Required to Turn Outlook into a Business Power Tool



Published by
Redmond Technology Press
8581 154th Avenue NE
Redmond, WA 98052
*www.redtechpress.com*

Library of Congress Catalog Card No: applied for

ISBN 1-931150-04-4

Printed and bound in the United States of America.

9 8 7 6 5 4 3 2 1

Distributed by
Independent Publishers Group
814 N. Franklin St.
Chicago, IL 60610
*www.ipgbook.com*

# Contents at a Glance


| | | |
|---|---|---|
| | Introduction | xvii |
| *Skill 1* | Getting Started with Outlook | 1 |
| *Skill 2* | Reading E-Mail | 31 |
| *Skill 3* | Sending E-Mail | 81 |
| *Skill 4* | Managing Your E-Mail | 127 |
| *Skill 5* | Using a Contacts List | 169 |
| *Skill 6* | Managing Your Time | 195 |
| *Skill 7* | Maintaining Outlook | 243 |

*Appendix A* **Using Notes** 271

*Appendix B* **Outlook and Exchange** 273

*Appendix C* **Automatically Processing Form Data** 287

**Glossary** 293

**Index** 301

# Contents

## Introduction xvii

What This Book Assumes About You ... xvii
How This Book Is Organized ... xviii
  Skill 1: Getting Started with Outlook ... xviii
  Skill 2: Reading E-Mail ... xviii
  Skill 3: Sending E-Mail ... xviii
  Skill 4: Managing Your E-Mail ... xviii
  Skill 5: Using a Contacts List ... xix
  Skill 6: Managing Your Time ... xix
  Skill 7: Maintaining Outlook ... xix
  Appendix A: Using Notes ... xix
  Appendix B: Outlook and Exchange ... xix
  Appendix C: Automatically Processing Form Data ... xx
Conventions Used in This Book ... xx

*Skill 1* **Getting Started With Outlook** 1

Getting an E-Mail Account ... 2
  Personal E-Mail ... 3
  One Box Is Not Enough ... 4

Setting Up Outlook .......... 4
Keep Home and Work Separate .......... 7
Using Outlook's Interface .......... 8
Be Careful What You Send .......... 10
Importing from Other Programs .......... 11
Importing E-Mail Messages and Addresses .......... 11
Importing E-Mail Account Settings .......... 13
Looks Matter .......... 15
Importing Data from Other Programs .......... 16
Setting Up Additional E-Mail Accounts .......... 21
Setting Up an LDAP Directory .......... 23
Getting Help .......... 25
Summary .......... 30

*Skill 2* **Reading E-Mail** **31**

Starting Outlook .......... 31
Checking for New Messages .......... 33
Sending and Receiving Mail .......... 33
Using the Send/Receive Progress Window .......... 34
Automatically Checking Your E-Mail .......... 36
Setting Up Send/Receive Groups .......... 38
Maximizing Slow or Expensive Internet Connections .......... 40
Maximizing High Speed Connections .......... 45
Reading Messages .......... 47
Get to the Point Already .......... 50

Working with Your Messages ........ 51
Sorting Messages ........ 51
Marking Messages You Want to Read Later ........ 53
Toolbar Tips ........ 58
Deleting Messages ........ 60
Saving Messages ........ 62
Nine Things You Can Do to Manage Your Messages ........ 65
Editing Messages ........ 67
Changing Message Fonts ........ 68
Printing Messages ........ 70
Working with Attachments ........ 72
Ask Before You Attach ........ 74
Protecting Yourself from Viruses and Hoaxes ........ 75
Using an Antivirus Program ........ 75
Don't Open Suspicious Attachments ........ 75
How to Spot a Hoax ........ 76
Using Outlook Today ........ 78
Summary ........ 80

*Skill 3* **Sending E-Mail** **81**

The Basics of Sending E-Mail ........ 81
Addressing Messages ........ 84
Entering an E-Mail Address or Name ........ 84
Selecting Addresses from a List ........ 86
Check Your Addresses ........ 88

Composing Messages ........................................................ 88
Writing Effective Messages ........................................................ 89
Avoid Flames ........................................................ 90
Changing Message Formats ........................................................ 91
Context Is King ........................................................ 95
Formatting HTML Messages ........................................................ 95
Postponing Messages ........................................................ 98
Attaching Files to Messages ........................................................ 102
Using E-Mail Signatures ........................................................ 104
Keep "Sigs" Simple ........................................................ 109
Changing the Appearance of Replies and Forwards ........................................................ 110
Writing in Another Language ........................................................ 115
Using Word as Your E-Mail Editor ........................................................ 115
Recovering a Message from a Crash ........................................................ 117
Sending and Delivering Messages ........................................................ 119
Preventing Immediate Message Delivery ........................................................ 119
Sending Mail with a Specific E-Mail Account ........................................................ 121
Sending (and Not Checking) E-Mail ........................................................ 122
Reviewing Sent Messages ........................................................ 123
Sent Mail's History Lesson ........................................................ 124
Summary ........................................................ 125

*Skill 4* **Managing Your E-Mail** **127**

Finding Messages ........................................................ 127
Finding Messages Related to Replies and Forwards ........................................................ 128
Sorting and Grouping Messages ........................................................ 129

Using the Find Tool ........ 131

Performing Advanced Searches ........ 134

Organizing Messages Using Folders ........ 137

Creating Folders ........ 138

Moving Your Messages ........ 140

Using the Organize Pane ........ 142

Using Message Templates ........ 143

Creating Message Templates ........ 143

Composing Messages Using Templates ........ 146

Adding Templates to the Outlook Bar ........ 147

Automatically Processing Your E-Mail ........ 151

Creating Rules Based on Existing Messages ........ 152

Creating Rules from Scratch ........ 156

Dealing with Junk Mail ........ 158

Control Your Address ........ 158

Nine Tips for Avoiding Spam ........ 159

Ignore and Delete ........ 160

Enabling Junk Mail Rules ........ 160

Adding to the Junk Senders List ........ 161

Creating More Powerful Junk Mail Rules ........ 162

Open to Interpretation ........ 167

Third-Party Anti-Spam Solutions ........ 167

Summary ........ 168

*Skill 5* **Using a Contacts List** **169**


Contacts and Address Book Overview ........ 170

Creating New Contacts ........ 172

Editing Contacts ........ 174

Creating Distribution Lists ........ 178

Finding Contacts ........ 180

  Browsing the Contacts Folder ........ 180

  Finding Contacts from the Toolbar ........ 181

  Searching for a Contact ........ 182

Using Contacts ........ 183

  Mapping Contacts ........ 183

  Viewing Items Related to a Contact ........ 184

  Printing Contacts ........ 185

  Sending Contact Information Across the Internet ........ 188

  Calling Contacts and Using the Journal ........ 188

Managing Address Books ........ 191

  Creating Multiple Contacts Folders ........ 191

  Controlling Message Addressing ........ 192

Summary ........ 193


*Skill 6* **Managing Your Time** **195**


Basic Terminology ........ 196

Viewing Your Calendar ........ 196

Finding Calendar Items ........ 198

Creating Appointments ........ 201

Creating Events ........ 202

Editing Calendar Items .......... 203
Editing Directly in the Calendar .......... 203
Editing Advanced Details .......... 205
Making Items Recur .......... 208
Scheduling Meetings .......... 209
Creating and Sending Meeting Requests .......... 209
Sending Updates and Tracking Responses .......... 212
Responding to Meeting Requests .......... 214
Finding Appropriate Times for Meetings .......... 215
Setting Up Internet Free/Busy Information .......... 217
Updating Your Free/Busy Information .......... 226
Printing from the Calendar .......... 227
Working with Tasks .......... 230
Creating Tasks .......... 231
Editing Tasks .......... 232
Assigning Tasks to Others .......... 235
Receiving Task Requests .......... 237
Updating Tasks .......... 238
Changing the Appearance of the Tasks Folder .......... 239
Using Reminders .......... 241
Summary .......... 242

*Skill 7* **Maintaining Outlook** **243**

Managing Outlook Data Files .......... 243
Cleaning Up Folders to Improve Performance .......... 244

Opening Other Outlook Folder Stores ..... 249
Creating New Folder Stores ..... 252
Managing E-Mail Accounts ..... 253
Sharing Data Between Computers ..... 255
Leaving Messages on the Server ..... 256
Sharing Your Folder Store on a Network ..... 258
Backing Up and Restoring Outlook Data ..... 259
Backing Up Your Outlook Data and Settings ..... 259
Restoring from a Backup ..... 262
Customizing Outlook ..... 263
Customizing the Outlook Bar ..... 263
Disabling Word as Your E-Mail Editor ..... 265
Troubleshooting Common Problems ..... 266
Locating Missing IMAP Folders ..... 266
Messages Are Stuck in the Outbox ..... 266
Mail Server Keeps Asking for a Password ..... 267
Repairing Your Outlook Folder Store ..... 268
Summary ..... 269

*Appendix A* **Using Notes** **271**
Creating Notes ..... 271
Working with Notes ..... 272

*Appendix B* **Outlook and Exchange** **273**
Server-Side Storage Overview ..... 273

Using Public Folders ........ 274

Reading Posts ........ 274

Posting Messages ........ 276

Creating New Public Folders ........ 278

Using Delegates ........ 279

Setting Up Offline Folders ........ 282

Using the Out Of Office Assistant ........ 284

*Appendix C* **Automatically Processing Form Data** **287**

Preparing a Form ........ 288

Using Outlook to Process Form Data ........ 289

**Glossary** **293**

**Index** **301**

# INTRODUCTION

Microsoft Outlook 2002 is more than just the most powerful e-mail program for business users on the market. It is a highly integrated software package that you can use to effectively manage your time, tasks, and messages.

Few business users have the time or interest to become an expert on every obscure feature of Outlook. Therefore, in *Effective Executive's Guide to Outlook 2002,* we focus on those tasks and features most important to users such as you.

This means that we cover the basic tasks quickly, but thoroughly. We don't insult your intelligence—we provide you with the information you need most, in a clear and concise manner.

It also means that we cover more advanced features and tasks than are discussed in most "beginner" books. Business users are power users of Outlook, so we make suggestions on how to make Outlook work more effortlessly and powerfully for you—without losing you in the details.

Since there is no linear way to work with e-mail and manage your time with Outlook, we have divided this book into the seven core skills that you need to work with Outlook. This allows you to quickly go to the skill you need help with, find the information you need, and get on with your workday.

## What This Book Assumes About You

This book makes two assumptions about you. First, the book assumes that you're not and don't want to become an Outlook guru. Rather, we assume you're a professional working in business, for a nonprofit organization, or perhaps in public service. We assume that you want to become more comfortable with Outlook's core features, as well as possibly learn how to use some other features that can make your work go smoother.

The book also assumes that you're familiar working with the Microsoft Windows operating system. In the pages that follow, as a result, you won't get detailed information about how to choose menu commands or select dialog box buttons and boxes. If you don't already possess this knowledge, you'll need to acquire it either by using the online help available in Windows, by getting a quick tutorial from a friend or coworker, or by reading a good introductory book.

# How This Book Is Organized

This book breaks the process of using Outlook into the following seven skills:

## Skill 1: Getting Started with Outlook

Before you can use Outlook, you need to set up Outlook and familiarize yourself with its interface. Skill 1 shows you how to do this, and includes some valuable tips on acquiring a good e-mail account and importing data and settings from other programs.

## Skill 2: Reading E-Mail

Reading e-mail is one of the most important skills to master and Skill 2 provides you with everything you need to know on the subject. This includes checking for new messages, reading messages, working with attachments, and protecting yourself from viruses and virus hoaxes.

## Skill 3: Sending E-Mail

Skill 3 shows you the basics of sending and delivering messages with Outlook, as well as the most important information on addressing, composing, and delivering e-mail messages. This includes tips on how to write better e-mail messages, which message formats you should use, how to attach files to your e-mails, and how to compose messages in other languages.

## Skill 4: Managing Your E-Mail

Most business users are flooded with e-mails. Skill 4 provides a sort of bilge pump you can use to better deal with your mail. It covers topics such as finding messages, using folders to organize your messages, and creating message templates for messages you send often. It also covers how to set up Outlook to automatically process your e-mail and filter out junk e-mail (spam).

## Skill 5: Using a Contacts List

Many business users live and die by their contacts list—fortunately, Outlook provides powerful contact management capabilities you can use to maintain a contacts list. Skill 5 discusses Outlook's Contacts folder, how to create and edit contacts and distribution lists, as well as how to locate contacts, send them to others, and manage multiple contacts lists.

## Skill 6: Managing Your Time

Outlook provides some powerful tools that you can use to manage your time, and Skill 6 shows you how to put them to good use. It covers how to use the Outlook Calendar to create and edit appointments, schedule meetings, and make printouts. It also discusses how to keep track of tasks that you need to accomplish and work with reminders you may have placed on various Outlook items.

## Skill 7: Maintaining Outlook

The final Outlook skill is that of keeping Outlook running well. This skill includes information on managing your Outlook data files and e-mail accounts, backing up your Outlook data files and settings, customizing Outlook, and dealing with some common errors.

## Appendix A: Using Notes

Notes are Outlook's version of the little yellow sticky pieces of paper that are probably all over your monitor. Appendix A briefly discusses how to use notes to keep track of miscellaneous information.

## Appendix B: Outlook and Exchange

Although Outlook works basically the same whether or not you use it with an Exchange Server, Outlook contains some additional functionality when coupled with an Exchange Server. Appendix B covers these features, such as the ability to use public folders, allowing delegates access to your Outlook folders, setting up Outlook to work offline, and how to use the Out Of Office Assistant.

## Appendix C: Automatically Processing Form Data

Appendix C presents information on how to set up message rules to automatically process e-mails sent from a form on a Web site.

NOTE Effective Executive's Guide to Outlook 2002 *also includes a glossary of Outlook and e-mail terms.*

# Conventions Used in This Book

This book uses a couple conventions worth mentioning here. The first is this. We view this book as a conversation among professionals. That means the pronoun *we* refers to us, the authors. And that means the pronoun *you* refers to you, the reader. In this case, this conversation style means you will frequently see the pronoun *we,* because two of us, Gerend and Bermant, wrote the book. Although *we* has sometimes been used as a stilted self-reference by writers, please don't take it that way. Think of us as workshop presenters or discussion group facilitators, with jackets off and ties loosened. Think of us, in other words, as colleagues. Think of this book as a conversation.

Another convention concerns references to the buttons and boxes in Outlook windows and dialog boxes. Even though they don't appear that way onscreen, this book capitalizes the initial letter of the words that label buttons and boxes. For example, the box that is actually labeled "Save as type" gets referenced in these pages as the Save As Type box. The initial caps, then, will be a signal to you that we're referring to a label.

NOTE *Outlook 2002, like virtually every new Microsoft product, has a feature called Personalized Menus And Toolbars. What this means is that Outlook will hide infrequently used menu commands to reduce clutter. If you can't find a menu command that we specify, click the down arrow at the bottom of the menu to display any hidden commands.*

*Skill 1*

# GETTING STARTED WITH OUTLOOK

## Featuring:

- Getting an E-Mail Account
- Setting Up Outlook
- Using Outlook's Interface
- Importing from Other Programs
- Setting Up Additional E-Mail Accounts
- Setting Up an LDAP Directory
- Getting Help

E-mail is one of the most important means of communication in today's business world, and it's essential that you learn how to effectively communicate via this medium. Outlook 2002 provides excellent e-mail services, as well as powerful contact management and calendar functions, making it an essential tool for business users.

In order to use Outlook, you first need to acquire an e-mail account. You then need to set up Outlook, import data from any other mail, contact, or calendar programs, set up any additional e-mail accounts you have, and learn the basics of Outlook's interface. In this skill we help you achieve these tasks, and also briefly show you where to get additional help if you need it.

## Getting an E-Mail Account

In order to send or receive e-mail, you need an e-mail account. In most cases, your company will provide you with one.

If your company isn't already set up for e-mail, then you need to choose an e-mail provider. If you have a Web site, it's usually most economical to obtain e-mail accounts from your Web hosting company. Otherwise, many Web hosting companies and Internet service providers (ISPs) will provide you with an e-mail account for $1 to $5/month (a typical price for multiple e-mail accounts is $12/month for 40 accounts). Either way, you can easily use your domain name for your e-mail address, for example, bettysmith@yourcompany.com.

NOTE *If your company or organization doesn't already have a Web site, we recommend that you consider creating one. For more information, pick up a copy of* New Webmaster's Guide to FrontPage 2002, *by Gerend and Nelson.*

Your e-mail hosting company should provide you with a sufficient number of e-mail accounts as well as the type of e-mail access you want. Three types of e-mail servers are commonly used on the Internet:

- POP servers. When using Post Office Protocol, or POP, servers, you download all mail from the server into your mail program (Microsoft Outlook). Most hosting companies use POP servers.
- IMAP servers. When using Internet Message Access Protocol, or IMAP, servers, all messages are stored on the mail server (and thus remain accessible from multiple locations). You view the messages using Outlook or another IMAP-compliant mail program.
- Web-based servers. When using Web-based servers (such as Hotmail), you access your messages using a Web browser. Although Web-based e-mail accounts are inappropriate for business use, many hosting companies provide Web access to POP- or IMAP-based e-mail accounts. This feature is ideal for retrieving e-mail when away from the office.

In general, we recommend that you stick with POP accounts unless the ability to access all e-mail messages from multiple locations is important, in which case we recommend using IMAP accounts. We also recommend that you consider Web access to your e-mail accounts a requirement, considering how convenient this feature is when you're away from your main computer. Figure 1-1 shows the Web interface for a POP-based e-mail account.

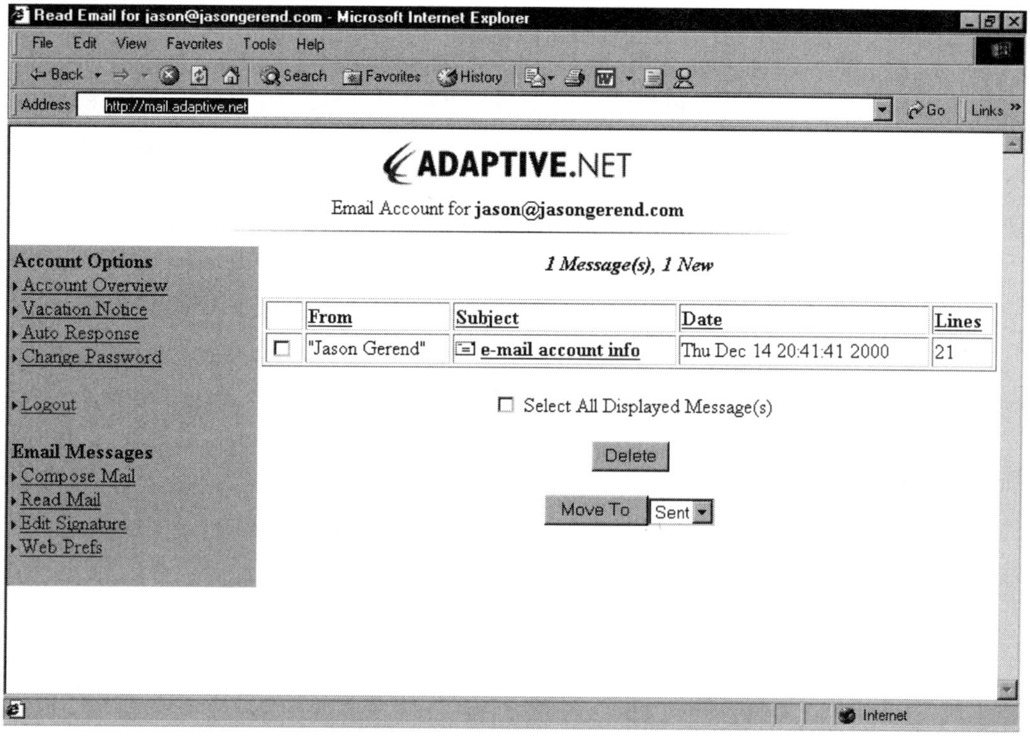


**Figure 1-1** Accessing a POP-based e-mail account through a Web page.

## Personal E-Mail

For personal e-mail, most people use either the e-mail account provided by their ISP or a free e-mail account such as one provided by Hotmail. While these both have the nicety of being free, there are drawbacks to them.

If you use an e-mail account provided by your ISP, you have to change your address if you change ISPs (unless you use a forwarding service such as *www.bigfoot.com*, which may delay your receipt of e-mail at times up to several days). Using a free e-mail account such as one provided by Hotmail (*www.hotmail.com*) or Yahoo!Mail (*mail.yahoo.com*) usually entails tolerating ads as well as unreliable e-mail servers and limited functionality.

If you take your personal e-mail seriously, we recommend that you take the same approach as a business would. This means acquiring your own permanent domain name and either redirecting mail to an existing e-mail account or paying for e-mail hosting just as you would a business e-mail account.

Using e-mail redirection (provided for free by some registrars, such as directnic.com) is a great way to use your domain name for your e-mail account without paying an extra monthly cost. With e-mail redirection, all mail sent to your new, permanent e-mail address (such as jasonj@gerend.com) is automatically forwarded to your existing e-mail account. If you change ISPs and get a different e-mail address, redirect your permanent e-mail address to your new account. The drawback of using e-mail redirection is that, like free forwarding services such as bigfoot.com, it may impart a delay while the messages are forwarded to your existing account, although this delay is usually minimal.

### One Box Is Not Enough

One electronic mailbox may not be enough. Consider this "real world" example: People don't always have the same mailing address for home and work. And even if you work at home, there is usually some way to differentiate personal and business correspondence.

So it makes sense to have multiple mailboxes to manage correspondence between different parts of your life. The most obvious use is to protect you from unwanted sales-oriented mass mailings, or *spam*. You can use one address for personal correspondence, given out only to close friends, and use a second to run e-commerce transactions and handle electronic newsletters. Another analog example is the idea of a private telephone line for important contacts.

Outlook supports this behavior with the ability to connect to different mailboxes and sort the messages into separate folders. This will make sense for some users, while others will set up a second account through Hotmail or another free service. Although free services have a number of disadvantages including unwanted ads, slow speeds and unreliable access, they may be adequate for secondary e-mail accounts.

## Setting Up Outlook

The first time you run Outlook you need to go through a setup process to enable it to work with your e-mail accounts as well as access any existing messages or contacts you may have.

In order to do this, follow these steps:

1. **Start Outlook.**

   To start Outlook, double-click the Microsoft Outlook icon on your desktop, or choose the Start menu's Programs command and then choose Microsoft Outlook from the list of programs.

NOTE *Outlook is installed by default when you install Office.*

2. **Click Next to start the Outlook Startup Wizard.**

   If you used a previous version of Outlook on your computer, Outlook automatically uses your existing settings and closes the Outlook Startup Wizard.

3. **Select the mail program to upgrade from.**

   If Outlook can automatically import settings from an existing e-mail program, it displays the E-Mail Upgrade Options screen. Select the mail program to upgrade from, click Next, and then verify the imported e-mail account settings. Alternatively, click the Do Not Upgrade option button, and click Next to skip the import process.

4. **Set up your e-mail.**

   Click the Yes option button in the E-Mail Accounts screen to set up your e-mail, and then click Next, as shown in Figure 1-2.

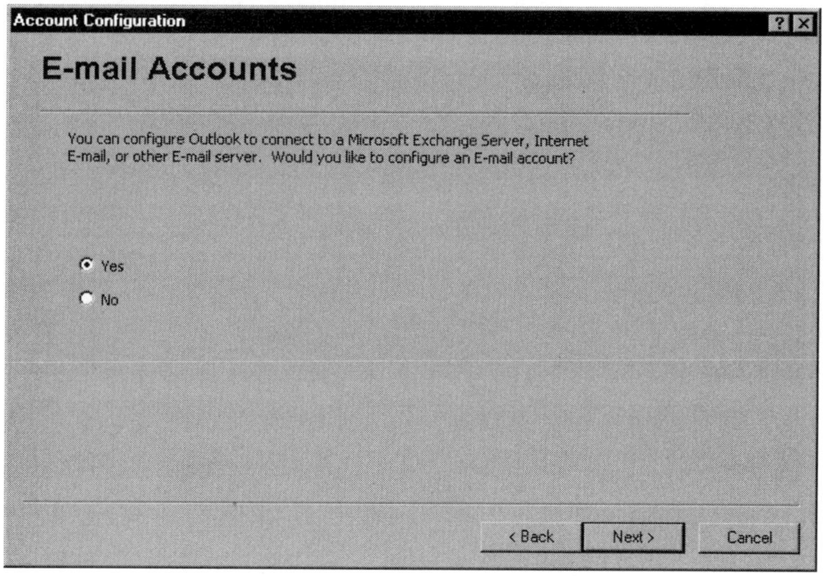


**Figure 1-2** Choosing to set up an e-mail account.

5. **Choose the server type.**

   In the Server Type screen, shown in Figure 1-3, select the type of mail server your mail account uses. This will most likely be POP3. Click Next to continue.

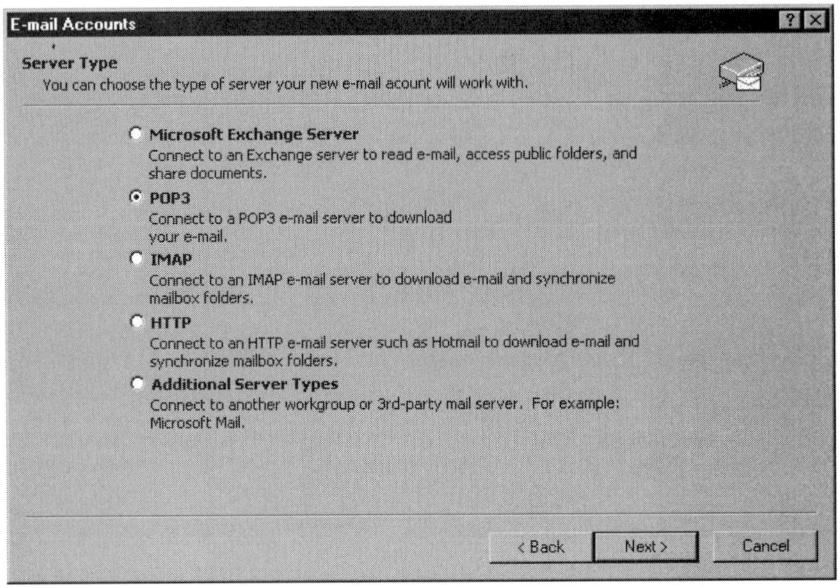


**Figure 1-3** Selecting the appropriate server type.

6. **Enter your name and e-mail address.**

   Enter the name you want to appear on your e-mails in the Your Name box, and enter your e-mail address in the E-Mail Address box, as shown in Figure 1-4.

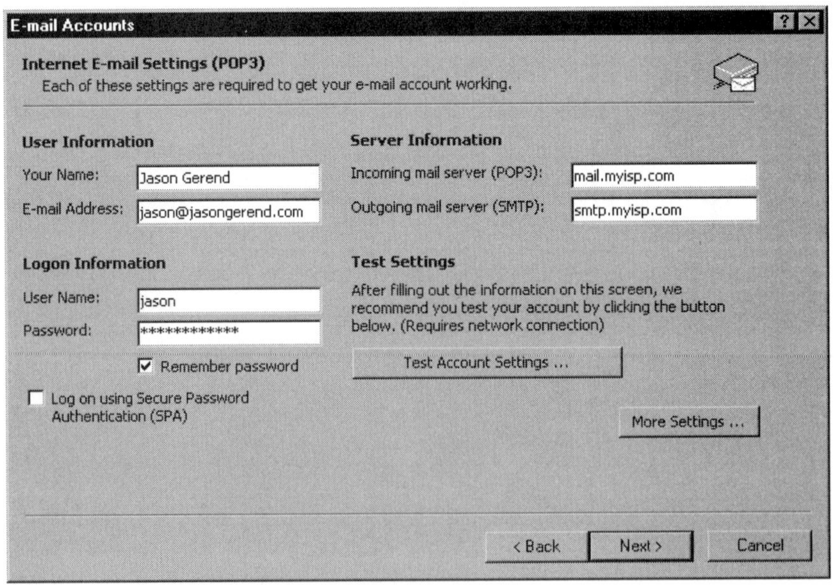


**Figure 1-4** Entering the account information for a POP3 server.

TIP *To receive replies with a different e-mail address, click the More Settings button In the Reply E-Mail box, enter the e-mail address you want to use to receive replies.*

**7. Enter your server information.**

In the Incoming and Outgoing Mail Server boxes, enter the mail server names provided to you by your network administrator or mail provider. Enter your e-mail user name and password in the User Name and Password boxes. Click the Test Account Settings button (POP3 accounts only) to test your settings.

If you're setting up an Exchange Server account, enter the name of the Exchange Server, and enter your Exchange Server user name. Click Next, and then click Finish.

TIP *For increased security, clear the Remember Password check box.*

## Keep Home and Work Separate

It's easy and convenient to send short personal messages from work. Still, you should refrain from using the work server to send more than the most rudimentary messages. It costs nearly nothing to get your own mailbox, and you can feel free to say what you want to anyone without fear of repercussions.

Businesses, however, no longer have that choice. Until recently, e-mail has been a company perk. You'd get an e-mail address that could be accessed at home. Your boss wouldn't care, as long as your usage wasn't abnormal. Besides, a corporate e-mail address gave the boss an open invitation into your home and your life after hours.

Companies are now finding that letting employees use a work e-mail address during nonwork hours is a really bad idea, and not just because some people spend a lot of work time e-mailing mom. It turns out that companies may become liable for any piece of mail sent through their servers and under their address. So if a company provides a "free" e-mail address to an employee who sends a sexist joke to a bowling buddy, the company could be liable.

For an analog comparison, consider company letterhead. A company takes some kind of responsibility for every piece of mail that is sent on its stationery. But think about it: Few people who want to send a letter to a friend will use company stationery to impart the latest about the spouse and the kids. You do this on e-mail because it's there and it's free. Furthermore, by changing your identity on the mail client a message will appear that it comes from a person rather than a company.

No matter who you are, you don't want to get fired and you don't want your boss to get sued because you shot off your mouth about something. So even the smallest companies are wise to establish an e-mail policy, to be included in the employee manual between Dress Code and Health Benefits. As the lines between work and life continue to blur, there needs to be an objective, specific guide as to what you can and cannot do. Individuals, also, can protect themselves by keeping their personal correspondence off of the company server.

## Using Outlook's Interface

Outlook's interface is not complex, allowing you to quickly become familiar with the different features and understand how they work. The following list describes some key aspects of the Outlook interface, as shown in Figure 1-5.

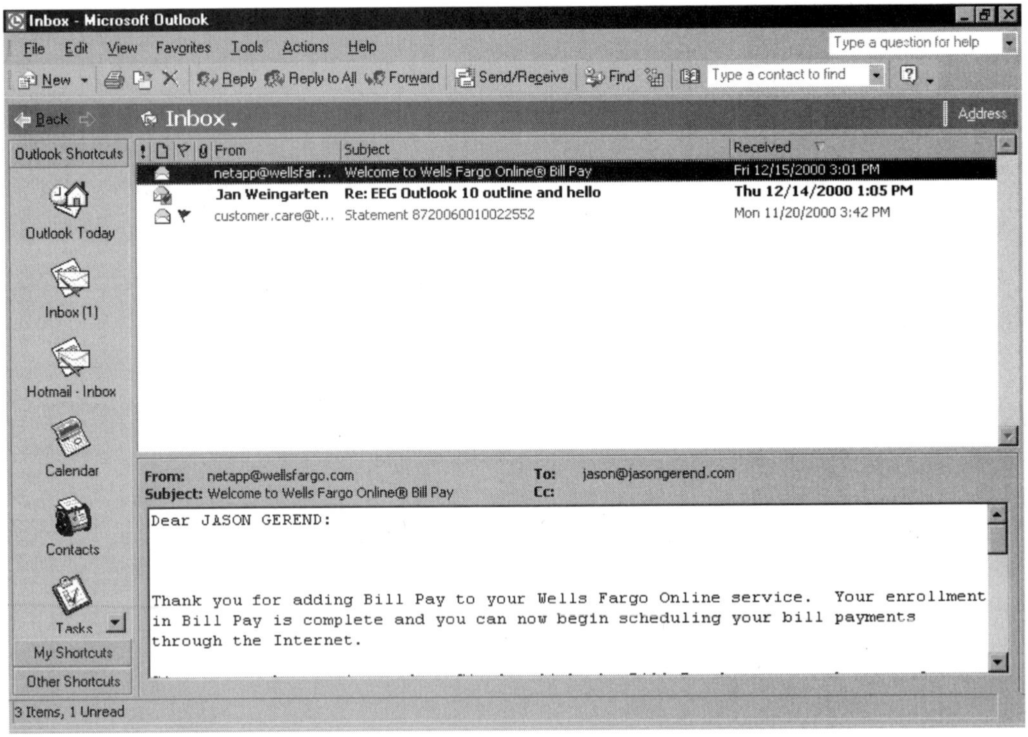


**Figure 1-5** The Outlook interface.

- The menu bar (at the top) provides a series of menus you can use to accomplish tasks in Outlook. If you don't see the command you want in a menu, click the double arrows at the bottom of the menu to display infrequently used commands. Of special note is the Actions menu, which provides a list of nearly every action you can perform on the selected item.

TIP *To prevent Outlook from hiding menu commands and toolbar buttons, right-click a toolbar and choose Customize from the shortcut menu. Click the Options tab, and then select the Always Show Full Menus and Show Standard And Formatting Toolbars On Two Rows check boxes.*

- The Standard toolbar (under the menu bar) contains buttons for frequently used commands. If you don't see the button you want, click the double arrows at the right side of the toolbar to display infrequently used buttons. Move the mouse over a button to see a description of the button.
- The Outlook bar (on the left) contains shortcuts (icons) to frequently used Outlook folders, such as the Inbox and Calendar. Click a shortcut to display its associated folder. At the bottom of the Outlook bar are two groups, My Shortcuts and Other Shortcuts, which contain additional shortcuts. Click a group name to display more shortcuts.
- The Information Viewer (the main part of the window) displays the contents of the current folder. Double-click an item to display it in its own window, as shown in Figure 1-6.

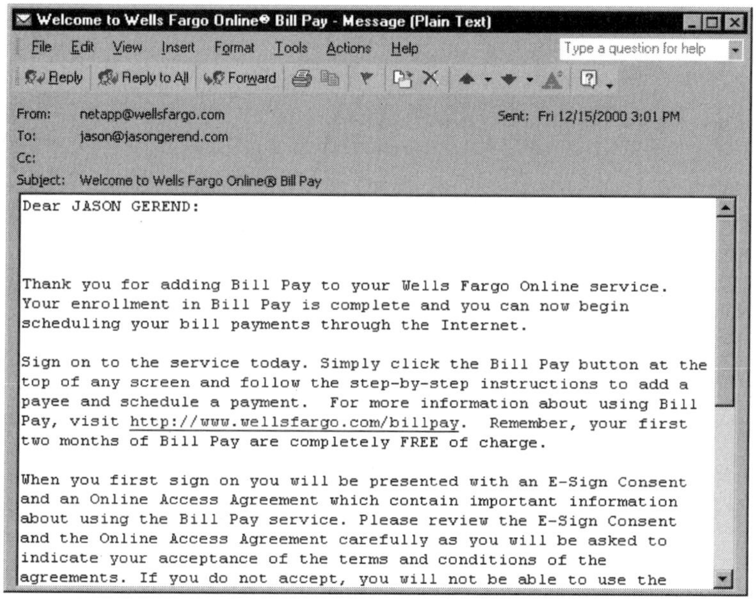


**Figure 1-6** An e-mail in its own window.

- The Preview pane (near the bottom of the window) displays the contents of the currently selected e-mail message.

- The status bar (the bottom of the window) displays information about the current folder and other information about Outlook, such as when it's checking for new e-mail messages.
- The Folder List (hidden) displays an Outlook Express-like listing of the folders contained in your Outlook Personal Folders File (the file that stores all Outlook items). To display the Folder List, click the current folder's title (such as Inbox) and click the pushpin button in the upper right corner to keep the Folder List open. To go back to a previous folder, click the Back button.

TIP *Right-click any item to display a shortcut menu listing the actions you can perform on the selected item.*

## Be Careful What You Send

While recent e-commerce attacks have made us all more security conscious, they also serve as a reminder that e-mail has never really been private.

Think of it this way: Any message you have ever sent to anyone since your first account lives on. Chances are it remains on the recipient's hard drive. Otherwise, it could linger on the server that either sent or received the original message. And if either the sender or the recipient used a corporate e-mail account, the message is probably backed up in two or three places.

Should we worry that an angry or indiscreet message written 10 years ago will come back to bite us? Probably not. Millions of messages fly back and forth every day, and it takes some real effort for a "spy" to catch a specific item. A stupid indiscretion is incredibly hard to isolate, and hardly worth the effort. In fact, the danger of such a mistake surfacing is just slightly more likely than a tape of your teen years' most embarrassing moment.

Even so, we need to be more careful, from this day forward. Remember that people drove cars for decades before it was necessary to add ignition keys. Up until now, everything has been a free ride. Starting tomorrow, we should send no message that we don't want to share with the rest of the world. Anything you say, at any time, can and will be used against you.

Those who care about your business are a tiny group, relatively speaking, and they probably won't bug your e-mail to find out about confidential products or strategies. But consider this: If we can stand behind every message and not write anything scurrilous or slimy, we will improve the quality of communications. And pretty soon being decent and straightforward will start to feel natural.

## Importing from Other Programs

If you have messages, address books, or e-mail account settings that Outlook didn't automatically import, you can import them separately at any time.

The procedure for importing data varies somewhat depending on the type of data you're importing. Use the following sections to import e-mail messages, e-mail addresses, e-mail account settings, and contact information and calendar schedules.

## Importing E-Mail Messages and Addresses

To import e-mail messages and addresses from Eudora, Netscape, or Outlook Express, open Outlook and follow these steps:

1. **Choose the File menu's Import And Export command.**

   This starts the Import And Export Wizard, as shown in Figure 1-7.

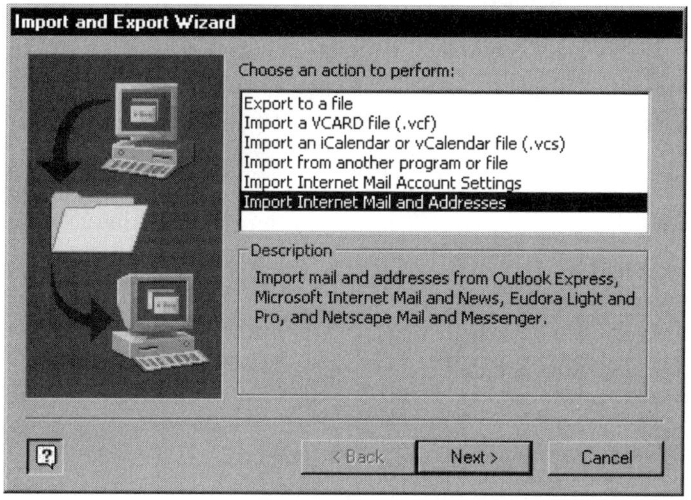


**Figure 1-7** The Import And Export Wizard.

2. **Select Import Internet Mail And Addresses, and then click Next.**
3. **Select the program to import from.**

   In the list provided, select the program from which you want to import data, as shown in Figure 1-8.

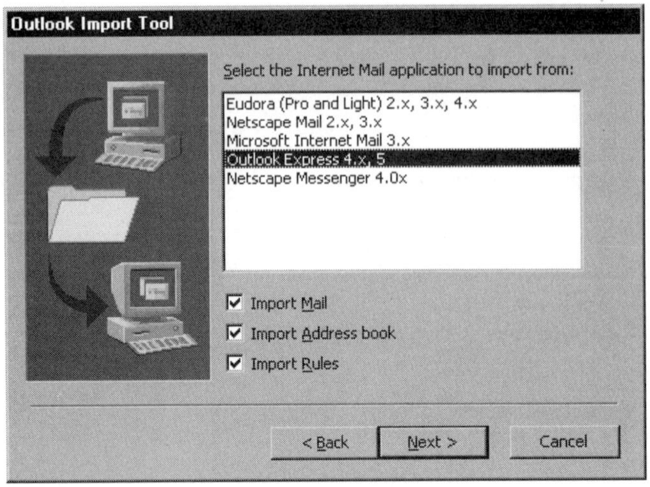


**Figure 1-8** Selecting a program to import from.

4. **Select the type of data to import.**

   Select the Import Mail check box to import e-mail messages, select Import Address Book to import e-mail addresses, and (if available) select Import Rules to import automated message-processing rules. Click Next to continue.

5. **Specify what to do with imported contacts.**

   To import e-mail addresses into the Contacts folder (a good idea), leave the Outlook Contacts folder option selected. To change the way Outlook handles instances when a contact being imported already exists in the Contacts folder, select the appropriate option, as shown in Figure 1-9.

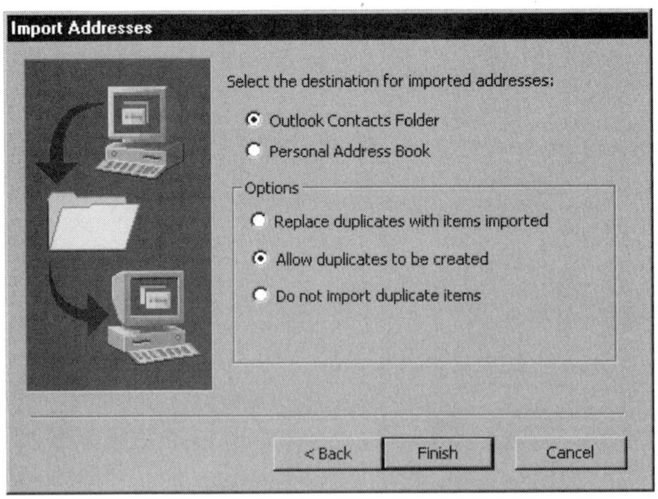


**Figure 1-9** Specifying how to import addresses.

TIP *For information on transferring data from a copy of Outlook on another computer or importing data from an existing Outlook file, see "Skill 7: Maintaining Outlook."*

## Importing E-Mail Account Settings

If you already have your e-mail account(s) set up in another e-mail program, such as Outlook Express, Netscape, or Eudora, you can import them into Outlook. This saves you the trouble of finding the appropriate settings and entering them in Outlook.

NOTE *Unfortunately, Outlook 2002 doesn't allow you to import mail accounts that were exported from previous versions of Outlook or Outlook Express to a file.*

Outlook attempts to import account settings automatically the first time you open it, but if it doesn't, manually import settings by following these steps:

1. **Choose the File menu's Import And Export command.**

   This starts the Import And Export Wizard, as shown in Figure 1-10.

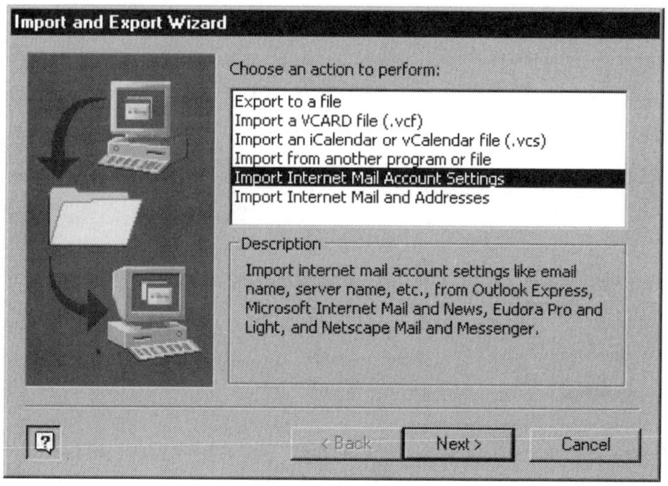


**Figure 1-10** The Import And Export Wizard.

2. **Select Import Internet Mail Account Settings, and then click Next.**
3. **Select the program to import accounts from.**

   Outlook displays a list of currently installed e-mail programs that it can import settings from, as shown in Figure 1-11. Select the program you want, and then click Next.

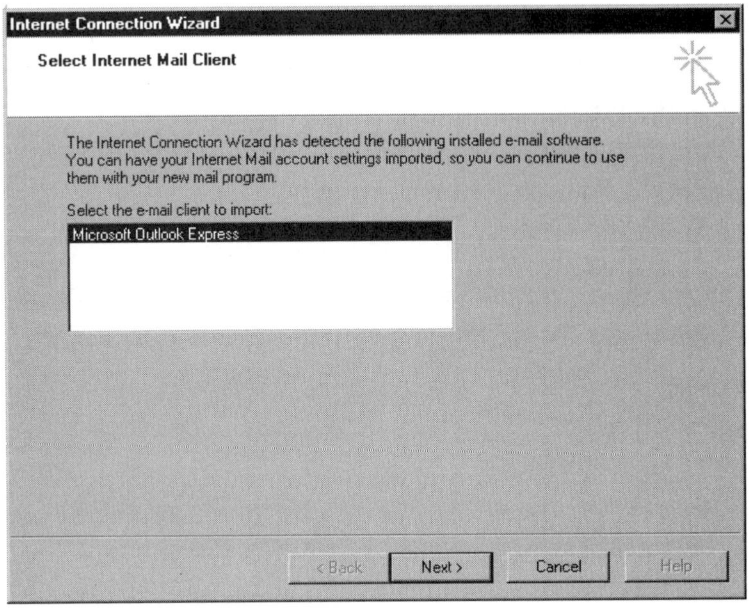


**Figure 1-11** Selecting a program from which to import account settings.

**4. Verify the imported settings.**

Use the Internet Connection Wizard to step through the imported settings and verify that they're correct, as shown in Figure 1-12. Click Next after each screen to move to the next settings. Click Finish to close the wizard.

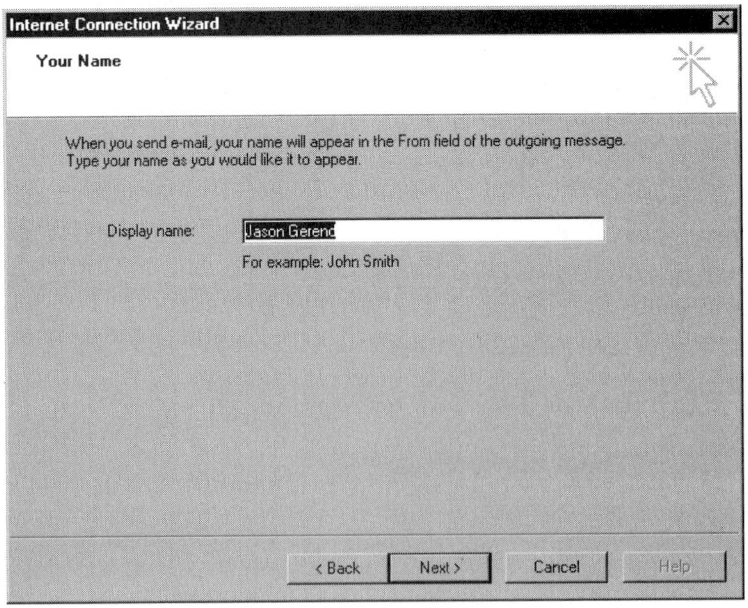


**Figure 1-12** Verifying imported settings.

## Looks Matter

When you start using e-mail, either from scratch or with a new box, you need to keep in mind the perception of that new e-mail address. Once, the slogan was "you are what you eat." Today, you have become an extension of your e-mail address, where recipients will draw certain conclusions based upon your domain name.

There are three types of domains: commercial (MSN, AOL, your local provider), custom or corporate, and promotional. These three types can overlap. For instance, if you work for joesgarage.com, you will probably use the mailbox for personal mail because this promotes the company. If you work for an identifiable company, you may choose to use a generic or promotional account for noncorporate mail just to keep things separate.

People who are really serious about e-mail impressions need to register and pay for their domain, as discussed earlier in this skill. Those who are less serious can have some fun with promotional names, setting up an account that brands them as a hyperintellectual or a frothing metal head. These more playful (and usually Web-based) options are appropriate for secondary e-mail accounts.

A company called Chek.com (*http://www.chek.com*) has turned this practice into a real blast. Chek manages promotional Web-based mail for thousands of companies, and has tied them together on their site. Log in and choose a category, and then pick an appropriate identity from more than 1,100 possible choices. The names on this page are only a fraction of those available from sites around the Web, but this gives you a good selection nevertheless. If you are looking for a secondary box to transmit a mood or a joke (*wishiwasgolfing.com*), this is the ticket. Once registered for this "free lifetime" account, you just log into the Chek (or the domain owner) site to send and receive.

Many of these sponsors need to get something out of this as well, so there may be some promotional or advertising slogans sent at the end of every message. It all leads back to image, or how recipients will interpret a domain name. Because you are sending along a short commercial, make sure you are comfortable with the site's message.

Remember, this is all an image game. In fact, drawing a conclusion about someone based on his or her domain name is only slightly more accurate than jumping to conclusions based on a person's appearance or the car they drive.

## Importing Data from Other Programs

Outlook can import contacts, calendar information and other information from a variety of other programs, such as Act!, Ecco, and Lotus Organizer. However, the import process isn't always foolproof. In fact, sometimes importing data from another program can wreak havoc with your existing contacts, tasks, or appointments.

Because of the danger involved with importing data from other programs, we recommend that you first create a separate folder in Outlook, import your data into this new folder, and then move the data into the appropriate folder. This is a somewhat involved procedure, so get comfortable and take your time. Getting everything right might take a while, but you'll probably find it faster than reentering 1,000 contacts by hand.

To import data from one of these programs, follow these steps:

1. **Create a new folder for your imported data.**

   Choose the File menu's New command, and then choose Folder from the submenu. (You might have to click the double arrows at the bottom of the menu to display this command.)

2. **Specify the type of items the folder will hold.**

   In the Create New Folder dialog box, as shown in Figure 1-13, click an icon to select the type of Outlook items you'll be importing—for example, Contact for address information or Calendar for scheduling information.

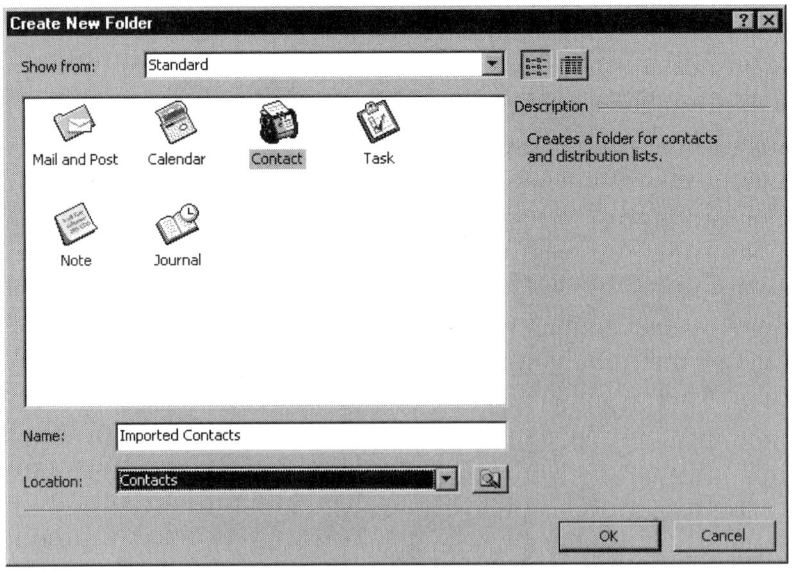


**Figure 1-13** Creating a new folder.

3. **Enter a name and location for the folder.**

   Enter a name for the folder in the Name box (such as Imported Contacts), and use the Location drop-down list box to select the folder in which to create your new folder. Click OK, and then click Yes if you want to create a shortcut on the Outlook bar.

4. **Display the new folder.**

   Click the My Shortcuts group on the Outlook bar, and then click the shortcut corresponding to the folder you created, as shown in Figure 1-14.

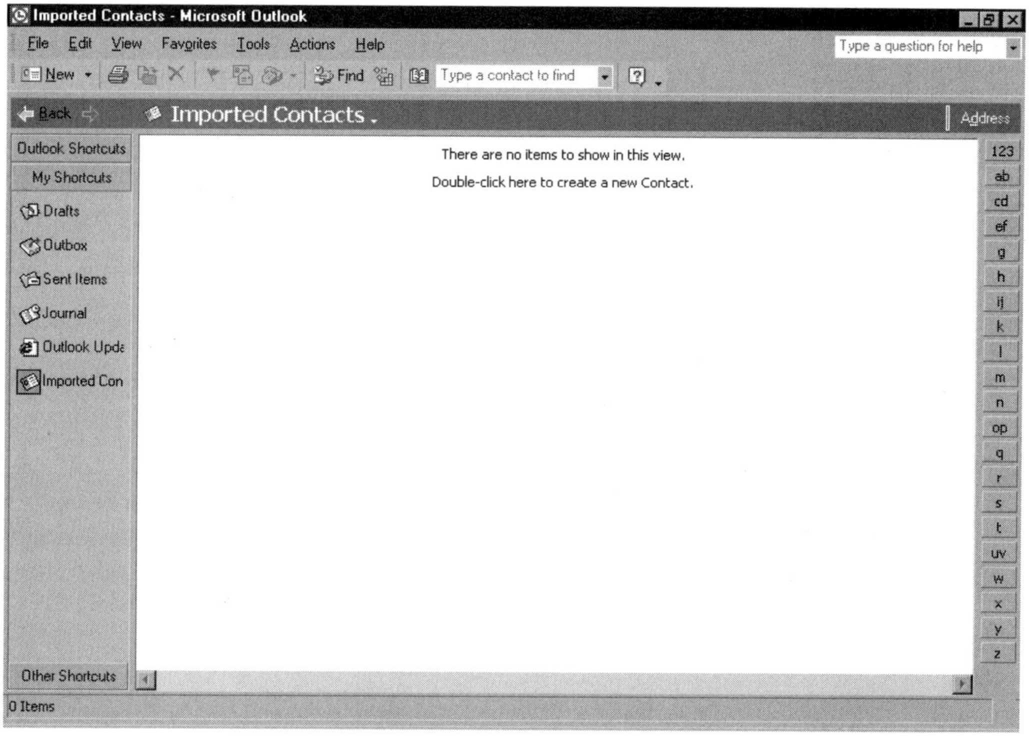


**Figure 1-14** The newly created folder.

5. **Choose the File menu's Import And Export command.**

   This starts the Import And Export Wizard, as shown in Figure 1-15.

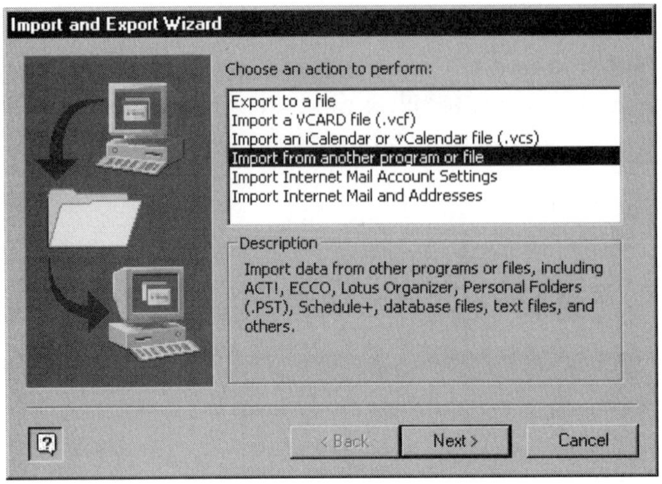


**Figure 1-15** The Import And Export Wizard.

6. **Select Import From Another Program Or File, and then click Next.**
7. **Select the file format to import.**

   In the list provided, select the file format of the data you want to import, as shown in Figure 1-16.

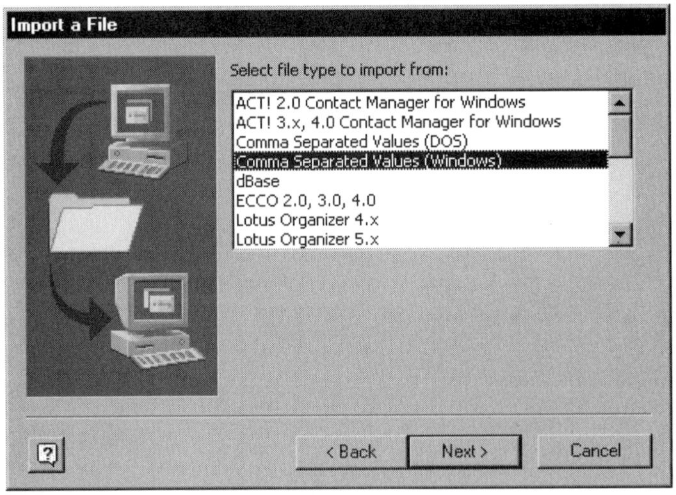


**Figure 1-16** Selecting the appropriate file format.

8. **Specify the file to import.**

   Click the Browse button, shown in Figure 1-17, to locate the file containing the data you want to import. Click Next to continue.

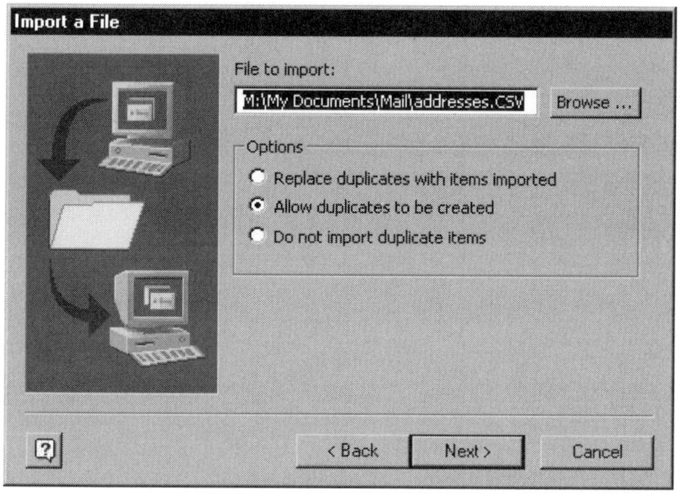


**Figure 1-17** Specifying the file to import.

9. **Specify where to place imported data.**

   Specify the Outlook folder in which to place the imported items (which should be the folder you just created), as shown in Figure 1-18. Click Next.

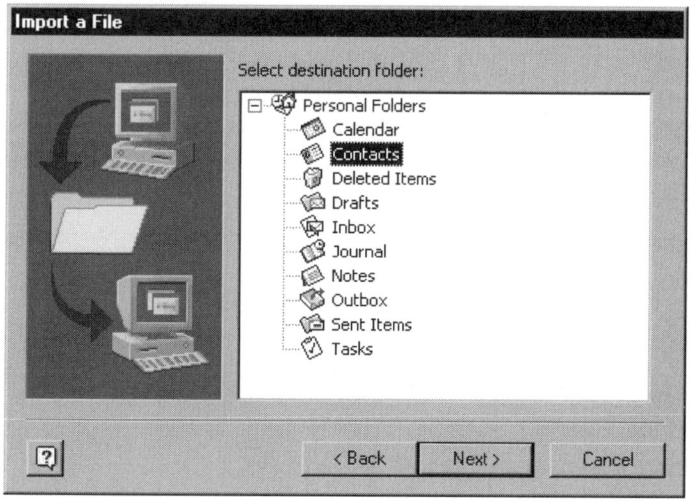


**Figure 1-18** Specifying the folder to place imported items.

10. **Check field mappings.**

    Click the Map Custom Fields button to check the way Outlook will import the various fields (pieces of data) in your data file. In the Map Custom Fields dialog box, shown in Figure 1-19, carefully examine the field mappings in the To box. The Field column of the To box lists the fields in Outlook. The Mapped From column lists the corresponding values from the imported file. The goal is to have fields and values match appropriately. To display hidden fields, click the plus sign next to a field. Use the Next and Last buttons to see how actual items are mapped.

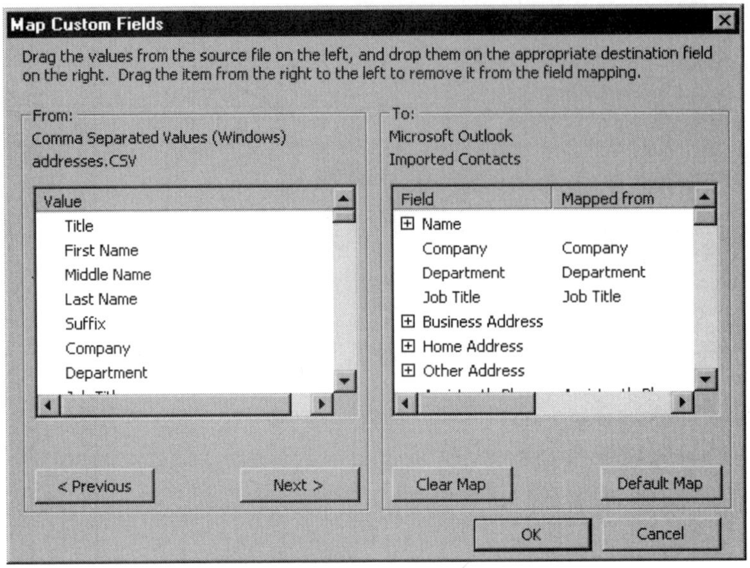


**Figure 1-19** Checking field mappings.

**11. Change field mappings as necessary.**

To replace or add a mapping, drag a value from the list of imported values on the left onto the corresponding field in Outlook, on the right side of the dialog box. Click OK when you're finished.

**12. Review the import settings, and click Finish.**

Outlook imports the data into the folder you created. Carefully check the imported items to make sure they imported properly. If necessary, delete all the items (select an item and press Ctrl-A to select all items) and repeat the import process with different field mappings.

**13. Move the items to the appropriate Outlook folder.**

If you want to integrate the items with your other Outlook items (for example, to place imported contacts in your main Contacts folder), select the items you want to move and drag them to the appropriate shortcut on the Outlook bar (hold the cursor over the Outlook Shortcuts group to redisplay your main Outlook folders).

**14. Deal with duplicate items.**

If some of the items you're moving already exist in the destination folder, Outlook prompts you to deal with the conflict, as shown in Figure 1-20. To update the existing contact with the new information, click the Update New Information From This Contact To The Existing One option button, or click the Add This As A New Contact Anyway option button to create a duplicate item. Then click Yes or click Yes To All to apply this action to all duplicate items. Alternatively, click Skip to move to the next item.

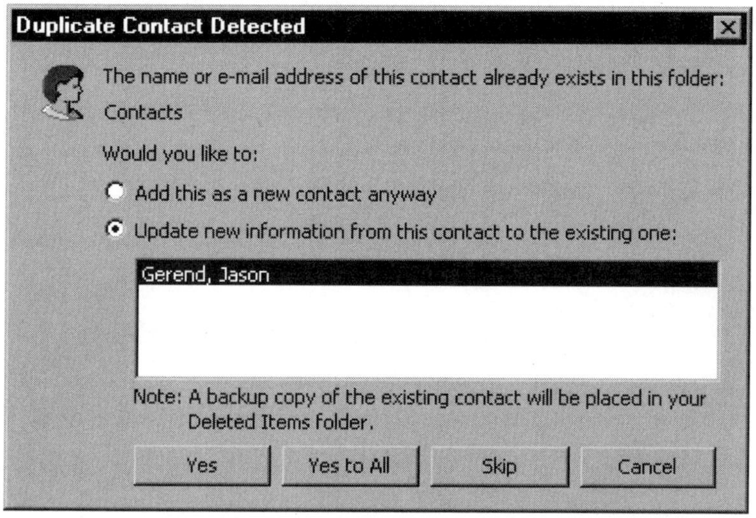


**Figure 1-20** Dealing with duplicate items.

NOTE *Outlook doesn't merge information from duplicate appointments, and instead simply creates duplicate items, so you might end up with identical appointments on your Calendar.*

## Setting Up Additional E-Mail Accounts

It's a rare business user who has only one e-mail account. If you have multiple e-mail accounts, Outlook can import the account settings for you, but only if they're currently set up on your computer in another e-mail program.

If you have an e-mail account that you haven't yet used on your computer, you need to set up the account in Outlook manually. To do so, open Outlook and follow these steps:

1. **Choose the Tools menu's E-Mail Accounts command.**
2. **Select an e-mail option, as shown in Figure 1-21.**

   Click the Add A New E-Mail Account option button, and click OK.

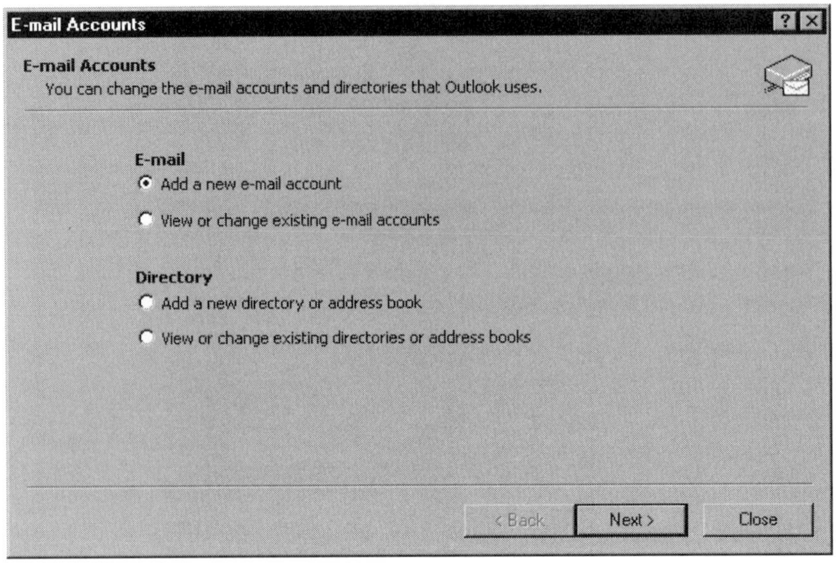


**Figure 1-21** The E-Mail Accounts dialog box.

**3. Choose the server type.**

In the Server Type screen shown in Figure 1-22, click an option button to select the type of mail server your mail account uses. This will most likely be POP3. Click Next to continue.

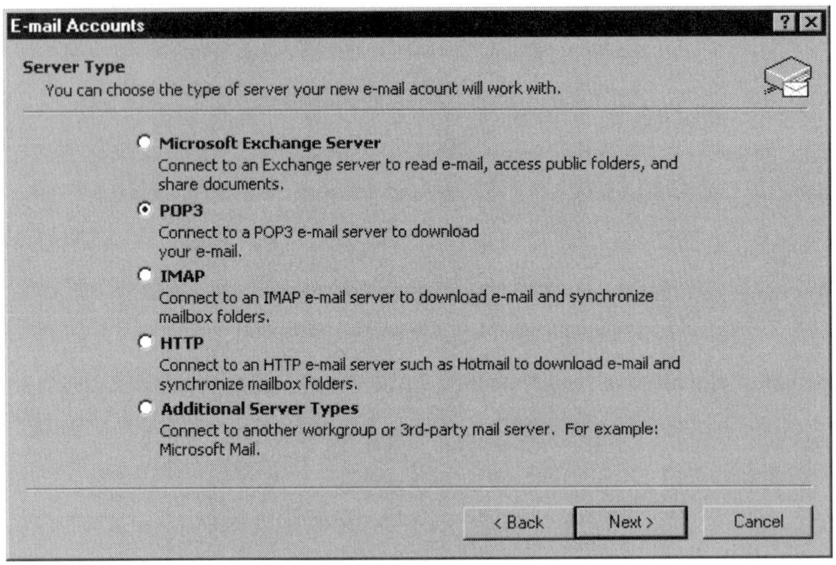


**Figure 1-22** Selecting the appropriate server type.

4. **Enter your name and e-mail address.**

   Enter the name you want to appear on your e-mails in the Your Name box, and enter your e-mail address in the E-Mail Address box, as shown in Figure 1-23.

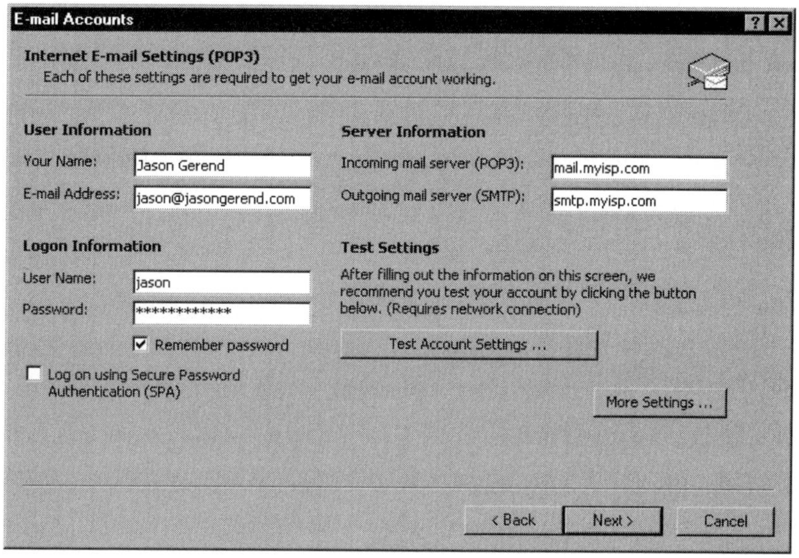


**Figure 1-23** Entering the account information for a POP server.

TIP *To receive replies with a different e-mail address, click the More Settings button. In the Reply E-Mail box, enter the e-mail address you want to use to receive replies.*

5. **Enter your server information.**

   In the Incoming and Outgoing Mail Server boxes, enter the mail server names provided to you by your network administrator or mail provider. Enter your e-mail user name and password in the User Name and Password boxes. Click the Test Account Settings button (POP accounts only) to test your settings.

   If you're setting up an Exchange Server account, enter the name of the Exchange Server and your Exchange Server user name. Click Next, and then click Finish.

TIP *For increased security, clear the Remember Password check box.*

## Setting Up an LDAP Directory

Many companies have a centralized address book of users that you can query, either via Exchange Server (as discussed in "Appendix B: Outlook and Exchange") or via the

Lightweight Directory Access Protocol (LDAP). In addition to any LDAP directories your company or organization provides, a number of companies provide LDAP directories for finding people on the Internet, such as Bigfoot.com.

Outlook can use any LDAP directory as an address book for looking up e-mail addresses. We have some caveats about this feature though.

- If you are on a Windows 2000 Server-based network, it might be useful to set up Outlook to access your company's Active Directory via an LDAP address book.
- Setting up Internet white pages directories, such as Bigfoot.com (*ldap.bigfoot.com*), is possible but slow, and not very useful.
- LDAP directories that are accessed across the Internet may not work well in Outlook. We recommend that you instead set up your Internet-based LDAP directories in Microsoft Windows' Find People tool.
- To find addresses on the Internet in general, use Windows' Find People tool, accessible by clicking the Start button, choosing Search, and then choosing Find People.

To configure an LDAP directory in Outlook, follow these steps:

1. **Choose the Tools menu's E-Mail Accounts command.**
2. **Select a directory option, as shown in Figure 1-24.**

   Click the Add A New Directory Or Address Book option button, and click OK.

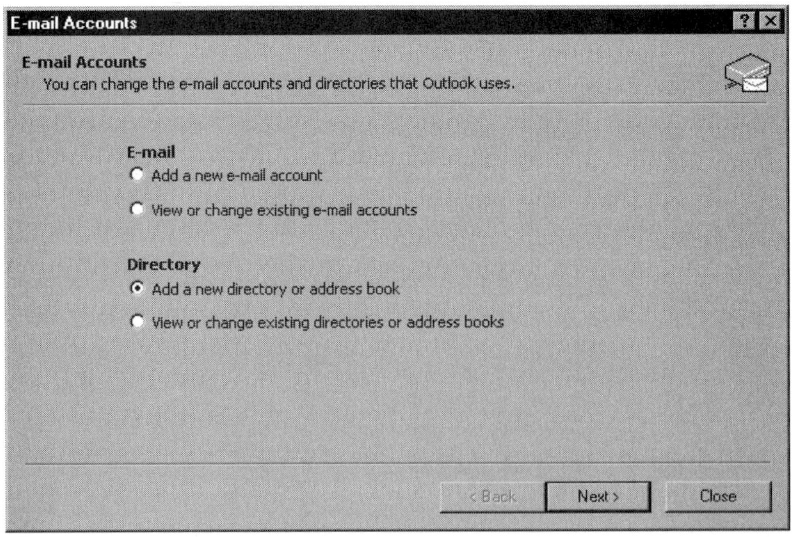


**Figure 1-24** The E-Mail Accounts dialog box.

3. **Select Internet Directory Service (LDAP), and click Next.**

4. **Enter the LDAP server information.**

   Enter the LDAP server name in the Server Name box, as shown in Figure 1-25. For example, Bigfoot.com's LDAP server is *ldap.bigfoot.com*. If the server requires you to log on, select the This Server Requires Me To Log On check box and enter your user name and password. If your directory service provider gave you a Search Base to enter, click the More Settings button, click the Search tab, and then enter the settings in the Search Base text box.

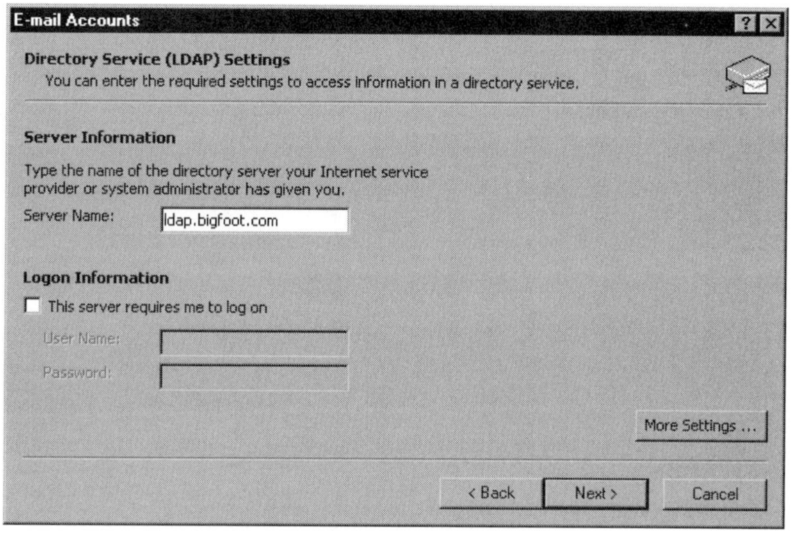


**Figure 1-25** Entering LDAP server information.

# Getting Help

If you need additional help with a feature or task that's beyond the scope of this book, try the following resources:

1. **Type a question in the Ask A Question box.**

   Enter a question in the Ask A Question box at the top right part of the Outlook window, as shown in Figure 1-26, and then press Enter. Outlook displays a pop-up menu with a list of possible topics. Click a topic to view more information.

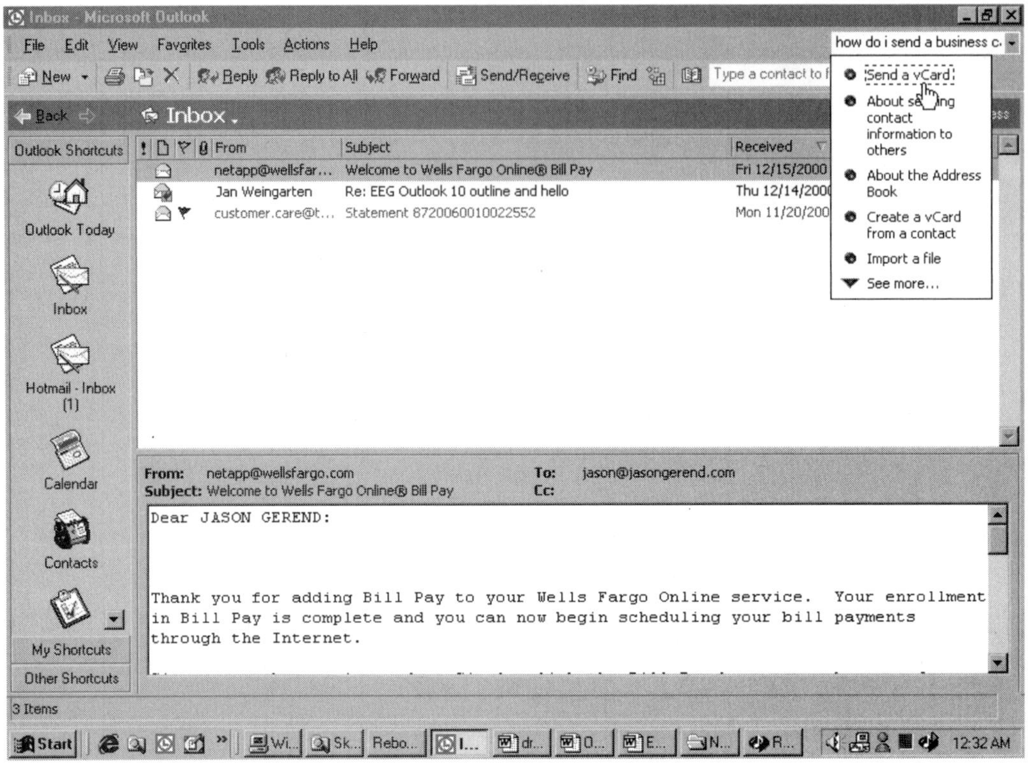


**Figure 1-26** Asking Outlook's Help system a question.

**2. Use the Help menu.**

Press the F1 key to display Help, or choose the Help menu's Microsoft Outlook Help command. Use the Contents tab, as shown in Figure 1-27, to browse a list of topics; click the Answer Wizard tab to ask a question; or click the Index tab to look up a specific word. To navigate topics you've already viewed, use the Back and Forward buttons at the top of the Help window.

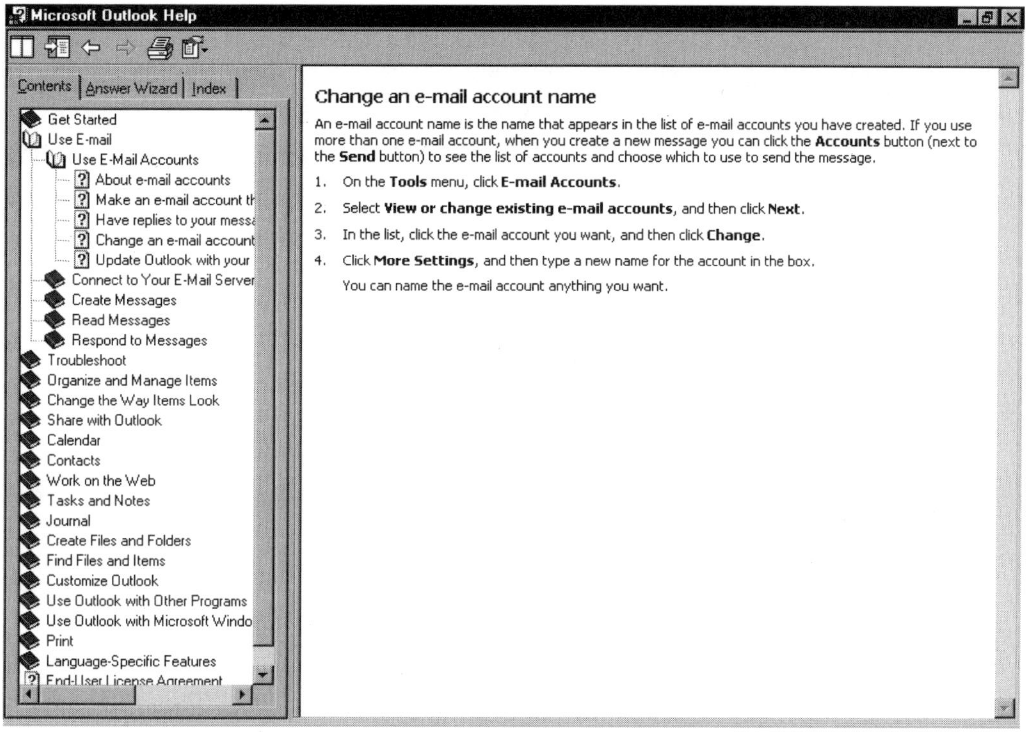


**Figure 1-27** Outlook's Help system.

**3. Use online support.**

When you first display Outlook Help, a listing of Web pages appears, including online lessons and Microsoft Support Services. Click a link to open the Web page directly within Help, as shown in Figure 1-28.

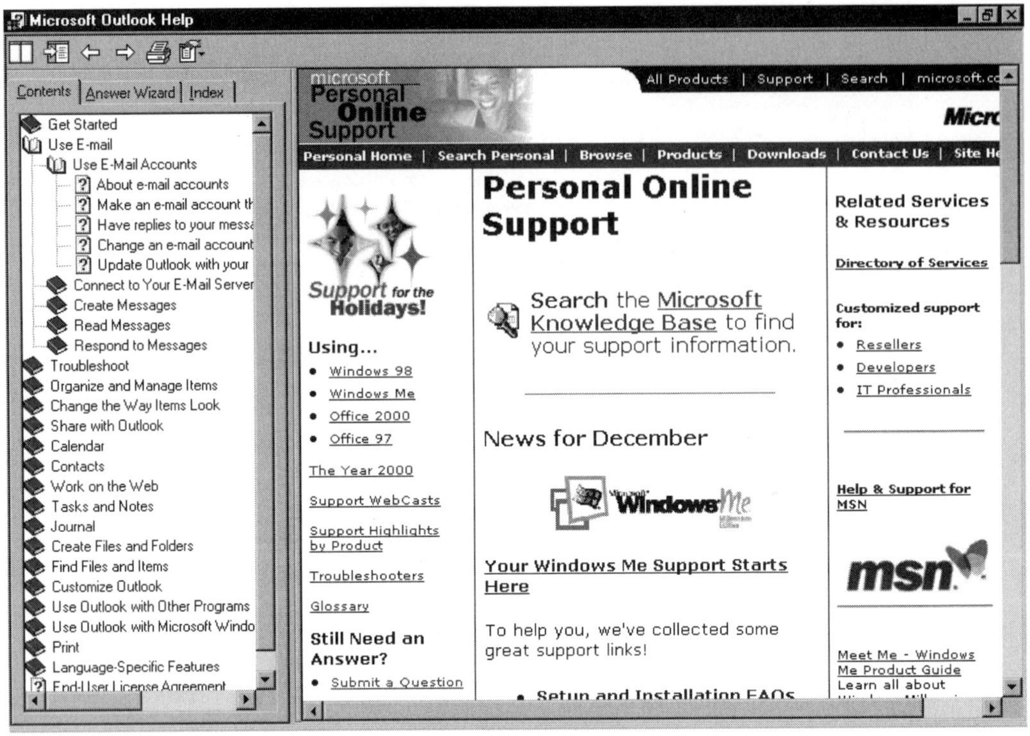


**Figure 1-28** Microsoft's online support Web site.

TIP *Use the Microsoft Knowledge Base to search for answers to questions that Outlook Help can't help you with. The Microsoft Knowledge Base, which you can get to from the Microsoft Support Services link within Help or directly at* http://support.microsoft.com, *is a repository of troubleshooting articles for all Microsoft products and is incredibly valuable when trying to solve a problem.*

4. **Use the Outlook newsgroups.**

   On the Microsoft Support Services Web site, click the Newsgroups link (you might have to look a bit, as the Web site changes occasionally). Microsoft maintains a large number of newsgroups specifically for Outlook users, as shown in Figure 1-29. Most Outlook questions have already been asked (and answered) on these newsgroups, so it's worth your effort to spend some time searching these newsgroups. You can also post a question here for other users and Microsoft to respond to.

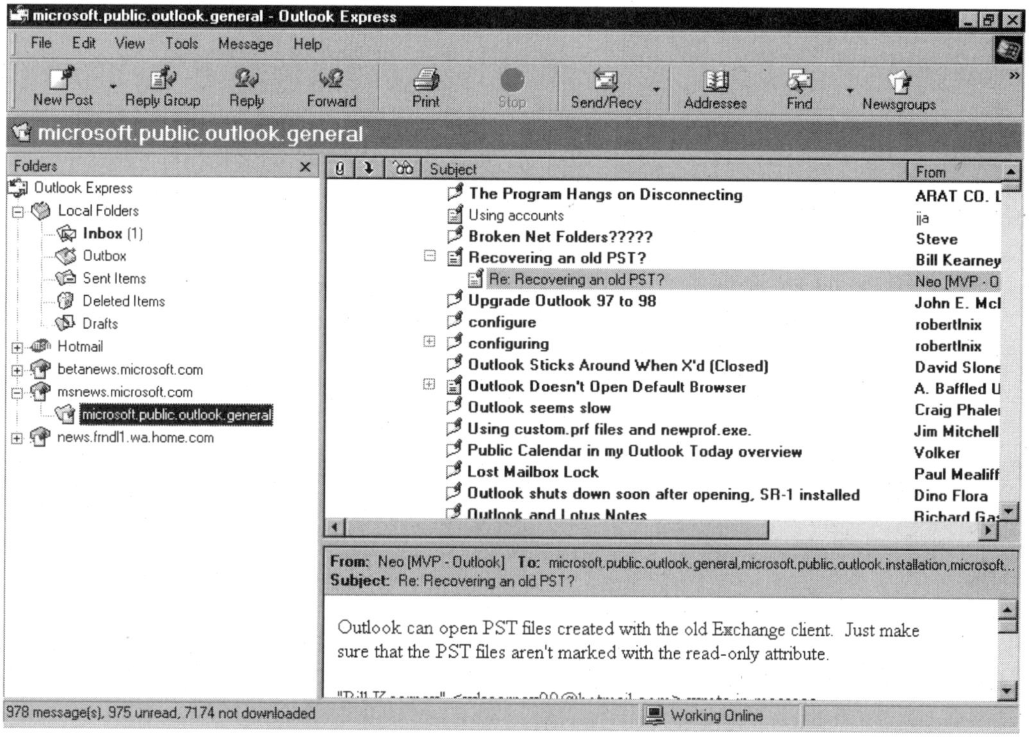


**Figure 1-29** An Outlook newsgroup in Outlook Express.

5. **Submit a question to Tech Support via e-mail.**

   If you still can't find a solution to your problem, e-mail Tech Support by using the Submit A Question (or similarly named) link on the Microsoft Support Services Web site. E-mail technical support is free—and often more convenient than telephone-based support—so try this option before resorting to picking up the phone.

6. **Call Tech Support.**

   Microsoft currently provides free telephone-based technical support for the first two problems you have with Microsoft Office. After you've used up your two free incidents, you can pay per-incident for additional support. If your problem is urgent, call Tech Support, at (425) 635-7056 Monday through Friday, 5 A.M. to 9 P.M. Pacific Standard Time, and Saturdays, 9 A.M. to 3 P.M. Pacific Standard Time, except holidays.

## Summary

To begin using Outlook, you need to acquire an e-mail account and set up Outlook to use it. After showing you how to set up Outlook, we briefly reviewed the different aspects of the Outlook interface and also walked you through importing data and settings from other programs. We also showed you how to set up additional e-mail accounts and presented ways of getting additional help with tasks and problems not covered in this book.

*Skill 2*

# READING E-MAIL

**Featuring:**

- Starting Outlook
- Checking for New Messages
- Reading Messages
- Working with Your Messages
- Working with Attachments
- Protecting Yourself from Viruses and Hoaxes
- Using Outlook Today

Business users depend on their e-mail more than any other type of user (with the possible exception of teenagers). As such, it's important to understand the basic tasks involved with reading your e-mail. In this skill we quickly demonstrate these basics so that you can immediately get started reading your messages.

However, because e-mail is so important to business users, we also show you some tricks and advanced techniques that will help you work with your e-mail most efficiently, powerfully, and safely.

## Starting Outlook

Starting Outlook is a simple procedure—use one of the following methods:

- Double-click the Microsoft Outlook icon on the desktop.

- Choose the Start menu's Programs command, and choose Microsoft Outlook from the list of programs.

You can start Outlook in two additional ways that can save you a few seconds every time you use Outlook:

- Drag the Microsoft Outlook icon from the desktop into the Windows Quick Launch toolbar, next to the Start button. (The Quick Launch toolbar is unavailable on Windows NT.) Click Yes when asked if you want to create a shortcut to the item. This places a button on the Quick Launch toolbar that you can use to launch Outlook with a single click.
- To force Outlook to start automatically when you start your computer, right-click the Start button and choose Open from the shortcut menu. Double-click the Programs folder, and then double-click the Startup folder. Drag the Microsoft Outlook icon from the desktop into the Startup folder and click Yes when prompted to create a shortcut, as shown in Figure 2-1. The next time you reboot, Outlook will start automatically.

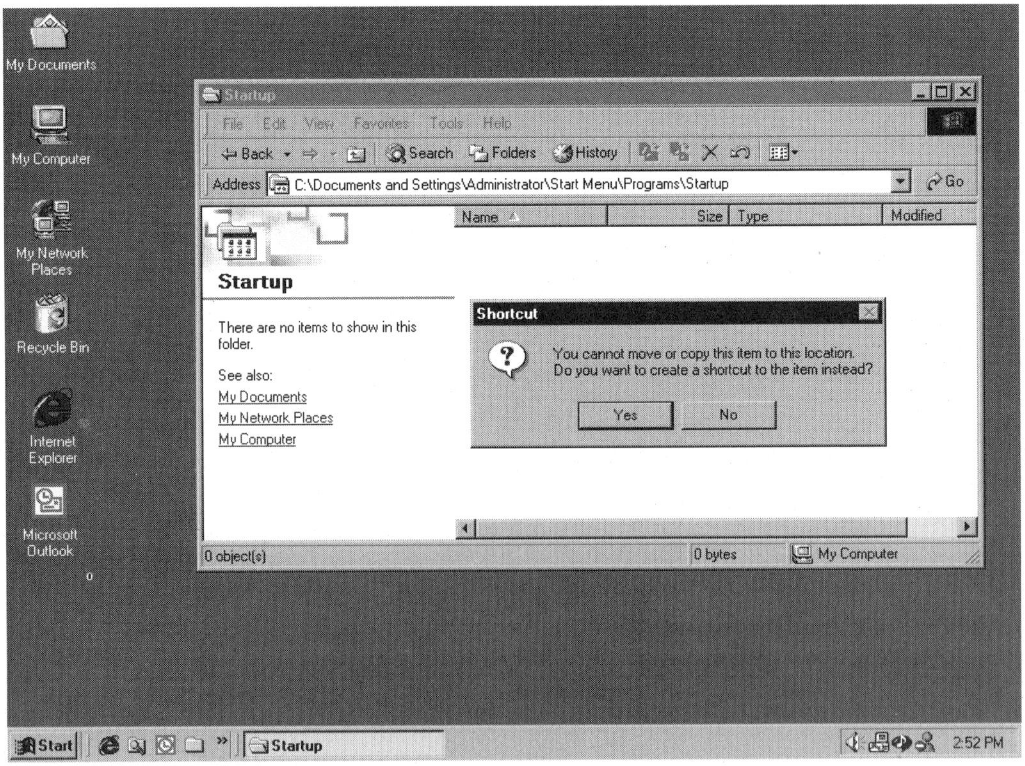


**Figure 2-1** Adding Outlook to the Startup folder.

# Checking for New Messages

Outlook doesn't automatically check for new e-mail messages. In order to receive e-mail, you need to manually check for new messages.

The next sections show you how to quickly check your messages, as well as some additional tasks you can perform to make the send and receive process work better, such as setting up Outlook to automatically check for new messages at set intervals.

## Sending and Receiving Mail

To check for new e-mail messages and send any messages you've written, use one of the following methods:

- Click the Send/Receive toolbar button.
- Press the F5 key.
- To check for new messages on a single e-mail account (if you have multiple), choose the Tools menu's Send/Receive command and then choose the e-mail account from the submenu, as shown in Figure 2-2.

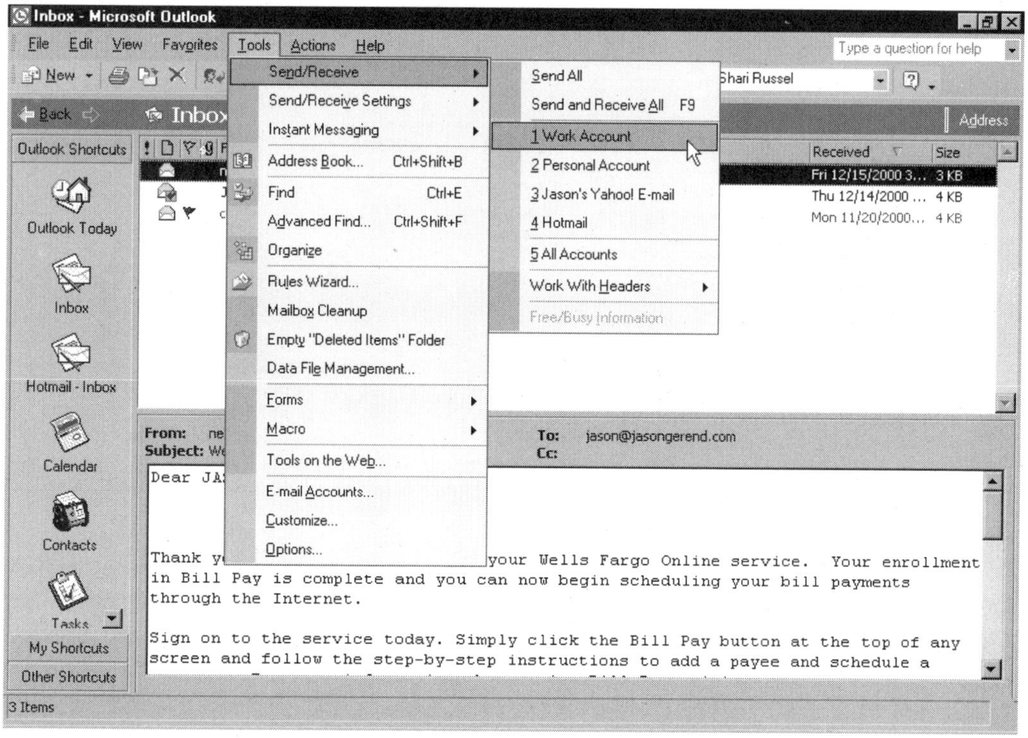


**Figure 2-2** Checking for new messages on a specific e-mail account.

If you're using a dial-up Internet connection, Outlook automatically connects to the Internet, and then disconnects when it's finished checking for new messages. (To change this behavior, choose the Tools menu's Options command, click the Mail Setup tab, and then use the Dial-Up section of the dialog box.)

If you have any new messages, Windows displays a small envelope icon in the System Tray, at the lower right corner of your computer screen. Outlook also displays the number of unread messages you have next to the Inbox icon on the Outlook bar.

NOTE *If you switch ISPs or dialing locations, you may need to adjust your e-mail account settings. For more information, see "Skill 7: Maintaining Outlook."*

## Using the Send/Receive Progress Window

When you click the Send/Receive toolbar button, Outlook connects to the Internet (if you're not already connected), and then displays the Outlook Send/Receive Progress window, as shown in Figure 2-3.

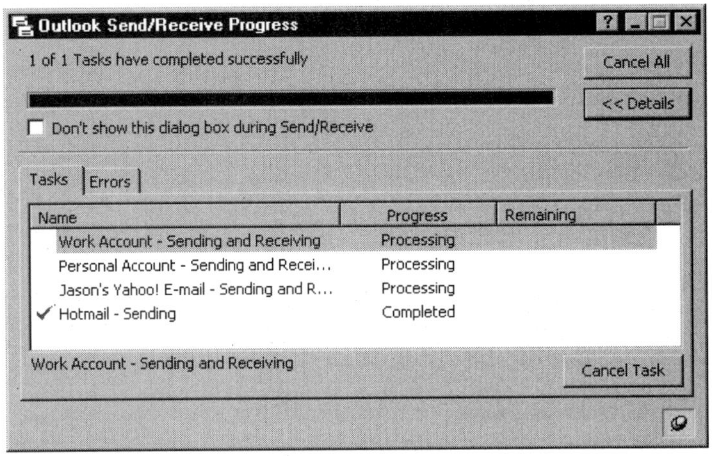


**Figure 2-3** The Outlook Send/Receive Progress window.

This Outlook Send/Receive Progress window shows the status of each e-mail account you're sending or receiving mail on, as described below:

- To prevent the Outlook Send/Receive Progress window from disappearing when all accounts are processed, click the pushpin button in the lower right corner of the window.
- The e-mail accounts Outlook is processing are listed on the Tasks tab in the Name column.

- To cancel a task, select an e-mail account from the list and click the Cancel Task button.
- To cancel all tasks, click the Cancel All button.
- To hide the bottom half of the window but still display a progress bar, click the Details button.
- To prevent this window from being displayed when you check for new messages, select the Don't Show This Dialog Box During Send/Receive check box. Outlook will instead display this information in Outlook's status bar, as shown in Figure 2-4.

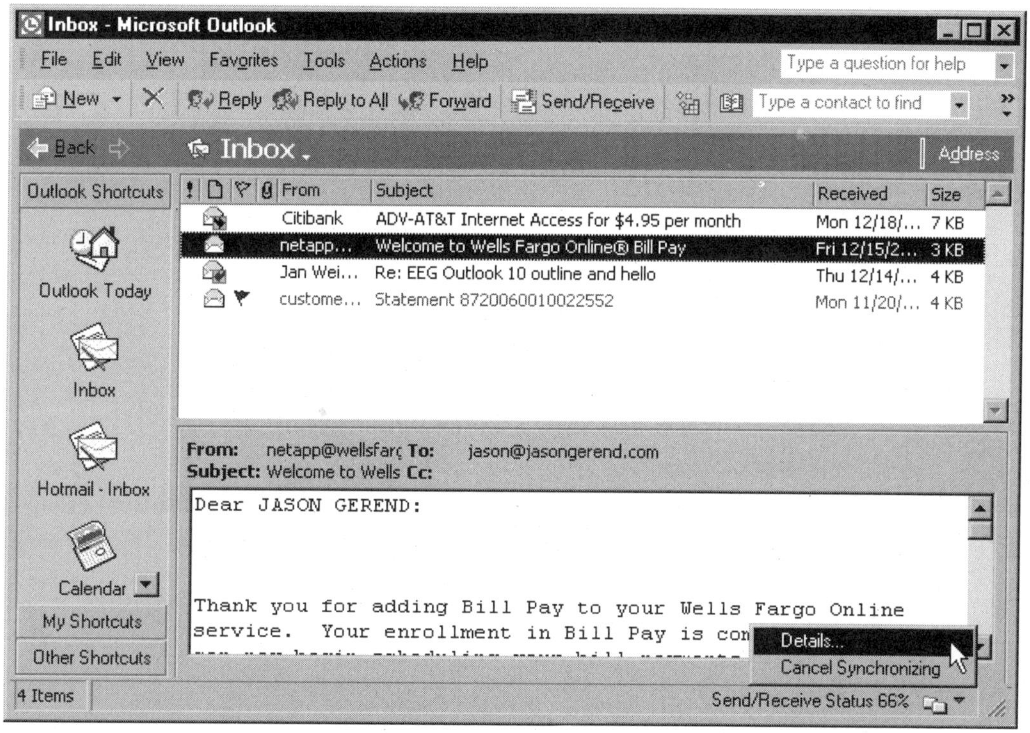


**Figure 2-4** Send/Receive progress information in the Outlook status bar.

TIP *Click the arrow next to the status information in Outlook's status bar to cancel the sending and receiving of e-mail or to display the Outlook Send/Receive Progress window.*

## Automatically Checking Your E-Mail

We recommend that you set up Outlook to automatically check for new messages at regular intervals, especially if you have a persistent Internet connection over your company network or over a DSL or cable modem connection. This saves you from having to check for new messages manually and ensures that you receive messages promptly.

To set up Outlook to automatically check for new e-mail messages, follow these steps:

1. **Open the Send/Receive Groups dialog box.**

   To do so, choose the Tools menu's Send/Receive Settings command, and then choose Define Groups from the submenu, as shown in Figure 2-5.

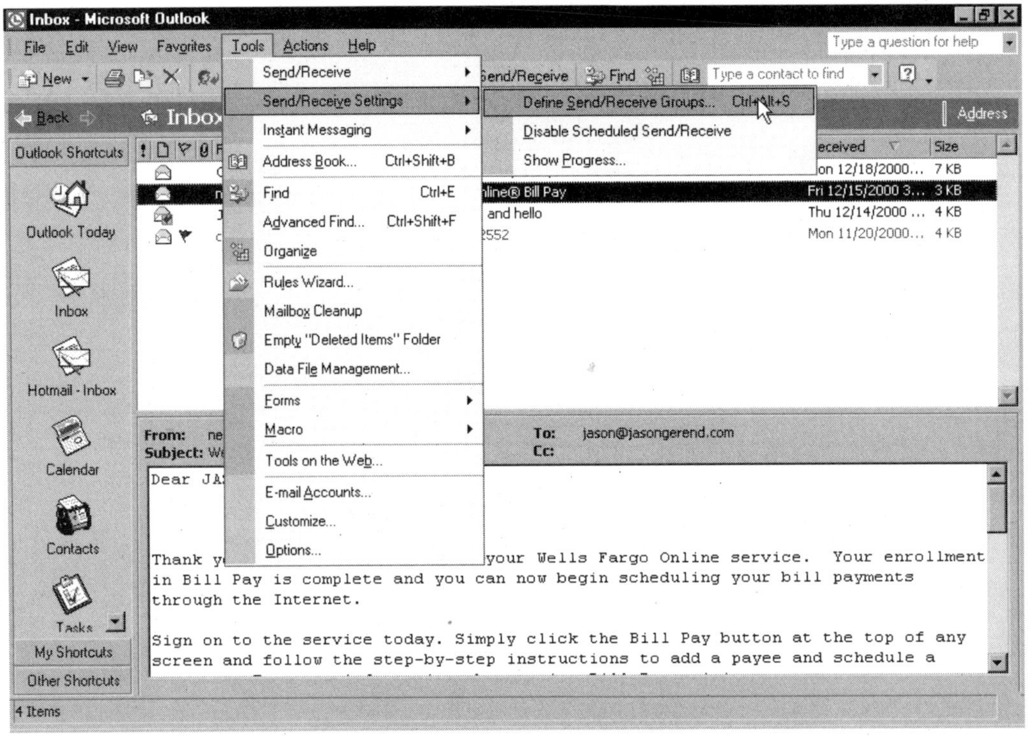


**Figure 2-5** Opening the Send/Receive Groups dialog box.

2. **Specify when Outlook should check for new mail.**

   Use the settings in the Send/Receive Groups dialog box, as shown in Figure 2-6, to specify when Outlook should check for new messages.

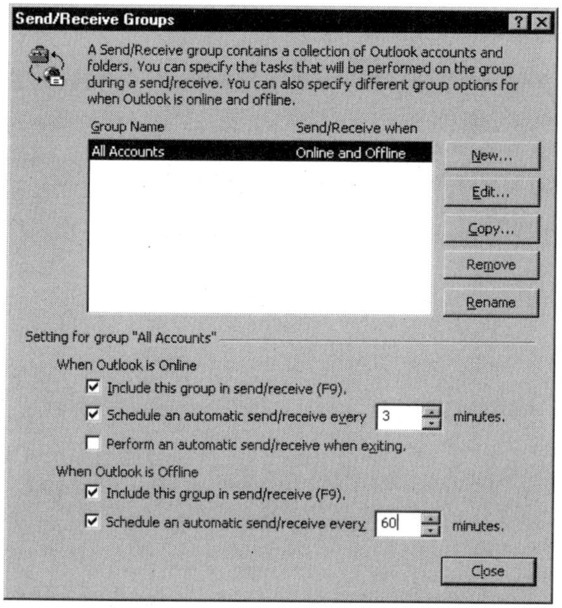


**Figure 2-6** The Send/Receive Groups dialog box.

You have the following options for scheduling mail delivery:

- To automatically send and receive mail according to a preset schedule, select the Schedule An Automatic Send/Receive check box, and then specify how often Outlook should send and receive new mail.
- To automatically send and receive messages when you close Outlook, select the Perform An Automatic Send/Receive When Exiting check box.
- To automatically send and receive messages even when in Offline mode (discussed later in this skill), select the Schedule An Automatic Send/Receive check box in the When Outlook Is Offline section, and then specify how often Outlook should connect to the Internet and check for new mail when you're offline.

## Setting Up Send/Receive Groups

Outlook 2002 now includes the convenient ability to group your e-mail accounts. This permits you to check different accounts at different intervals.

For example, you might set up Outlook to automatically check your work accounts every five minutes and your personal accounts every two hours. You can create a group for accounts you rarely use, and then schedule it to be checked infrequently or only when you check for new messages manually.

To set up Send/Receive groups, follow these steps:

1. **Open the Send/Receive Groups dialog box.**

   To do so, choose the Tools menu's Send/Receive Settings command and then choose Define Groups from the submenu. This displays the Send/Receive Groups dialog box, shown in Figure 2-7.

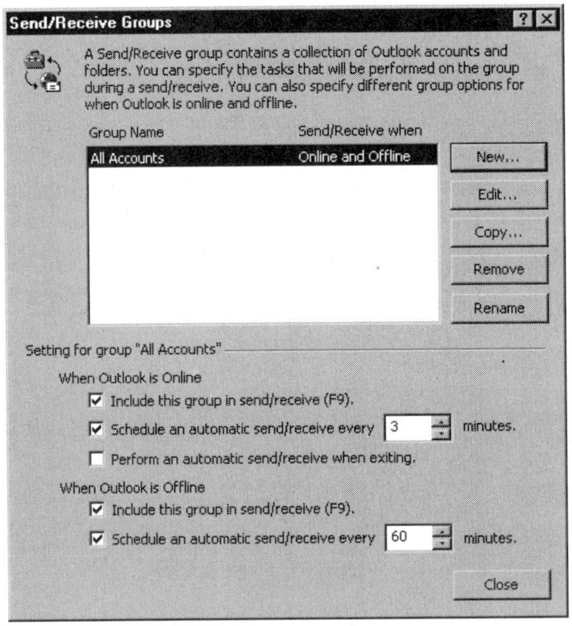


**Figure 2-7** The Send/Receive Groups dialog box.

TIP *If your e-mail accounts are set up to work with different dial-up accounts, Outlook may prompt you to hang up and dial a different connection when checking your e-mail. To force Outlook to always use the current dial-up connection instead of hanging up and dialing another, choose the Tools menu's Options command, click the Mail Setup tab, and then select the Always Use An Existing Dial-Up Connection check box.*

2. **Create a new group.**

   Click the New button, enter a descriptive name for the Send/Receive group, and then click OK, as shown in Figure 2-8.

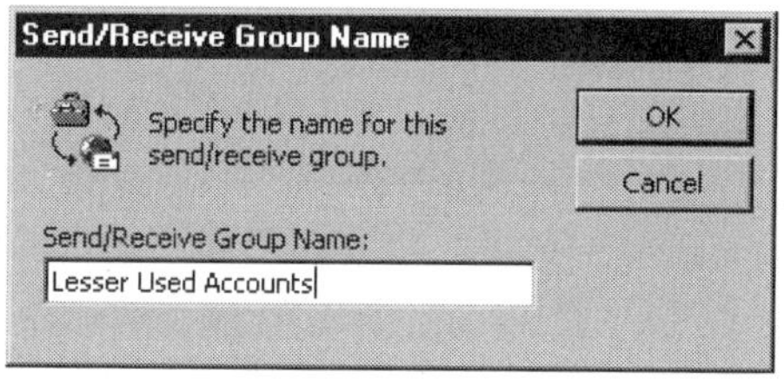


**Figure 2-8** Creating a new Send/Receive group.

3. **Specify which mail accounts to include.**

   In the Send/Receive Settings dialog box, as shown in Figure 2-9, select an e-mail account you want to include in the new group from the Accounts list, and then select the Include Account In This Send/Receive Group check box.

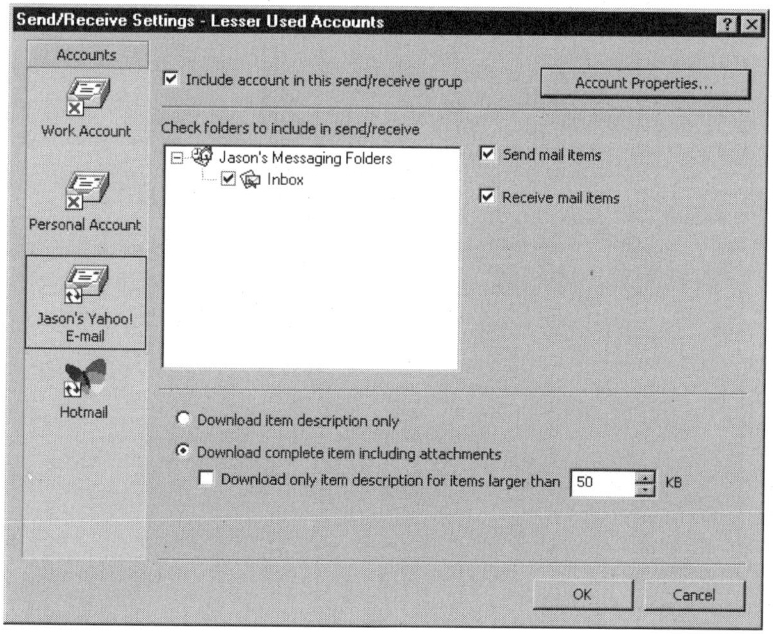


**Figure 2-9** Specifying e-mail accounts to include in a Send/Receive group.

4. **Specify which folders to check for new messages.**

   For IMAP and Web-based accounts (Hotmail), select the folders you want to check for new messages (the Inbox) by selecting the check box next to the folder's name. Click OK when you're finished.

5. **Modify the group's Send/Receive schedule.**

   In the Send/Receive Groups dialog box (see Figure 2-7), select the new group and use the dialog box to specify when Outlook should check for new messages, as discussed earlier.

NOTE *You may want to remove accounts from the All Accounts group that you added to your new group so that you're not checking the same accounts in both schedules. Alternatively, consider creating a group for just the accounts you check frequently and then setting Outlook to infrequently check the All Accounts group.*

# Maximizing Slow or Expensive Internet Connections

If your Internet connection is slow and/or expensive, you can take some steps to maximize your connection, as described in the following sections.

## Adjust Your Send/Receive Settings

To make checking your e-mail take as little time as possible, follow these steps:

1. **Make sure Outlook disconnects after checking for new mail.**

   Choose the Tools menu's Options command, and then click the Mail Setup tab. In the Dial-Up section, make sure the Hang Up When Finished With A Manual Send/Receive check box is selected, as shown in Figure 2-10. Also consider clearing the Automatically Dial During A Background Send/Receive check box so that Outlook connects to the Internet only when you instruct it to.

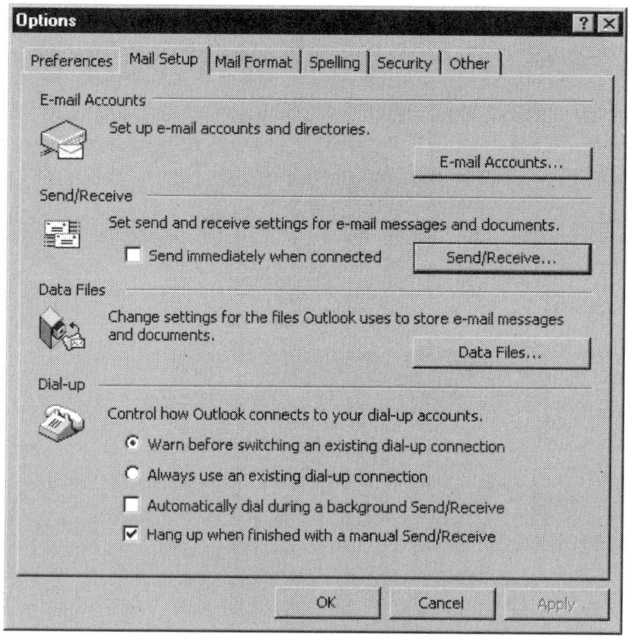


**Figure 2-10** Verifying that Outlook disconnects after checking for new mail.

**2. Click the Send/Receive button to open the Send/Receive Groups dialog box.**

**3. Adjust the Send/Receive schedules.**

Select each Send/Receive group, and adjust its schedule as appropriate, as shown in Figure 2-11.

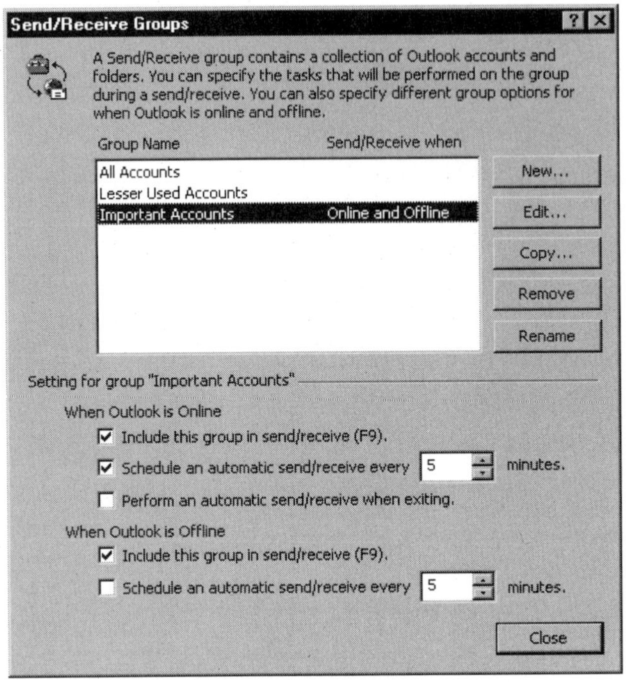


**Figure 2-11** Adjusting send/receive schedules.

Here are some suggestions:

- Clear the Schedule An Automatic Send/Receive check box in the When Outlook Is Offline section so that Outlook never automatically connects to the Internet.
- Prevent Outlook from checking inessential groups for new messages by clearing all check boxes for the group. (You can force Outlook to check these groups later by choosing the Tools menu's Send/Receive command and then selecting the group from the list.)

4. **Edit individual account settings.**

Select a Send/Receive group, click the Edit button, and then select an e-mail account from the Accounts list, as shown in Figure 2-12.

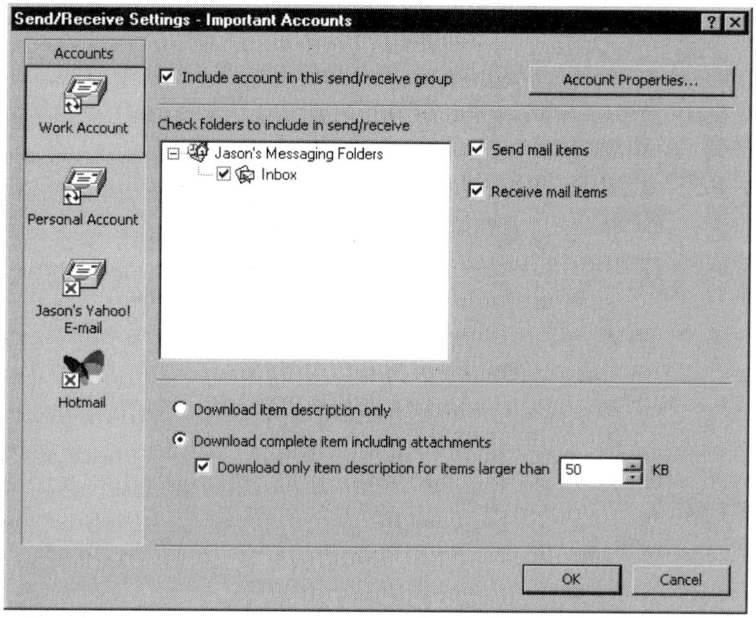


**Figure 2-12** Changing a POP3 account's download settings.

Here are some suggestions:

- To download only message headers (the sender and subject), click the Download Item Description Only option button. This permits you to read the subjects of messages and then download the messages you want to read later, as described in the next section.
- To download all messages, but limit the size of the messages that are downloaded, click the Download Complete Item Including Attachments option button (POP3 accounts only), and then select the Download Only Item Description For Items Larger Than check box.
- For IMAP and Hotmail accounts, check for new messages only in your Inbox and any other essential folders. To do this, clear the check boxes next to all inessential folders.

## Reading Mail Offline

You can use Outlook's Offline mode in combination with message headers to reduce the time you spend online to a bare minimum.

When you check for new messages, Outlook downloads only the headers (subject and sender) of new messages, sends any messages you've written, and then immediately disconnects. You can then peruse the downloaded message headers, mark the ones you want to read, and download them to read them while disconnected.

To work with messages while offline, follow these steps:

1. **Configure your mail accounts to download item descriptions only.**

   Follow the steps described in the previous section.

2. **Choose the File menu's Work Offline command.**

   This instructs Windows to disconnect from the Internet (if you're already connected), and try to accomplish everything it can while offline. Outlook then displays a disconnected icon on the right side of the status bar to indicate that you're offline.

3. **Check for new messages.**

   Click the Send/Receive toolbar button, or choose the Tools menu's Send/Receive command and select the e-mail account or group that you want to check from the submenu. Outlook connects to the Internet, downloads new message headers, and then disconnects.

4. **Mark the messages you want to download.**

   Right-click any messages you want to read, and choose Mark To Download Message(s) from the shortcut menu, as shown in Figure 2-13. This changes the icon next to the message to display a small blue arrow, indicating the message is marked for download.

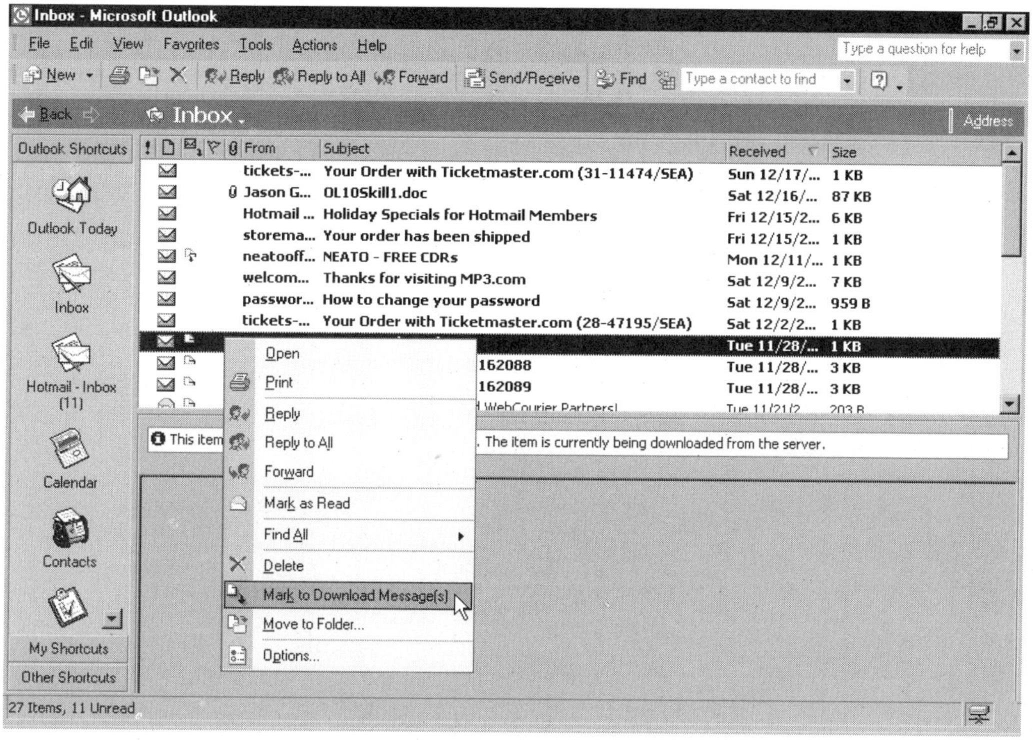


Figure 2-13 Marking a message to download later.

**5. Download marked messages.**

Click the Send/Receive toolbar button to check for new messages, as well as download the message bodies for any messages you marked. Once the messages are downloaded, you can read them and work with them as you would any other message.

## Maximizing High Speed Connections

If you have a persistent, high-speed Internet connection, such as access via a corporate network, DSL, or a cable modem, you can maximize your e-mail speed in a couple of ways.

Besides setting up Outlook to automatically check for new messages (discussed earlier), you can tell Outlook to download complete messages (as opposed to just the subjects) from IMAP and Hotmail accounts. To do so, follow these steps:

**1. Open the Send/Receive Groups dialog box.**

Choose the Tools menu's Send Receive Settings command, and then choose Define Send/Receive Groups from the submenu. This displays the Send/Receive Groups dialog box, shown in Figure 2-14.

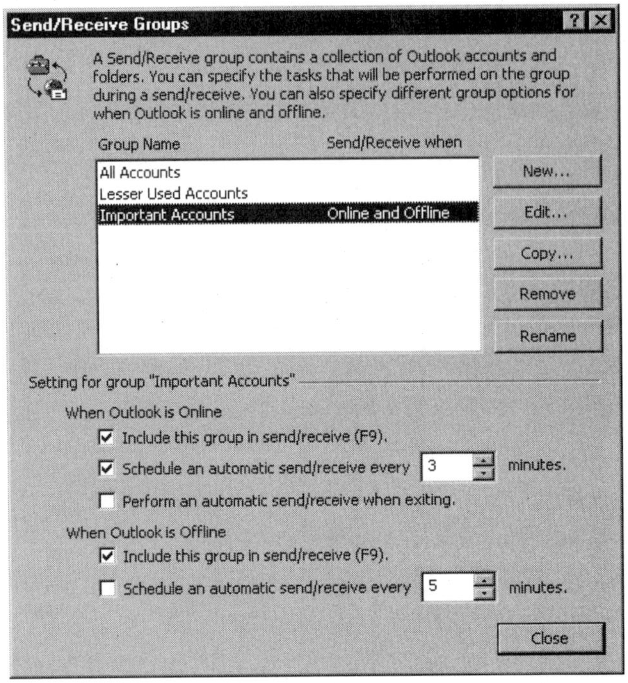


**Figure 2-14** The Send/Receive Groups dialog box.

2. **Select the Send/Receive group.**

   Select a group from the list box, and click Edit.

3. **Select the IMAP or Hotmail account.**

   Choose the IMAP or Hotmail account from the Account list on the left.

4. **Set the download options for the folders.**

   Select the folder from which you want to download complete messages (most likely the Inbox folder), and click the Download Complete Item Including Attachments option button, as shown in Figure 2-15.

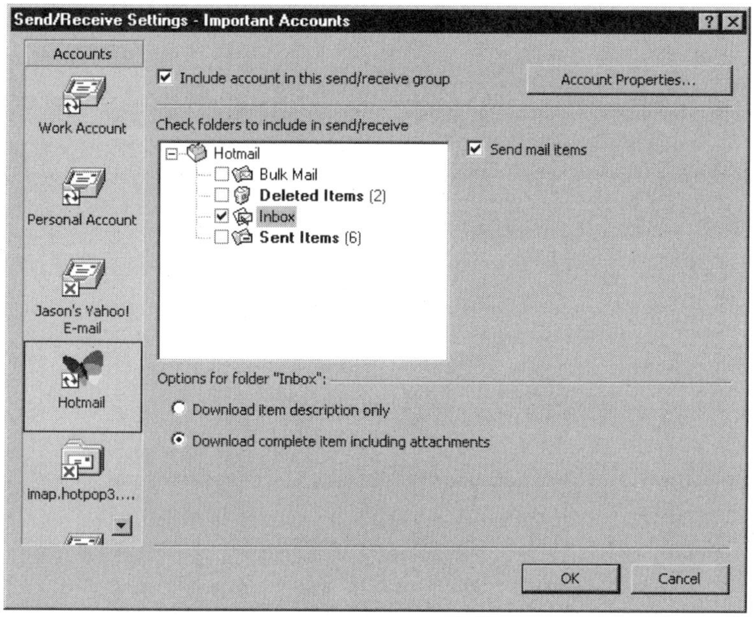


**Figure 2-15** Changing an account's download settings.

# Reading Messages

To read your e-mail, you first need to display your Inbox by clicking the Inbox shortcut on the Outlook bar. If you have an IMAP or Hotmail account, click the shortcut corresponding to your account (located under the Inbox shortcut on the Outlook bar), as shown in Figure 2-16.

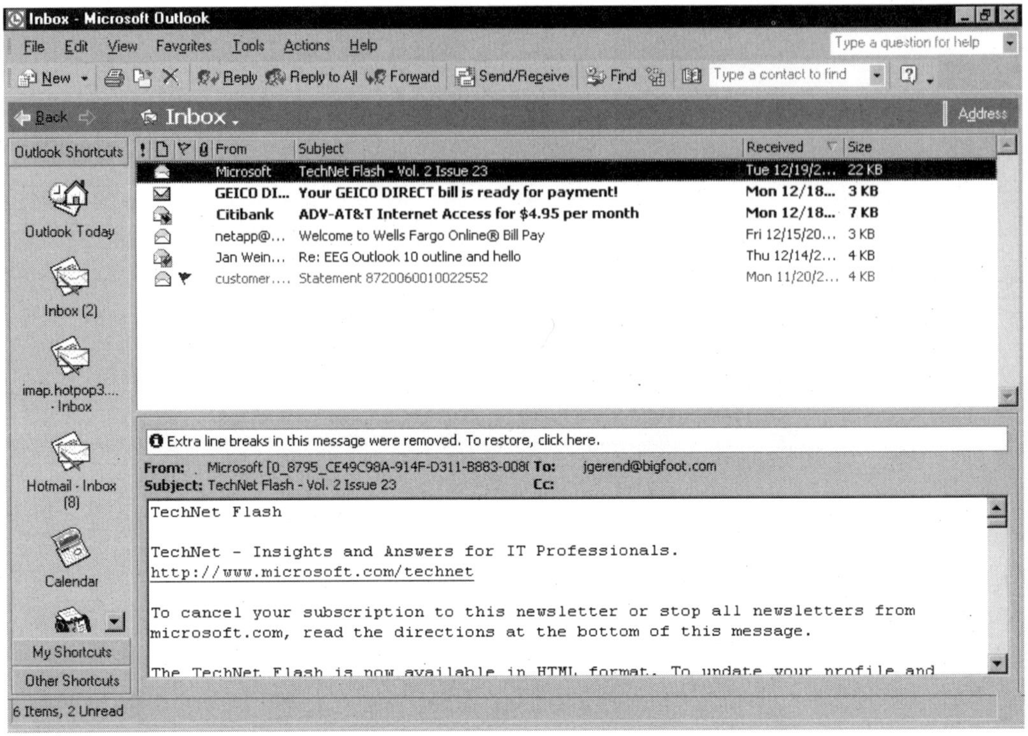


**Figure 2-16** Outlook with multiple Inboxes.

NOTE *If you didn't set up any e-mail accounts the first time you started Outlook, and it didn't find any on its own, your Inbox shortcut may be in the My Shortcuts group. To display it, click the My Shortcuts group on the Outlook bar. You can then drag the Inbox shortcut onto the Outlook Shortcuts group to move it back to where it should be.*

New mail is delivered to the Inbox folder, where it appears in bold text with a closed envelope icon next to it. To read your messages, as well as perform a few other common tasks, use the following list:

- Preview the message. Select the message from the list to automatically display the contents of the message in the Preview pane (see Figure 2-16). Press the spacebar to quickly scroll through the current message, and use the up and down arrow keys to view the next or previous message.
- Open the message. Double-click the message you want to open in a separate window, as shown in Figure 2-17.

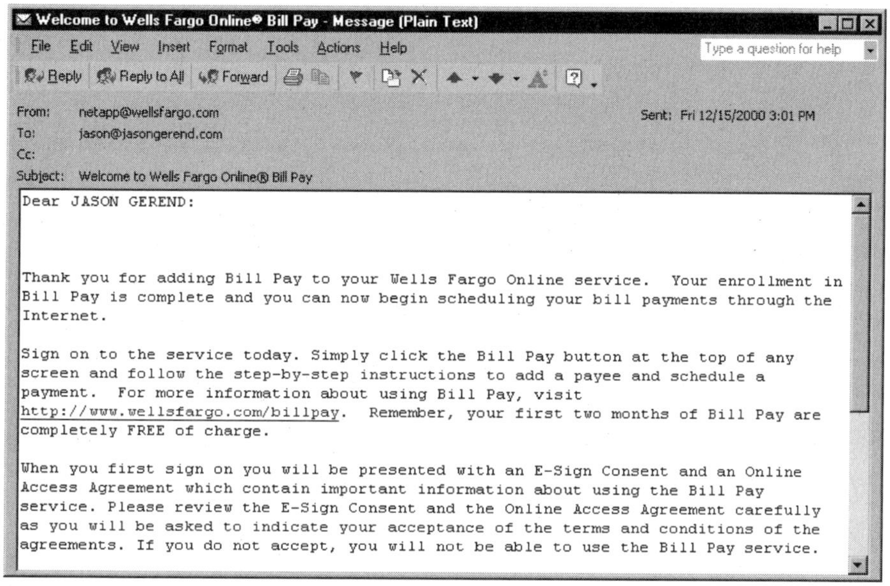


**Figure 2-17** A message open in its own window.

- Reply to a message. Select or open the message, and then click the Reply toolbar button.
- Forward a message. Select or open the message, and then click the Forward toolbar button (composing e-mail is discussed extensively in "Skill 3: Sending E-Mail").
- Add the sender to your Contacts folder. Select or open the appropriate message, right-click the sender's name in the From field, and then choose Add To Contacts from the shortcut menu, as shown in Figure 2-18.

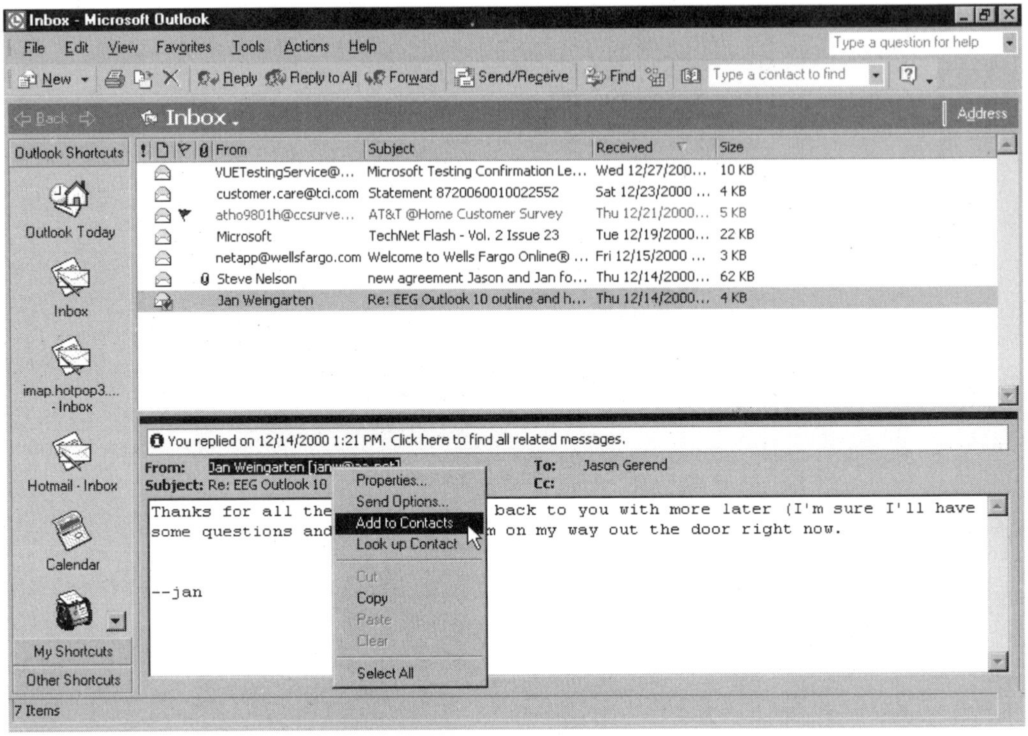

**Figure 2-18** Adding a sender to your Contacts folder.

NOTE *If you can't access your IMAP inbox, you might have the incorrect IMAP server settings. Click the Tools menu's E-Mail Accounts command, click Next, select the IMAP account from the list of accounts, and then click Change. Verify that the settings in the Internet E-Mail Settings (IMAP) dialog box are correct. If you need to enter a root folder path for your account, click the More Settings button, click the Advanced tab, and then enter the path (which is often mail) in the Root Folder Path text box.*

## Get to the Point Already

Most messages don't need to be any larger than a screen-full of text, and you should rarely send anything longer.

This is actually more than enough. Using most of today's programs, a screen full of verbiage is between 800 and 900 words. Your total may vary, but the limits are clear. If what you say exceeds these parameters, you need to think seriously about whether to click the Send button in the first place.

There are exceptions, of course. People who are communicating on a personal level and really like each other should go on as long as they want. Ditto for those who are actually interesting. But the rest of us need to be brutally economical in our use of words.

One guideline: We need to act as if we are not only being charged to send a message, but as if the assessment is according to size. Those who go on too long face some real dangers. Many people skim their messages, so an important fact buried toward the end of the communiqué is bound to be ignored.

If you get the reputation for sending long-winded or uninteresting messages, your correspondence will remain unread. And if you become a true bore, your recipients may set up a macro to send your mail directly to the Deleted folder.

Look at it this way: Abraham Lincoln would need less than half a screen to post the Gettysburg Address online. Anything we have to say today is certainly less substantial, so there seems to be little reason for it to take more space.

# Working with Your Messages

Besides simply checking for new messages and reading your mail, you can use a few techniques to work with e-mail more efficiently, as discussed in the following sections.

## Sorting Messages

Although Outlook's default method of displaying messages in your mail folders is usually optimal, you may want to sort the messages differently. For example, if you want to quickly locate all the messages sent to you by a certain business contact, you could sort the messages by sender. Alternatively, you could sort messages based on whether you've read them yet, or by subject.

The following list describes how to change the way that Outlook sorts messages:

- To sort messages by a different field, such as the From field, click the column heading. A small triangle appears in the column you clicked, indicating that messages are being sorted based on this field.
- To change the order in which messages are displayed—for example, from most recent to oldest, click the column heading messages are sorted by. The triangle next to the column heading flips over to indicate the sort order is reversed.

- To resize a column, drag the line separating two columns until the column is sized appropriately.
- To make a column fit the content best, right-click the column heading and choose Best Fit from the shortcut menu, as shown in Figure 2-19.

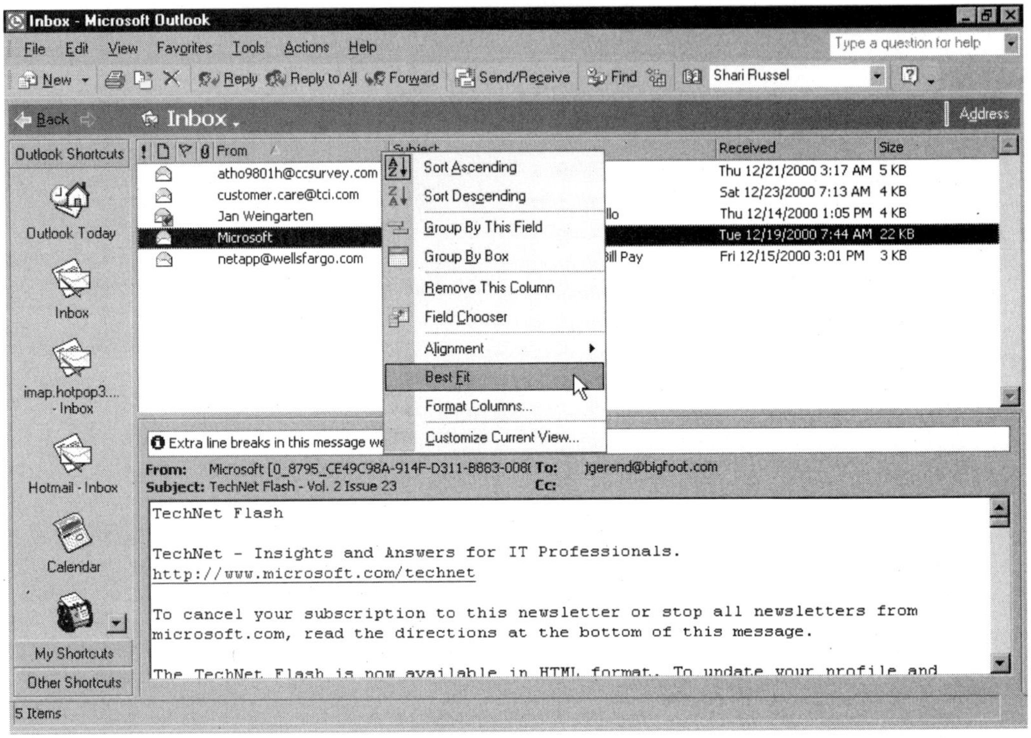


**Figure 2-19** Adjusting a column's properties.

- To move a column, drag the column heading to the desired location. Drag the heading down to remove it.
- To add a column, right-click a column heading and choose Field Chooser from the shortcut menu. In the Field Chooser window, locate the field you want to add, such as Categories, and then drag it to the appropriate location in the column headings, as shown in Figure 2-20.

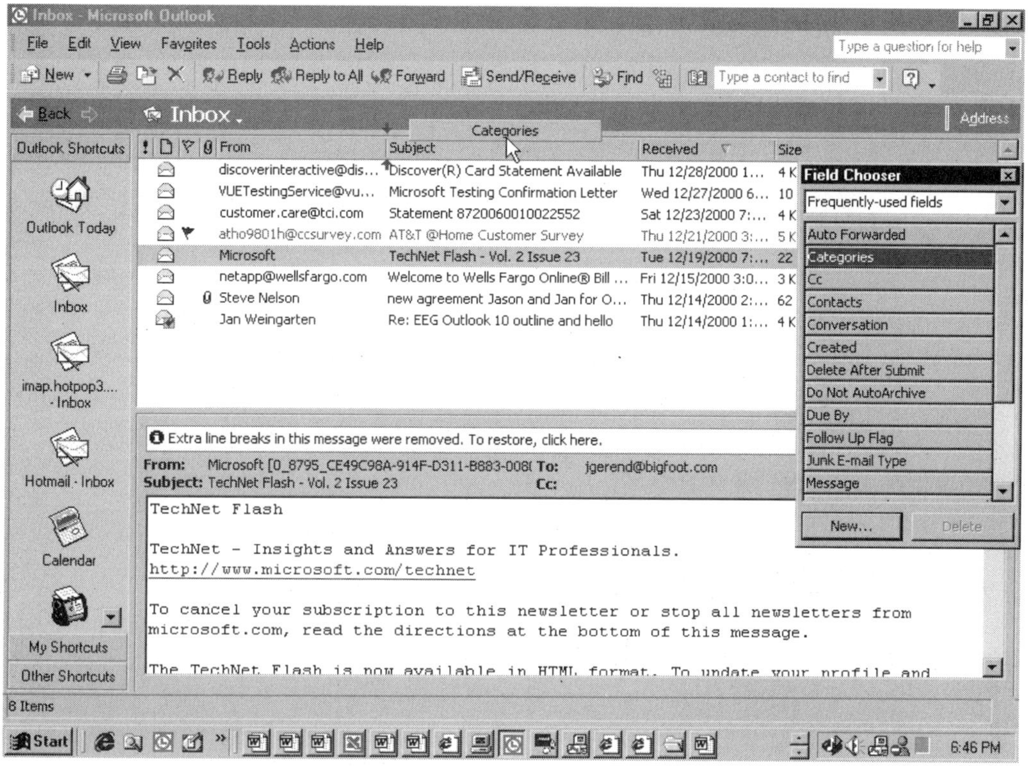


Figure 2-20 Adding a column.

# Marking Messages You Want to Read Later

Although it may be tempting to immediately read every message you receive, doing so can interrupt your workflow and distract you from your projects. To make more efficient use of your time, you can mark messages as unread (if you've already viewed them) or flag them to remind yourself to read them at a more convenient time.

## Marking Messages as Unread

Outlook marks a message as read if you view it and then view another message—even if you don't actually read the message. If you haven't actually read a message that Outlook marked as read, or you feel you should reread the message, the easiest thing to do is mark the message as unread.

- To make a message appear as if you haven't read it, right-click the message and choose Mark As Unread from the shortcut menu, as shown in Figure 2-21.
- To mark multiple messages as unread, hold down the Ctrl key and select each message you want to mark as unread, right-click one message, and choose Mark As Unread from the shortcut menu.

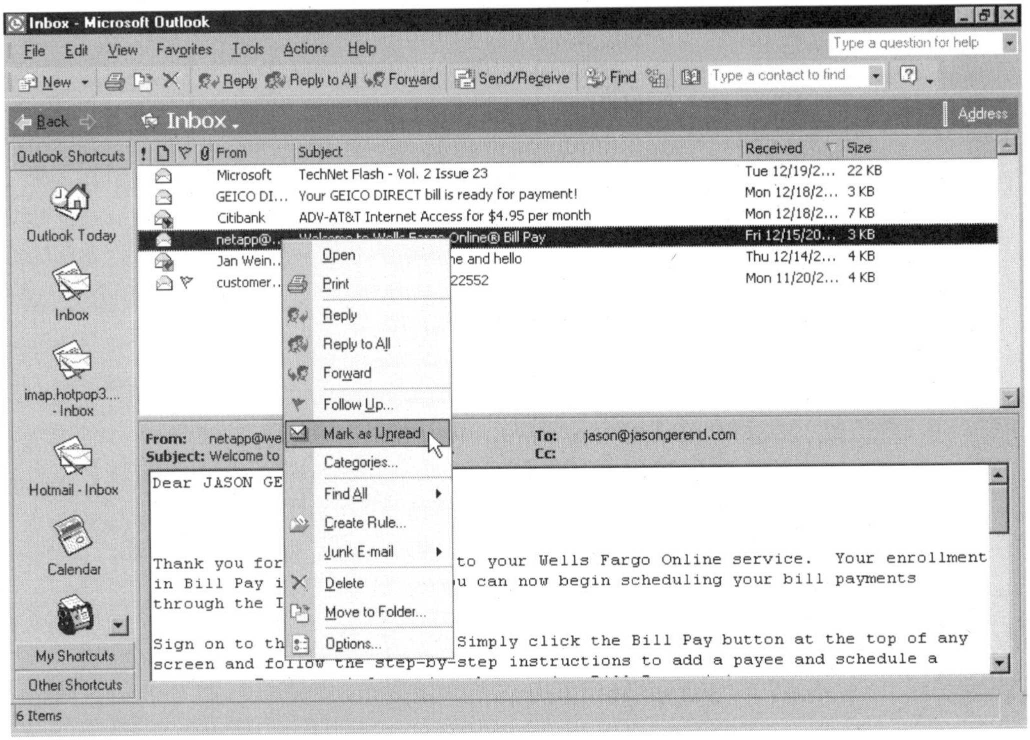


**Figure 2-21** Making a message appear as if you haven't read it yet.

## Flagging Messages

Besides simply marking a message as read or unread, you can also flag a message to help you remember to deal with it later. Flagging a message provides a number of benefits:

- A small red flag appears next to the message in your Inbox (or wherever the message is located), which serves as a visual reminder that you need to take action with the message.
- You can specify what action you need to perform when you flag the message, such as Follow Up or Reply.

- You can use flags to mark interesting or important messages so that they're easier to find later. You can also use the Do Not Forward flag so that you or your collaborators know not to pass along the message.
- You can set a due date for the item, which will display a reminder for you at the specified date and time.

To flag a message, follow these steps:

1. **Open the Flag For Follow Up dialog box.**

   Right-click the message, and choose Follow Up from the shortcut menu, as shown in Figure 2-22, or open the message in its own window and click the flag icon on the toolbar.

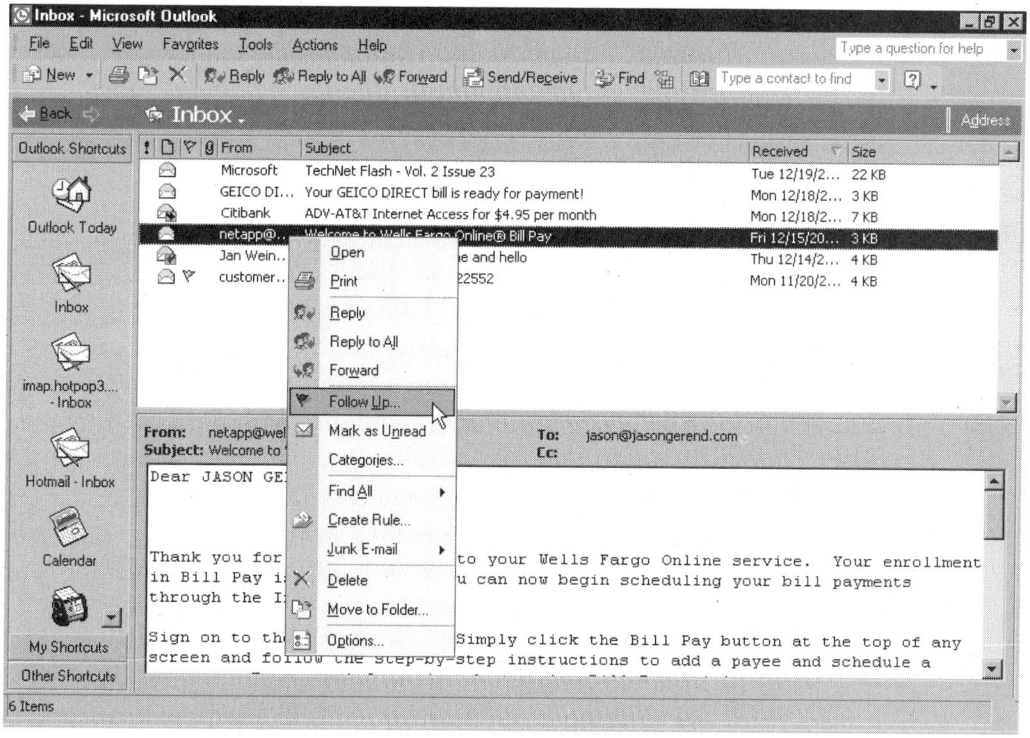


**Figure 2-22** Opening the Flag For Follow Up dialog box.

2. **Specify what you need to do with the message.**

   In the Flag To box, select the action that you need to take with the message, as shown in Figure 2-23. You can also enter your own action directly in the Flag To text box.

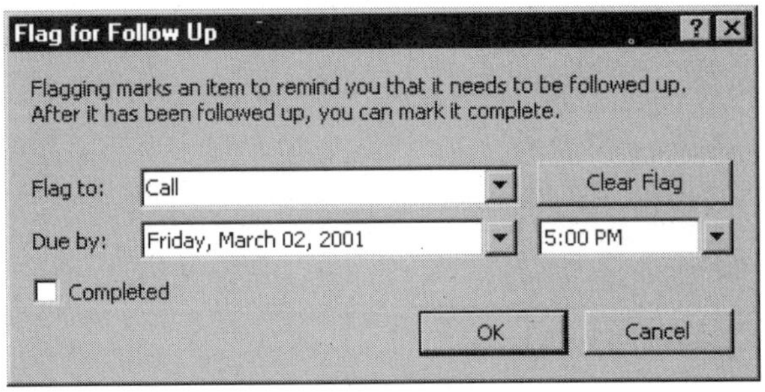


Figure 2-23 The Flag For Follow Up dialog box.

3. **Enter the due date for the flag.**

   Use the Due By text boxes to specify when you want to be reminded of the task (if you do). Enter the date and time in the boxes provided, or click the down arrows to select a date and time from pop-up menus.

TIP *Most of Outlook's date fields can interpret a date entered in many different ways. For example, you could enter 3/2, March 2, Friday, next Friday, or tomorrow. Outlook fills in the actual date when you move to the next field.*

4. **Click OK when you're finished.**

   Outlook redisplays the current mail folder (most likely your Inbox) with a small red flag next to the message, as shown in Figure 2-24.

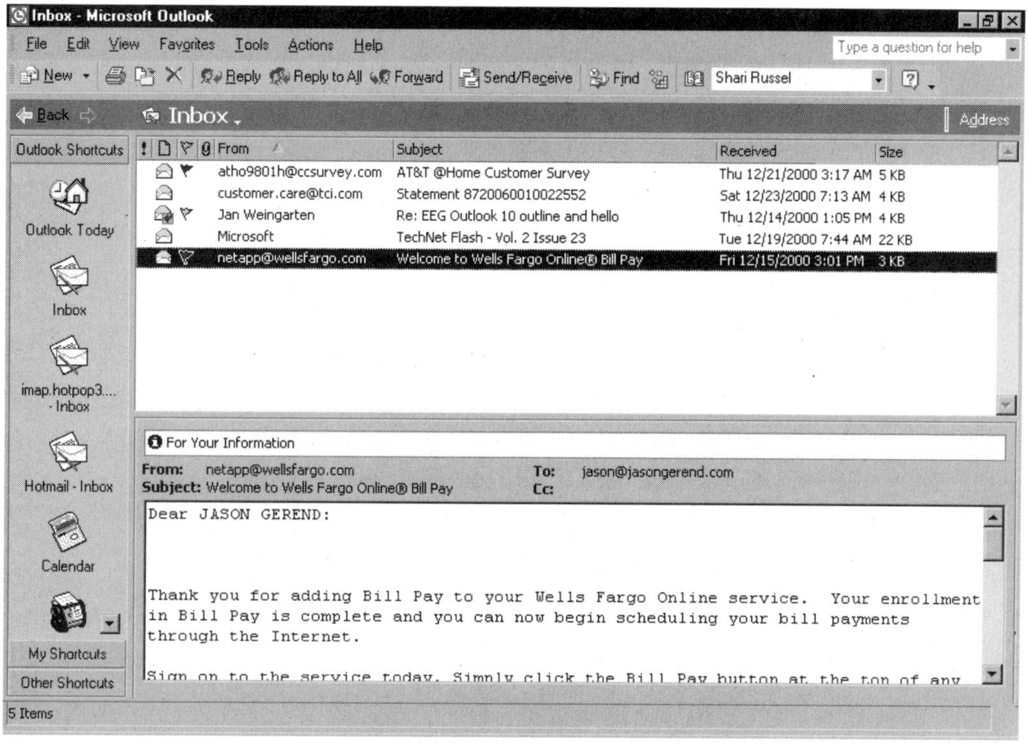


Figure 2-24 Several flagged messages in the Inbox.

5. **Clear or delete completed flags.**

   When you deal with a flagged message, you may want to delete the flag, or indicate that you completed the task (completed flags are colored in gray). To do so, right-click the flagged message and choose Flag Complete or Clear Flag from the shortcut menu.

## Toolbar Tips

Along the top of the toolbar is a button marked with an exclamation point, which you can use to set the priority for each message. Although the default is Medium, you can easily attach greater importance to a certain missive with a click of the mouse so that the recipient knows the message deserves the fullest attention.

Resist this temptation—not because some of your messages may be more important than others but because so many people have abused it in the past by attaching this tag to specious messages. Allow your recipients to decide whether a message is so worthy.

In contrast to the high-priority toggle is the button marked with a flag, which allows you to tag messages that arrive and indicate yourself whether they are worthy of some kind of follow-up. Using this button turns your Inbox into a simple to-do list: You tag the messages that require attention tomorrow, and then sort the folder by tags.

Software's best feature is the ability to give you more control over your life and work. Flagging messages for follow-up is a great example of this, because you manage the incoming flow. The priority flag is the opposite, however, because it hands over the control to someone else (if you are the recipient) and is generally ineffectual (if you are the sender).

Which makes us wonder about the third button, the down arrow that indicates low priority. In general, if a message isn't that important, instead of marking it as low priority, just don't send it. If, as the sender, you don't think the message is meaningful, your recipient probably won't either. It's like a big sign that says, "You don't have to read this." And since life is too short, you don't.

## Assigning Categories to Messages

Outlook categories can make it much easier to find related items of all types. For example, you can assign the Competition category to e-mails you receive from or about your competitors, as well as competitors' contacts, meetings, etc. You can then perform a search (discussed in "Skill 4: Managing Your E-Mail") based on the Competition category and quickly locate all of these various Outlook items.

Because assigning categories to items does involve extra work, we recommend that you set up Message Rules to automatically do this for you, as discussed in "Skill 4: Managing Your E-Mail." However, you'll also probably want to manually assign categories to messages that aren't included in your rules, as well as other types of Outlook items, such as Tasks and Appointments.

NOTE *The more you use this feature, the more you'll get out of it. Categories aren't that useful if you don't consistently assign them to your Outlook items.*

To assign categories to messages (or any Outlook item), follow these steps:

1. **Select the items you want to categorize.**

   To select multiple items, hold down the Ctrl key and click each item.

2. **Open the Categories dialog box.**

   Right-click the item(s), and choose the shortcut menu's Categories command, as shown in Figure 2-25.

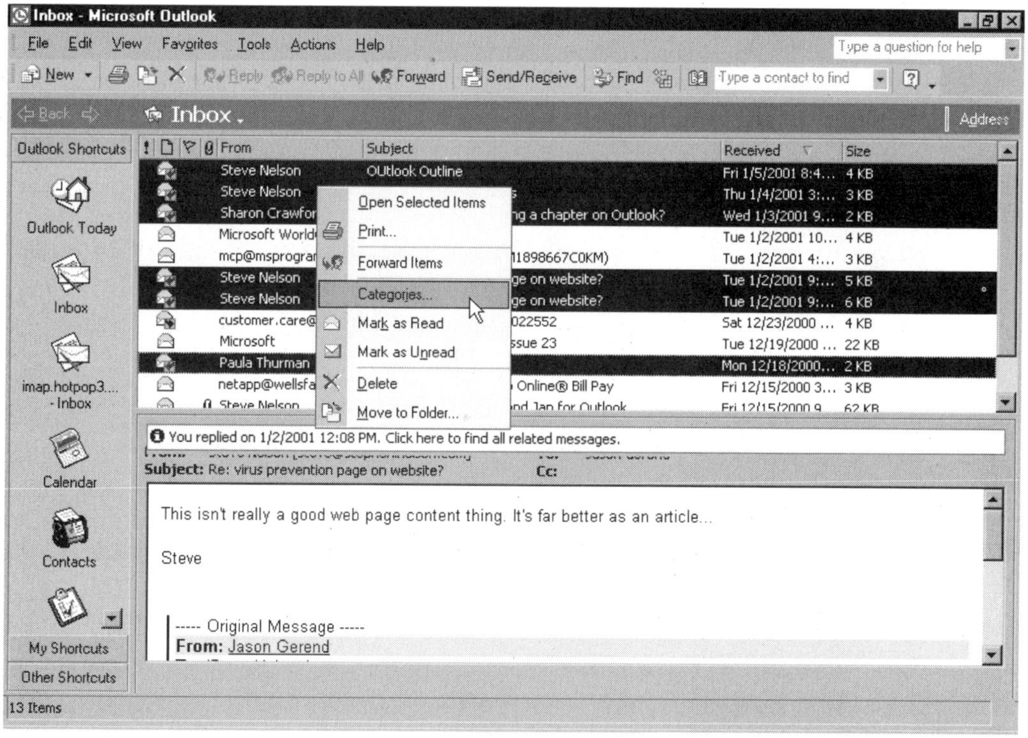

**Figure 2-25** Opening the Categories dialog box.

3. **Select a category for the items.**

   Select the check box next to the appropriate category for the items. Optionally, assign multiple categories, as shown in Figure 2-26. To add new categories, click the Master Category List button, enter the category name, and click Add.

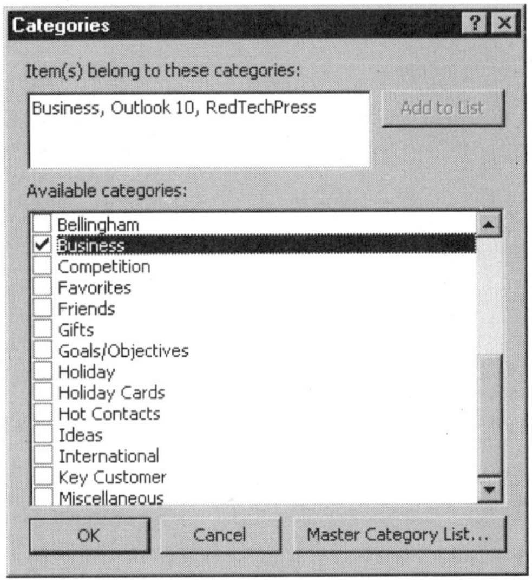


**Figure 2-26** The Categories dialog box.

## Deleting Messages

Deleting messages you no longer want is an important Outlook housekeeping task. Doing so reduces the hard drive and memory usage of Outlook, which keeps Outlook from slowing down. Deleting unwanted messages also makes it easier to locate those messages that you do want. Of course, deleting messages also saves you from repeatedly seeing certain messages you'd rather not view—advertisements, billing notices, and so forth.

WARNING *Owing to limits in Outlook's Personal Folders File (.pst) file format, if your Personal Folders File exceeds 2 GB in size, Outlook will fail and you won't be able to access your data. For more information on managing your file size, see "Skill 7: Maintaining Outlook."*

To delete a message, follow these steps:

1. **Select the messages you want to delete.**

   Click the message you want to delete. To delete multiple contiguous messages, click the first message, hold down the Shift key, and then click the last message in the list. To select multiple messages that aren't next to each other in the list, hold down the Ctrl key and click each message, as shown in Figure 2-27.

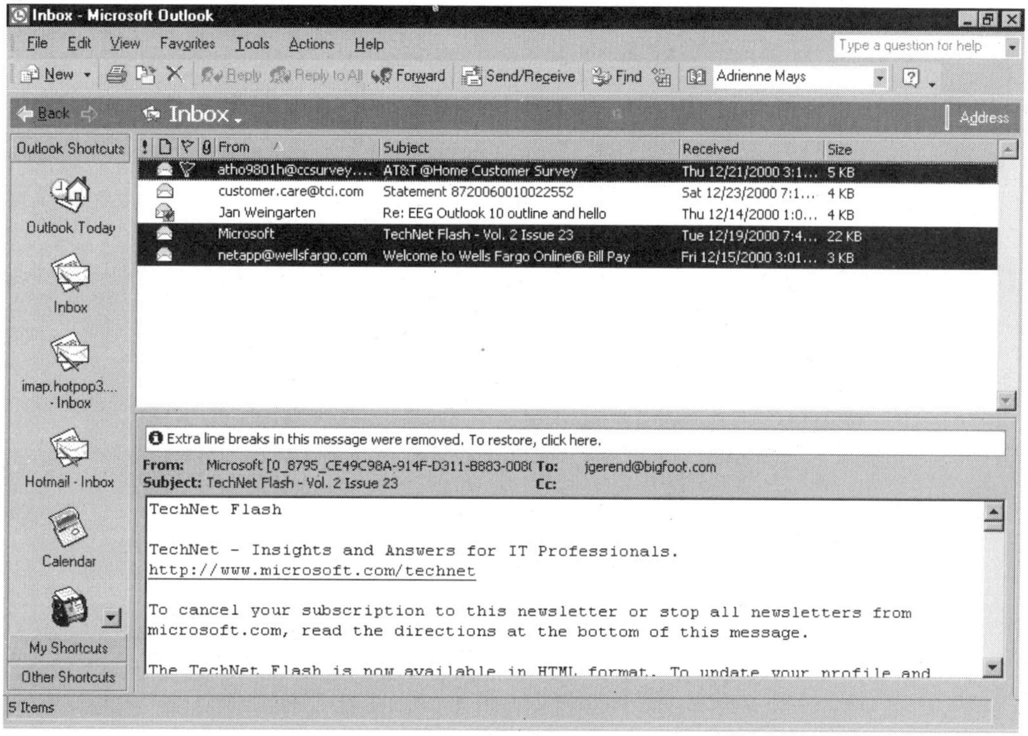


**Figure 2-27** Deleting several individual messages.

2. **Click the Delete toolbar button.**

   Outlook sends the messages you selected to the Deleted Items folder. If you're using an IMAP account, a line appears through the message, indicating the message is marked for deletion.

3. **Optionally, recover deleted messages.**

   To recover messages you deleted, click the Deleted Items shortcut on the Outlook bar (you may need to click the down arrow at the bottom of the Outlook bar to locate it), select the messages you want to recover, and drag them to the Inbox shortcut on the Outlook bar, as shown in Figure 2-28. For IMAP accounts, right-click a deleted message and choose Undelete from the shortcut menu. For information on emptying the Deleted Items folder, see "Skill 7: Maintaining Outlook."

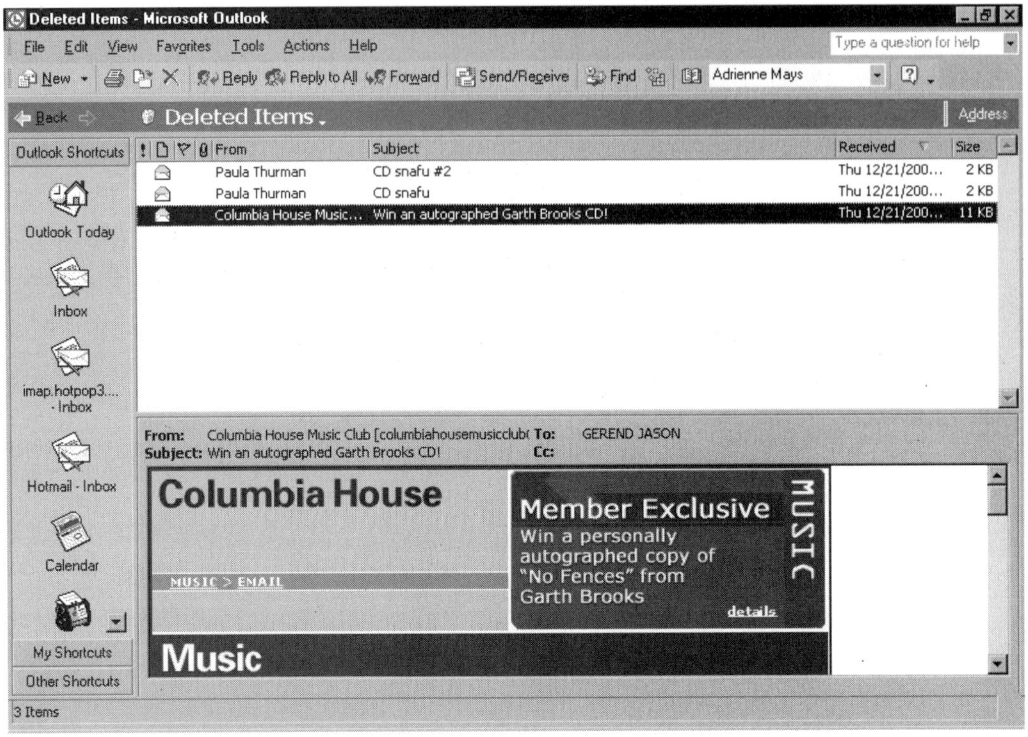


**Figure 2-28** Viewing the Deleted Items folder.

TIP *Because messages in an IMAP folder are simply marked for deletion rather than explicitly deleted, your Inbox is still as cluttered as before. To remedy this, you can either permanently delete all marked messages by choosing the Edit menu's Purge Deleted Items command or you can hide deleted messages by choosing the View menu's Current View command and then choosing Hide Messages Marked For Deletion from the submenu.*

## Saving Messages

All messages you receive are automatically saved in your Inbox. Standard POP3 e-mail accounts store their messages in Outlook's Personal Folders File on your hard drive, while other account types store their messages in the Inbox stored on your mail server.

If you want to save some messages in a different location, you have a couple options. You can save the messages in another folder on your hard drive or mail server, or you can save the messages as separate message files on your hard drive or removable disk.

## Saving Messages to Outlook Folders

Saving messages to folders other than the Inbox in Outlook offers you a few benefits. You can save messages to different folders to group them together and make them easier to find. You can also save messages to server-based mail accounts such as IMAP accounts or Hotmail so that you can access them from other locations.

To save a message to a different folder in Outlook, follow these steps:

1. **Select the message(s) you want to save.**
2. **Display the Folder List.**

   Click the Inbox heading (next to the Back button above the Outlook bar), and then click the pushpin button in the top right corner of the Folder List to lock the Folder List open, as shown in Figure 2-29.

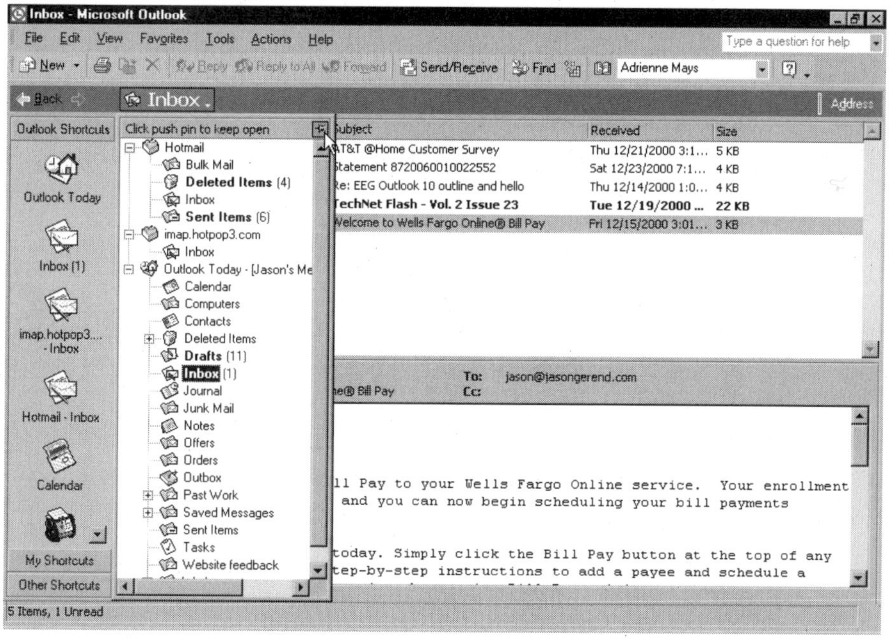

Figure 2-29 Displaying the Folder List.

3. **Drag the messages to the desired folder.**

   Outlook moves the messages to the folder you drag them to. (This process might take a while if you're moving them to a folder on a sever-based e-mail account.) To display subfolders, click the plus sign next to the parent folder. For more information on using folders, see "Skill 4: Managing Your E-Mail."

## Saving Messages as Files

If you want to save an individual message to a file for transporting on a removable disk (such as a floppy or CD-RW disk) or to store on your hard drive or network, follow these steps:

1. **Select the message(s) you want to save.**

   If you select more than one message, the contents of all selected messages will be saved in a single text or HTML file (depending on the format of the selected messages).

2. **Choose the File menu's Save As command.**

3. **Specify the location in which to save the file.**

   Use the Save As dialog box to specify where to save the file. Most likely you'll want to click either the My Documents or Desktop shortcuts in the Places bar to save the file in the My Documents folder or on your desktop. To save the file to a removable disk, select the drive from the Save In drop-down list box, as shown in Figure 2-30.

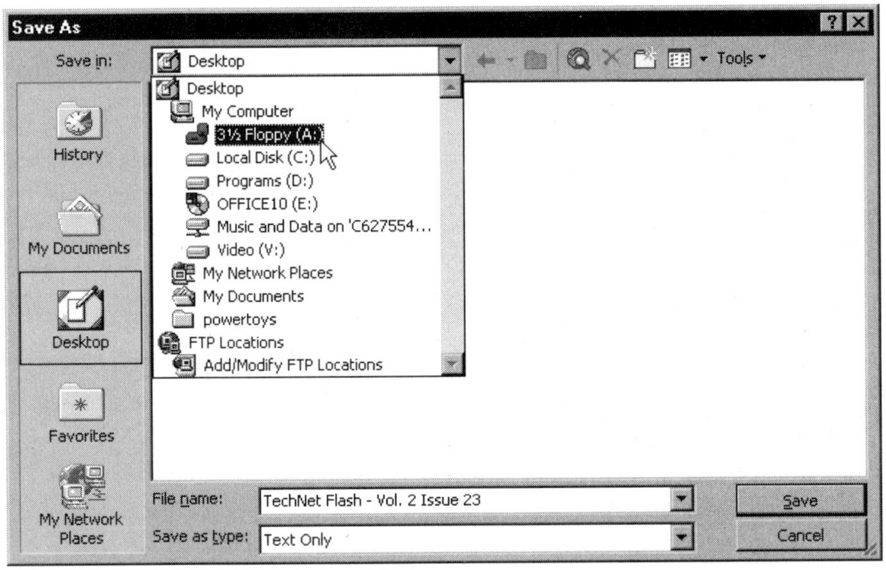


Figure 2-30 Choosing a location in which to save the file.

4. **Enter a filename.**

   In the File Name text box, enter a descriptive name for the file. If you anticipate using the file on a Unix or Linux operating system, or you are sending the file to someone who does, don't use spaces in the filename.

5. **Choose a file format.**

   In the Save As Type drop-down list box, select the file format you want to use:

- Text Only saves the file in a plain text format, which can be read by any computer.
- HTML saves the file as a Web page, which can be read by any Web browser (only available for messages written in HTML format).
- Outlook Template saves the file as a template that you can use to create new messages based on the message you selected. See "Skill 4: Managing Your E-Mail" for more information on templates.
- Message Format saves the file as an Outlook message, which you can open only in Outlook or Outlook Express. This format allows you to reply to the message or work with the message like a message stored within Outlook.

6. **Click Save.**

## Nine Things You Can Do to Manage Your Messages

Everyone who gets on to the e-mail train finds they have too many messages before they get two stops down the line. With this in mind, you can take some steps to manage a multitude of messages.

1. Use folders. In the same way that you can't eat a 72-ounce steak in one sitting, a 1,000-message Inbox will be incomprehensible until you establish an organizational order step by step. Take the time to list 10 important categories and create a corresponding folder for each. Moving every existing message into one of the folders will be frustrating and time consuming, but it is a job you need to do only once—as long as you shift all incoming messages into the appropriate spot.
2. Use filters. Folders are greatly enhanced by filters. E-mail software lets you apply certain conditions to incoming messages, automatically sorting them into the proper folder—or the Deleted Items folder. Here, you can determine the content or subject of a message and separate it from the rest. For instance, you may be working on a project called "Convention," and so you instruct your correspondents to use that word in the header of every pertinent message.

   Or you can search the body of each message for certain terms and move those messages to a specific location. The hardest part of using filters is the planning; you need to spend a lot of time determining the nature of the messages you are to receive. And because no filter in the world is foolproof, you'll always have to check other folders to make sure you haven't missed anything.

3. Deal with everything right away. This is your mother speaking: "Clean your room now, or the junk will pile up and be messy forever." If you never listened to her, you won't listen to me, but we're right: Sort the mail as soon as it comes in. Answer what you can. Create folders that reflect different parts of your e-mail life, and move messages to the appropriate ones as soon as they come in. Keep your Inbox small, and use it to hold only the most important messages.

4. Use the flag. Outlook allows you to set priorities on messages and tag them for follow up. If you are really snowed under, flag the messages that are important and assume the rest is drivel.

5. Sort and delete by correspondent. If you have a thousand messages in your Inbox, sort by the sender's name and hack away at the messages that don't scream "Read me!" Those who are really swamped might just sort by date and delete everything prior to the day before yesterday.

6. Change the rules. Most e-mail slaves see a message of nebulous value and save it for later. The safe way to approach these messages is to save them, if there is any question whether you need them later. But if you are getting too many messages, it may be wiser to reverse the equation. That is, if the value of a message isn't immediately clear, dump it. At the end of each week (month? year?) you can wade through the Deleted Items folder to see if there's anything you missed. Or don't.

7. Reply to e-mail only at certain times of the day. If you stay online all the time and reply immediately to messages other people may feel like they should respond immediately as well. So the amount of messages received will naturally grow. If you log on only a few times a day, you won't be so inclined to waste your breath.

8. Get Nelson. The Nelson Organizer, downloadable from *www.caelo.com* (free for a month, $30 thereafter), is an Outlook add-on that sorts messages in a number of different views. You can see messages by date or correspondent, and it automatically sorts all bulk mail into a separate folder. You can also reset the Inbox to see only the very newest messages.

9. Nip it in the bud. To continue the gardening analogy, every e-mail you send is like a seed, to bloom at a later date. So if you are getting too much mail, you may consider sending less. More directly: If you don't send frivolous messages, maybe you won't receive them.

## Editing Messages

Most e-mail programs don't allow you to edit messages you receive. Although this does prevent you from manipulating other people's words, there are times that you may want to edit a message, for example, to correct mistakes or eliminate sensitive information before saving the message in Outlook. (If you're replying to a message or forwarding it, you can simply edit the inserted message text before sending it.)

To edit a message, follow these steps:

1. **Open the message.**

   Double-click the message to open it in a new message window.

2. **Choose the Edit menu's Edit Message command, as shown in Figure 2-31.**

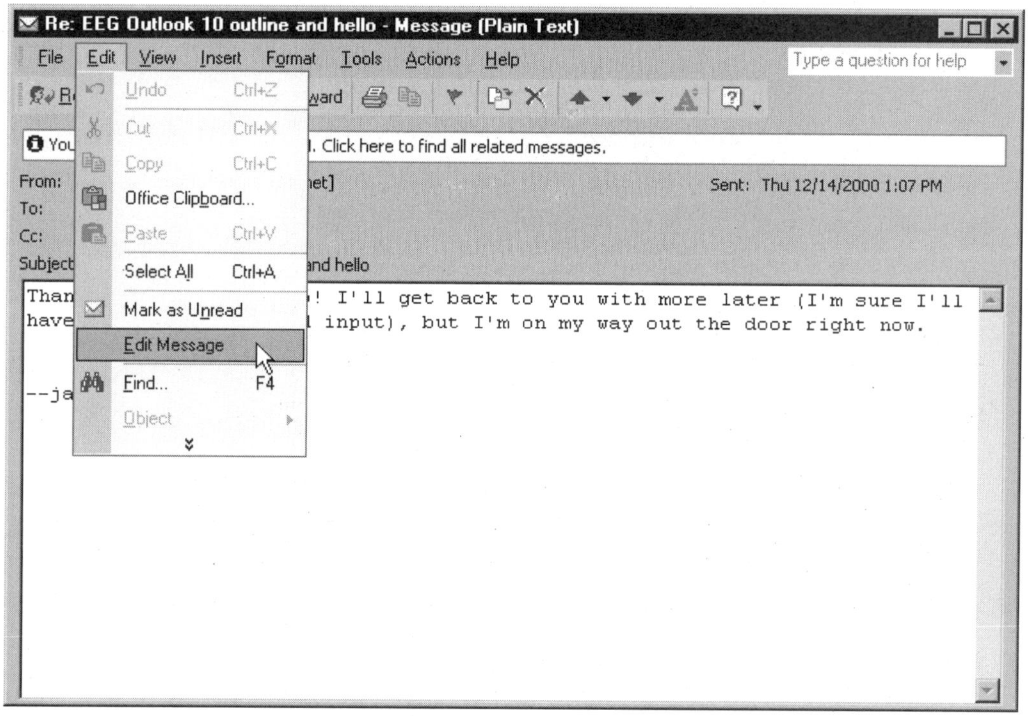


**Figure 2-31** Accessing the editing function.

3. **Edit the message.**

   Edit the message as if you were composing the message yourself. (For more information, see "Skill 3: Sending E-Mail.")

## Changing Message Fonts

By default, Outlook displays all plain text e-mail messages using the Courier New font, at 10-point size. If you find this font hard to read or displeasing to your eyes, you can change it to something more desirable. Doing so doesn't affect the way messages you send appear to others—only the way they look on your computer.

To change the font Outlook uses to display plain text e-mails, follow these steps:

1. **Display the Inbox, and then choose the Tools menu's Options command.**

   This displays the Options dialog box.

2. **Click the Mail Format tab, as shown in Figure 2-32.**

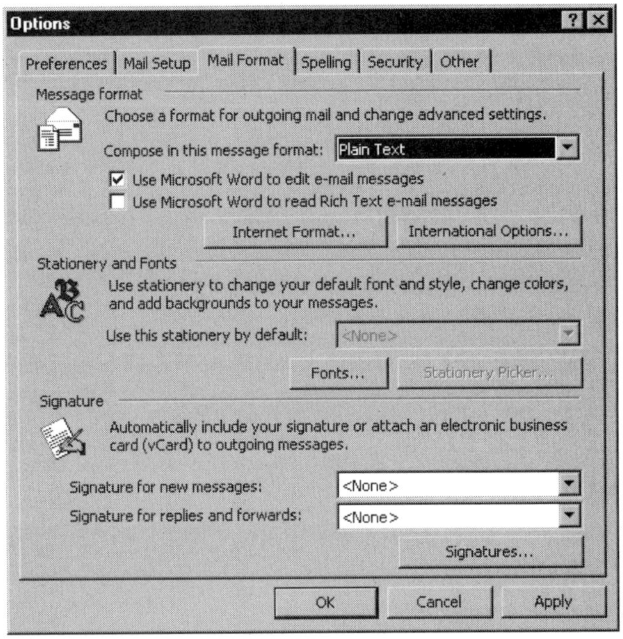


**Figure 2-32** The Mail Format tab of the Options dialog box.

3. **Click the Fonts button to open the Fonts dialog box.**

   Click the third Choose Font button in the Fonts dialog box, as shown in Figure 2-33.

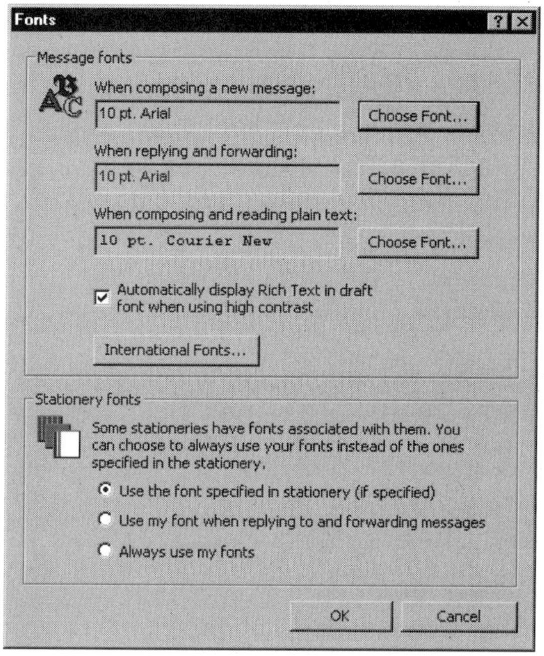


**Figure 2-33** The Fonts dialog box.

4. **Specify the font and font options.**

   In the Font dialog box, shown in Figure 2-34, select the font, font style, size, and color you want, and then click OK.

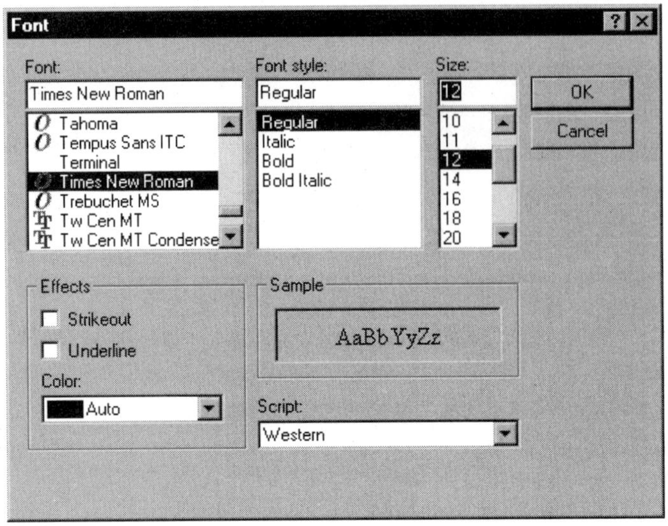


**Figure 2-34** Changing the font used to display plain text messages.

## Printing Messages

The utopia of the paperless office is still just fantasy. Reality is that whether it's directions to a new client's office or a new business contract, sometimes you're going to want to print out e-mail messages.

To do so, select the message and click the Print toolbar button to print using the default settings or follow these steps:

1. **Select the message you want to print.**
2. **Choose the File menu's Print command.**
3. **Specify the printer to use.**

   Choose the printer you want from the Name box at the top of the Print dialog box, as shown in Figure 2-35. To modify print options, such as color and resolution, click the Properties button.

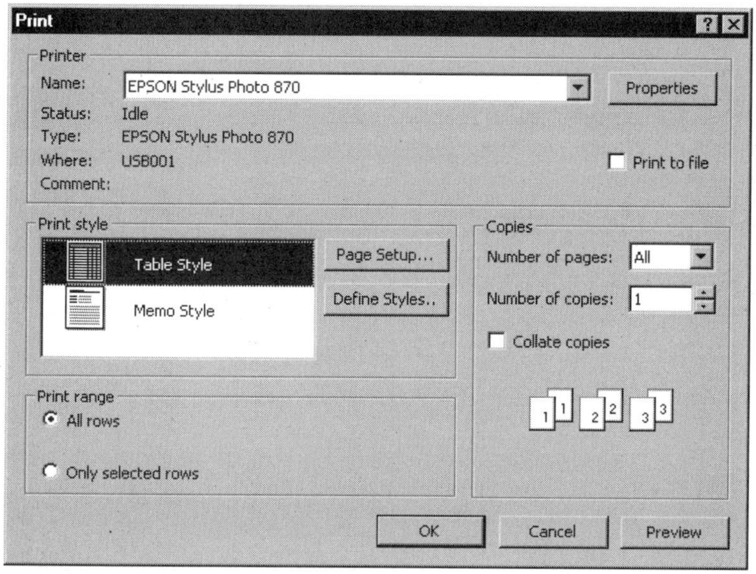


**Figure 2-35** The Print dialog box.

4. **Choose a print style.**

   In the Print Style box, select either Table Style to print just the message headers or Memo Style to print the entire message(s).

5. **Specify the number of pages and copies.**

   Use the Number Of Pages and Number Of Copies drop-down list boxes to specify how many pages of the message to print, as well as the number of copies. Select the Collate Copies check box to print each copy in its entirety before printing the next copy.

6. **Preview the print job.**

   Click the Preview button to display the Print Preview window, as shown in Figure 2-36. Click the Print toolbar button to return to the Print dialog box.

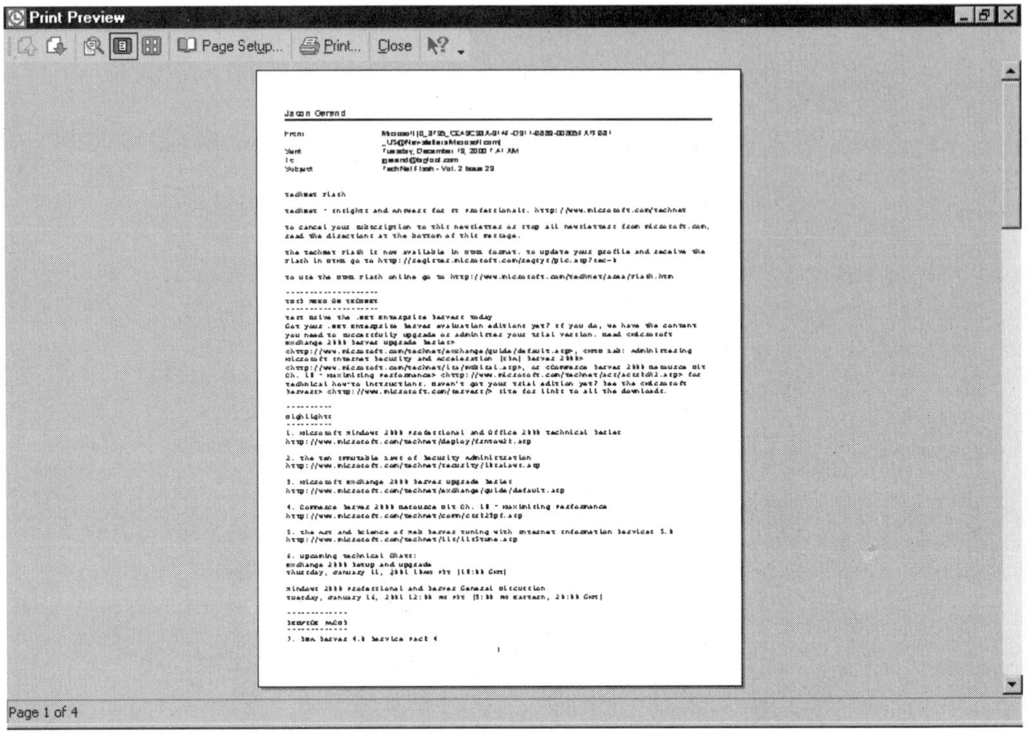


**Figure 2-36** The Print Preview window.

7. Click OK.

   Outlook sends the print job to your printer, which then prints the message.

# Working with Attachments

E-mail attachments cause more pain and frustration than any other aspect of e-mail. Many users have trouble opening and saving files that are attached to e-mail messages, and if that weren't enough, attachments are one of the biggest sources of computer viruses. However, e-mail attachments are a vital and useful tool for today's businessperson, so it's essential that you learn how to make use of them.

E-mails with attached files appear different in two ways. First, a small paper-clip icon appears next to the message in the Inbox, as shown in Figure 2-37. Second, Outlook displays an Attachments field for the message, listing the attached files.

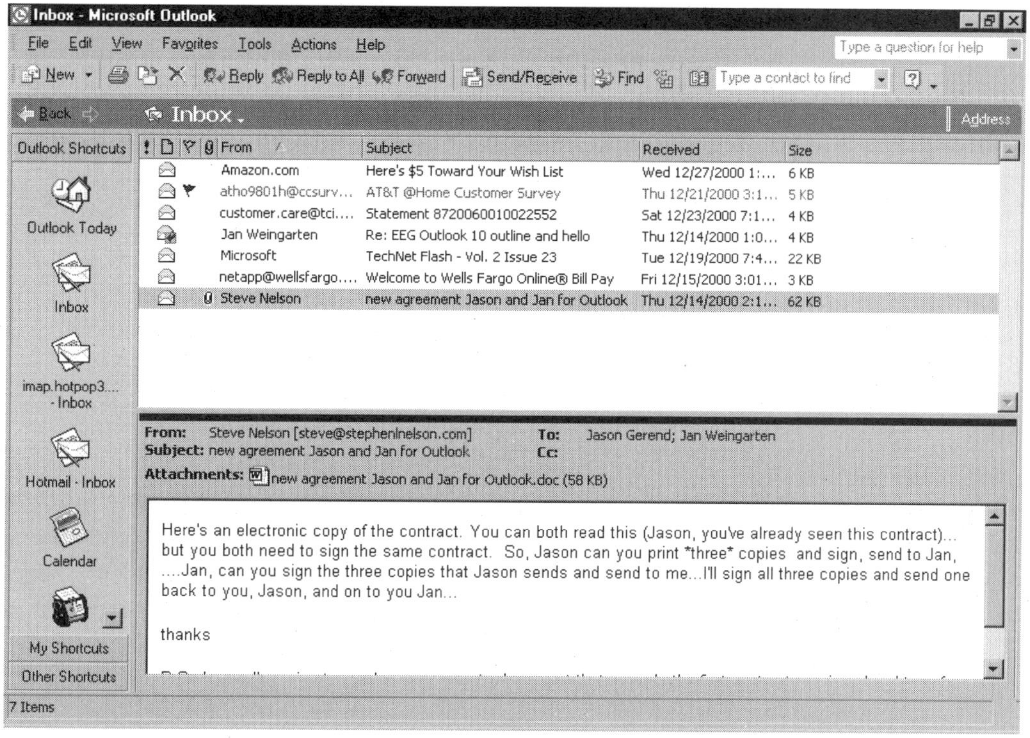


**Figure 2-37** The Inbox showing a message with an attachment.

Use the following list to work with attachments:

- To open an attachment, double-click its icon in the Preview pane or message window. Click the Open It option button in the Opening Mail Attachment dialog box, as shown in Figure 2-38, and click OK.

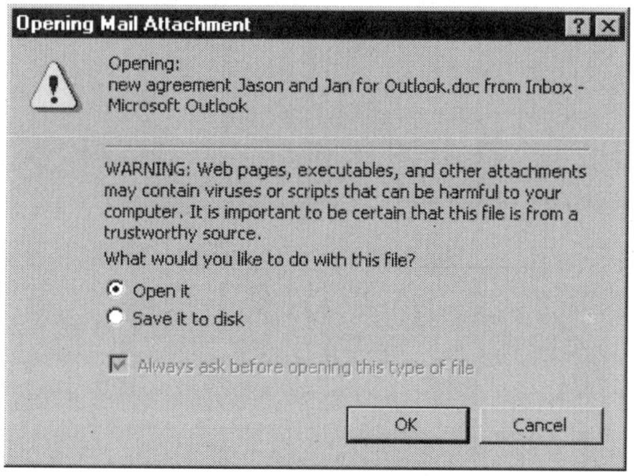


**Figure 2-38** The Opening Mail Attachment dialog box.

- To save an attachment, right-click the attachment, choose Save As from the shortcut menu, and use the Save Attachment dialog box to specify where to store the file.
- To remove an attachment from an e-mail message (perhaps to save hard drive space), double-click the message in the Inbox to display it in a separate window, right-click the attachment, and then choose Remove from the shortcut menu.

NOTE *Large attachments can sometimes fail to download properly, preventing you from accessing further messages. To deal with this situation, see "Skill 7: Maintaining Outlook."*

## Ask Before You Attach

The ability to send attachments with messages gave e-mail a new versatility and boosted it into the realm of the useful. Still, it contributed to the general downfall of online manners. To wit, too many people send off attachments without asking the permission of the recipient.

Viruses notwithstanding, there is still too much that can go wrong. An attachment—even a relatively "small" one—can take several minutes to download and tie up the phone line. Once arrived, there is a better-than-even chance that it will not open automatically. Although one preferred use for attachments is the ability to send along family pictures, it's not easy to teach the naive recipient about file size or association properties.

For this reason, you should always ask potential recipients before sending an attachment, specifying the file content, its size, and purpose. For instance, a query like "I'd like to send along a 3 MB PowerPoint presentation that shows you how we've renovated our house" gives them the opportunity to accept or decline the invitation.

This will eventually save them from the anguish of wondering why their e-mail program reads "downloading message 1 of 17" for half an hour. It is also essential to make sure the recipient has the software needed to read your file.

Better yet, we should set a polite limit for attachment size, say 100 kilobytes. Any larger, and you should ask permission. (The size of an attachment is always noted next to its icon in your mail program.)

For safety's sake, it makes sense to send along a text version of a document as backup for the attachment. Come to think of it, this also causes duplication. So the only time you should send an attachment is when it is expected or when the formatting is absolutely essential.

# Protecting Yourself from Viruses and Hoaxes

More damage has been done via so-called worm viruses spread via e-mail attachments than any other type of virus. However, it's actually very easy to avoid getting a virus, if you take a few precautions. The following sections show you how to stay safe, as well as how to spot virus hoaxes and stop their spread.

## Using an Antivirus Program

Antivirus programs that can scan incoming e-mail are the best first-line of defense for your e-mail. Two leading antivirus programs are Norton AntiVirus (*www.symantec.com*) and McAfee VirusScan (*www.mcafee.com*).

Antivirus programs don't work magic, however; you need to set them up properly and keep them updated in order for them to work optimally. Follow the procedures described below:

- Use an antivirus program compatible with Outlook 2002. Because older versions of these programs weren't designed to work with Outlook 2002, you may have to either manually configure the software to work with Outlook or upgrade to a newer version.
- Update your virus definitions frequently. Antivirus programs rely primarily on virus definitions—text files used by antivirus programs to identify known viruses. Because new viruses appear daily, it's important to update your virus definitions often—at least every two week. (Schedule automatic updates to occur daily for the greatest protection.)
- Protect all of your e-mail accounts. When you install an antivirus program, make sure that you enable e-mail protection for all of your e-mail accounts. If you set up a new e-mail account, make sure to set up your antivirus software to protect this account also (it won't automatically be protected).

## Don't Open Suspicious Attachments

Since e-mail viruses can spread nationwide in a matter of hours, you often get exposed to dangerous viruses before virus prevention companies can update their software.

Therefore, even more important than using an antivirus program is being careful about which attachments you open. Below are some guidelines to use every time you receive an attachment:

- Open only those attachments you can identify. Many people refuse to open any attachments they didn't specifically request, but we feel that if you can positively identify what the attachment is, you should be okay if you have up-to-date virus software.
- Don't open attachments you're unsure of. If you can't identify an attachment, or if the message text seems strange, e-mail the person who sent you the attachment and ask for an explanation. If you don't get a response back, delete the message.

## How to Spot a Hoax

Almost as bad as viruses are virus hoaxes. Virus hoaxes are e-mails sent to warn people of supposedly dangerous viruses that in reality don't exist.

Despite their seemingly innocuous appearance, virus hoaxes are a form of information terrorism, and they cost companies real money. Virus hoaxes incite unneeded fear in people who believe them and cause a loss in productivity from the time spent reading, forwarding, and worrying about the perceived virus threat. Worried users often call your Help Desk or support company, further increasing costs. The e-mails sent also consume precious network bandwidth, slowing down your network as well as the Internet in general.

The following list helps you identify virus hoaxes:

- Virus hoaxes warn of dire consequences. Most proclaim to be worse than the last bad virus epidemic. Ask yourself, if this virus is so bad, why haven't I heard of via the news media yet?
- Hoaxes don't provide verifiable references. All well-written e-mails about real viruses include references you can check for more information, such as a URL to Symantec's Antivirus Research Center (*http://www.symantec.com/avcenter*).
- Virus hoaxes ask you to forward them to everyone you know. Since the point of a virus hoax isn't to inform but to spread the hoax, there is a strong call to action at the end of the hoax, informing you to forward it to everyone you know.

To help stop the spread of virus hoaxes, follow these recommendations:

- Don't forward any virus warnings. Many people receive a multitude of real virus warnings, which can quickly become almost as bad as an actual virus hoax. If you feel the need to educate a friend or colleague about viruses, loan them this book, or direct them to Symantec's Antivirus Research Center.

- Check out urban legends and other chain letters. Virus warnings aren't the only hoaxes circulating via e-mail. In general, you should never forward any chain letter that you haven't personally verified (this includes charity letters, by the way). If no sources are listed, check Scambusters.org (*http://www.scambusters.org*) or Hoaxbusters (*http://hoaxbusters.ciac.org*) to see if they're scams or hoaxes.
- Check the accuracy of virus warnings you receive. Use Symantec's Antivirus Research Center Web site at *http://www.symantec.com/avcenter* to check for information on a suspected virus or virus hoax, as shown in Figure 2-39.

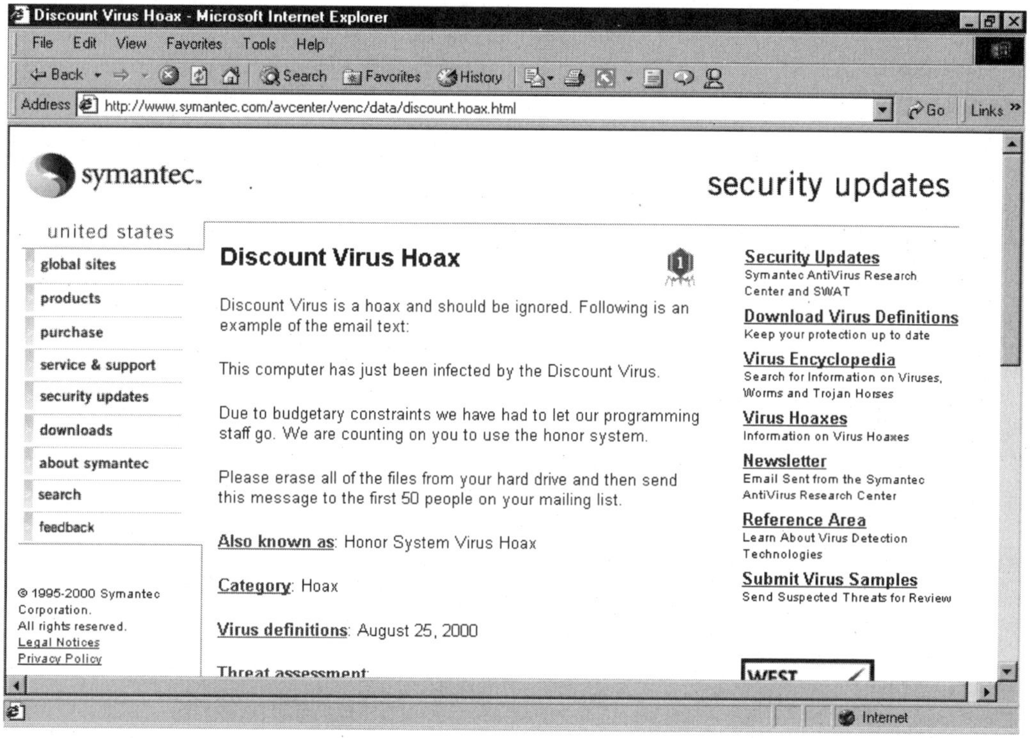


**Figure 2-39** Virus hoax information on Symantec's Web site.

# Using Outlook Today

Outlook Today is a special view that you can use to quickly get an overview of your information in Outlook. It lets you see any appointments you have scheduled for the next several days, any tasks you have, as well as a listing of how many unread e-mail messages you have. As such, many people find it a useful to look at Outlook Today from time to time, usually at the beginning of the day.

To use Outlook Today, follow these steps:

1. **Click the Outlook Today shortcut on the Outlook bar.**

   This displays Outlook Today, as shown in Figure 2-40.

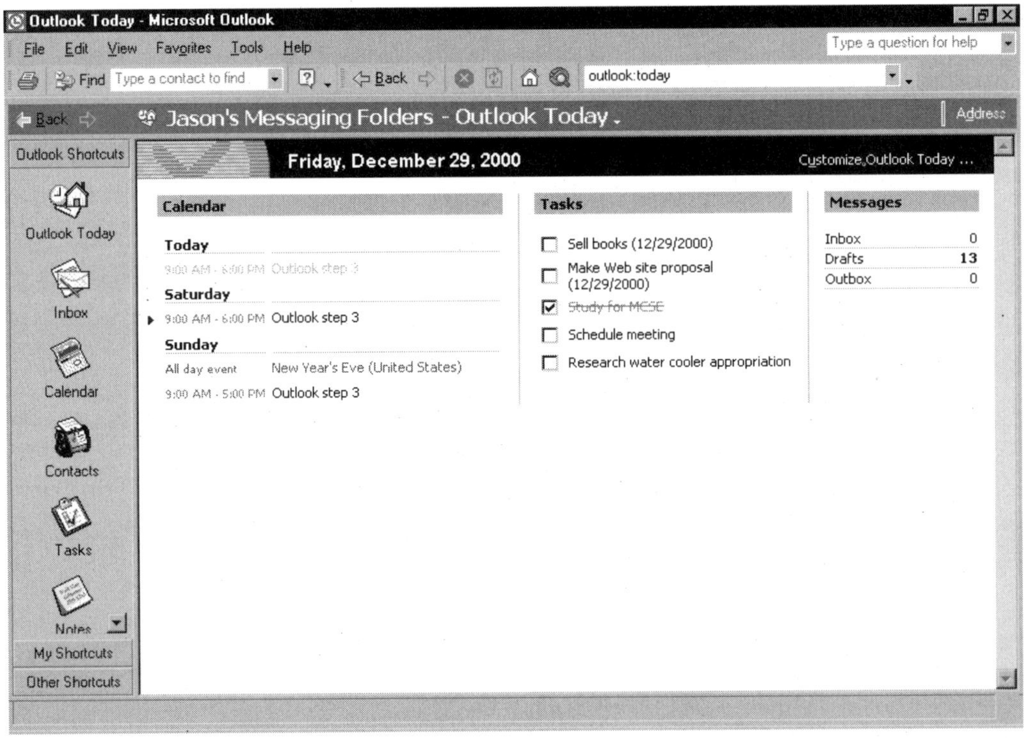


**Figure 2-40** Outlook Today.

2. **View any important items.**

   Click an item's description to open the item. Click the Calendar, Tasks, or Messages heading to display the Outlook Calendar, Tasks folder, or Inbox.

3. **Customize Outlook Today.**

   Click the Customize Outlook Today link at the top right of the Outlook Today window to display the Customize Outlook Today window, as shown in Figure 2-41.

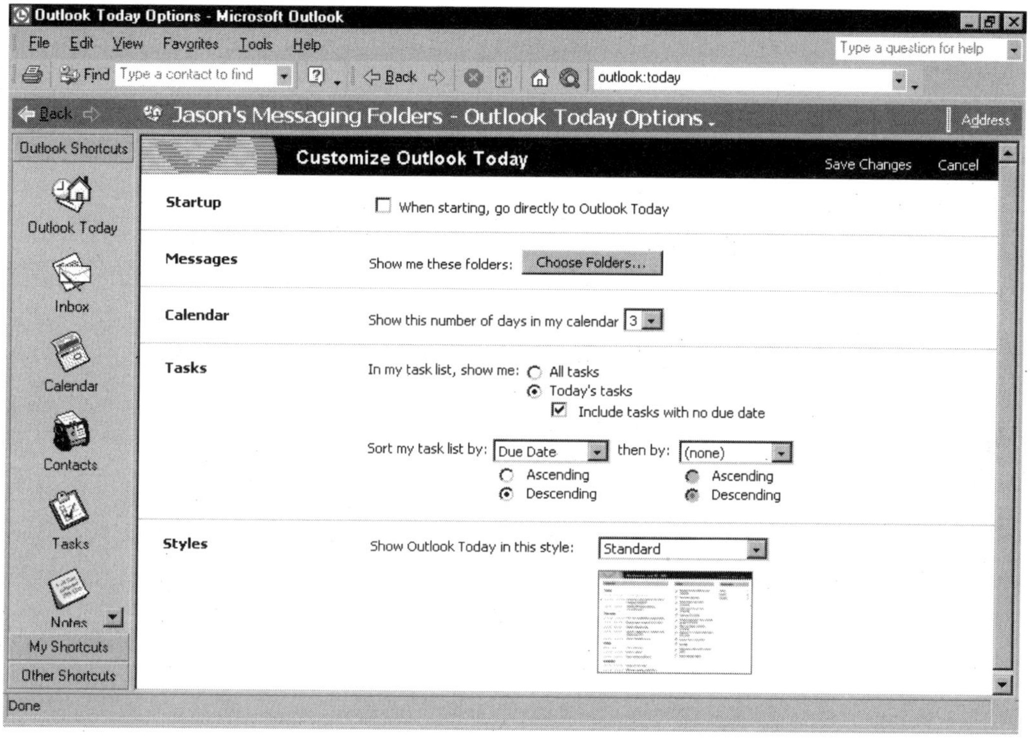


**Figure 2-41** Customizing Outlook Today.

4. **Specify whether to open Outlook Today by default.**

   Select the When Starting, Go Directly To Outlook Today check box if you want to view Outlook Today every time you open Outlook.

5. **Specify which message folders to display.**

   If you have multiple message folders, click the Choose Folders button to select those for which you want to display information in Outlook Today.

6. **Specify the number of days to display in your Calendar.**

7. **Specify what tasks to display.**

   To only see current tasks, click the Today's Tasks option button in the Tasks section. Optionally, select the Include Tasks With No Due Date check box, and use the Sort My Task List By boxes to change how tasks are sorted.

8. **Choose a visual style for Outlook Today.**

   Select a style from the Show Outlook Today In This Style drop-down list box to change the color scheme and layout of Outlook Today.

## Summary

Perhaps the most important thing you'll do with Outlook is read your e-mail. In this skill we showed you everything you need to know to effectively read your e-mail with Outlook, including how to open Outlook, check for new messages, read and work with the messages you receive, as well as how to deal with attachments and avoid viruses and virus hoaxes. We also showed you how to use Outlook Today to get an overview of your information in Outlook, as well as customize it to better suit your needs.

*Skill 3*

# SENDING E-MAIL

## Featuring:

- The Basics of Sending E-Mail
- Addressing Messages
- Composing Messages
- Writing in Another Language
- Recovering a Message from a Crash
- Sending and Delivering Messages

Sending e-mail, like reading e-mail, is one of the most important communications activities of today's businessperson. In this skill we show you the basics that you need to get started quickly, and then present more in-depth information on addressing messages, composing effective e-mails, and modifying the way Outlook sends and delivers messages.

## The Basics of Sending E-Mail

The basics of composing and sending an e-mail message are straightforward. The following procedure walks you through creating, addressing, composing, and sending an e-mail message. Later sections go into detail on each aspect, providing you with more advanced techniques that you can use to more effectively compose messages.

To create and send an e-mail message, follow these steps:

1. **Create a new message.**

Display the Outlook Inbox, as shown in Figure 3-1.

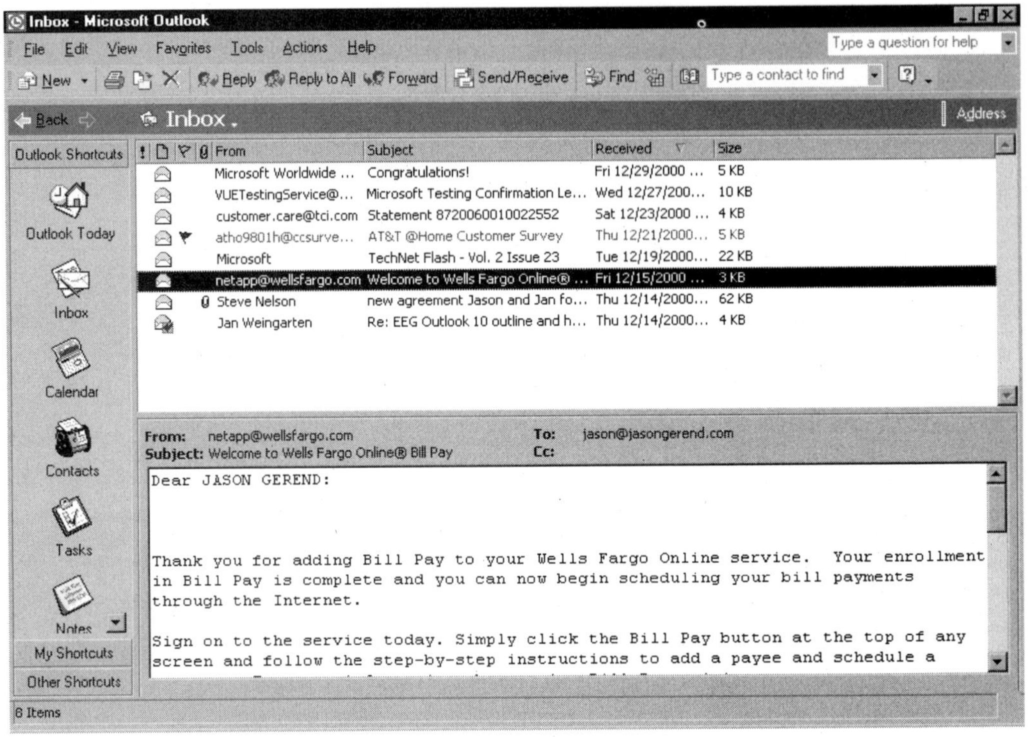

**Figure 3-1** The Inbox.

Use one of the following techniques to create a new message:

- To create a new blank message, click the New toolbar button, or press Ctrl-N.
- To reply to a message, select an existing message and click the Reply toolbar button.
- To reply to all recipients of the selected message, click the Reply To All toolbar button.
- To forward the selected e-mail to another person, click the Forward toolbar button.

TIP *You can also send e-mail from within Microsoft Internet Explorer or Windows Explorer. To send a link to a Web page in Internet Explorer, choose the File menu's Send command and then choose Link By E-Mail. To send a file from within Windows Explorer, right-click the desired file, choose Send To from the shortcut menu, and then choose Mail Recipient from the submenu.*

2. **Address the message.**

   Enter the recipient's name or e-mail in the To field, and then press the Tab key to move to the Cc box, as shown in Figure 3-2. To send a copy of the message to someone else, enter a name in the Cc box and then press the Tab key again.

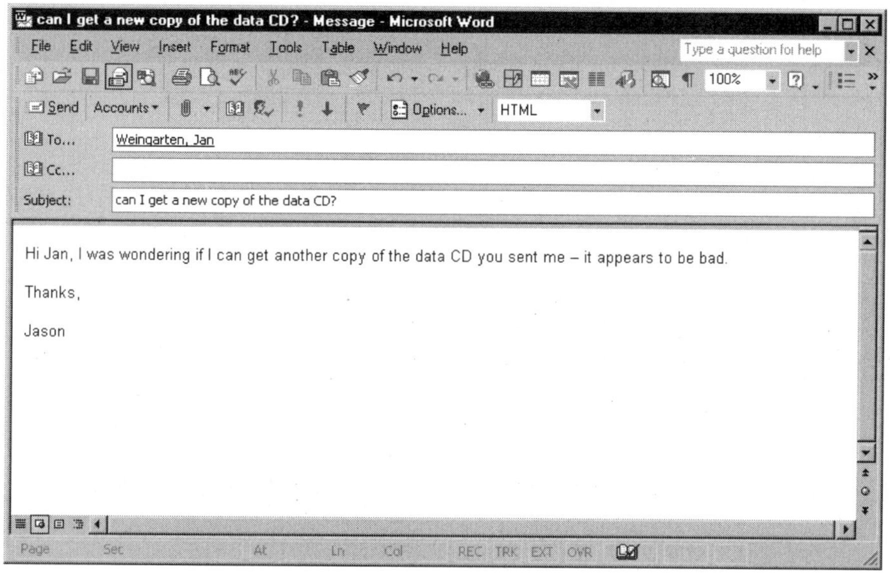


**Figure 3-2** Composing a new mail message.

3. **Enter a subject.**

   In the Subject box, enter a subject for the e-mail. Make it short (5 to 10 words or less) and descriptive so that it's easy to identify the contents of the message. Press the Tab key to move the cursor into the main message body.

4. **Compose the message.**

   Enter text in the main message body just as you would in a word processor or any other messaging program.

5. **Spell check your message.**

   Bad spelling reflects poorly on the sender, so check for spelling mistakes before sending any e-mail. If you have Microsoft Word 2002 installed, Outlook will underline misspelled words as you type, just like in Word. Right-click an underlined word to display a list of alternatives. If you don't have Word 2002, choose the Tools menu's Spelling command.

6. **Click the Send toolbar button.**

   If you're connected to the Internet, Outlook automatically delivers the message when you click Send. If you're not connected to the Internet (or if you disabled this feature), Outlook places the message in the Outbox for delivery the next time you press the Send/Receive button.

# Addressing Messages

You can address an e-mail message in Outlook in two ways: First, you can enter the recipient's name or e-mail address directly in the To or Cc box. Second, you can click the To or Cc button to select the recipient's name from a list of addresses. The following sections describe how to use each method.

## Entering an E-Mail Address or Name

The easiest way to address a new message is to enter the recipient's name or e-mail address in the To or Cc box. The following list provides further details:

- If the recipient's e-mail address is already in your Contacts folder, simply enter their name in the To or Cc box.
- Use the To box to indicate the primary recipient(s) of the message.
- Use the Cc box to indicate contacts to whom you're sending a courtesy copy.
- To send a Blind Carbon Copy (a secret copy), click the To button, select the address from the list (as described in the next section), and click the Bcc button.
- Outlook may try to guess the name you're entering; if it does, it will either fill in the name for you or display a pop-up menu with a couple of possibilities, as shown in Figure 3-3. If the correct name is listed, select it, and then press Enter. Otherwise continue typing.

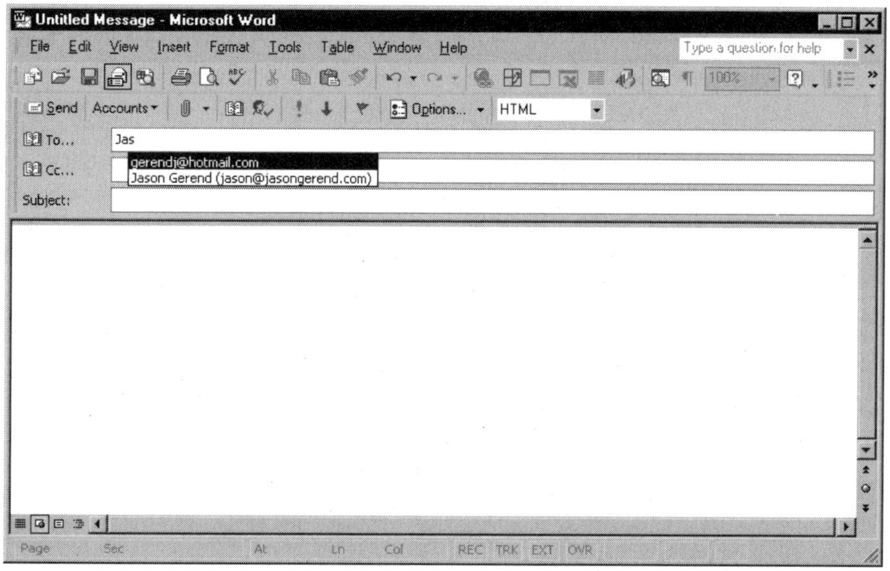


**Figure 3-3** Outlook may try to complete the name as you type.

- You can enter a valid e-mail address directly in the To or Cc box.
- To enter multiple names, separate them with semicolons.
- Use the Tab key after entering the recipient's name to move on to the Cc or Subject boxes.
- Outlook underlines names for which it finds an e-mail address. If a name is underlined with a red squiggly line or a green dotted line, Outlook found more than one match. Right-click the name and choose the correct match from the shortcut menu, as shown in Figure 3-4.

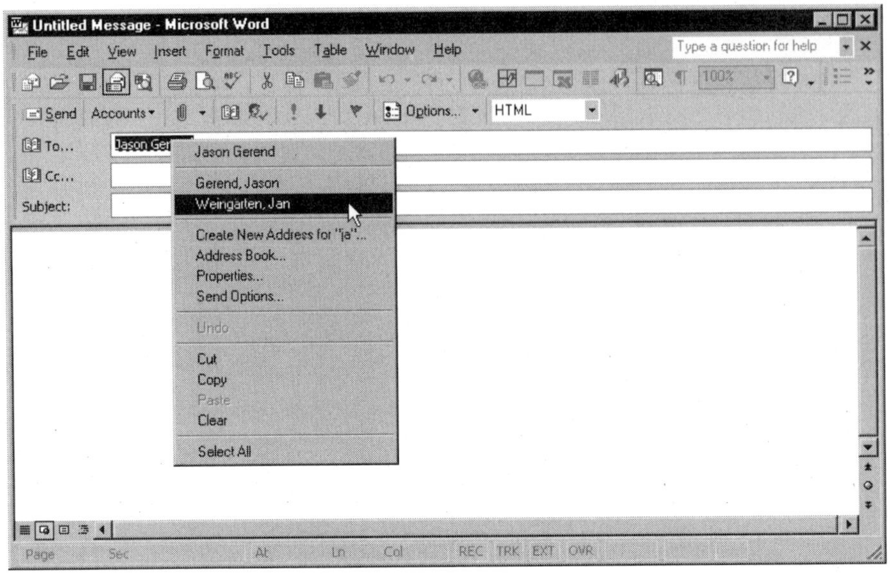


**Figure 3-4** Choosing the correct name for a recipient.

- If the contact has multiple e-mail addresses, Outlook chooses the first one listed. To choose an alternate, right-click the name (if it is underlined) and choose one of the other entries.

NOTE *When selecting another e-mail address from the list, chances are good that you won't know which e-mail address you're choosing because Outlook doesn't list the e-mail address, just the contact's name. To try to determine the address you're sending to, right-click the name listed in the To or Cc box and choose Properties from the shortcut menu. Click the triangle next to the E-Mail box in the Contacts window to view all e-mail addresses associated with the contact.*

## Selecting Addresses from a List

You can use the Select Names dialog box to pick names from the Contacts folder or another address book. To do so, create a new message and then follow these steps:

1. **Click the To button.**
2. **Select the address book that contains the desired contact(s).**

   To choose names from an address book other than the Contacts folder (such as an Exchange Server address book), select the appropriate address book from the Show Names From The drop-down list box, as shown in Figure 3-5.

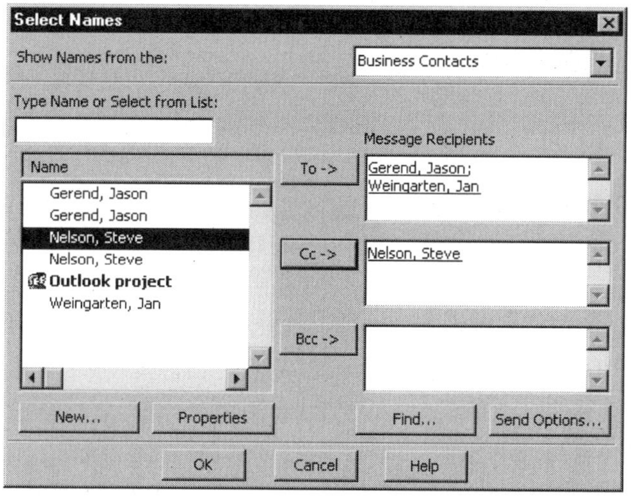


**Figure 3-5** Choosing recipients.

3. **Locate the recipient(s)**

   Enter the first few letters of the recipient's name in the box provided, and then select the desired contact(s) from the list (hold down the Ctrl key to select multiple names). Distribution Lists (discussed in "Skill 5: Using a Contacts List") have a small icon next to them. If you choose an LDAP address book and no names are listed, click the Find button to search for the contact.

4. **Click the To, Cc, or Bcc button.**

   Use the To button if you want to indicate that the message is intended primarily for the selected contact(s), or use the Cc button to send a courtesy copy to the contact(s). To send a secret copy to the selected contact(s), use the Bcc button. If you don't want any of the contacts to see the other recipients' names, add all recipients using the Bcc button—leave the To and Cc fields blank.

NOTE *Contacts are listed once for every e-mail address they have. The first instance of the contact in the list corresponds to the contact's primary e-mail address, the second instance to their second e-mail address, and so on. To view the e-mail addresses for the contact, select the contact, click the Properties button, and then use the down arrow next to the E-Mail box in the Contacts window to select and view the contact's second and third e-mail addresses.*

## Check Your Addresses

It's easy to make a mistake and send a piece of e-mail to the wrong person. But many people are not willing to forgive or forget these little slips.

These mistakes are too commonplace. Not too long ago, a Chamber of Commerce employee issued a standard instruction to a colleague and clicked the wrong button, sending the message to a 1,000-member distribution list. Despite a heartfelt apology sent out less than an hour after the inadvertent spam attack, the errant message soon took on a life of its own.

People started sending "Please delete me" messages to everyone on the list. Finally, a wise soul wrote (necessarily this time) to the whole list: "If you don't want to get more mail from an inadvertent mailing (obviously the case here), then just restrain that itchy Reply All finger, e-mail the original sender (not the whole list), delete the message, and get on with your life."

Even after this, several people felt the need to get their e-licks in, reflexively clicking the Reply button with frivolous "Me too" messages.

A lot of the unwanted mail that arrives in our Inboxes is annoying because the sender doesn't have a clue that we don't want to hear a joke, receive an attachment, or join their little chain. Still, there is a clear difference between deliberate and accidental. For some people, any unwanted mail generates huge waves of anger, but these are the same folks who will say "No problem" when accidentally jostled on the street or who toss away piles of weekly junk mail with no complaint.

So one piece of unwanted mail is a drop in the digital bucket and does not warrant a reaction. For the sender, the solution is simple, even if it goes against the e-mail culture's prevailing behavior: Go slow. Be careful. Understand the difference between Reply and Reply To All. And double-check the address line before sending every message.

# Composing Messages

Writing an e-mail is no more complicated than simply placing the cursor in the message body and typing.

The following sections show you how to write effective e-mail messages, change message formats, stylize messages, and write messages in other languages.

## Writing Effective Messages

Writing e-mail messages is easy, but writing powerful and effective messages requires a little savvy. The following list provides some suggestions for making your messages more successful with their intent.

- Don't write when you're angry. If you're tempted to fire off an irate note—don't. Give yourself a chance to cool off. The immediacy of e-mail can escalate a minor difference into World War III.
- Keep your e-mails short and focused. It's better to send a couple short e-mails on separate topics than one long e-mail.
- Write a subject that accurately describes the message. This allows recipients to quickly identify the message, and deal with it as appropriate. Good subjects are critical when trying to locate messages later.
- Keep your sentences tight. Conciseness is power. Short, clear, complete sentences are easier to digest than sentence fragments or longer sentences with too many ideas.
- Reread for clarity and tone. It's prudent to reread important messages to ensure that the messages are clear and the tone is appropriate. Because e-mail lacks verbal and non-verbal cues, it's easy to be misconstrued, especially when in a rush. Be clear, even forceful if you must, but be careful to not be aggressive unless you're willing to brave the potential fallout.
- Avoid clichés. By definition they're overused and tired—let them rest in peace.
- Don't abuse abbreviations. FYI, abbreviations are distracting and often misunderstood, IMHO. BTW, if your recipient misunderstands your message and doesn't ask for clarifications ASAP, you're SOL.
- Check for errors. Few things reflect more poorly upon the sender than spelling and grammar mistakes, even in the supposedly informal e-mail medium.
- Don't press the Enter key at the end of a line—only at the end of a paragraph. If you press Enter at the end of every line, the lines won't wrap well in different sized windows. To manually create a new line within the same paragraph, press Shift-Enter.
- Use restraint with smileys. Smileys (J or :) ) and other emoticons are often used to change the tone of an e-mail, but are overused and unprofessional. Try to use an appropriate tone in your writing rather than leaning on emoticons to soften it.

- Compose marketing e-mails with care. Use the Bcc line to keep each recipient's e-mail address private. State your most important information first. Include the URL of your Web site. Never buy lists of e-mail names and never e-mail people who haven't contacted you first.

## Avoid Flames

People don't always get along. And since e-mail reflects human behavior, it isn't always nice.

The word *flame* is evoked to define any piece of e-mail that is especially mean, nasty, or critical. These missives are on a level with a temper tantrum or a reaming by the boss. Like these encounters, it's not fun to be on the receiving end here. Flames are often fearsome, and receiving such a communiqué can knock the wind out of a person.

When you receive a flame, it is a good idea to try to respond rationally. In this case it may be wise to include the text of the original letter, to show the sender that you can act like an adult even if he or she finds it necessary to rely upon cheap shots and below-the-belt punches.

As for those who would write flames, show some restraint. If you are angered by someone's behavior, it may help to let out some steam to say so in the most vitriolic way. But that doesn't mean you should actually send the thing. Once completed, let the flame simmer for at least two hours. Chances are, once you've cooled down and reread the message a cooler head will prevail.

Another reason to show restraint has to do with e-mail's permanent nature. If you throw a virtual temper tantrum, there is nothing you can do to prevent the recipient from making it public. This will cause no end of embarrassment, especially if you ever attempt to win a congeniality title at a company picnic.

# Changing Message Formats

Although Outlook uses the HTML message format by default, we feel that it's most appropriate to use plain text instead. The next sections discuss the advantages of using plain text, how to make plain text your default message format, and how to choose plain text or HTML formatting on a message-by-message basis.

## The Case for Using Plain Text

We recommend that you send the majority of your e-mail messages using plain text for the following reasons:

- Plain text is faster. Over a slow 14.4 Kb modem (such as is common in handheld computers and cell phones), an HTML message 25 KB in size might take 14 seconds to download, and only 3 seconds if the message were formatted using plain text.
- Plain text is more compatible. Every e-mail program and device can read plain text messages, including America Online, old e-mail programs, cell phones, handheld computers, and terminal-based e-mail clients.
- Plain text is easy to read. Because there is no formatting, unnecessary backgrounds, or other distractions, nothing distracts a recipient from what's important—your text.

## Changing Your Default Message Format

To change the message format used by Outlook to send e-mail messages from HTML to plain text, follow these steps:

**1. Open the Options dialog box.**

Open the Inbox, and then choose the Tools menu's Options command, as shown in Figure 3-6. If you don't see the Options command, click the down arrows at the bottom of the menu to display hidden commands.

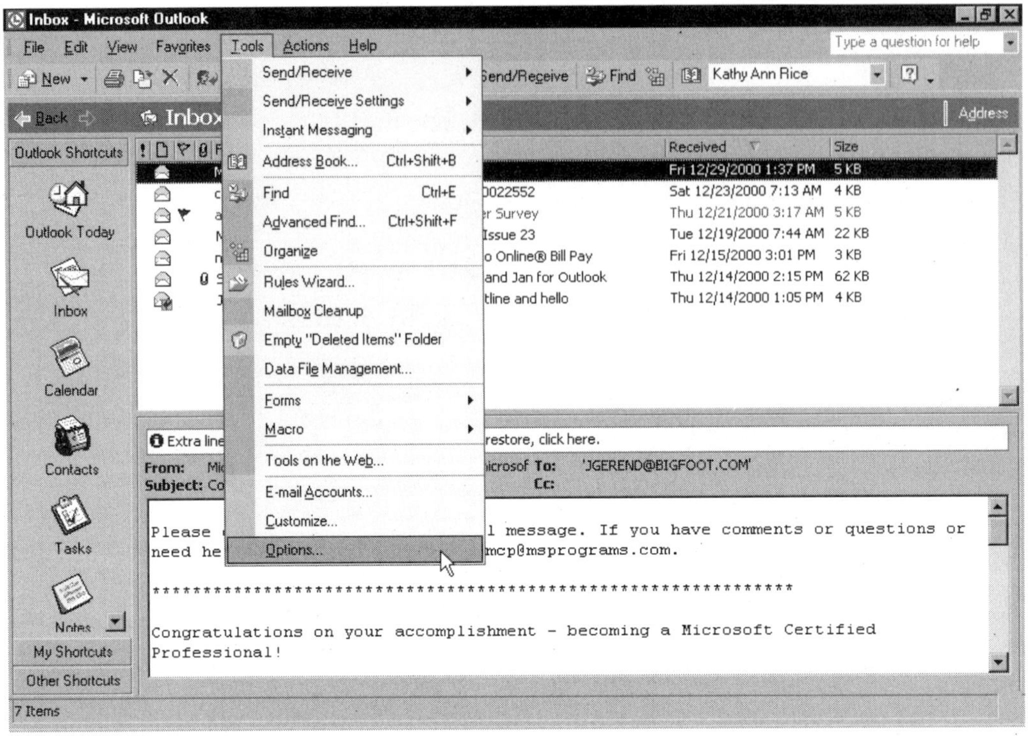

Figure 3-6 Opening the Options dialog box.

2. **Click the Mail Format tab.**
3. **Switch the message format to plain text.**

   Select Plain Text from the Compose In This Message Format drop-down list box at the top of the tab, as shown in Figure 3-7.

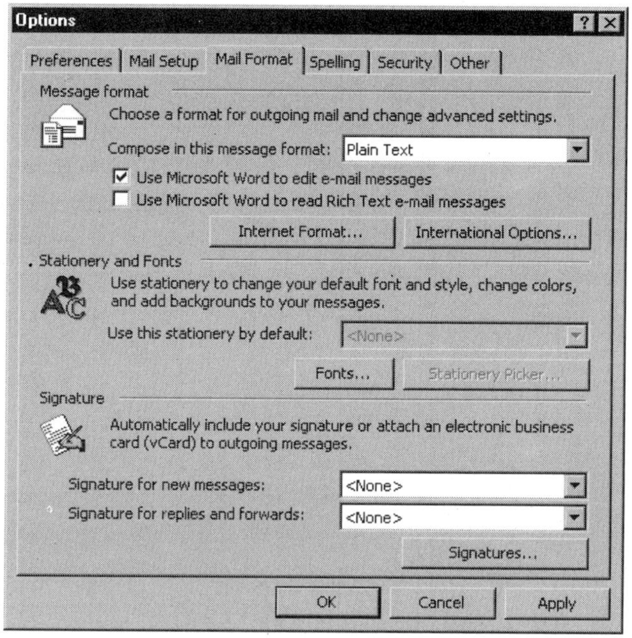


**Figure 3-7** Switching the default message format to plain text.

## Changing the Message Format for Individual Messages

Whatever message format you use by default, there are times when you'll want to send a message using the other format. Perhaps you want to use HTML to create a bulleted list or headings in an e-mail, and you know the recipient can read HTML messages. Or perhaps you want to send a quick e-mail to someone's cell phone and you need to switch to plain text.

To switch the message format, follow these steps:

1. **Create a new message.**

   Click the New Mail Message toolbar button in the Inbox and create a new message.

2. **Change the message format.**

   Select the appropriate message format from the Message Format box on the toolbar, as shown in Figure 3-8.

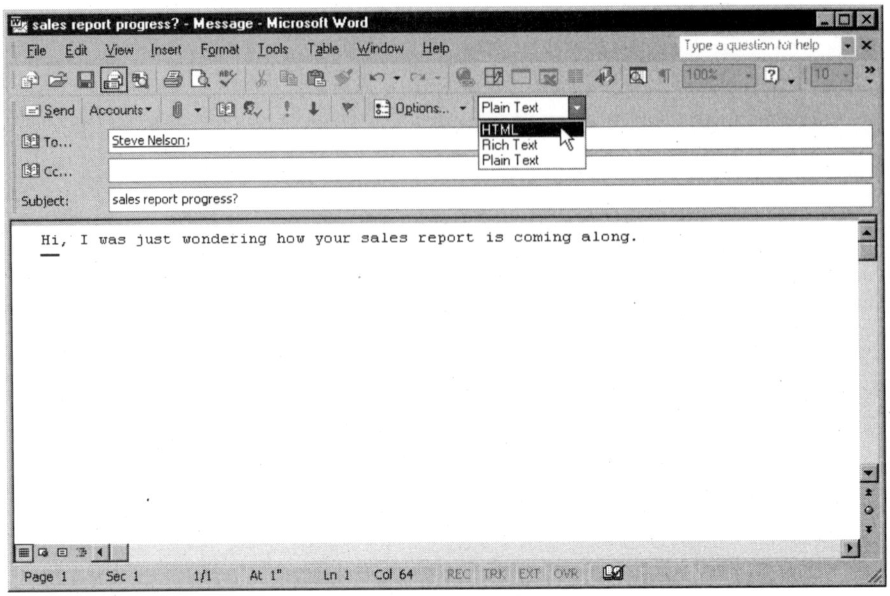


Figure 3-8 Switching the message format for a single message.

3. **Review the changes Outlook will make.**

   If you switch to plain text from HTML, Outlook displays a dialog box summarizing how it will convert your formatted text to plain text, as shown in Figure 3-9.

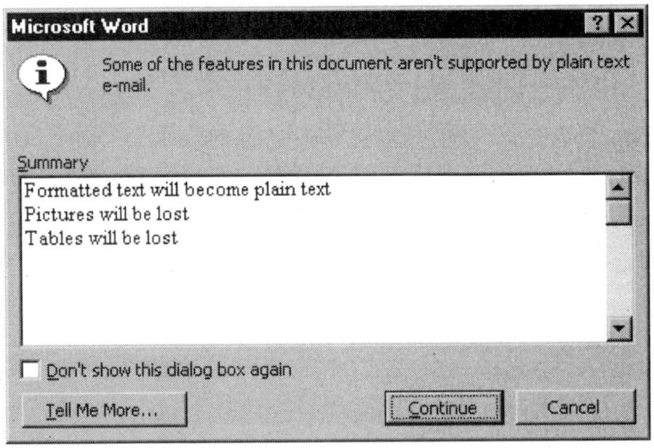


Figure 3-9 Reviewing the process of converting HTML to plain text.

## Context Is King

By clicking Reply or Reply To All you can return the original message to the sender and add your own spin to the top. This is easy and convenient, but it is a lazy way to do things.

While answering a message with a simple "yes" without any context will be confusing, you can get away with it here. So if you send a note asking if a friend is coming for Thanksgiving dinner, a "yes" will actually suffice.

But it can get complicated. If you send the message to 10 people and they all respond "yes" while including your original message, you'll have 10 additional copies of the same text residing on your PC. Your guests may then ask for directions and it starts again (especially as they all include the previous correspondence with each reply). Even if there are times when you want a running account of the correspondence, reply text is in most cases extraneous.

Then there are repliers who parse your original message into separate segments, interspersing their responses throughout. There may be times when you send a list of questions when this tactic truly is appropriate. But splitting messages as a default option is easily the most annoying and obnoxious e-mail practice around.

There are two solutions.

The easy way is to delete all of the reply text as you answer the message, except the most relevant section.

The "hard" way is to just send a new message; from scratch: "Yes, I am coming to Thanksgiving." A simple complete sentence, with a subject, verb, and object.

In the e-mail world, it will at least get points for uniqueness.

# Formatting HTML Messages

Although we recommend that you use HTML formatting with restraint, you may occasionally find it appropriate to apply additional formatting to your messages, such as bulleted lists, headings, and italicized words.

Before you send a message in HTML format, make sure that the message meets the following criteria:

- The formatting truly adds to the readability of the message, as is often the case with lists, headings, and italicized or boldfaced words.
- You know that the recipient uses an HTML-capable e-mail program. If you've received an HTML message from them in the past, this is probably OK.
- The message isn't time critical. If the recipient is checking e-mail using a cell phone or other limited device, they may choose to not read your message until they're back in the office, since HTML messages can be difficult to read and time-consuming to download for some e-mail devices.

To format a message, follow these steps:

1. **Create a new message.**

   Click the New Mail Message, Reply, or Forward toolbar buttons in the Inbox.

2. **Switch to HTML format.**

   In the new message window, select HTML from the Message Format box on the toolbar.

3. **Format your text.**

   Select the text you want to format, and then use the toolbar buttons to add the formatting, as shown in Figure 3-10.

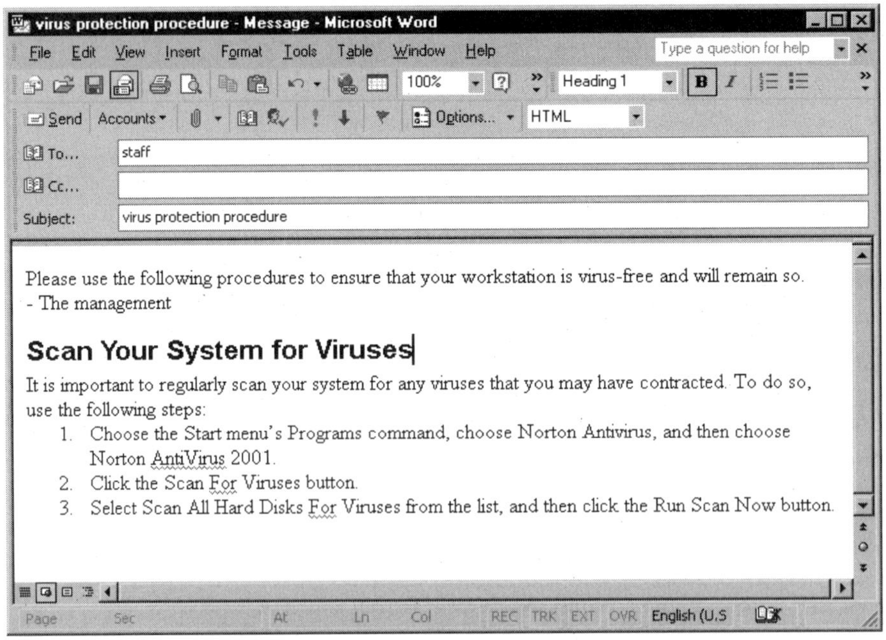


**Figure 3-10** An HTML message with limited formatting applied.

Choose from the following formatting options:

- To make the selected text boldfaced or italicized, click the Bold or Italic toolbar buttons.
- To create numbered or bulleted lists, click the Numbering or Bulleted toolbar buttons.
- To apply a style, such as Heading 1, to the selected text, use the Styles drop-down list box on the toolbar.
- To insert a small picture in your message, choose the Insert menu's Picture command and then choose From File from the submenu. Select the picture you want, and click Insert. We recommend that you use this feature sparingly, because pictures greatly increase download time.
- Avoid using different fonts, themes, or stationery; adding a background image; or inserting drawings in your messages. These formatting options simply aren't appropriate for business communications.

**4. Create hyperlinks.**

To create a hyperlink, simply enter the address, such as *www.redtechpress.com*—Outlook automatically converts the text into a hyperlink. Alternatively, select the text you want to make a hyperlink, click the Insert Hyperlink toolbar button, and then use the Insert Hyperlink dialog box, as shown in Figure 3-11, to specify the page to which you want to link.

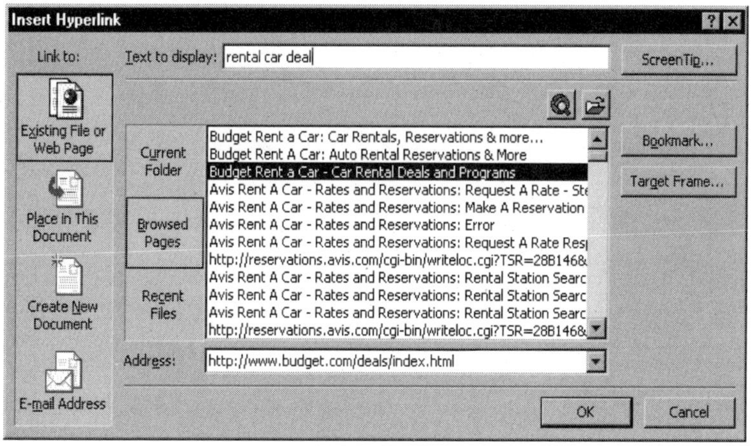


**Figure 3-11** Creating a hyperlink.

## Postponing Messages

Outlook allows you to postpone messages in two ways: First, you can save the message as a draft and continue writing it later. Second, you can send the message, but specify that it shouldn't be delivered before a certain time.

### Working with Drafts

If you decide that you want to continue composing a message later, you can save it as a draft. To do so, follow these steps:

1. **Compose your message.**

   Address and compose your message as you would normally, as shown in Figure 3-12.

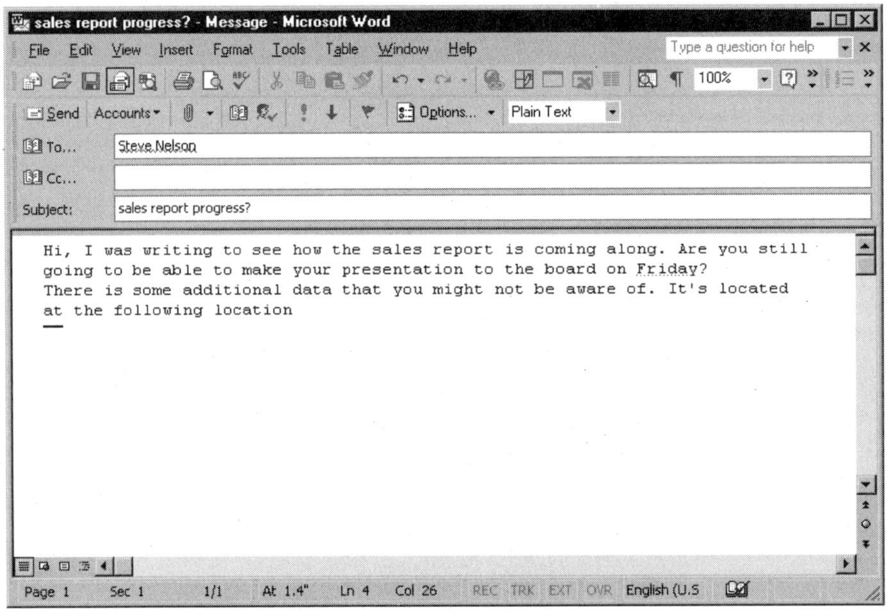


**Figure 3-12** Composing a message.

2. **Click the Save toolbar button.**

   Outlook saves a copy of the message to the Drafts folder. Alternatively, you can simply close the message, at which point Outlook will ask if you want to save the message. Click Yes to save the message to the Drafts folder.

NOTE *Outlook periodically saves a copy of the message you're composing to the Drafts folder so that in the event that Outlook crashes, you won't lose all of your work.*

3. **Display the Drafts folder.**

Click the My Shortcuts group in the Outlook bar, and then click the Drafts shortcut. Outlook displays the contents of the Drafts folder, as shown in Figure 3-13.

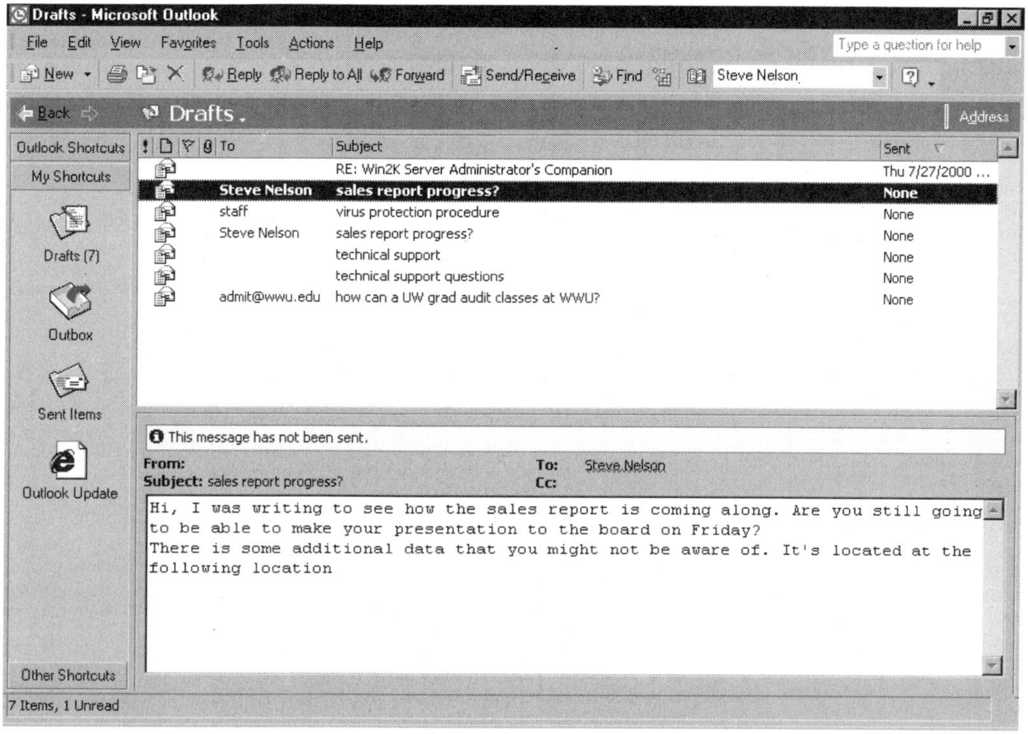


**Figure 3-13** A draft message.

4. **Edit the draft message.**

Double-click the draft you want to continue editing. Finish editing the message and click the Send toolbar button to send the message, or click the Save toolbar button and close the message to continue editing it later.

## Postponing Message Delivery

After you click the Send toolbar button, Outlook sends the message as quickly as it can —immediately if you're connected to the Internet, or the next time you (or Outlook) checks for new messages. (See the "Sending and Delivering Messages" section later in this skill for more information on this process.)

If you want to ensure that a message isn't delivered before a particular time—for example, to prevent a press release from being delivered until after a scheduled press conference, follow these steps:

1. **Compose your message.**

   Address and compose your message as you would normally, as shown in Figure 3-14.

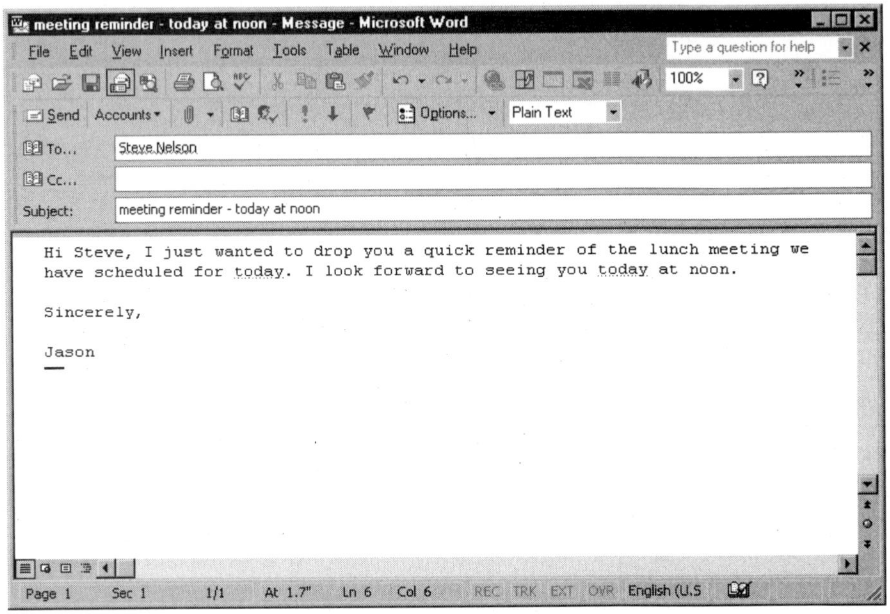


**Figure 3-14** Composing a message.

2. **Click the Options toolbar button.**

   This displays the Message Options dialog box, as shown in Figure 3-15.

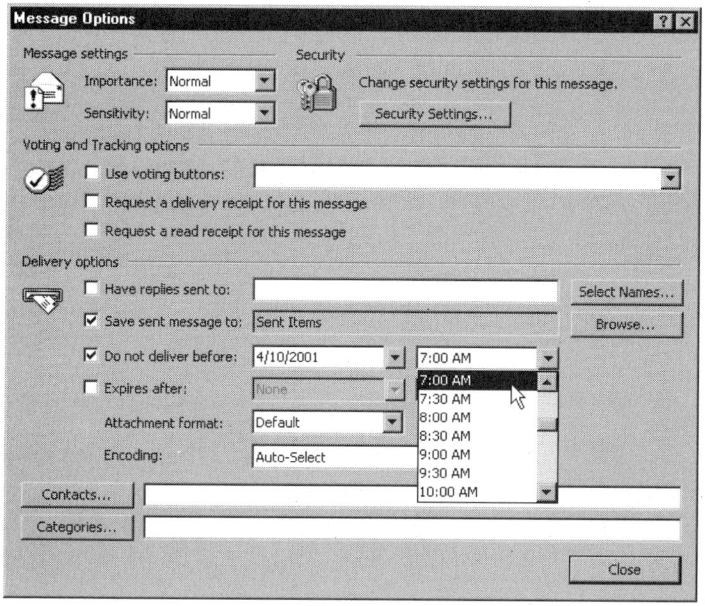


**Figure 3-15** The Message Options dialog box.

3. **Select delivery options.**

   In the Delivery Options section, select the Do Not Deliver Before check box.

4. **Specify the earliest possible delivery time.**

   Use the date and time drop-down list boxes to specify the earliest date and time that Outlook can deliver the message, as shown in Figure 3-15. Click Close when you're finished.

## Attaching Files to Messages

Like opening file attachments (discussed in "Skill 2: Reading E-Mail"), sending file attachments is frequently a challenge to business users. Although the process may not be completely transparent, attaching a file to an e-mail message is straightforward—simply use the following steps:

1. **Compose your message.**

   Address and compose your message, making sure to adequately describe the attached file so that your recipient knows exactly what it is and why you're sending it, as shown in Figure 3-16.

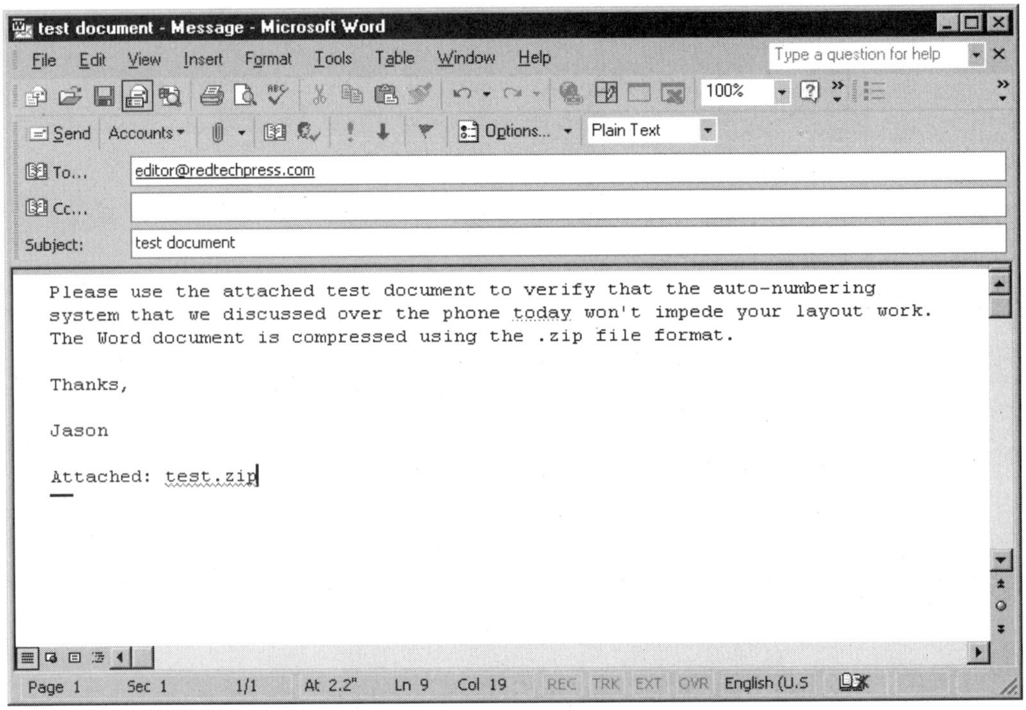


**Figure 3-16** Composing a message.

2. **Click the Insert File (paper clip) toolbar button.**

   This displays the Insert File dialog box, as shown in Figure 3-17. Alternatively, to attach an Outlook item for another Outlook user, click the down arrow next to the Insert File toolbar button and choose Item from the pop-up menu. Then use the Insert Item dialog box to locate the desired Outlook contact, message, appointment, or other item.

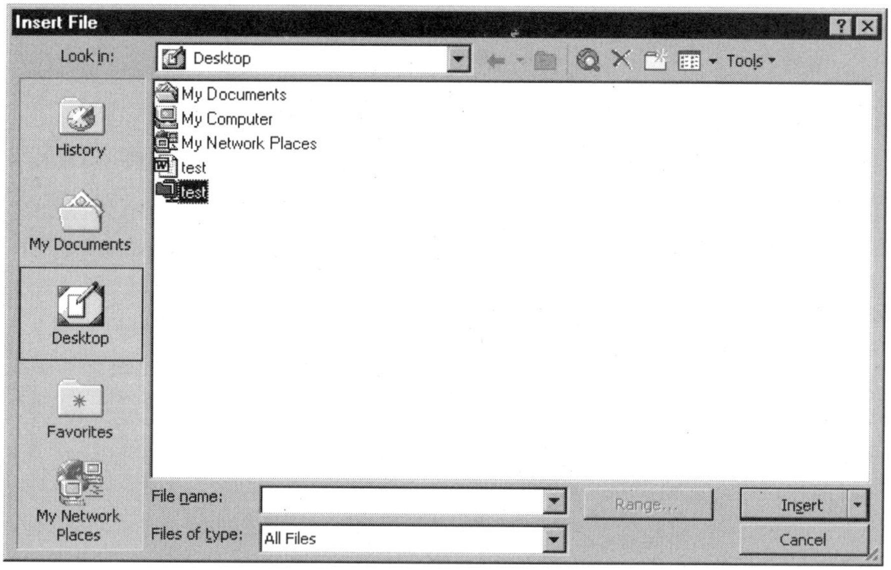


**Figure 3-17** The Insert File dialog box.

**3. Choose a file to attach.**

Use the Insert File dialog box to select the file you want to attach. Here are some points to consider when attaching files:

- Scan your system for viruses before sending attachments.
- Limit the size of your attachments. The smaller the better, in general you should limit attachments to 100 KB in size or less unless you've previously verified that it's okay to send larger attachments. Large attachments take a long time to download over slow connections, may not send properly, and can overflow the recipient's mail account, causing other messages to be returned.
- Use a file compression utility, such as WinZip (available at *www.winzip.com*), to compress your attachments using the .zip file format.

TIP *Another compression utility you might want to check out is StuffIt, especially if you exchange large files with Mac users. If you send them a file compressed with WinZip, they'll be able to uncompress it and read it, but if they send you a file compressed with StuffIt, you won't be able to uncompress it and read it unless you also have StuffIt on your computer. To download StuffIt, go to* www.aladdinsys.com/stuffitwin/index.html.

4. **Click the Insert button.**

   Outlook displays the attached file in the new Attach field of the message, as shown in Figure 3-18.

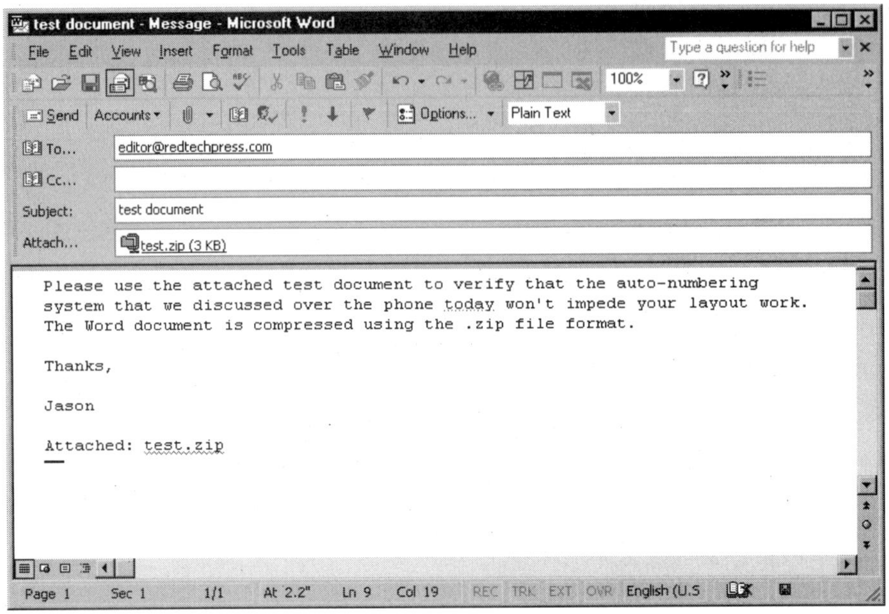


**Figure 3-18** An e-mail message with an attachment.

NOTE *You can click the down arrow next to the Insert button to optionally insert the contents of the file directly into the message. This is often preferable for short text files, since the message recipient doesn't have to open any attachments—something many users have trouble with.*

# Using E-Mail Signatures

E-mail signatures can be a great time-saver for business users. They allow you to quickly insert text that you use in all your messages—for example, a closing signature giving your name, company, and contact information.

## Creating Signatures

Before you can insert a signature in your messages, you need to create one. To do so, follow these steps:

1. **Open the Options dialog box.**

   Display the Inbox, and then choose the Tools menu's Options command, as shown in Figure 3-19. If you don't see the Options command, click the down arrows at the bottom of the menu to display hidden commands.

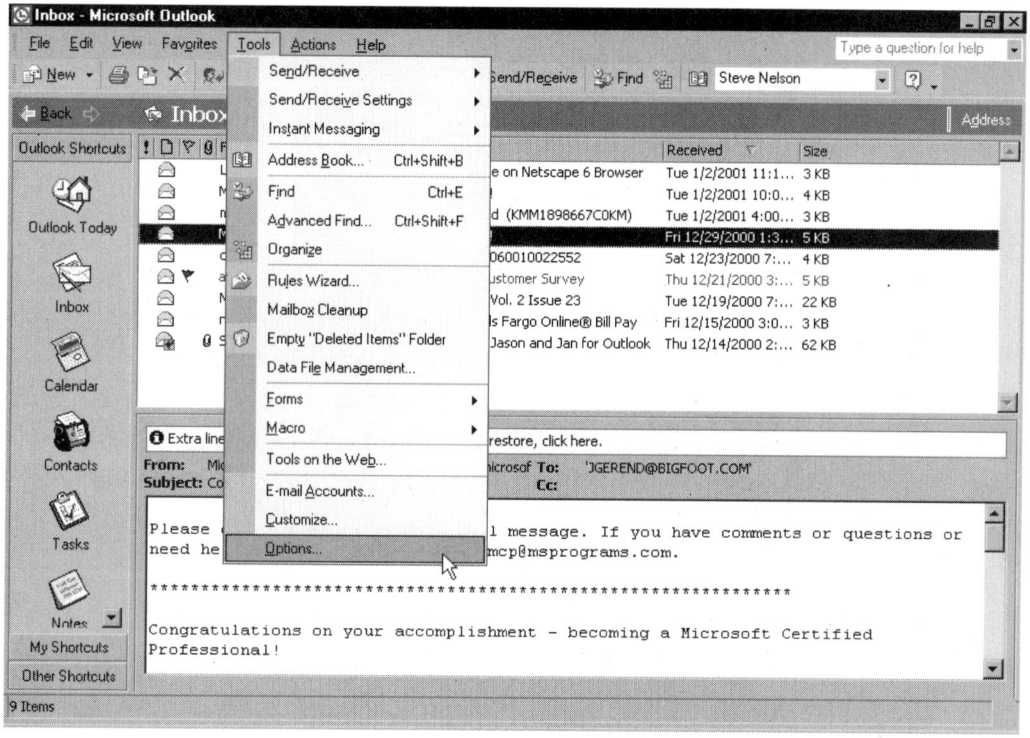


Figure 3-19 Opening the Options dialog box.

2. **Click the Mail Format tab.**

   This displays the Mail Format tab of the Options dialog box, as shown in Figure 3-20.

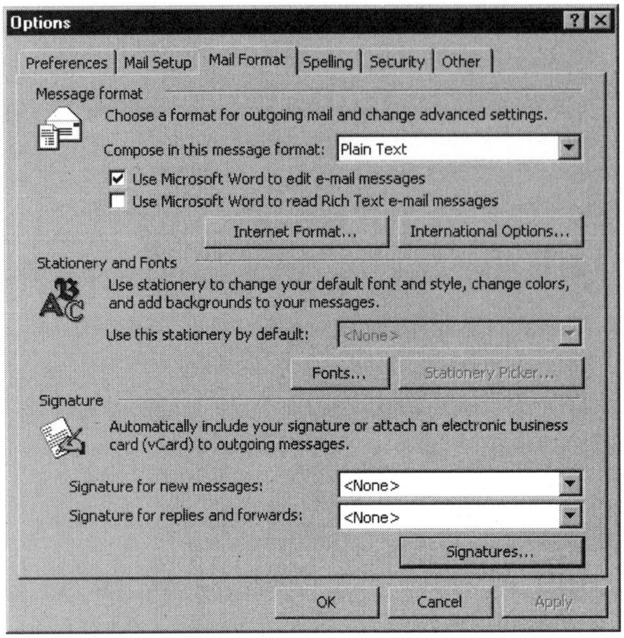


**Figure 3-20** The Mail Format tab of the Options dialog box.

3. **Click the Signatures button.**

   Outlook displays the Create Signature dialog box.

4. **Click the New button to create a new signature.**

   Outlook displays the Create New Signature dialog box, as shown in Figure 3-21.

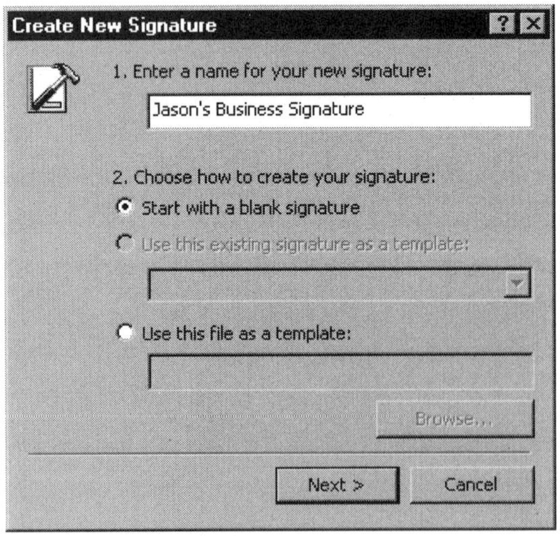


**Figure 3-21** Creating a new signature.

5. **Name the new signature.**

   Enter a descriptive name for the signature, and then click Next.

6. **Create your signature.**

   In the Edit Signature dialog box, as shown in Figure 3-22, enter your signature text, and then click OK. Click the New button in the Create Signature dialog box to create additional signatures, or click Close to finish.

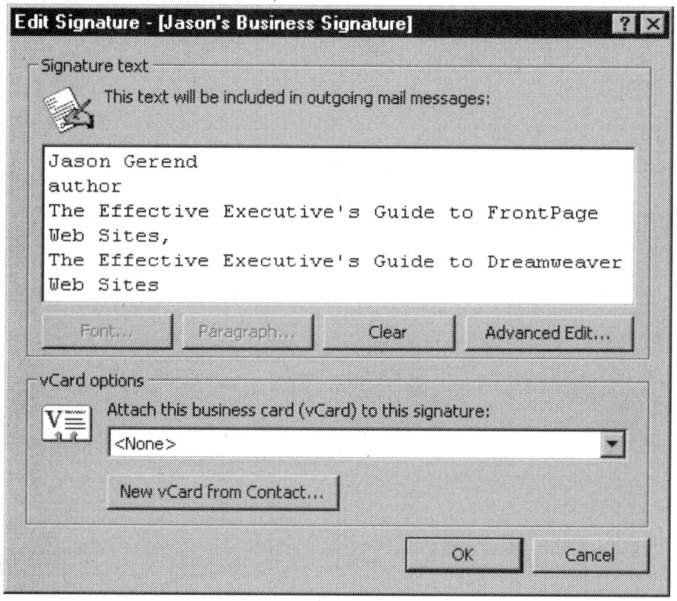


**Figure 3-22** Creating a new signature.

## Adding Signatures to Your Messages

You can either add signatures individually to messages (unless you're using Word as your e-mail editor) or assign a default signature to apply to all messages.

To insert a signature into a single e-mail message, choose the Insert menu's Signature command and then choose your signature from the submenu, as shown in Figure 3-23.

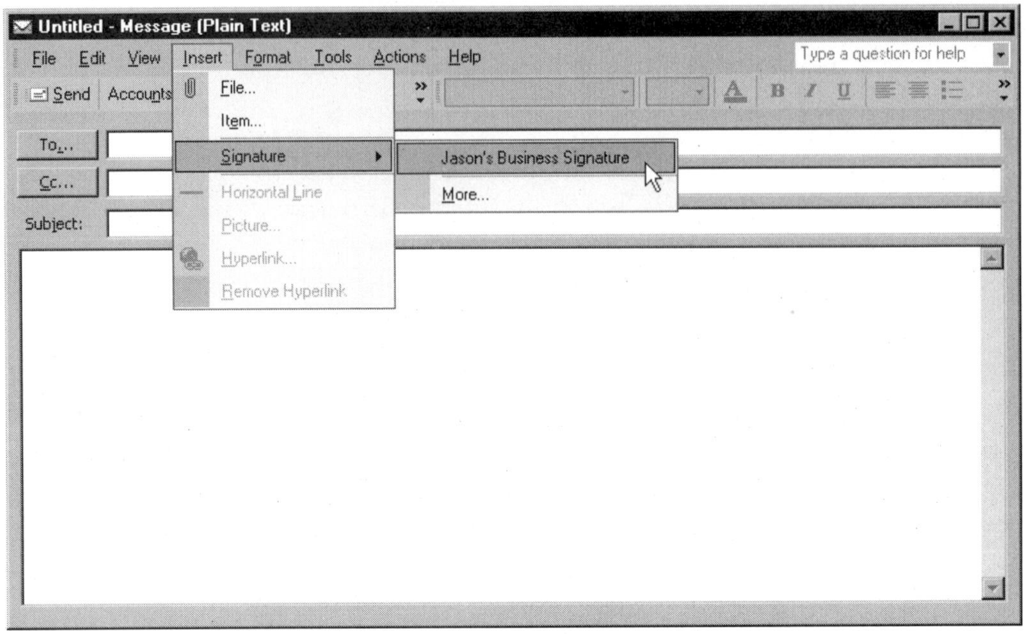


**Figure 3-23** Inserting a signature.

To set a default signature for your messages, follow these steps:

1. **Open the Options dialog box.**

   Display the Inbox, and then choose the Tools menu's Options command.

2. **Click the Mail Format tab.**

3. **Choose your default signatures.**

   Use the Signature For New Messages drop-down list box to select the signature you want to use for all new messages, as shown in Figure 3-24. Select a signature to use for replies and forwards from the Signature For Replies And Forwards drop-down list box.

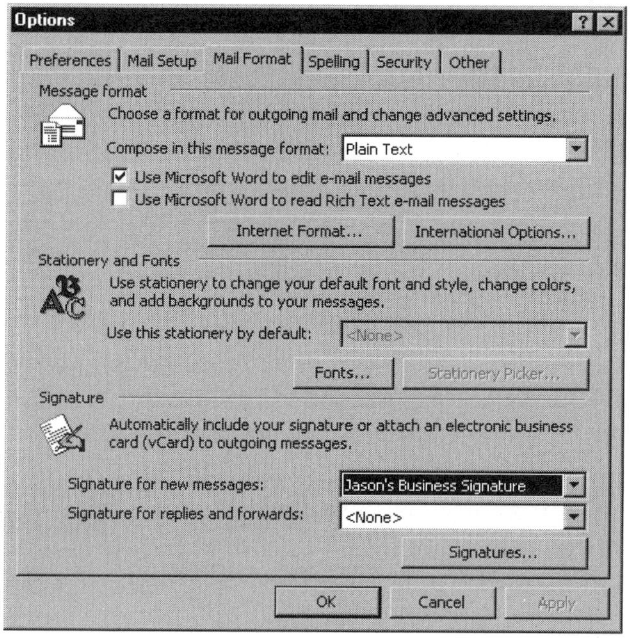


**Figure 3-24** Selecting default signatures.

TIP *You can easily delete signatures from messages that you create. Simply select the inserted text and press the Delete key.*

## Keep "Sigs" Simple

Signature (or "sig") files are a great idea, but for every useful function there seems to be an equal and opposite irritation. In one of the most annoying recent e-mail trends, many people add various sayings, words of wisdom, and even jokes to their sig files. This effort to add levity or wisdom and underscore the personality of the sender falls flat and becomes less amusing with each message and makes the sender appear terminally unimaginative.

This is reminiscent of when people get their first telephone answering machine. They will spend hours producing complicated and clever messages that are wonderfully compelling—the first time you call. Pretty soon they wise up and realize the best messages provide just the facts and nothing more.

The first time you get a message from someone with a cutesy sig file you may laugh. But it's not cute anymore when you swap 10 messages a day with someone and get a copy of the "wisdom" each time. And while it may take a while for extraneous sig files to eat up even a single megabyte, this is an annoying waste of time and storage—sort of like meeting someone at a party who tells you the same joke three times.

How do we escape this torture? Mail software of the future may give us the option of sending rotating sig files drawn from a database of different sayings (as does Outlook Express for the Macintosh). However, a better and more immediate solution is to actually show some restraint. Keep the sig files simple: Your address, company name, phone/fax numbers, and Web page are a good place to start, and finish.

Simplifying sig files gives correspondence the opportunity to channel the imagination toward the body of the message, where it belongs. Recipients will appreciate this and will refer to your messages if they have misplaced your phone number. They will not, on the other hand, search your correspondence to determine your stand on cursing the darkness.

## Changing the Appearance of Replies and Forwards

Many people don't like the way Outlook handles messages that you reply to or forward. You may want to prevent Outlook from including the original message text with the message you're replying to or forwarding, or perhaps you want to prevent Outlook from automatically coloring HTML messages that you reply to or forward in blue.

To change the way Outlook formats your replies and forwards, follow these steps:

1. **Open the Options dialog box.**

   Display the Inbox, and then choose the Tools menu's Options command. If you don't see the Options command, click the down arrows at the bottom of the menu to display hidden commands.

2. **Open the E-Mail Options dialog box.**

   On the Preferences tab, as shown in Figure 3-25, click the E-Mail Options button.

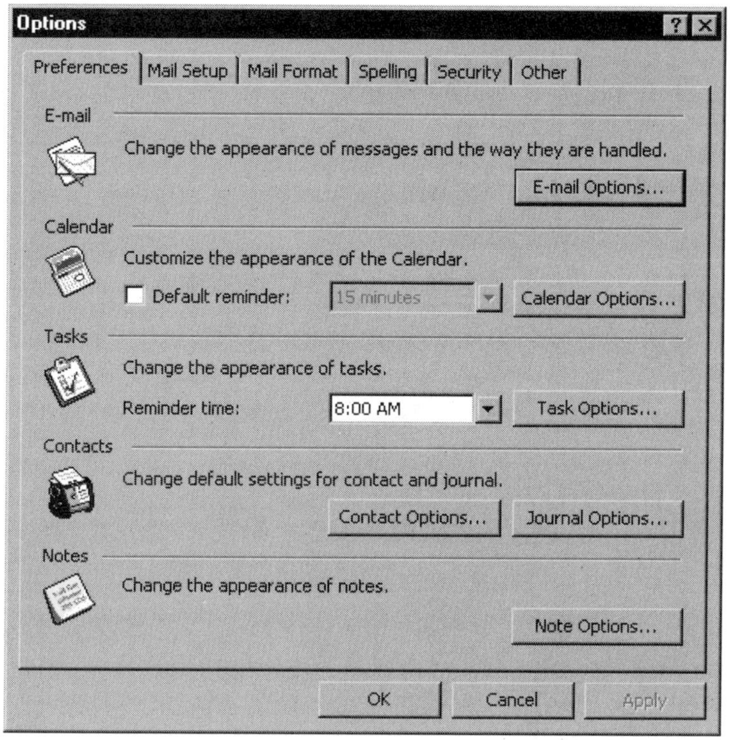


**Figure 3-25** The Preferences tab of the Options dialog box.

3. **Specify whether to include the original message.**

   Choose what you want Outlook to do with the original message you're replying to or forwarding, as shown in Figure 3-26.

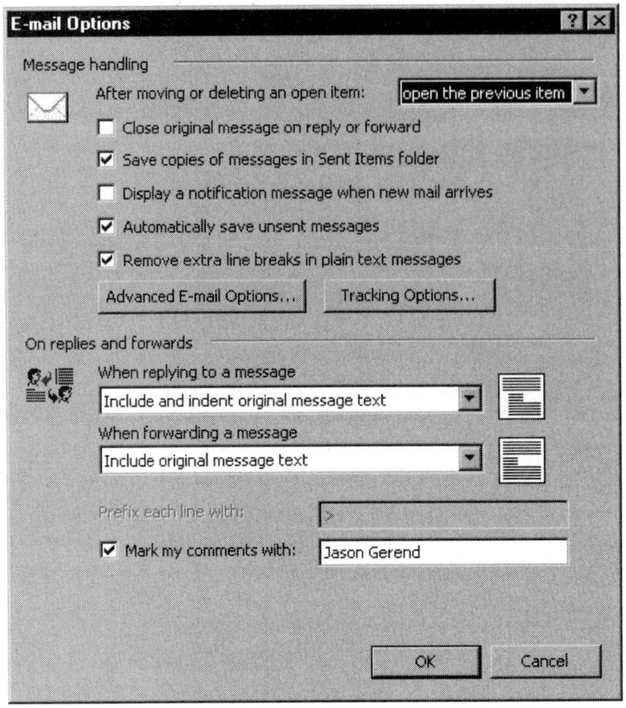


**Figure 3-26** The E-Mail Options dialog box.

You have the following options in the When Replying To A Message and When Forwarding A Message drop-down list boxes:

- Do not include original message.
- Attach original message.
- Include original message text.
- Include and indent original message text.
- Prefix each line of the original message.

NOTE *Many people have trouble with attachments and are rightly wary of their virus-carrying potential, so we recommend that you avoid the Attach Original Message setting. We also recommend that you avoid the Prefix Each Line Of The Original Message setting, as this setting often makes it more difficult to read or quote sections of the message.*

4. **Display the Mail Format tab.**

   Click OK in the E-Mail Options dialog box, and then click the Mail Format tab of the Options dialog box, as shown in Figure 3-27.

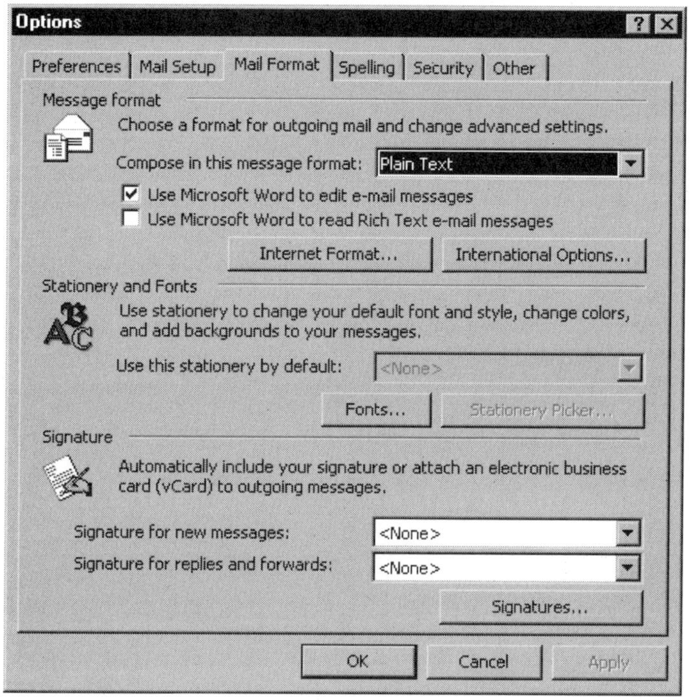


**Figure 3-27** The Mail Format tab of the Options dialog box.

5. **Click the Fonts button.**
6. **Open the Choose Font dialog box for replies and forwards.**

   Click the Choose Font button next to the When Replying And Forwarding box, as shown in Figure 3-28. (If you use HTML as your default message format, you can change your default font by using the first Choose Font button in this dialog box.)

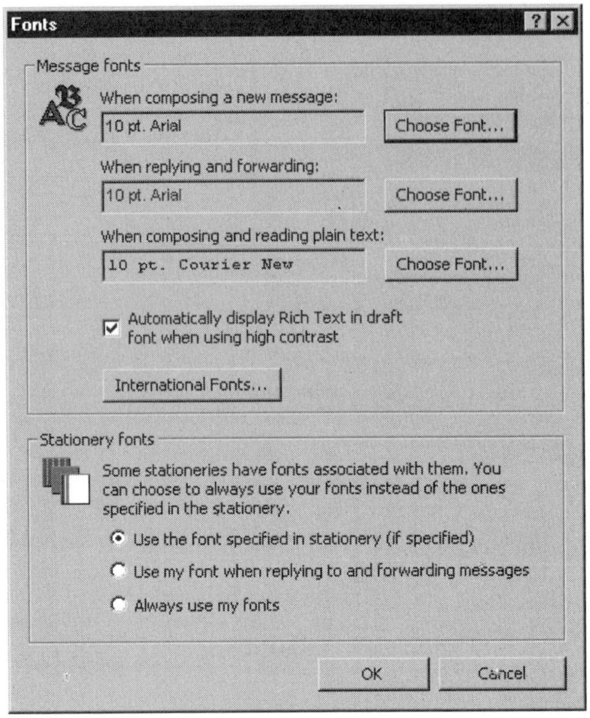


**Figure 3-28** The Fonts dialog box.

**7. Specify the font and font options.**

In the Font dialog box, as shown in Figure 3-29, select the font, font style, size, and color you want, and then click OK. Most people will want to change the color from blue to black.

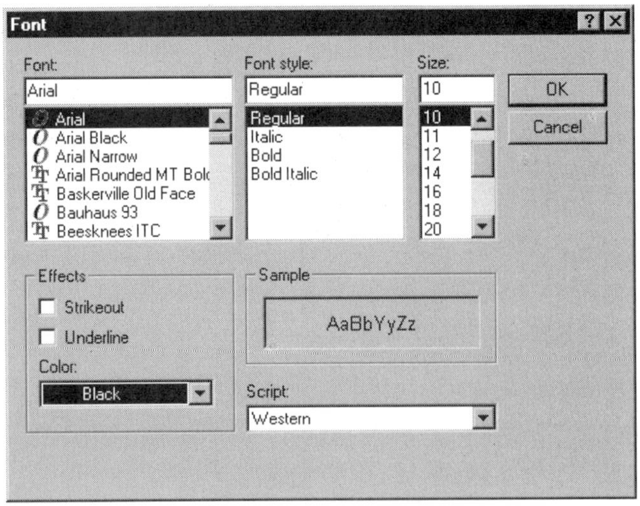


**Figure 3-29** Changing the way text appears in replies and forwards.

# Writing in Another Language

Thanks to the Internet and an international marketplace, it is an increasingly common requirement for businesspeople to be able to carry on at least limited communication in other languages, especially via e-mail.

Outlook itself doesn't provide any multilingual capabilities. If you want to compose a message using a different character set, such as Greek or Kanji, use the Text Input Settings applet in the Microsoft Windows Control Panel to switch your input language to the appropriate language.

TIP *Check messages you compose in another language carefully for spelling and grammar mistakes. Ideally, you should have a native speaker proofread important messages for language and cultural mistakes.*

# Using Word as Your E-Mail Editor

If Word 2002 is your default e-mail editor, you can use Word's additional language capabilities to compose messages in other languages, as described in the following steps:

1. **Create a new mail message.**

   Display the Inbox, and click the New Mail Message toolbar button.

2. **Compose your message.**

   Word automatically recognizes the language you're typing in, and switches the dictionary used for spell checking to the appropriate language (if you have that dictionary installed. You may need to use the Office Language Pack CDs to install additional dictionaries). If you don't have the appropriate dictionary installed, Word disables spell checking.

3. **Manually specify the language if necessary.**

   If Word doesn't automatically recognize the language in which you're typing, select the text and choose the Tools menu's Language command, choose Set Language from the submenu, and then use the Language dialog box, as shown in Figure 3-30, to select the correct language.

**Figure 3-30** Manually specifying a language.

**4. Enter special characters, such as accents and umlauts.**

Choose the Insert menu's Symbol command. Select the character you want to insert, and click Insert, as shown in Figure 3-31. Notice that Word provides a modifiable keyboard shortcut for most characters. (Click the Shortcut Key button to change the shortcut.)

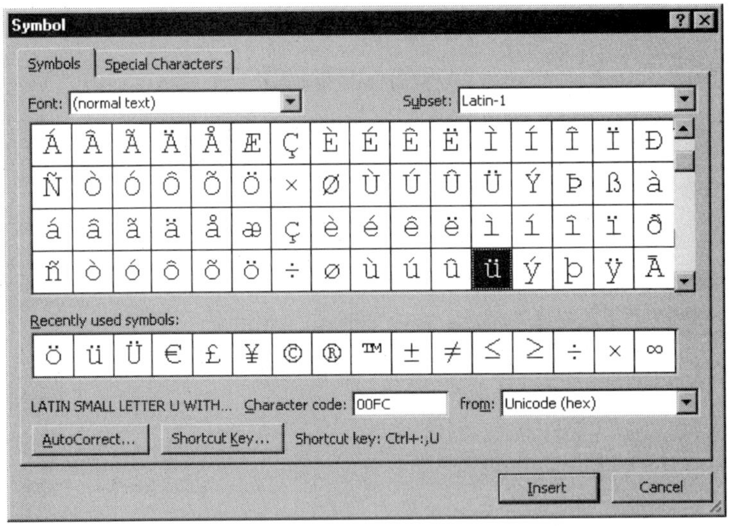


**Figure 3-31** Inserting a special character.

**5. Translate text as necessary.**

To translate a word or section of text from one language to another, select the text, choose the Tools menu's Language command, and then choose Translate from the submenu. Outlook then displays the Translate task pane. Select the dictionary to use for the translation from the Dictionary drop-down list box, and click Go, as shown in Figure 3-32.

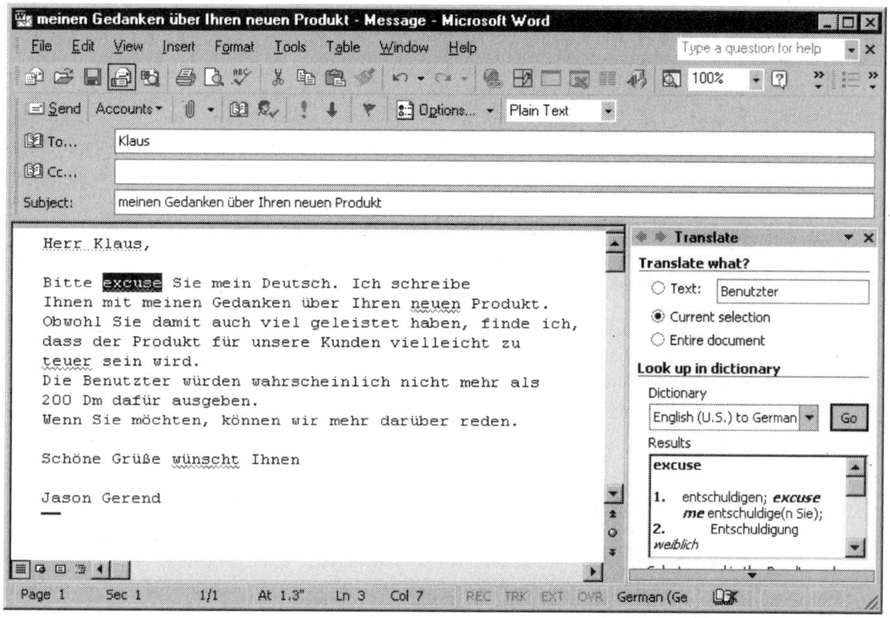


**Figure 3-32** Translating text.

WARNING *Word's translations don't always convey the meaning you intend. You can also use the Translate Via The Web feature at the bottom of the Translate task pane, or go to* http://babelfish.altavista.com, *but none of these solutions are going to be 100 percent accurate.*

# Recovering a Message from a Crash

In the event that Outlook or Word crashes (quits unexpectedly), Outlook uses special recovery information that it had saved at set intervals to recover any unsaved e-mails you were composing. If you have Word 2002 installed and are using it as your e-mail editor (enabled by default), Word will control the recovery process.

To recover from a crash of Outlook or Word, follow these steps:

1. **When Word or Outlook crashes, click the Send Error Report button.**

   Verify that the Recover My Work And Restart Microsoft Word (or Outlook) check box is selected, and then click the Send Error Report button, as shown in Figure 3-33. Outlook then connects to the Internet and sends the crash information to Microsoft and checks to see if there are any updates that address the cause of your crash. Alternatively, click the Don't Send button.

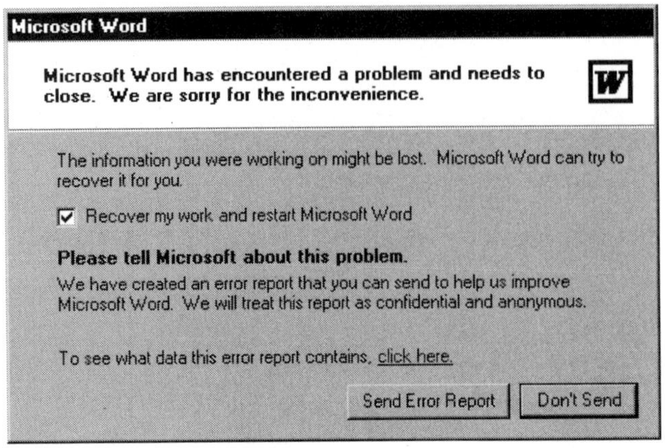


Figure 3-33 The dialog box Word displays when it crashes.

2. **Select the message to recover.**

   When you restart Word after a crash, it automatically displays any documents and messages it managed to recover, as shown in Figure 3-34. Select the message version you want to use from the Document Recovery task pane.

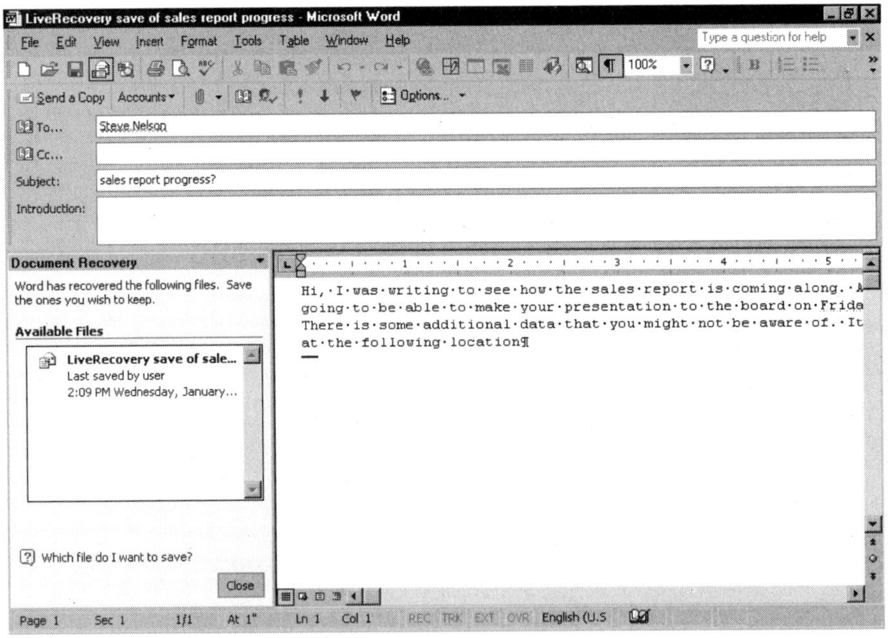


Figure 3-34 A recovered message.

3. **Review the message and save or send it.**

   Review and edit the message as you would any other message. Click the Save toolbar button to save a draft, or click the Send or Send A Copy toolbar button to send the message.

NOTE *To change how frequently Outlook saves a draft of your messages, choose the Tools menu's Options command, click the E-Mail Options button, click the Advanced E-Mail Options button, and then use the AutoSave Unsent Every setting to adjust how frequently Outlook saves drafts of your unsent messages.*

# Sending and Delivering Messages

To send a message you've composed, simply click the Send toolbar button. Outlook then immediately delivers the message (if you're connected to the Internet), or places the message in the Outbox for later delivery.

The following sections show you how to prevent Outlook from immediately delivering messages, send e-mail from a specific e-mail account, deliver messages but not check for new mail, and review messages you've already sent.

## Preventing Immediate Message Delivery

Outlook sends messages that you write immediately after you click the Send button. If you find that you often remember things that you wanted to say in an e-mail shortly after sending it, consider disabling this feature.

When you disable the Send Immediately When Connected feature, Outlook places all messages you send in the Outbox folder. Messages in the Outbox are then delivered the next time you click the Send/Receive toolbar button or when an automatic send and receive is scheduled.

To prevent Outlook from immediately delivering messages that you send, follow these steps:

1. **Open the Options dialog box.**

   Display the Inbox, and then choose the Tools menu's Options command, as shown in Figure 3-35. If you don't see the Options command, click the down arrows at the bottom of the menu to display hidden commands.

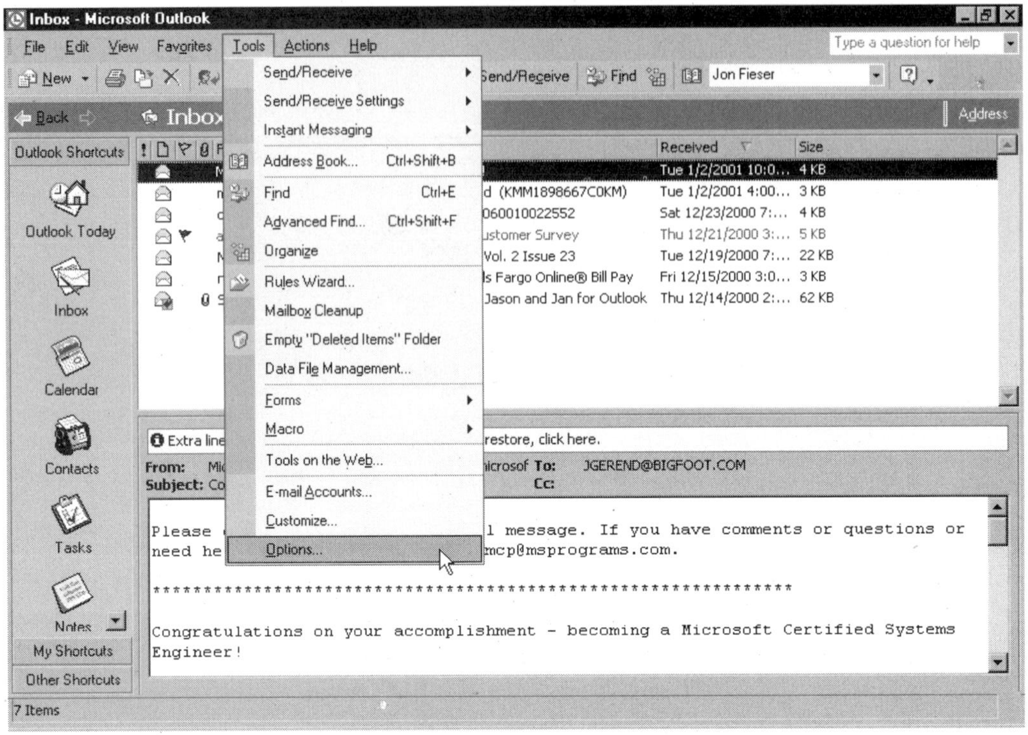

Figure 3-35 Displaying the Options dialog box.

2. **Click the Mail Setup tab.**

   This displays the Mail Setup tab of the Options dialog box, shown in Figure 3-36.

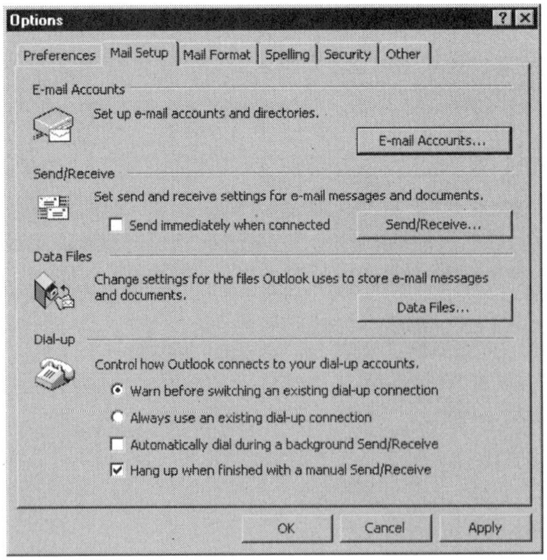

Figure 3-36 The Mail Setup tab of the Options dialog box.

3. **Clear the Send Immediately When Connected check box.**

   Click OK when you're finished.

## Sending Mail with a Specific E-Mail Account

If you have multiple e-mail accounts set up in Outlook, all mail is sent using your default mail account. To send a message using an alternate e-mail account, such as a personal e-mail account, follow these steps:

1. **Compose your message.**

   Address and compose your message as you would normally.

2. **Select the account to use.**

   Click the Accounts toolbar button, and choose the e-mail account you want to send the message with, as shown in Figure 3-37.

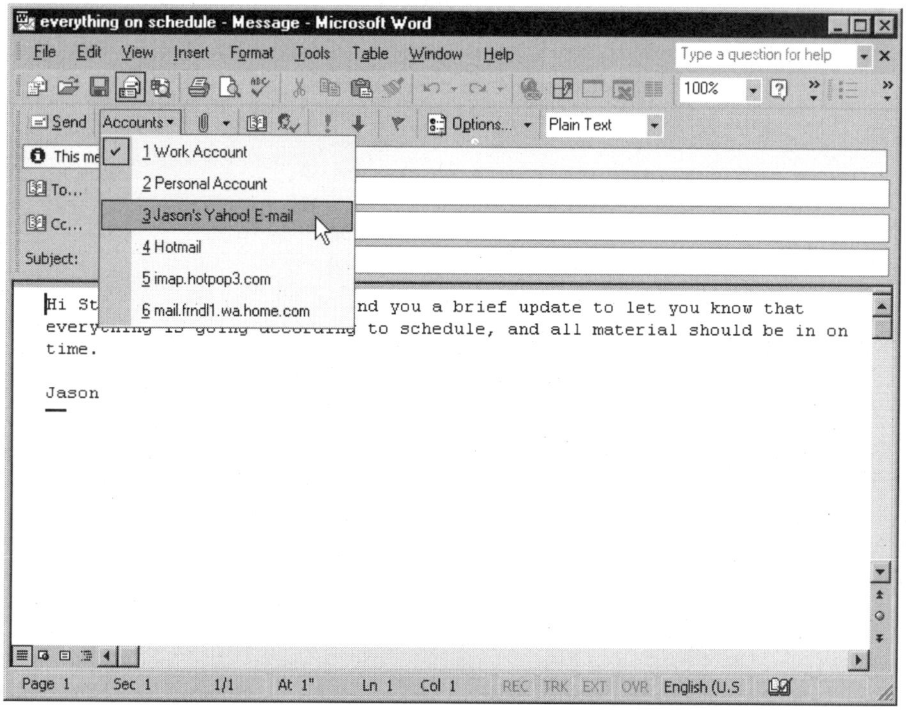


**Figure 3-37** Choosing which e-mail account with which to send a message.

3. **Click the Send toolbar button.**

Outlook then delivers the message using the specified e-mail account.

## Sending (and Not Checking) E-Mail

Sometimes you may want to only send e-mail messages and not check for new messages. You might do this because you're on a slow Internet connection or because you are sending messages with an account that's not included in your Send/Receive schedule.

To do so, choose the Tools menu's Send/Receive command and then choose Send All from the submenu, as shown in Figure 3-38.

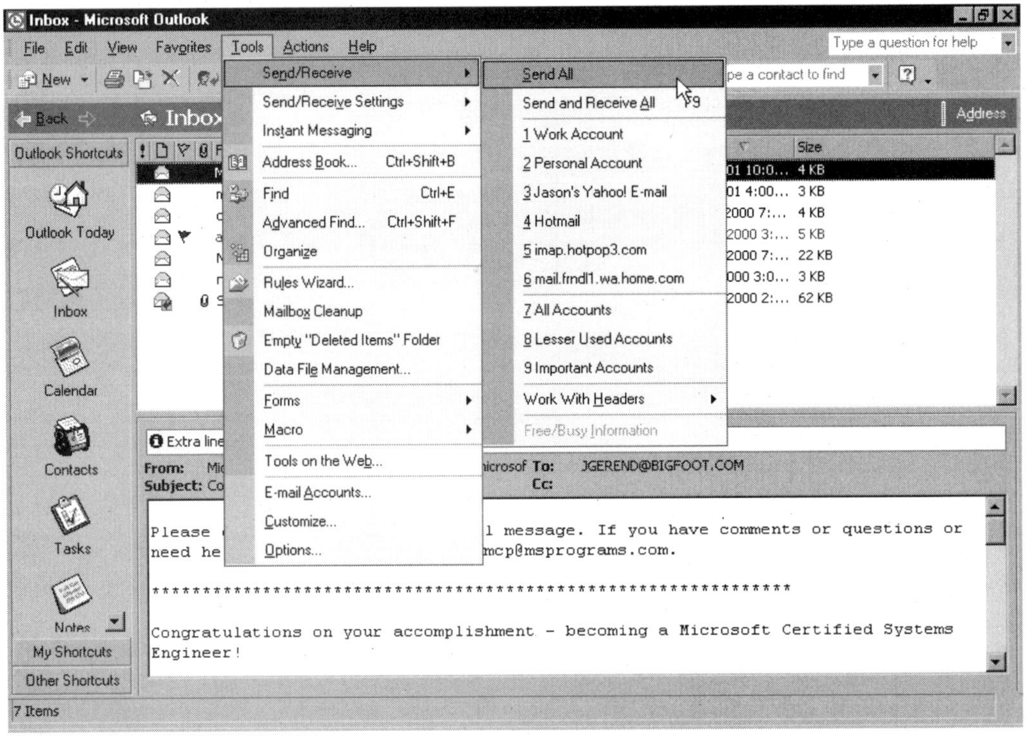


**Figure 3-38** Sending messages without checking for new mail.

TIP *If you have e-mails that refuse to leave the Outbox when you click the Send/Receive button, try using the Send All command. This will send messages on all accounts—even accounts that may be excluded from the normal Send/Receive schedule. For more information on troubleshooting messages that don't send properly, see "Skill 7: Maintaining Outlook."*

## Reviewing Sent Messages

Outlook automatically stores a copy of every e-mail message you send in the Sent Items folder. This makes it easy to review what you said in a prior message, as well as resend messages as necessary.

To review messages you've sent, follow these steps:

1. **Display the Sent Items folder.**

   Click the My Shortcuts group on the Outlook bar, and then click the Sent Items shortcut. This displays the Sent Items folder, as shown in Figure 3-39.

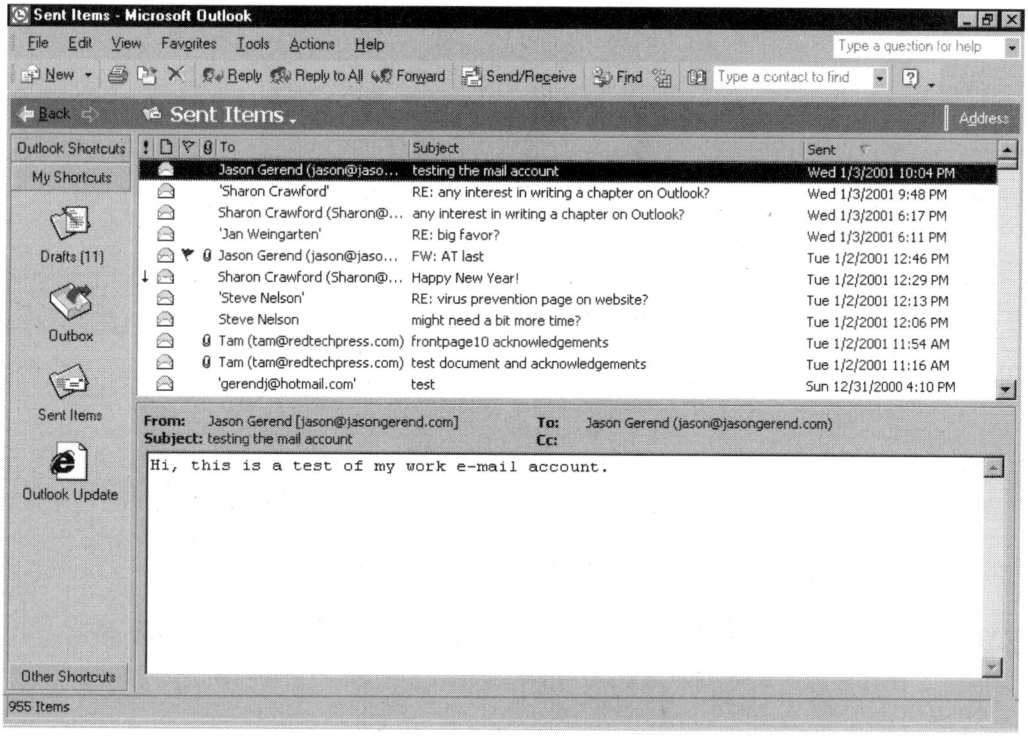

**Figure 3-39** The Sent Items folder.

2. **Open the message you want to read or resend.**

   Double-click a message to open it.

3. **Optionally, resend the message.**

   To do so, choose the Actions menu's Resend This Message command, as shown in Figure 3-40. Optionally, edit the message, and then click the Send toolbar button.

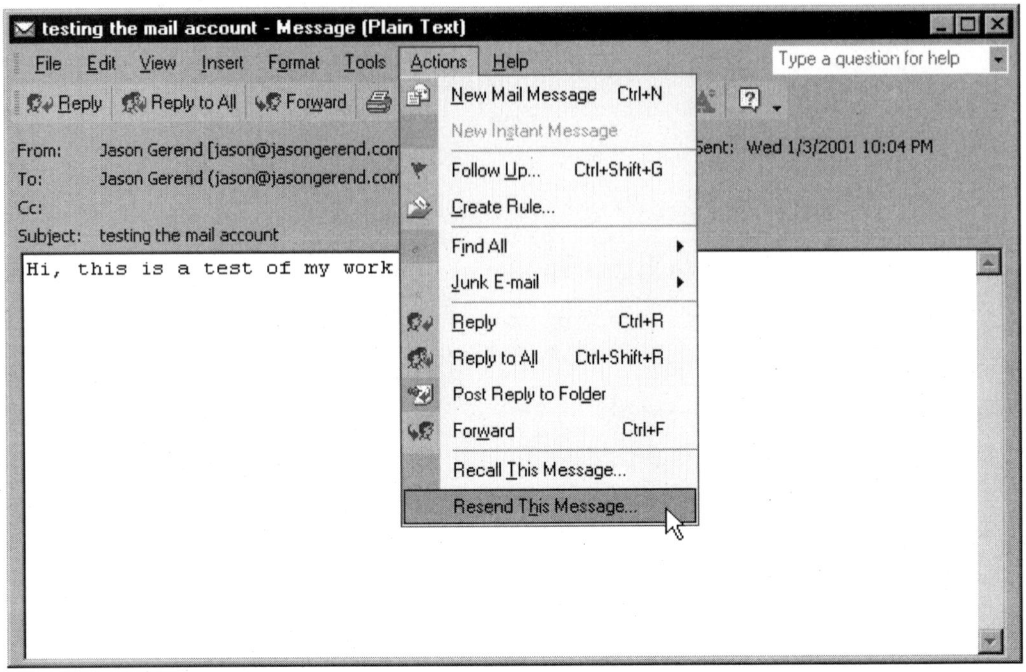


**Figure 3-40** Resending a message.

## Sent Mail's History Lesson

While the Inbox folder provides the immediate component of your e-mail system, the Sent Mail folder is just as essential to the experience—and its contents are a little more selective.

Many users who clean out their Inbox on a moderately regular schedule will only deign to erase messages from Sent Mail when the computer system begins to crawl and they're willing to try anything. This may not be a bad thing. Because you never really know if something will become important, it is better to save an eventually unneeded message than toss something that could help to support litigation.

While your Inbox shows how many people are chasing after your time—spam and all—Sent Mail can be an accurate log of your daily accomplishments. The quantity/quality equation isn't absolute here, and one size decidedly does not fit all.

On an incredibly productive day you may send out 20 messages. This is either a huge accomplishment or laugh-out-loud pathetic, depending on your perspective. But it is a pretty clear, detailed record for that particular day.

A Sent Mail folder can go way back, so if someone accuses you of slacking, the evidence (for or against) is at your fingertips. Too many times, someone may say they lost (or didn't receive) something you sent. Rifling through the Sent Mail folder to find the particular e-mail is a whole lot easier than tracking down a lost fax or phone message.

In that way, the Sent Mail folder is a part of history that keeps you from repeating yourself.

## Summary

Sending e-mail messages is a basic task that you can delve into deeper for more control. In this skill we covered the basics of sending messages, and we provided more in-depth information on addressing, composing, sending, and delivering messages.

*Skill 4*

# MANAGING YOUR E-MAIL

## Featuring:

- Finding Messages
- Organizing Messages Using Folders
- Using Message Templates
- Automatically Processing Your E-Mail
- Dealing with Junk Mail

Managing the deluge of messages you receive can become a full-time job in itself. Fortunately, Outlook provides a number of tools and techniques that you can use to organize and find your messages, saving you time and reducing distractions.

Besides showing you how to find and organize your messages, in this skill we also document how to create and use message templates to streamline the creation of similar messages, as well introduce methods you can use to reduce the amount of unsolicited advertisements you find in your Inbox.

## Finding Messages

Finding a particular message can sometimes seem hopeless, especially in a cluttered Inbox. The following sections give you some powerful techniques for quickly finding a particular message or messages.

## Finding Messages Related to Replies and Forwards

To find all messages related to a message you replied to or forwarded, including messages you sent as well as received, follow these steps:

1. **Select the message you replied to or forwarded.**

   This displays the message in the Preview pane, along with an information bar across the top of the Preview pane. This information bar, shown in Figure 4-1, tells you when you replied to or forwarded the message.

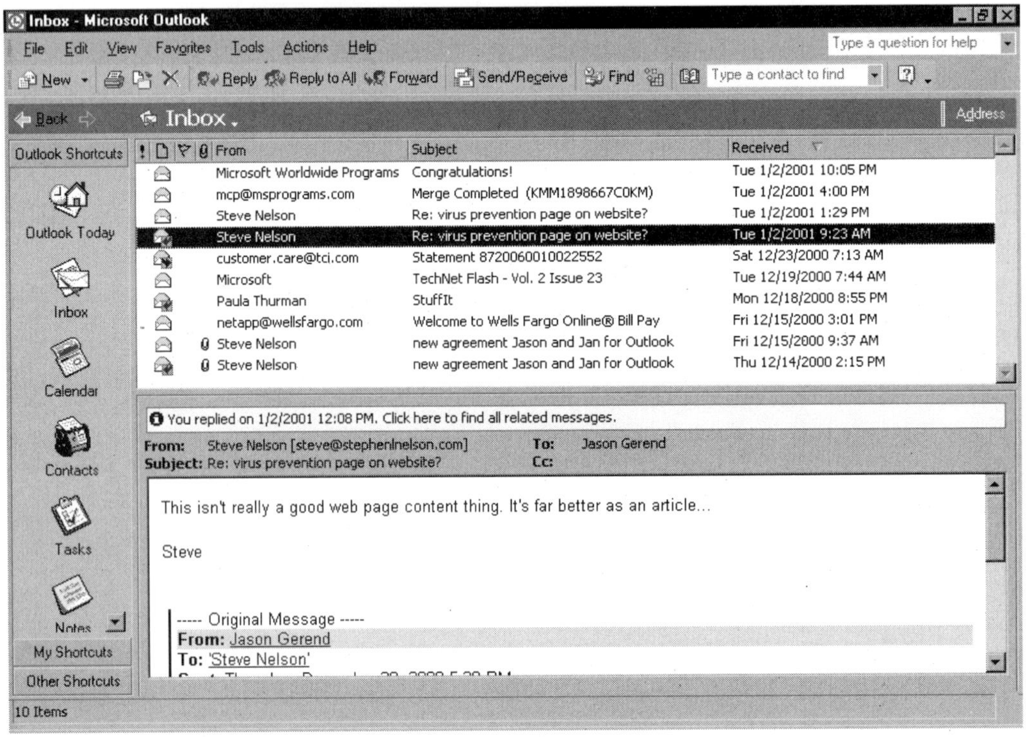


**Figure 4-1** The information bar of a message reply.

2. **Click the information bar in the Preview pane.**

   Outlook then opens the Advanced Find tool and performs a search for all related messages, as shown in Figure 4-2.

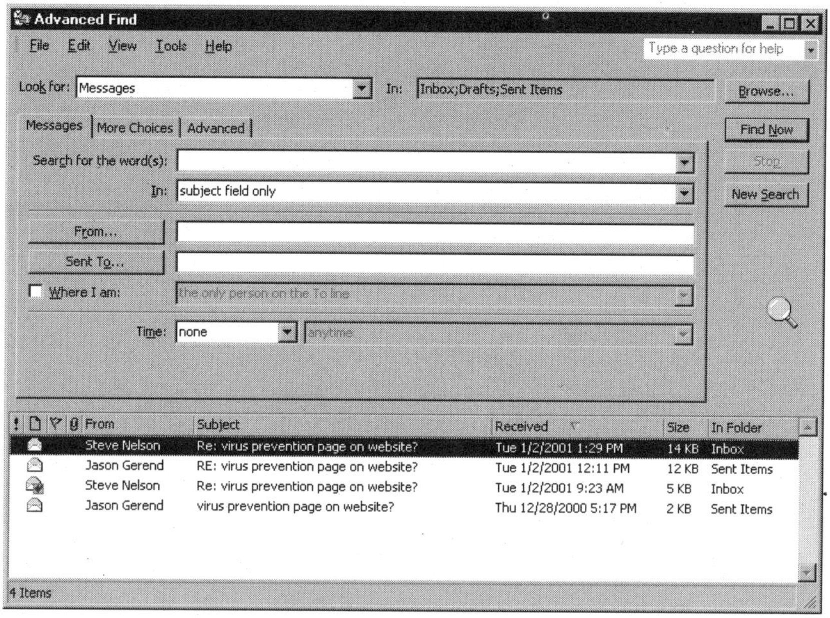


**Figure 4-2** Finding related messages.

## Sorting and Grouping Messages

You can also quickly find related messages in the same folder by sorting or grouping messages by sender or subject.

- To sort messages by sender or subject, click the Subject heading or the From heading and then scroll to the appropriate message, as shown in Figure 4-3.

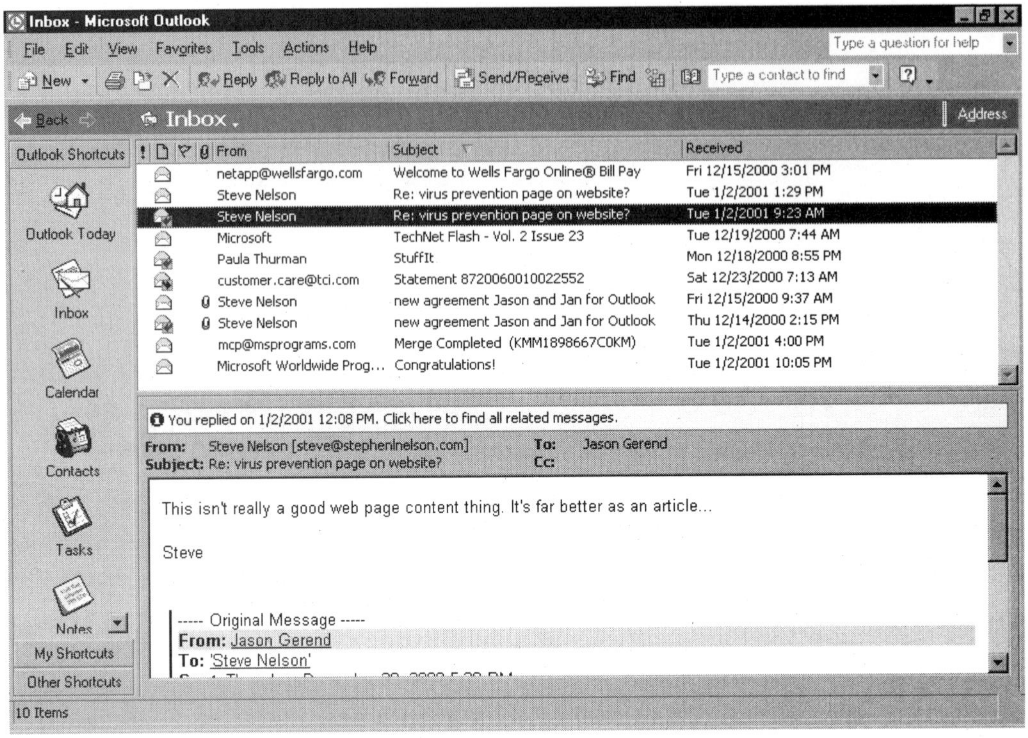


**Figure 4-3** The Inbox with messages sorted by subject.

- To group messages by topic, choose the View menu's Current View command and choose By Conversation Topic from the submenu. To view messages pertaining to a topic, click the plus sign next to the topic, as shown in Figure 4-4.

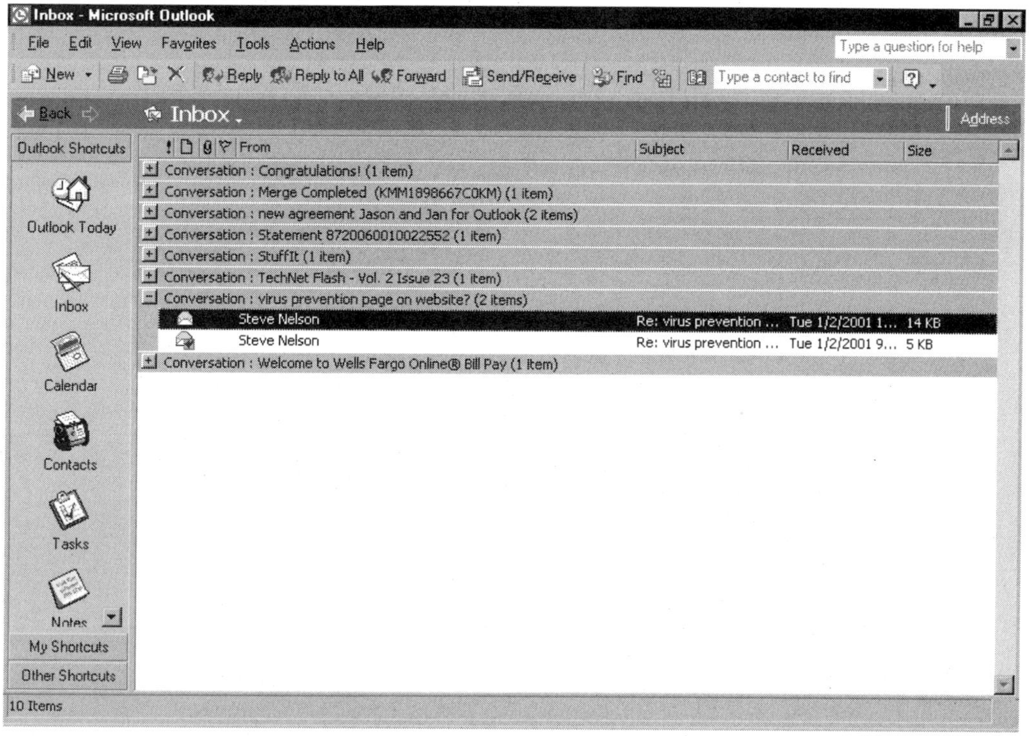

Figure 4-4 Grouping messages by conversation topic.

## Using the Find Tool

To find a message containing a specific string of text—either in the From field, the Subject field, or the message body, use the Find tool. Follow these steps:

**1. Click the Find toolbar button.**

This displays the Find bar, as shown in Figure 4-5.

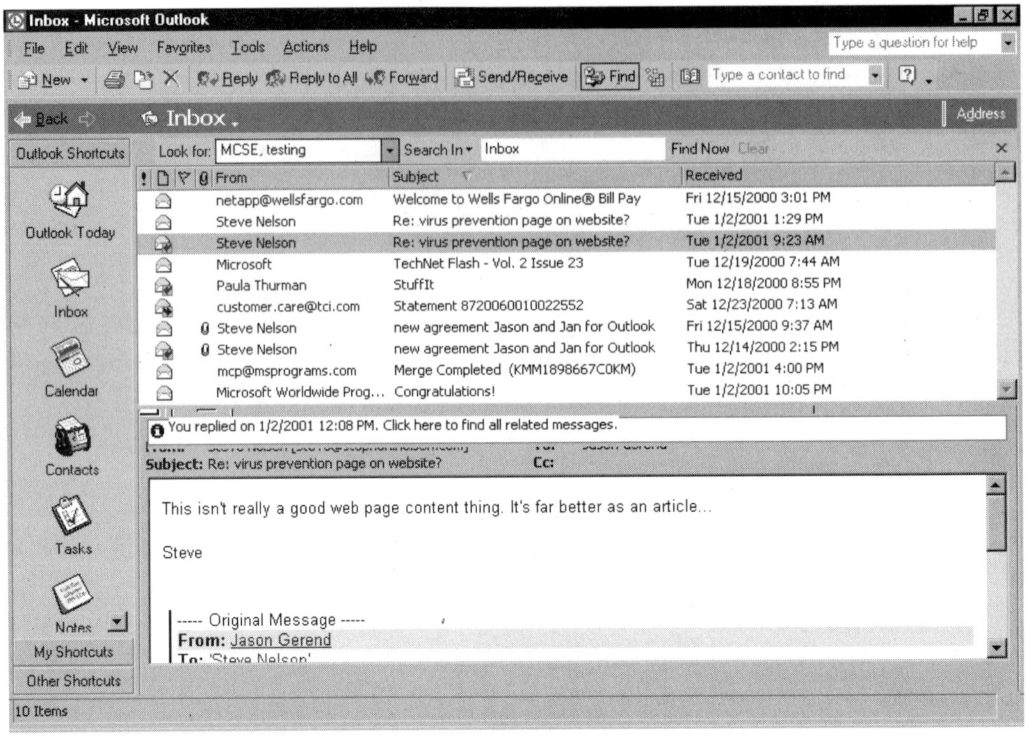


**Figure 4-5** Searching for messages using the Find tool.

**2. Enter the words for which you want to search.**

In the Look For box, enter the words for which you want to search. Here are some tips for searching with the Find tool:

- By default, Outlook searches for any messages with all the words listed.
- To search for messages with any of the words (the Boolean OR command), separate the search words with commas.
- To perform a search you previously performed, click the down arrow next to the Look For box to display a list of previous searches.
- To search only for messages you sent or that are specifically addressed to you, click the Search In button and choose Mail I Received or Mail I Sent from the pop-up menu.

3. **Select the folder(s) in which to search.**

Click the Search In button to select a different folder to search in from the pop-up menu, as shown in Figure 4-6. If the folder in which you want to search isn't listed or you want to select multiple folders, choose the Choose Folders command from the pop-up menu, use the Select Folders dialog box to select the folders you want to search in, and then click OK, as shown in Figure 4-7.

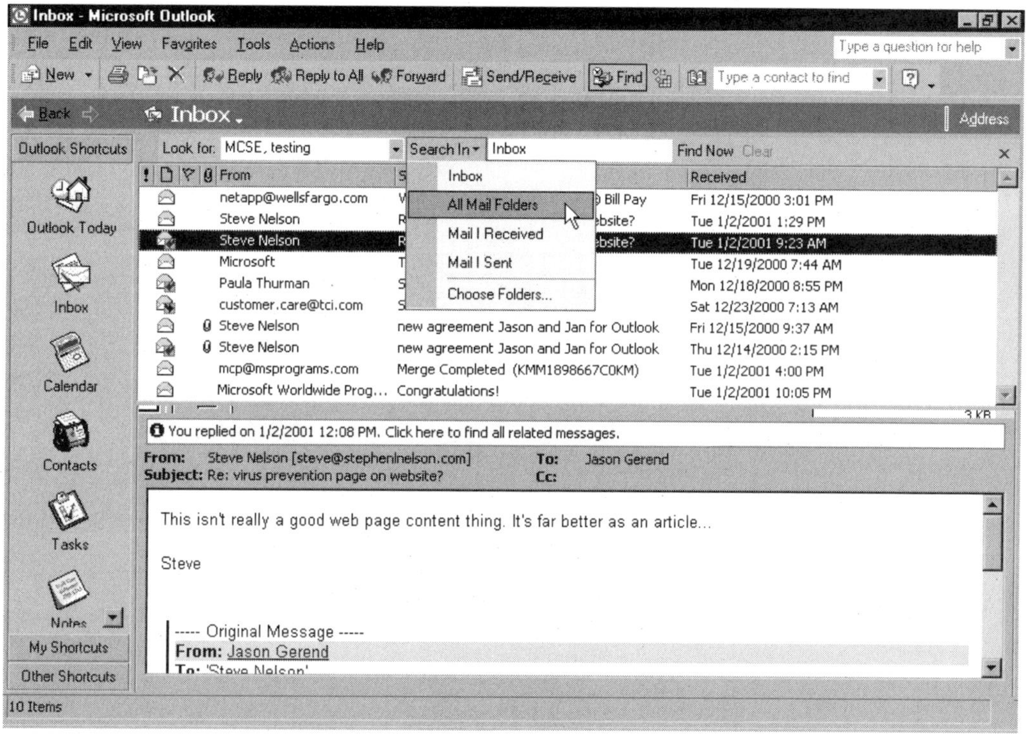


**Figure 4-6** Selecting a folder in which to search.

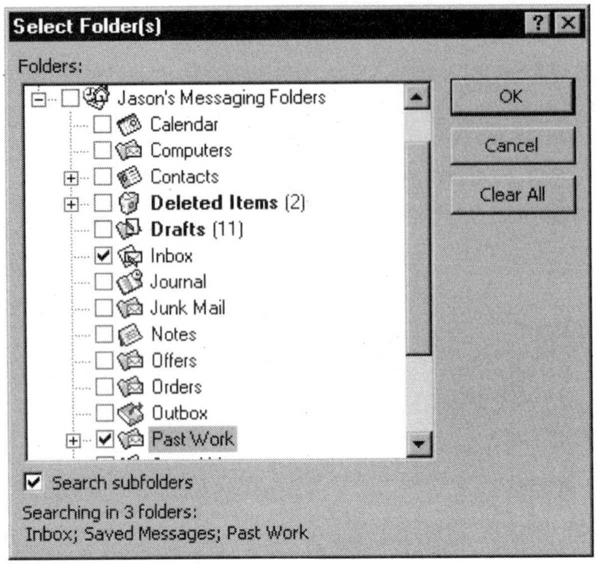


**Figure 4-7** Selecting multiple folders in which to search.

4. **Click Find Now.**

   Outlook displays the messages it finds in the current view. Open and work with the messages normally, but keep in mind that if you switch folders, the search results will disappear. You can also clear the search results by clicking the Clear button.

5. **Close the Find bar.**

   Click the X at the far right end of the Find bar to close it.

## Performing Advanced Searches

To perform a more sophisticated search than the Find bar allows, you need to use the Advanced Find tool. This tool allows you to search for any Outlook item, based on just about any criterion you can think of.

To use the Advanced Find tool to locate a message or other Outlook item, follow these steps:

1. **Open Advanced Find.**

   Choose the Tools menu's Advanced Find command, or right-click the folder you want to search in and choose the shortcut menu's Advanced Find command.

2. **Specify the type of Outlook item to look for.**

   In the Look For drop-down list box at the top of the Advanced Find window, as shown in Figure 4-8, select the type of Outlook item to look for (most likely Messages).

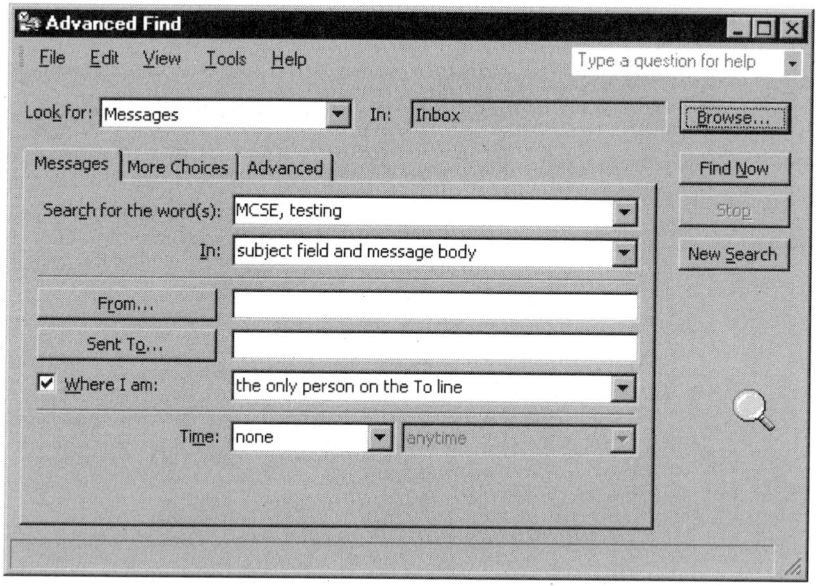


**Figure 4-8** The Advanced Find window.

TIP *If you've been assigning categories (as discussed in "Skill 2: Reading E-Mail") to your Outlook items, you might want to search solely on Category. To do so, skip ahead to step 7.*

3. **Enter your search terms.**

   As with searches from the Find bar, there are a few things to note about entering search terms in the Advanced Find window:

   - By default, Outlook searches for any messages with all the words listed.
   - To search for messages with any of the words (the Boolean OR command), separate the search words with commas.
   - To perform a search you previously performed, click the down arrow next to the Look For box to display a list of previous searches.

4. **Specify which fields to search.**

   You'll most likely want to select Subject Field and Message Body from the In drop-down list box.

5. **Specify which folders to search.**

   Click the Browse button to select a different folder to search in, use the Select Folders dialog box to select the folders you want to search in, and then click OK.

6. **Click Find Now.**

   Outlook performs the search and displays any matching messages, as shown in Figure 4-9. Click New Search to clear the search and start over.

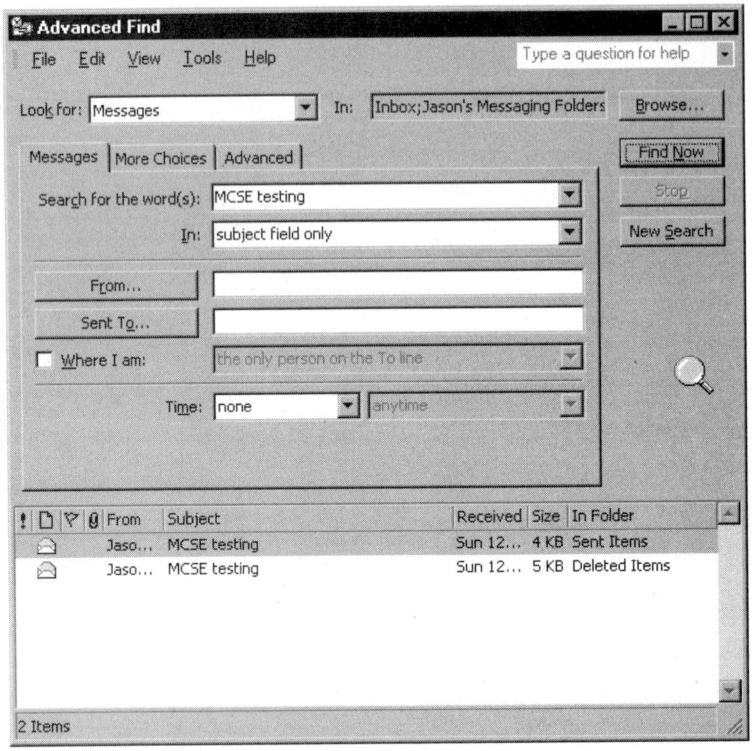


**Figure 4-9** The results of a search in the Advanced Find window.

TIP *If you find yourself frequently performing a complex search, save it. To do so, choose the File menu's Save Search command, enter a filename and location for the search, and click OK. To load the saved search, choose the File menu's Open Search command. (Click the down arrows at the bottom of the menu to display this command, if it's hidden.)*

7. **Refine your search.**

   If your search returns too many items (or the wrong ones), you can further limit your search using the other fields in the Advanced Find window:

   - Use the From button and text box to limit the search to messages only from a specific contact.

- Use the Sent To button and text box to limit the search to only messages sent to a specific contact (you'll most likely want to enter one of your e-mail addresses here).
- Use the Where I Am check box to limit the search to messages sent only to you, or to you and others.
- Use the Time box to specify when the messages should've been received, sent, and so forth.
- Click the More Choices tab to further refine your search by category, whether items are unread, or have attachments or to search by size.
- Click the Advanced tab for full control over your search. Choose a field from the Field drop-down list box, select a condition for the field, enter a value for the field, and then click Add To List. Repeat this until your search is constructed, as shown in Figure 4-10, and then click Find Now.

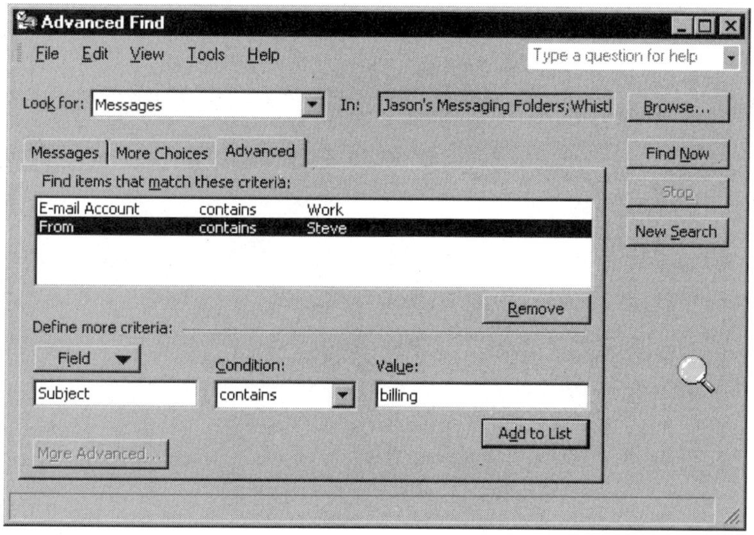


**Figure 4-10** Manually constructing a search.

# Organizing Messages Using Folders

The best way to tidy up your Inbox is to move messages you want to save into other folders within Outlook. This allows you to find messages of interest to you, as well as deal more effectively with the new messages that you receive.

To organize messages with folders, you first need to create the folders and then move your messages into them.

## Creating Folders

By default, Outlook provides only a single folder for you to store your messages in—the Inbox. Most users find that this folder quickly overflows with messages, making it difficult to find any but the few most recent.

The solution to the full Inbox problem is to create extra folders in Outlook to store those messages you want to keep. To do so, follow these steps:

1. **Display the Inbox.**

   Open Outlook, and click the Inbox shortcut on the Outlook bar.

2. **Create a new folder.**

   Choose the File menu's New command, and then choose Folder from the submenu, as shown in Figure 4-11. (If you can't find the command, click the down arrows at the bottom of the menu.)

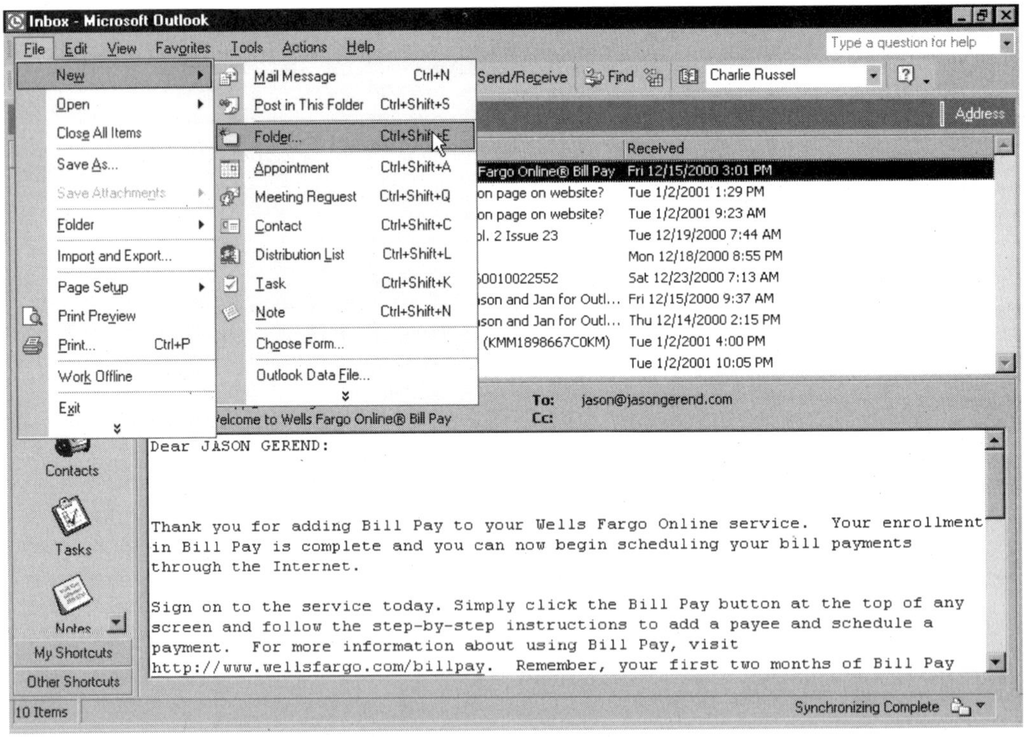


**Figure 4-11** Creating a new folder.

3. **Choose the type of items the folder should store.**

   Select Mail And Post to create a folder for e-mail messages, as shown in Figure 4-12. Alternatively, select a different Outlook type if you want to create additional Calendar, Task, Contact, or Note folders.

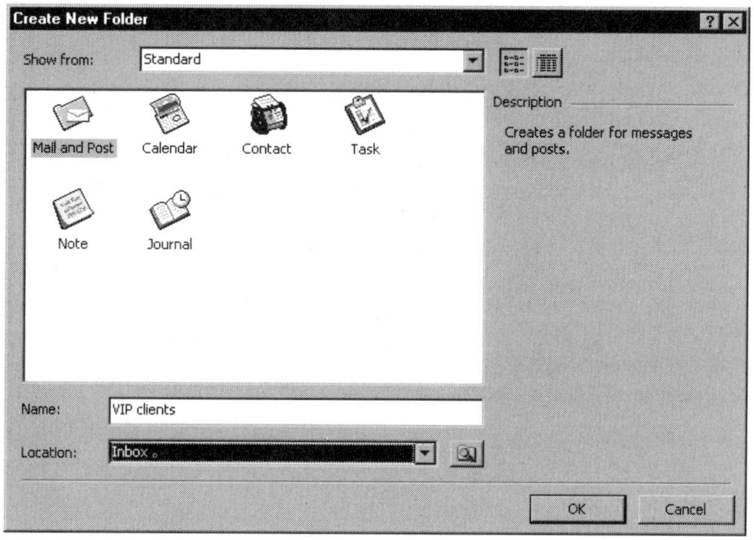


**Figure 4-12** Specifying the folder type, name, and location.

4. **Name the folder.**

   Enter a short but descriptive name for the folder in the Name box.

5. **Specify where to place the folder.**

   Use the Location drop-down list box to select the folder in which you want to store your new folder. (We recommend either your local Inbox or the Inbox on your IMAP, Exchange, or Hotmail server, if you have one.) Alternatively, click the folder icon next to the box to visually select a folder, as shown in Figure 4-13.

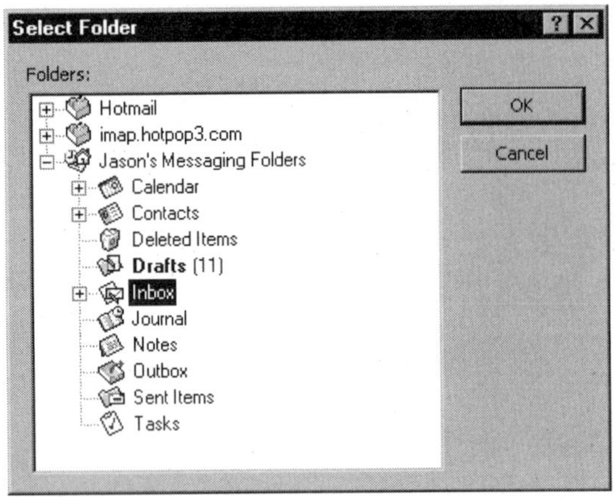


**Figure 4-13** Visually selecting a parent folder.

**6. Click OK.**

When Outlook asks if you want to create a shortcut to the folder on the Outlook bar, click Yes. Outlook creates the folder and adds a shortcut to the My Shortcuts group on the Outlook bar.

# Moving Your Messages

The simplest way to move messages to a new folder is to display the new folder and drag the messages into it. (You can also use the Organize pane to do this, as discussed in the following section.)

To move your messages, follow these steps:

**1. Open the Inbox.**

**2. Locate the shortcut to your new folder.**

Click the My Shortcuts group on the Outlook bar to display the shortcut to your new folder, as shown in Figure 4-14.

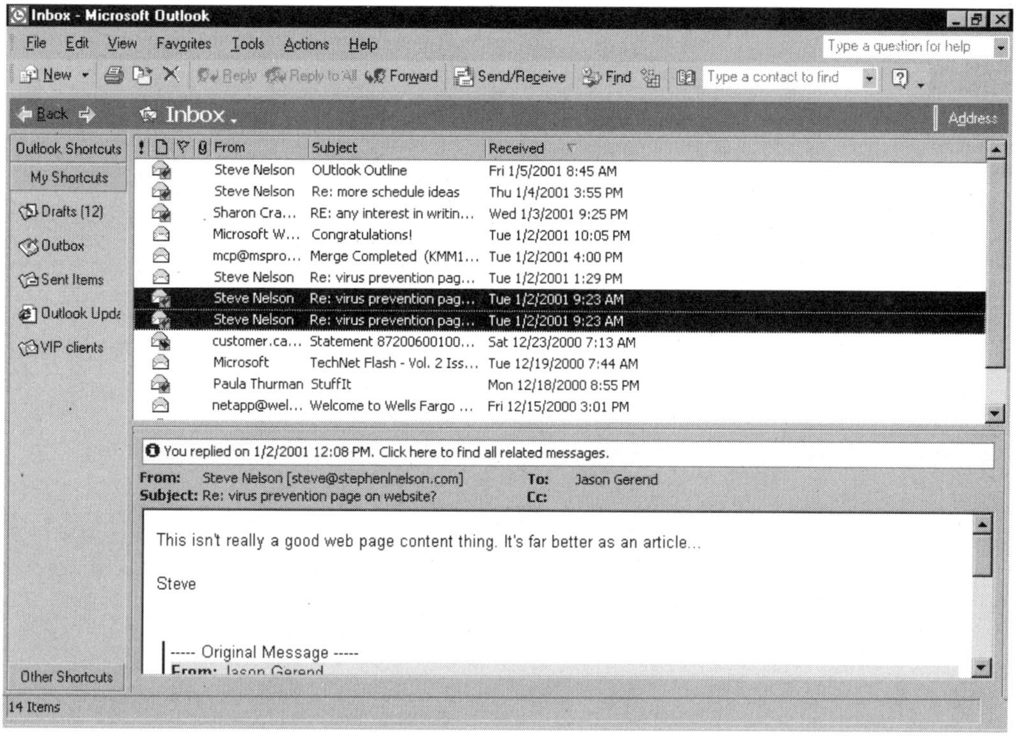


**Figure 4-14** The My Shortcuts group in the Outlook bar.

3. **Select the messages you want to move.**

   To select multiple messages, click the first message you want to move, hold down the Shift key, and then click the last message you want to select. Outlook selects every message in between. To select individual messages, hold down the Ctrl key and click each message.

4. **Drag the messages to the new folder.**

   Drag the messages onto the shortcut to your new folder. Outlook then moves the messages into that folder. (To copy messages instead, hold down the Ctrl key while dragging them.)

TIP *To move and copy messages as if you were using Windows Explorer or Outlook Express, open the Folder List. To do so, click the Inbox folder title (next to the Back button) and click the pushpin button to lock it open.*

## Using the Organize Pane

Outlook's Organize pane helps you tidy up your Inbox or other folders. Although most of the Organize pane's functionality is available through other means, it provides a convenient hub from which you can carry out a number of organizational tasks:

- To display the Organize pane, open the folder you want to organize and then click the Organize toolbar button.
- To move messages to another folder, select the messages you want to move and then use the Move Message section of the Organize pane to select the folder into which you want to move the messages. Click the Move button to move the messages.
- To create a rule that automatically sends all messages from a particular person to a different folder, select a message from the person, choose the folder into which you want you want to move their messages, and then click Create, as shown in Figure 4-15.

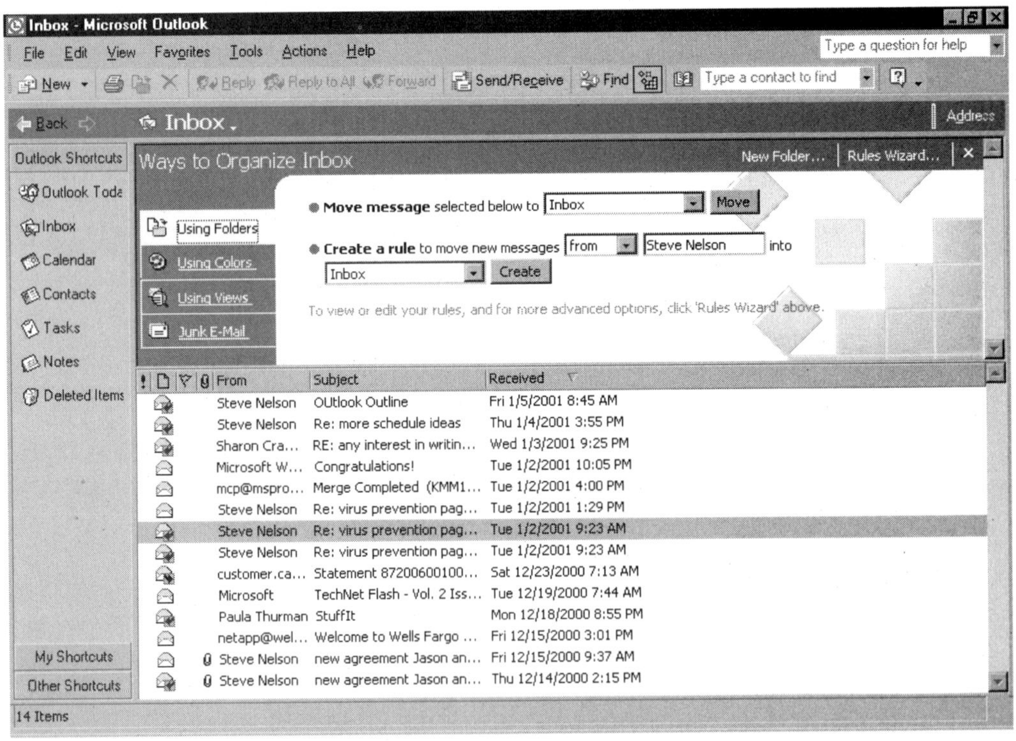


**Figure 4-15** Using the Organize pane to move messages.

- To color messages, perhaps sent from certain people or sent only to you, click the Using Colors tab in the Organize pane and use the settings provided to adjust the message coloring.
- To select a different view for the folder, such as Unread Messages, a view that displays only the messages you haven't read, click the Using Views tab and select a view from the list.
- To filter your messages for junk mail and adult content, click the Junk E-Mail tab. For more information, see the "Dealing with Junk Mail" section later in this skill.

## Using Message Templates

If you find yourself writing many similar e-mail messages, consider creating some message templates. A message template is a special type of message that you can create and then use as a sort of cookie cutter to quickly create identical e-mails (which you can then edit to suit your needs). Here are some subjects that you might want to create message templates for:

- Requests from employees for such things as more hours, time off, or a raise.
- Responses to job openings.
- Answers to frequently asked questions about your company or products.
- Press releases or information packets that you routinely send.

NOTE *You can also use message templates in conjunction with message rules to send out automatic replies. The templates are chosen automatically based on the subject of the incoming messages. For more information on this procedure, see "Appendix C: Automatically Processing Form Data."*

## Creating Message Templates

To create a message template, follow these steps:

1. **Disable Microsoft Word as your e-mail editor.**

   Unfortunately, you can't use Word to create message templates. To use Outlook's own editor for composing messages (you can switch back once you've created your templates), choose the Tools menu's Options command, click the Mail Format tab, and then clear the Use Microsoft Word To Edit E-Mail Messages check box, as shown in Figure 4-16. Click OK.

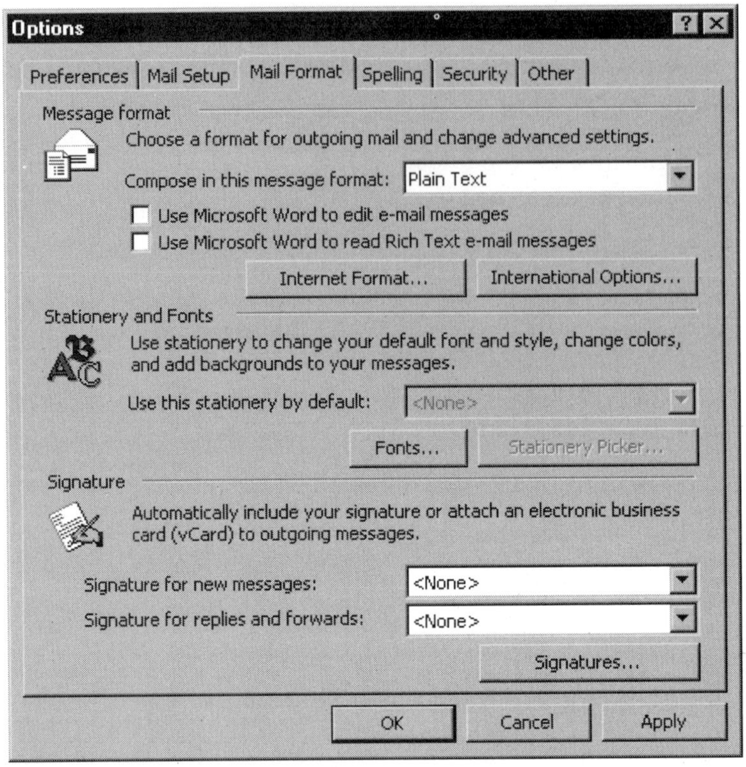


**Figure 4-16** Disabling Word as your e-mail editor.

2. **Create a new message.**

   Click the New Mail Message toolbar button to open a new message.

3. **Enter the standard text.**

   Enter a subject for the message, and enter any text that will apply to all messages you create with the template, as shown in Figure 4-17. (Don't address the message and exclude comments that pertain solely to one person, unless you'll use the template primarily when writing to that person.)

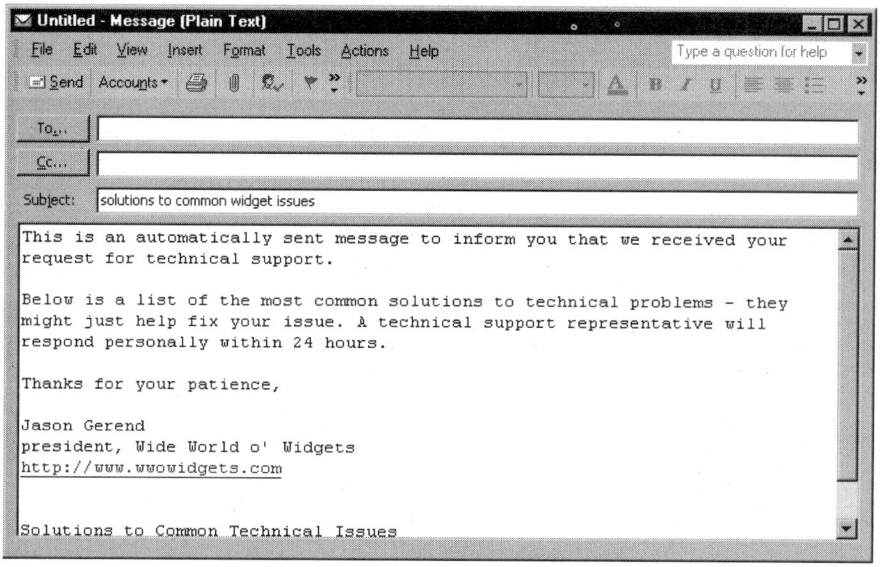


**Figure 4-17** Creating a message template.

**4. Choose the File menu's Save As command.**

This displays the Save As dialog box.

**5. Specify that you want to use the Outlook Template file format.**

Select Outlook Template from the Save As Type drop-down list box, as shown in Figure 4-18. Outlook then displays the Templates folder for your user profile, which is where we recommend that you save the template.

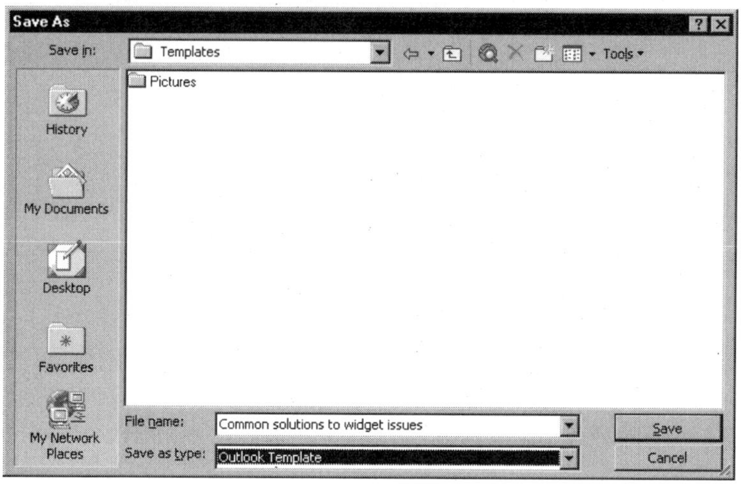


**Figure 4-18** Saving a message template.

**6. Click Save.**

# Composing Messages Using Templates

Once you've created a message template, you can use it to quickly create new messages based on the template. To do so, follow these steps:

1. **Open the Choose Form dialog box.**

   Click the down arrow next to the New Mail Message toolbar button, and then select Choose Form from the shortcut menu, as shown in Figure 4-19.

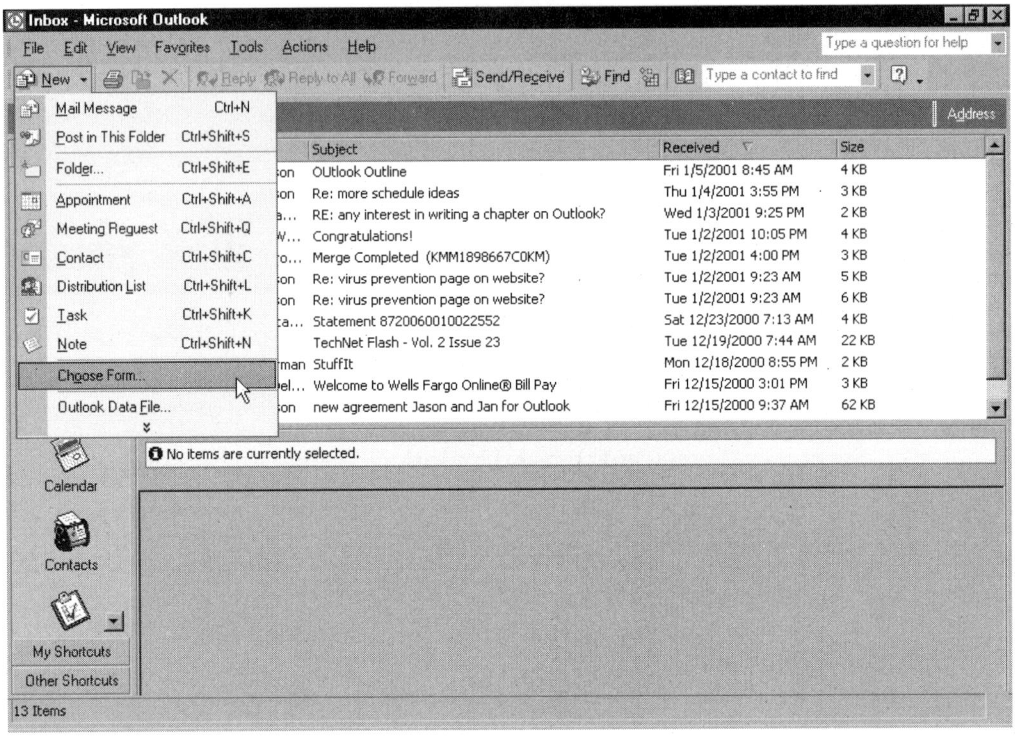


**Figure 4-19** Opening the Choose Form dialog box.

2. **Select User Templates In File System from the Look In box.**

   Outlook then displays any templates you created, as shown in Figure 4-20.

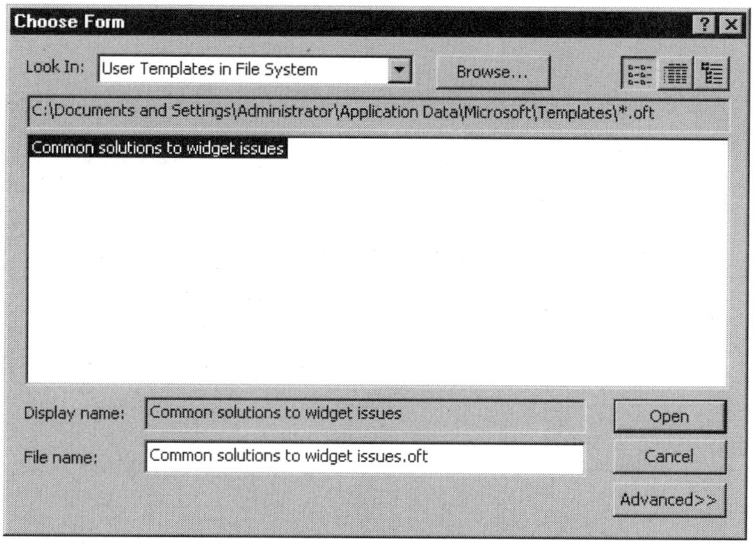


**Figure 4-20** Choosing a template in the Choose Form dialog box.

3. **Select the template you want, and click Open.**

   Outlook creates a new message with the template's text inserted.

## Adding Templates to the Outlook Bar

If you often use templates to create messages, you'll quickly get tired of using the Choose Form dialog box to select your template.

Although it takes a bit of effort to set up, a faster way to create messages using templates is to create a group on the Outlook bar for your templates and then create shortcuts in this group for all of your templates. To do this, follow these steps:

1. **Create a new group for your templates.**

   Right-click a group in the Outlook bar, choose Add New Group from the shortcut menu, and then enter a name for the group, as shown in Figure 4-21.

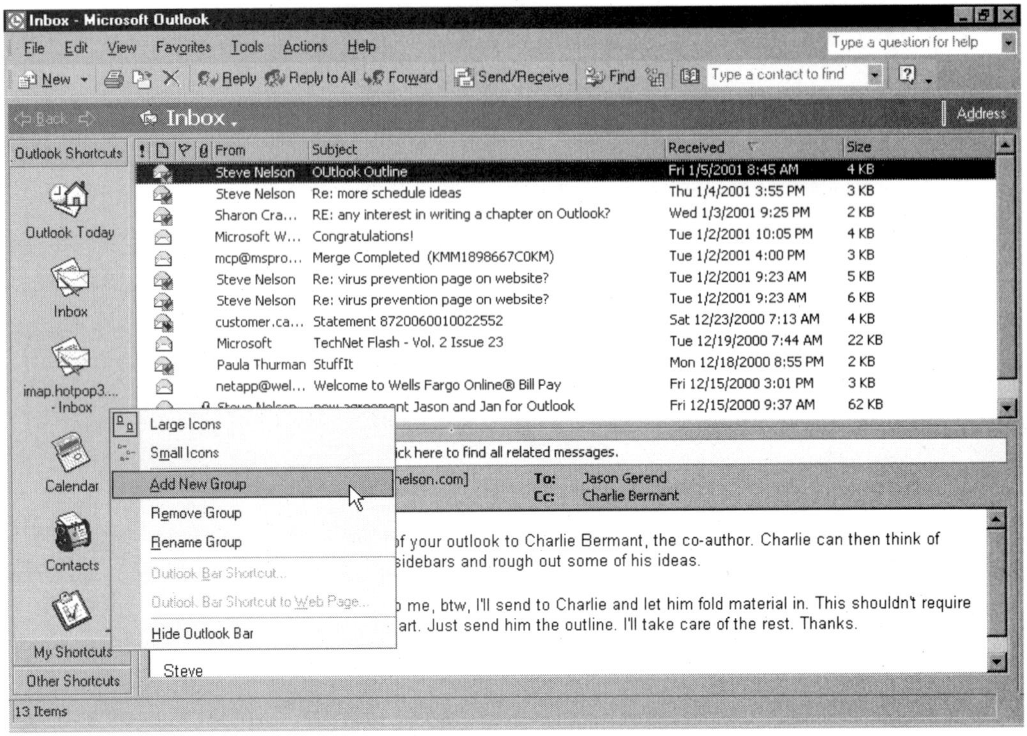


**Figure 4-21** Creating a new group for message templates.

2. **Open Microsoft Windows' Search tool.**

   In Windows 2000, click the Start button, choose Search, and then click For Files Or Folders (other versions of Windows may vary slightly).

3. **Enable the display of hidden files.**

   Because Outlook marks templates as hidden files, you need to tell Windows to display hidden files before searching for any templates. To do so, in Windows 2000's Search Results window, choose the Tools menu's Folder Options command, click the View tab, select the Show Hidden Files And Folders option, and then click OK, as shown in Figure 4-22.

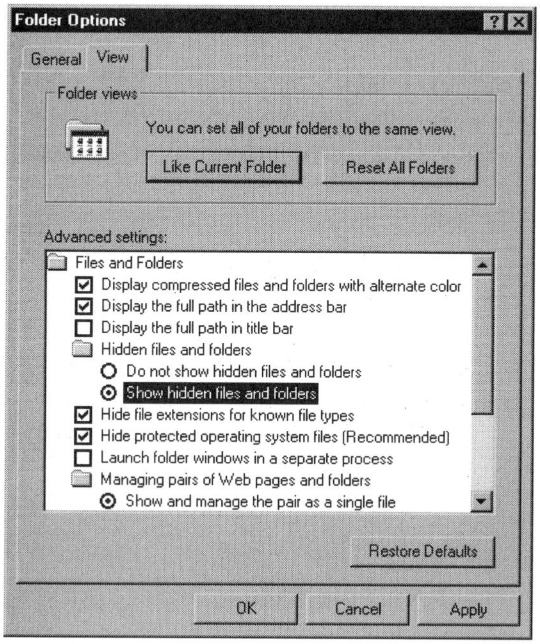


**Figure 4-22** Enabling the display of hidden files in Windows.

NOTE *For other versions of Windows, use the Help system to search for "display hidden files," and then follow the instructions provided.*

**4. Search for .oft files.**

In the Search Results window, enter **.oft* in the Search For Files Or Folders Named box, and select Local Harddrives from the Look In box.

**5. Click Search Now.**

Windows displays your templates, as shown in Figure 4-23.

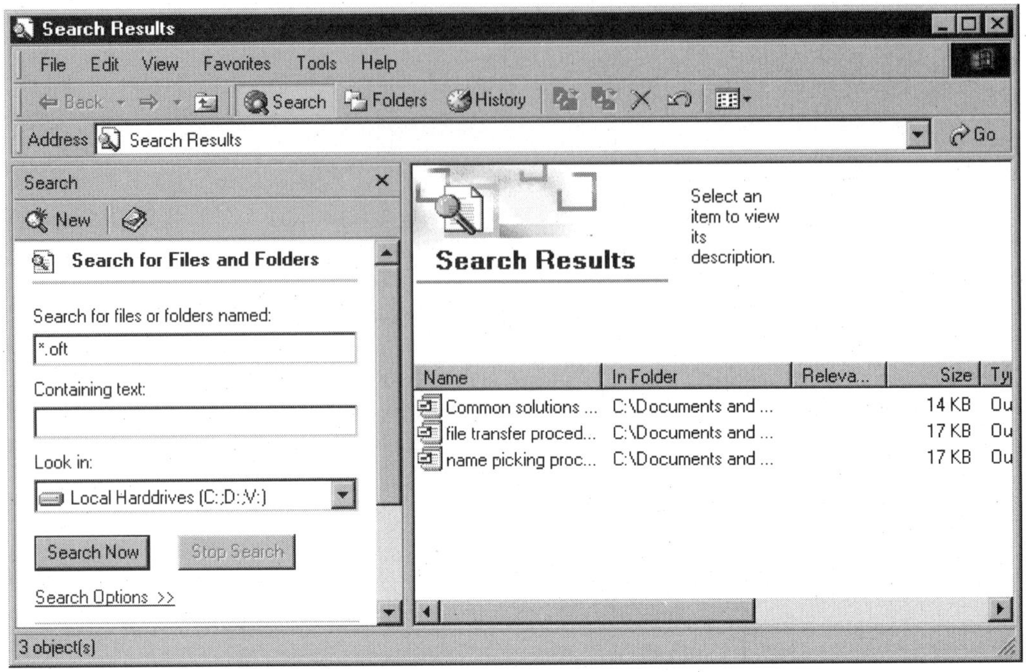


**Figure 4-23** Searching for your templates.

**6. Drag the templates into the new Outlook group.**

Resize the Search Results window and the Outlook window so that you can view both simultaneously, open the new Outlook group by clicking its name, and then drag the templates one by one into the new group, as shown in Figure 4-24.

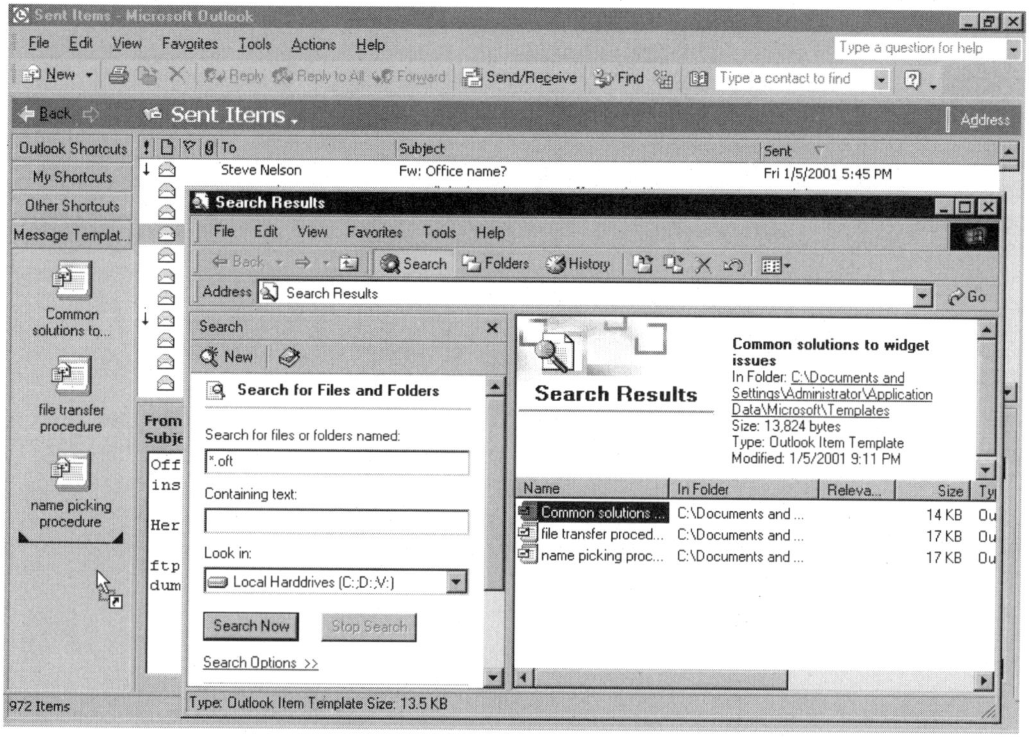

**Figure 4-24** Creating shortcuts to your templates.

7. **Create messages with your templates.**

   To create a message with your new template shortcuts, simply open the Message Templates group and click the desired template.

# Automatically Processing Your E-Mail

Perhaps the single most powerful feature in Outlook is its ability to automatically process your e-mails using message rules.

You can create message rules to select messages based on the sender (which can include mailing lists), keywords in their subjects or bodies, or with which e-mail account they were received. Once Outlook selects the messages, it can perform the following actions (as well as some others):

- Move the messages to a different folder.
- Assign categories to the messages to make them easier to find.
- Delete the messages.
- Forward the messages to another contact.
- Reply to the messages using a template you created. ("Appendix C: Automatically Processing Form Data" discusses this task in detail.)

You can also process messages you send—for example, you can sort messages you send into different folders or delete messages that are too large.

TIP *Message rules are very powerful, but they are also complex. We recommend that you plan your rules carefully and, ideally, test them out by applying them to messages already in your Inbox. If the rules don't work as you intend, edit them and retest.*

## Creating Rules Based on Existing Messages

The easiest way to create a message rule is to start with an existing message. When you use an existing message as a starting point for a message rule, Outlook examines the message and presents some possible criteria for your rules, based on the message.

To create a new rule based on an existing message, follow these steps:

1. **Select the message from which you want to make a rule.**

   In the Inbox, select a message that matches the criteria you'd like to use to automatically select messages for processing. For example, select a message with a specific subject or from a particular person.

2. **Start the Rules Wizard.**

   Right-click the message, and choose Create Rule from the shortcut menu, as shown in Figure 4-25, to start the Rules Wizard.

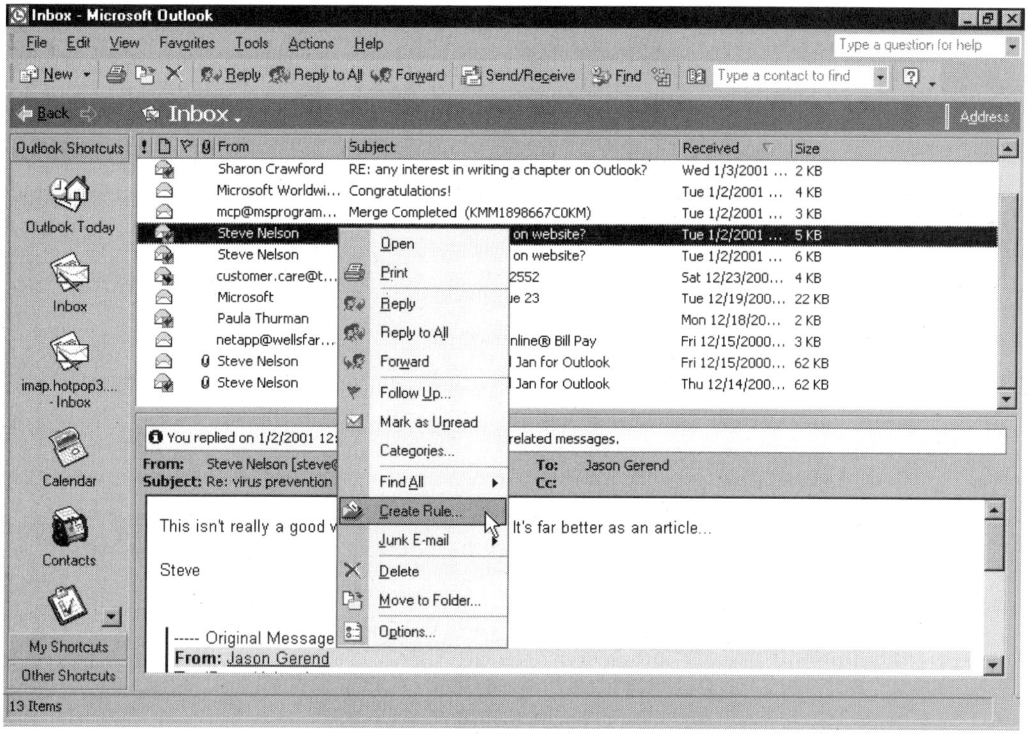


Figure 4-25 Creating a rule based on an existing message.

3. **Choose which conditions you want to use to select messages.**

   Select the check box next to each condition a message must meet in order to be selected for automatic processing, as shown in Figure 4-26.

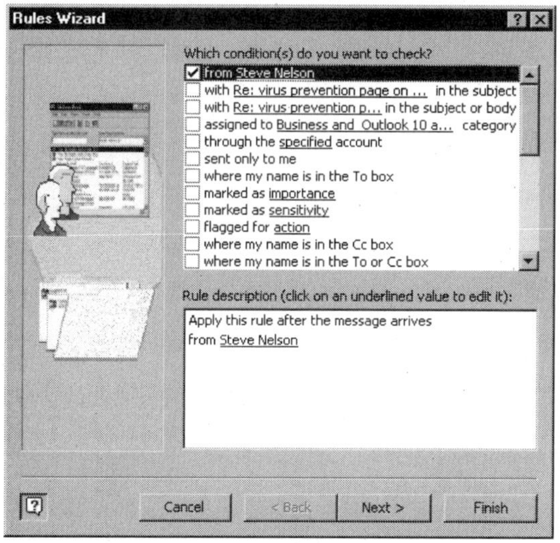


Figure 4-26 Specifying the conditions for inclusion in the message rule.

WARNING *When selecting messages based on sender, Outlook recognizes only the first e-mail address for a contact. To make sure Outlook processes all messages from this contact, click the contact's name in the Rules Wizard dialog box to open the Rule Address dialog box, select each instance of the contact, and then click the From or To button.*

4. **Edit the conditions.**

   After selecting a condition, you can edit the values for the condition by clicking the underlined words at the bottom of the dialog box. This permits you to specify values and add other names or words to your selection criteria. Click Next to continue.

5. **Specify what to do with the messages.**

   In the next dialog box, select the check box next to the actions you want to perform with the messages, such as Move It To The Specified Folder, as shown in Figure 4-27. Edit the actions as necessary by clicking the underlined words. Click Next to continue.

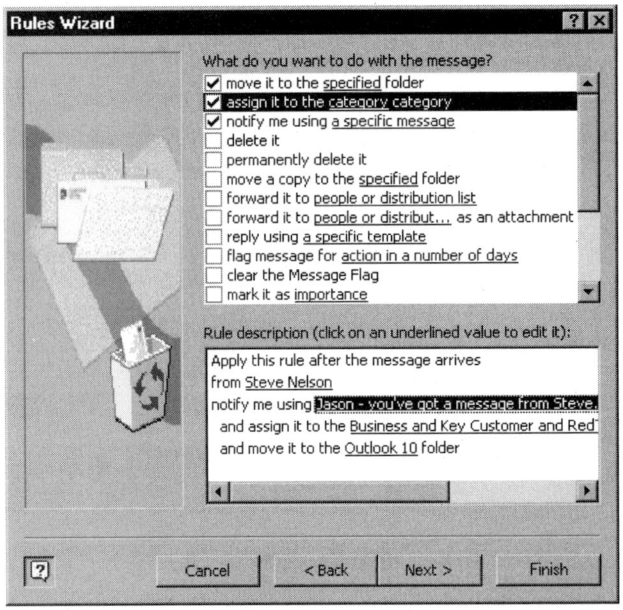


**Figure 4-27** Specifying what to do with selected messages.

6. **Add any exceptions to your rule.**

   To make exceptions to your rule, select check boxes in the next screen, as shown in Figure 4-28. Messages that match the exceptions criteria won't be processed and will be delivered to your Inbox as normal. Click Next to continue.

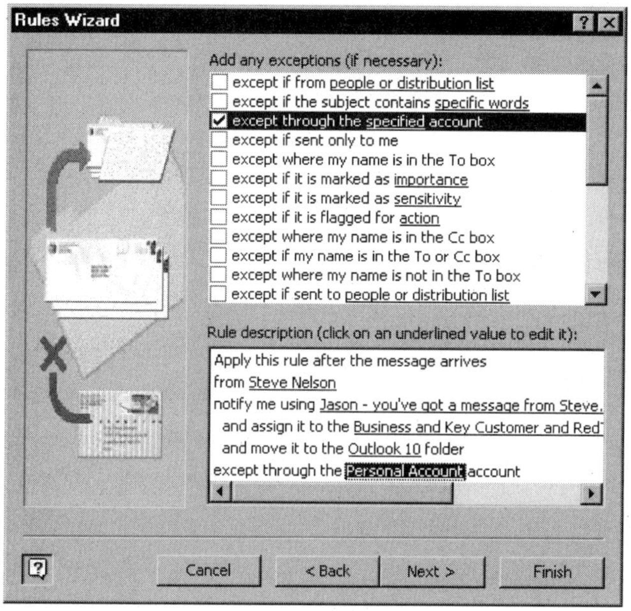


**Figure 4-28** Adding exceptions to a rule.

TIP *If you create a rule to automatically move messages to another folder, consider using the Notify Me Using A Specific Message action to display a dialog box listing the messages Outlook processed. This helps to ensure that you'll notice new messages that appear but that a rule immediately moves to a folder other than the Inbox.*

7. **Review and name the rule.**

   Use the last Rules Wizard dialog box to review your rule and make any changes necessary, as well as enter a name for the rule, as shown in Figure 4-29. To run the rule on messages already in your Inbox, select the Run This Rule Now On Messages Already In "Inbox" check box. Click Finish.

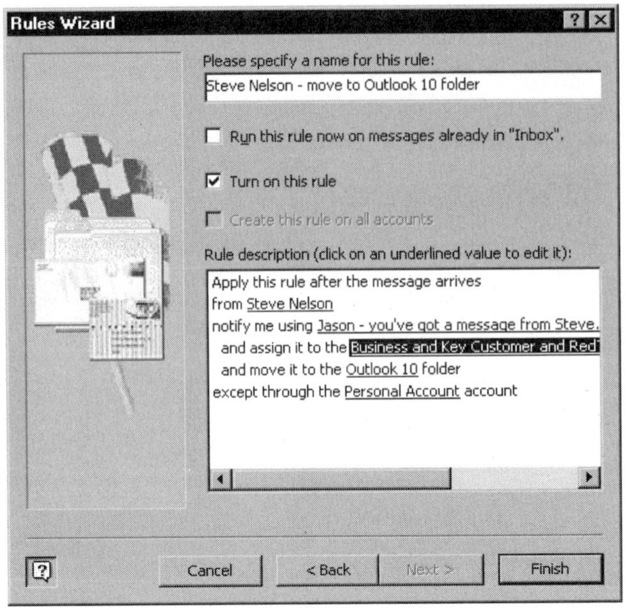


**Figure 4-29** Reviewing and naming a rule.

# Creating Rules from Scratch

Creating rules from scratch is much like creating rules based on existing messages, except that you have a couple more options, most notably the ability to move or categorize messages you send to others.

To create a rule from scratch, display your Inbox and then follow these steps:

1. **Choose the Tools menu's Rules Wizard command.**

   This starts the Rules Wizard with a list of any message rules you currently have.

2. **Select the Inbox to which you want to apply the rule.**

   If you have a POP3 account and an IMAP account, or multiple IMAP accounts, choose the appropriate Inbox from the drop-down list box at the top of the dialog box.

3. **Click New in the Rules Wizard dialog box.**

4. **Select a template.**

   Select a template to use as a basis for the rule, as shown in Figure 4-30, or click the Start From A Blank Rule option button to create a rule completely from scratch. Click Next to continue.

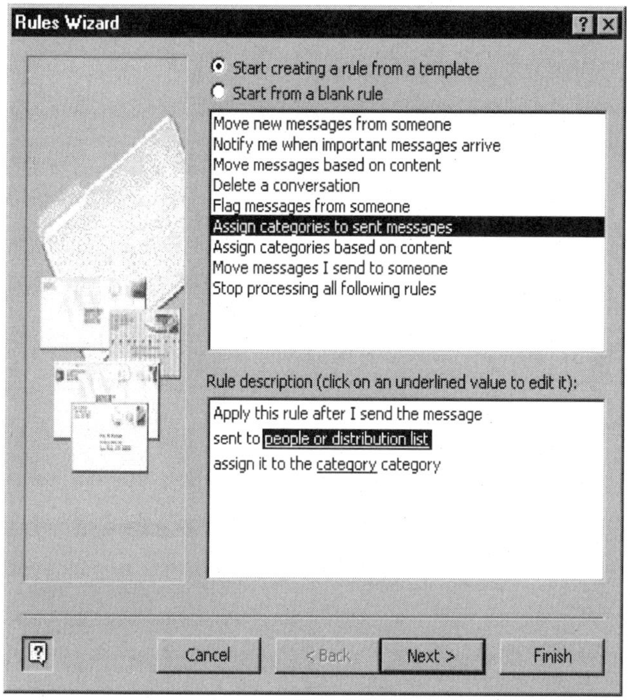


**Figure 4-30** Selecting options in the Rules Wizard dialog box.

5. **Choose which conditions you want to use to select messages.**

   Select the check box next to each condition a message must meet in order to be selected for automatic processing.

6. **Edit the conditions.**

   After selecting a condition, edit the values for the condition by clicking the underlined words at the bottom of the dialog box. Click Next to continue.

7. **Specify what to do with the messages.**

   Select the check boxes next to the actions you want to perform with the messages. Click Next to continue.

8. **Add any exceptions to your rule.**

   To make exceptions to your rule, select check boxes in the next dialog box. Messages that match the exceptions' criteria won't be processed. Click Next to continue.

9. **Review and name the rule.**

Use the last dialog box of the Rules Wizard to review your rule and make any changes necessary, as well as enter a name for the rule. To run the rule on messages already in your Inbox, select the Run This Rule Now check box. Click Finish.

# Dealing with Junk Mail

Unsolicited e-mail advertisements, otherwise known as junk mail or *spam*, are the scourge of e-mail users everywhere, and particularly busy businesspeople.

Spam is bad, but it's not a reason to get agitated. The following sections will help you reduce the amount of spam you have to face, but for the rest, we recommend that you just delete them and move on with your day.

NOTE *Avoid businesses that send spam—it's generally a sign of a disreputable company.*

## Control Your Address

Some firms have started giving away "premiums"—hats, T-shirts, and other trinkets—in exchange for an e-mail address. Anyone who approaches you with this exchange should be shown the door; it is the worst, most lopsided deal since the Dutch gypped the Native Americans out of Manhattan.

We all complain about spam, but we could cut it down considerably if we treated our electronic addresses as valuable commodities. But e-mail is still young, and people don't really know the value of their electronic address and what can happen when it gets out of their control. It takes only one breach to make your life miserable.

These merchants make promises about privacy, which are pretty worthless. They "personally" would never pass on your address, and their bosses may also have the best intentions. But what if the company is sold or gets into trouble and gets a lucrative offer for its mailing list? Will the CEO stand fast and say, "I made a promise to not give up these addresses, and for that my children will not attend Stanford."

There are two lessons here: Guard your primary address carefully, and don't sell it cheap. And if folks make an insulting offer for this address, be polite. They probably don't know the offer is completely ridiculous.

## Nine Tips for Avoiding Spam

Although some advertisers do send to random e-mail addresses in the hope of finding a valid user, most advertisers purchase a list of valid e-mail addresses. These lists are generated from a variety of sources, including e-mail directories, any companies you register products with using your e-mail address, and newsgroup posts.

To reduce your spam, take these measures:

1. Get a separate e-mail account that you use exclusively for high-risk activities, such as registering products or e-mailing companies for product information. This directs spam to a little-used account instead of your more vital e-mail accounts.
2. Don't give your e-mail address out to companies you don't want e-mailing you. Just because they ask for your e-mail address doesn't mean you need to give it to them. If they require an e-mail address, but they don't use it to send anything important, consider using a fake e-mail address.
3. Look closely for options to be excluded from e-mail offers when registering anything, anywhere.
4. Don't register your e-mail address with e-mail directories such as Bigfoot and WhoWhere. If you want to be listed, make sure the directory hides your actual address. People can still contact you through the directory without ever learning your address.
5. Don't post to newsgroups using your real e-mail address. If you want people to be able to reply to your posts, append deleteme or nospam somewhere in your e-mail address—for example, jason.deleteme@wwowidgets.com. Then tell people in your message to remove the deleteme from your address when replying.
6. Don't include your e-mail address in the body of any newsgroup messages. Automated e-mail-address-collection programs used by spammers can pick up e-mail addresses from the message body as well as the message header.
7. If you send messages to mailing lists that are mirrored on a Web site, take the same precautions you would with newsgroup messages.
8. If your ISP provides spam filters, turn them on.
9. Don't reply to spam, even if they promise to unsubscribe you from their list. (Make an exception for advertisements that clearly weren't intended as spam—for example, messages sent from companies that you registered products with.)

## Ignore and Delete

You can set up rules to get rid of spam. You can forward complaints to your ISP. You can report the senders to the chamber of commerce or the authorities.

Or you can just not bother and press the Delete key (or the more permanent Shift+Delete) when you get a piece of mail that is trying to sell you something. This could be a better strategy in a lot of cases. Sometimes it just doesn't pay to get so worked up about this stuff.

This depends on volume. If you get fewer than 10 of these things a day, it's a no-brainer. It is so easy to just cut and forget. Any more, well, that's up to your mood and that can vary even from day to day. Bottom line: Preventive action is necessary, and annoyance can be justified. But sometimes spam is inevitable and you shouldn't let it get under your skin.

# Enabling Junk Mail Rules

Outlook provides junk mail and adult content filters that you can use to deal with junk mail. These filters search the messages you receive for keywords and phrases, such as "money-back," "order now," and "adults only." Outlook then processes matching messages either by displaying them with a different color or by moving them to the folder you specify.

To enable junk mail filters, follow these steps:

1. **Display the Inbox.**

   If you have multiple Inboxes (for example, if you have any IMAP-based e-mail accounts), open the one for which you want to turn on junk mail filters.

2. **Click the Organize toolbar button.**

   This displays the Organize pane.

3. **Click the Junk E-Mail tab.**

4. **Specify what to do with junk mail.**

   To move junk and adult messages to a different folder (such as a Junk Mail folder or the Deleted Items folder), select Move from the first drop-down list box and then select the appropriate folder from the second drop-down list box, as shown in Figure 4-31. To create a new folder, choose Other Folders from the list and click New in the resulting dialog box.

   To color messages, select Color from the first drop-down list box and then select a color from the second drop-down list box.

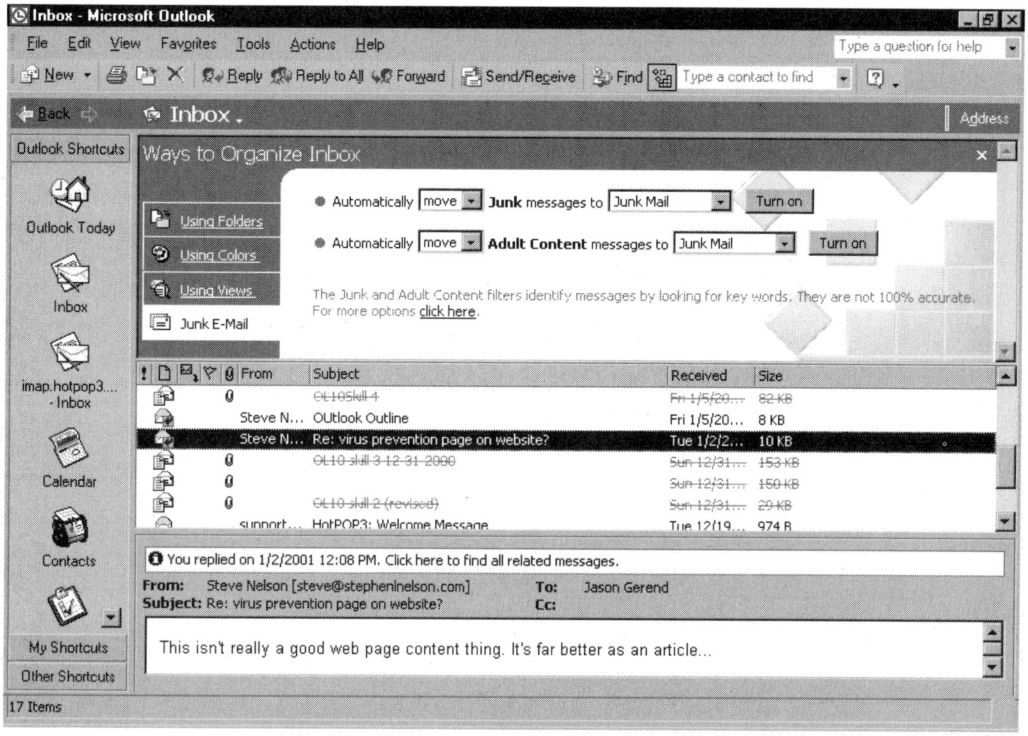

**Figure 4-31** Turning on junk mail and adult content rules.

TIP *We recommend that you initially use the junk mail filters to move messages to a Junk Mail folder that you create. Once you're certain you won't lose any important messages, you can change the junk mail rules to move messages directly to the Deleted Items folder. However, you should still look in your Deleted Items folder for important messages that are unread before you empty it.*

**5. Click the Turn On buttons.**

Outlook then creates the new junk mail and adult content rules, which you can later edit using the Tools menu's Rules Wizard command, as described earlier in this skill.

## Adding to the Junk Senders List

Outlook's junk mail rules aren't infallible, and some spam will always slip through into your Inbox. When you receive spam, the best thing to do is add the sender of the junk mail to your Junk Senders list so that future messages from the sender are automatically processed as junk mail.

To add the sender of a message to your Junk Senders list, right-click the message, choose Junk E-Mail from the shortcut menu, and choose Add To Junk Senders List from the submenu, as shown in Figure 4-32. Alternatively, choose Add To Adult Content Senders List to add the sender to the separate (but functionally identical) Adult Content Senders list.

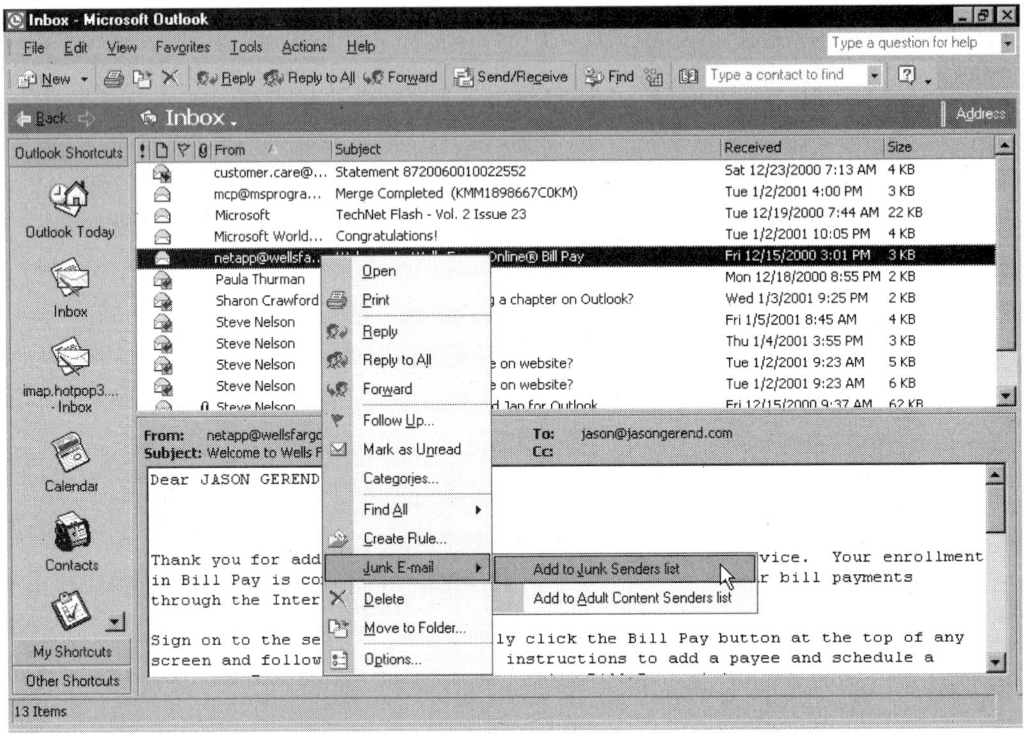


**Figure 4-32** Adding a sender to the Junk Senders list.

TIP *To add to a list of people excluded from junk mail processing, choose the Tools menu's Rules Wizard command, select the Exception List rule, click the Exception List hyperlink, and add the e-mail addresses.*

## Creating More Powerful Junk Mail Rules

Outlook's Junk Mail filters are intentionally conservative—Microsoft didn't want to make the filters remove important messages. (The company was sued because an earlier version of the filters did just that.)

However, you can create two additional mail rules with Outlook to further limit the spam that appears in your Inbox. Both of these rules can be much more aggressive than

Outlook's standard filters, so make sure to watch the results closely to avoid missing important e-mails.

## Filter Out Additional Keywords

Outlook's standard junk mail and adult content filters search for a small set of keywords. (Use Windows' Search tool to locate the *filters.txt* for a complete listing.) To create your own junk mail rule that filters out additional words that you find frequently in the spam you receive (and not in normal messages), follow these steps:

1. **Choose the Tools menu's Rules Wizard command.**
2. **Select the Inbox to which you want to apply the rule.**

   If you have a POP3 account and an IMAP account, or multiple IMAP accounts, choose the appropriate Inbox from the drop-down list box at the top of the dialog box, as shown in Figure 4-33.

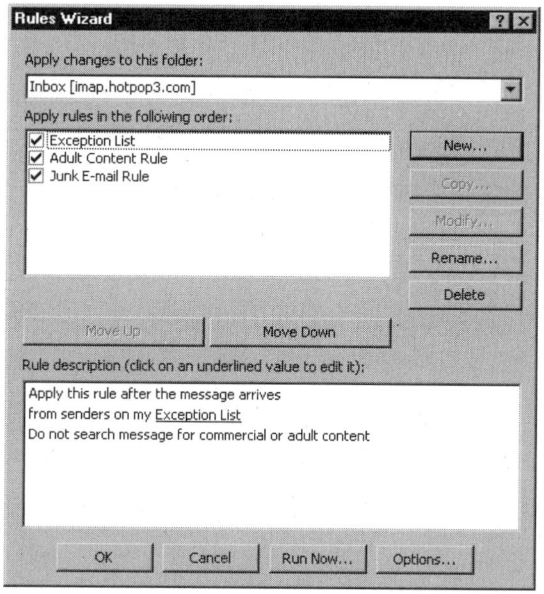


**Figure 4-33** The Rules Wizard dialog box.

3. **Click New in the Rules Wizard dialog box.**
4. **Select the Move Messages Based On Content template, and click Next.**
5. **Choose the With Specific Words In The Subject condition.**

   Click the Specific Words hyperlink to enter a list of keywords you want to use. Click Next.

6. **Specify the folder to which you want to move spam.**

   Click the Specified hyperlink to specify the Junk Mail folder you created (Click the New button in the resulting dialog box to create this folder if you haven't already.) Click Next.

7. **Select the Except If Sender Is In The Specified Address Book.**

   After selecting this exception, click the Specified hyperlink and choose your primary Contacts folder. This prevents Outlook from applying this filter to messages you receive from people in your Contacts folder.

8. **Review and name the rule.**

   Review and name your rule, as shown in Figure 4-34, and then click Finish.

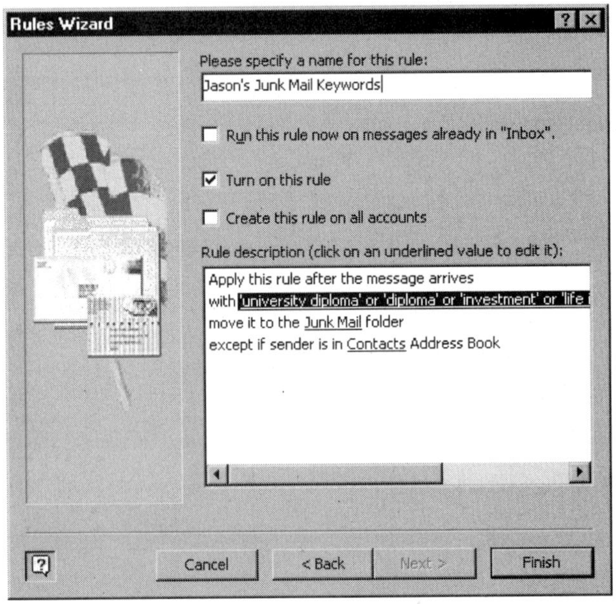


**Figure 4-34** Naming and reviewing a custom junk mail rule.

## Filter Messages Secretly Sent to You

A more aggressive strategy you can take to reduce the spam you receive is to filter out all e-mail messages where your name isn't in the To or Cc field (for example, you're listed in the Bcc field). Because this is one of the preferred ways to send spam, doing this can drastically reduce the amount of spam you receive.

To create a rule that filters out messages sent to you with your name in the Bcc field, follow these steps:

1. **Choose the Tools menu's Rules Wizard command.**
2. **Select the Inbox to which you want to apply the rule.**

   If you have a POP3 account and an IMAP account, or multiple IMAP accounts, choose the appropriate Inbox from the drop-down list box at the top of the dialog box that Outlook displays.
3. **Click New in the Rules Wizard dialog box.**
4. **Start from a blank rule.**

   Click the Start From A Blank Rule option button, select Check Messages When They Arrive, and then click Next, as shown in Figure 4-35.

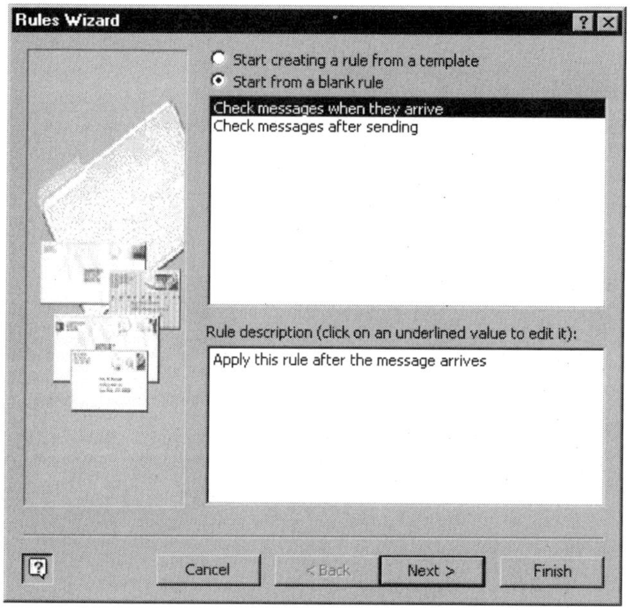


Figure 4-35 Creating a rule from scratch.

5. **Click Next in the Conditions screen.**

   Click Yes in the dialog box Outlook displays stating that the rule will be applied to every message you receive.
6. **Choose the Move It To The Specified folder action.**

   Click the Specified hyperlink to select the folder to which you want to move suspected junk mail (for example, a folder named Junk Mail), and then click Next.

7. **Select Except Where My Name Is In The To Or Cc Box.**

   Because Outlook looks only for your primary e-mail address, if you have multiple e-mail accounts, you should also select Except With Specific Words In The Recipient's Address, click the Specific Words hyperlink, and enter the other e-mail addresses you use with Outlook.

8. **Select Except If Sender Is In The Specified Address Book.**

   After selecting this exception, click the Specified hyperlink and choose your primary Contacts folder. This prevents Outlook from applying this filter to messages you receive from people in your Contacts folder.

9. **Review and name the rule.**

   Review and name your rule, as shown in Figure 4-36, and then click Finish.

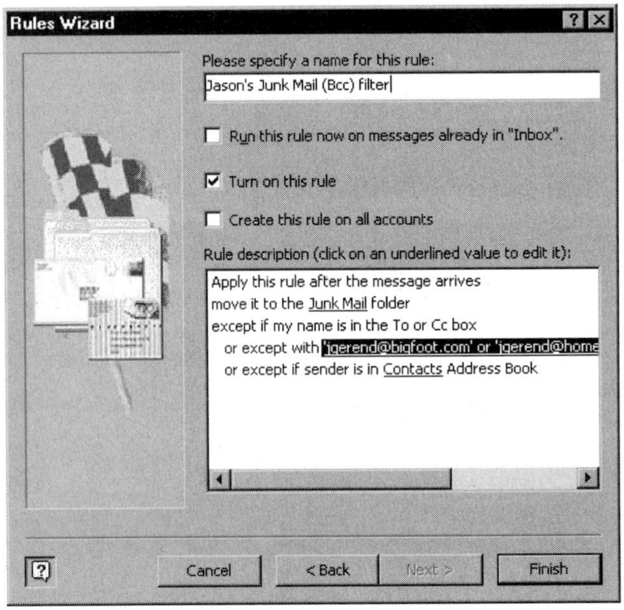


**Figure 4-36** Naming and reviewing a custom junk mail rule.

## Open to Interpretation

Spam can be subjective. In the first place—and this is a radical thought—one day you may actually find something of interest in a sales-oriented e-mail. The anti-spam authorities get on their high horses and avoid these messages on principle, but sometimes that attitude is closed-minded.

The truth is, the concept of spam can be assigned at will. A friend of yours may send a fundraising solicitation for a local clinic to their entire mail list. Someone else may send along a family progress report around Christmas time. The annoyed recipient will then designate these messages as spam even if they don't fit the accepted definition.

You may also sign up for newsletters and soon find they are not so interesting anymore. In many cases, people will wait a month or two before taking the proactive step to be removed from that list. In the meantime, they perceive the unwanted correspondence as spam.

The issue is control. We want to be able to get our wheat while filtering out all the chaff. But definitions change. The CNN dispatch that you so eagerly added two years ago is now boring and is usually discarded unread. Now when you see these messages arrive you immediately label them as spam. But this isn't really fair, and it's not Ted Turner's fault that you changed your mind.

# Third-Party Anti-Spam Solutions

If Outlook's junk mail tools simply aren't filtering out enough spam and the situation really bothers you, consider using a third-party solution for spam filtering.

Brightmail (*www.brightmail.com*) is a free, server-based solution that filters spam out of your e-mail before it reaches your computer. It works with most POP3 e-mail accounts and doesn't require installing any software on your computer.

In addition to server-based solutions, you can also use third-party utilities to reduce spam. These programs work in conjunction with Outlook to filter messages as you download them. Perform a search at *www.zdnet.com/downloads* for a list of available anti-spam programs, such as Mail Snoop and Spam Killer.

## Summary

In this skill we presented effective methods for locating messages, organizing messages using folders, and using templates to streamline composing messages, as well as creating message rules to automatically handle your e-mail and redirect or reduce the amount of unsolicited advertisements you receive.

*Skill 5*

# USING A CONTACTS LIST

## Featuring:

- Contacts and Address Book Overview
- Creating New Contacts
- Editing Contacts
- Creating Distribution Lists
- Finding Contacts
- Using Contacts
- Managing Address Books

In the ever-changing social landscape of the modern world, it is difficult for most of us to remember every business associate's name, let alone how to reach them. Outlook enables you to supplement your built-in contact list with a more reliable, external-to-your-brain storage location for contact information—the Contacts folder.

You can use Outlook's Contacts folder to store just about any possible contact information and use it to address e-mail messages, meeting and task requests, locate maps, and dial phone numbers, as well as print out your contacts or share them with others via e-mail.

In this skill we begin with an overview of Outlook's Contacts folder (and the difference between it and the Address Book) and then delve into the details of putting contacts to work.

NOTE *You can also synchronize your contacts with online address books and personal digital assistants (PDAs), although this process varies depending on what you want to synchronize with, and so we leave that to your device's manual or online service's help system.*

## Contacts and Address Book Overview

The Contacts folder is the primary location for storing contact information (addresses, phone numbers, and so on) and e-mail addresses in Outlook. All information is stored in individual contact entries in the Contacts folder, which is located within your Outlook Personal Folders File (the file in which Outlook stores all your items).

You can access contacts through a variety of methods:

- Through the Select Names dialog box that you can access from many Outlook items by pressing the To button in the message, meeting request, or task request (it is called various names depending on how you open it)
- Through the Address Book window, an alternate interface to the Contacts folder
- Directly from the Contacts folder by clicking the Contacts shortcut on the Outlook bar, as shown in Figure 5-1

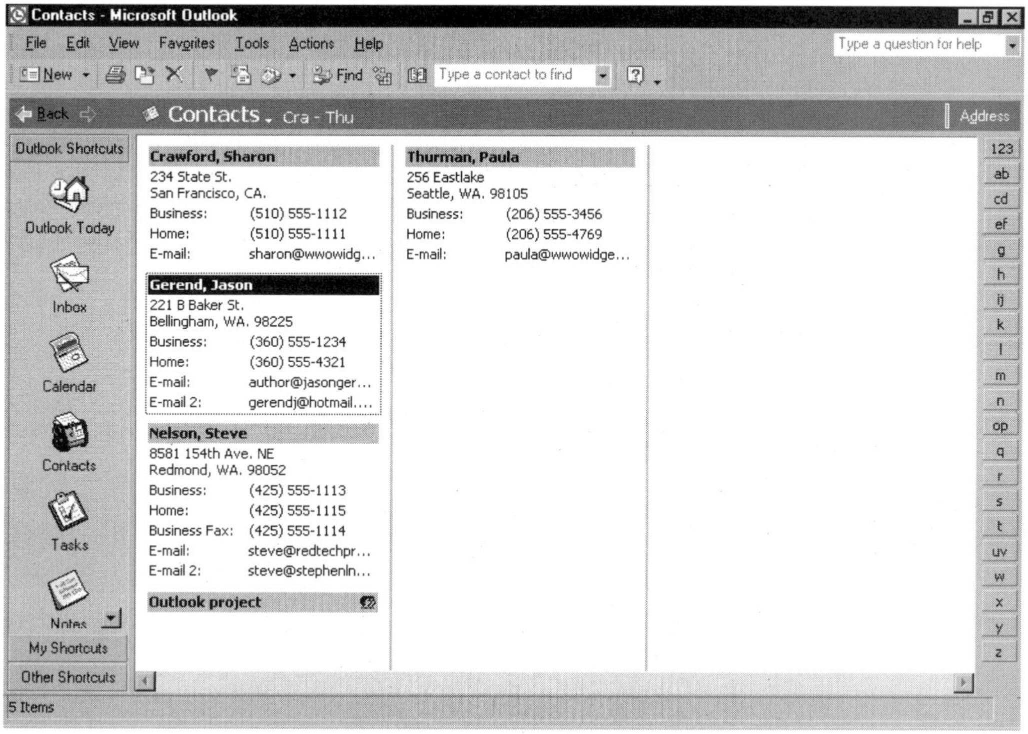


**Figure 5-1** The Contacts folder.

Most users will never have to concern themselves with any other address books. However, there may be additional address books to which you have access, such as a Global Address List, the Active Directory, an LDAP directory maintained by your company, or a Personal Address Book. You can access any additional address books through the Address Book interface or through the Select Recipients dialog box, as shown in Figure 5-2. Managing your various address books is discussed in the "Managing Address Books" section at the end of this skill.

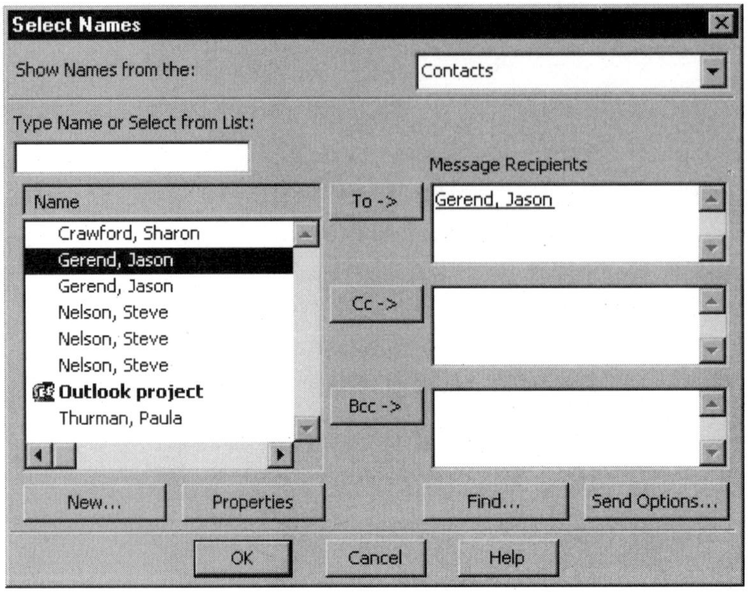


**Figure 5-2** The Select Names dialog box.

# Creating New Contacts

Record all your contact information for the people you correspond with in contact entries stored in the Contacts folder. If you don't already have a contact entry for the person, use one of the following methods to create one:

- Select or open a message from the person for whom you want to create a contact entry, right-click the sender's name in the From field, and then choose Add To Contacts from the shortcut menu, as shown in Figure 5-3.

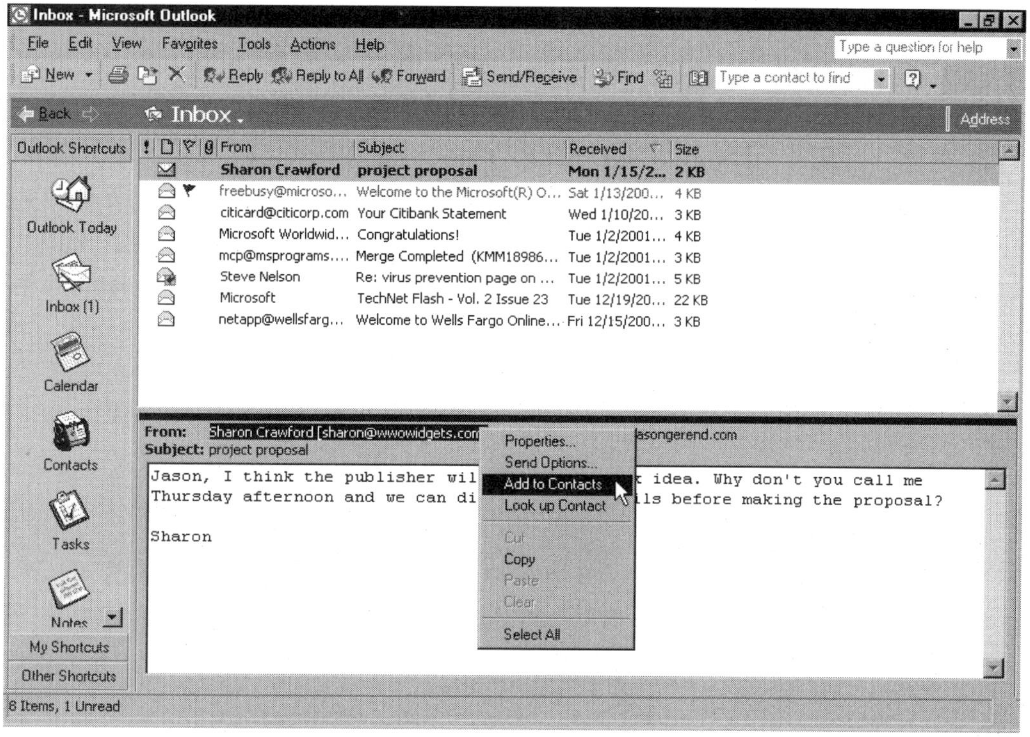

Figure 5-3 Adding a sender to your Contacts folder.

- Display the Contacts folder by clicking the Contacts shortcut on the Outlook bar, and then click the New Contact toolbar button. Outlook creates a blank contact entry, which you can then edit.

TIP *It's a good idea to create a contact for yourself. You can then forward this contact to others as a sort of virtual business card.*

- Drag any type of Outlook item to the Contacts shortcut on the Outlook bar. Outlook creates a new contact entry with the contents of the item inserted in the body of the Contact and fills in any contact information it recognizes, such as the e-mail address.

- Press Ctrl-Shift-C.

TIP *To create a contact based on an existing contact from the same company, open the existing contact and choose the Action menu's New Contact From Same Company command. Outlook uses the information from the existing contact as a template to create a new contact with the same business phone numbers and addresses.*

# Editing Contacts

After creating a contact, you need to fill in the details, such as phone numbers, e-mail addresses, and so forth. You may also need to update these details as time goes on and information changes.

To edit a contact, follow these steps:

1. **Open the contact.**

   If the contact isn't already open, display the Contacts folder by clicking the Contacts shortcut on the Outlook bar, and then double-click the contact you want to edit, as shown in Figure 5-4. Alternatively, enter the contact's name in the Find A Contact text box on the Standard toolbar, and press Enter.

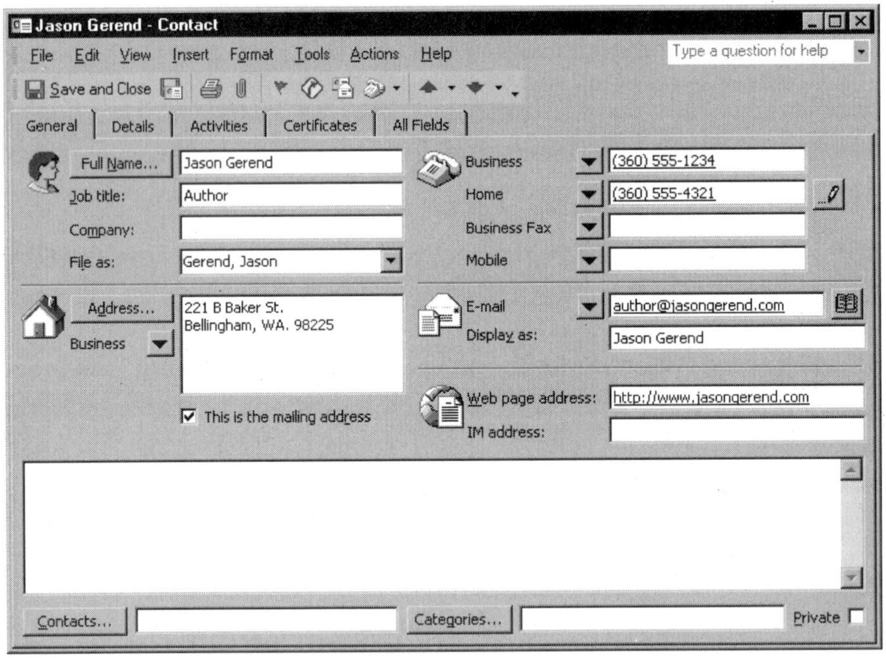


**Figure 5-4** Opening a contact to edit.

TIP *To delete a contact, select or open the contact and click the Delete toolbar button.*

2. **Enter the contact's full name in the Full Name box.**
3. **Enter the contact's job title and company.**
4. **Select how Outlook should display the contact's name.**

   In the File As box, enter the name Outlook should use to display and sort the contact in the Contacts folder, the Address Book, and the Select Names dialog box. Outlook's default method for filing contacts—last name followed by first name—is suitable for most users. However, you can enter anything you want in the File As box, or select a suggestion from the drop-down list box.
5. **Enter the contact's phone numbers.**

   Enter the contact's phone numbers in the phone number fields. Note the following about these fields:

   - If you don't specify an area code, Outlook fills in your current area code.
   - To enter a phone number for a different device, for example, a pager or car phone, click the down arrow next to the phone number field and select a phone number field from the list.
   - To enter a phone number from another country, enter the phone number and then click the pencil icon to the right of the text box to display the Check Phone Number dialog box, as shown in Figure 5-5. Select the appropriate country from the Country/Region drop-down list box, and verify that the city code is correctly formatted. (Outlook usually formats numbers with a three-digit city code, even though many countries use only a two-digit code.)

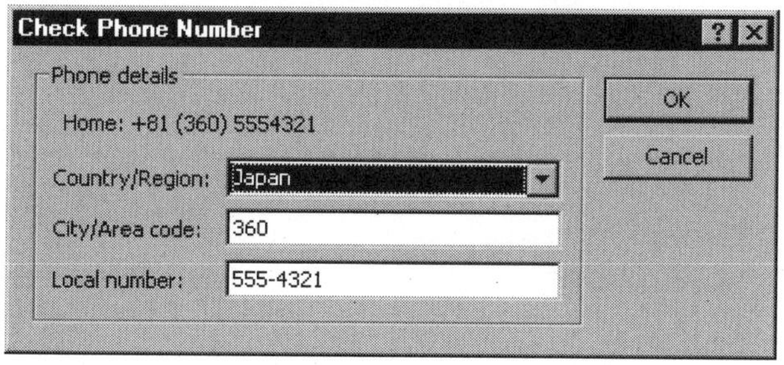


**Figure 5-5** Specifying the appropriate country code.

TIP *If you often need to send messages to a contact's secondary e-mail addresses, consider creating a second (and possibly third) contact for this person. Add to the contact's name a short description of the e-mail address, such as Personal. This allows you to circumvent the fact that Outlook chooses the primary e-mail address by default and doesn't make it easy to clearly choose alternates.*

6. **Enter the contact's e-mail addresses.**

   Enter the contact's primary e-mail address in the E-Mail box. To enter additional addresses, click the down arrow next to the E-Mail box and select E-Mail 2 or E-Mail 3 from the list.

TIP *Although we recommend setting your default message format to plain text (as described in "Skill 3: Sending E-Mail"), you may want to explicitly specify that Outlook should use only plain text when sending to a particular e-mail address (such as one accessed via a cell phone). To do so, right-click the e-mail address and choose Properties from the shortcut menu. In the E-Mail Properties dialog box, select the format you want from the Internet Format drop-down list box.*

7. **Enter the contact's physical addresses.**

   In the Address box, enter the physical address of the contact's workplace. To enter a home address or other address, click the down arrow under the Address button, and choose the desired address.

   Select the This Is The Mailing Address check box to specify the address to which you should send mail. (Word uses this to determine which address to use when using Word's Letters And Mailings feature.)

8. **Enter the contact's Web page and instant messaging address.**

   In the Web Page address box, enter the contact's Web page address, if they have one. Similarly, in the IM Address box, enter the contact's MSN Messenger instant messaging address (such as username@hotmail.com).

9. **Enter any notes about the contact.**

   In the main text box, enter any additional information you may have about the contact.

10. **Link the contact to other Outlook items.**

    If the contact relates to any other contacts, such as a manager, spouse, or assistant, click the Contacts button to select the related contacts (hold down the Ctrl key to select multiple contacts). Double-click a linked contact's name to open the contact.

To link the contact to another type of item, choose the Action menu's Link command, choose Item from the submenu, and then select the item to which you want to link the contact. This is a powerful way to associate contacts and items.

11. **Assign the item to one or more categories.**

    Click the Categories button, and then choose the category or categories the item belongs to, as shown in Figure 5-6. Taking the time to assign categories and link to associated contacts now makes it much easier to locate related items later.

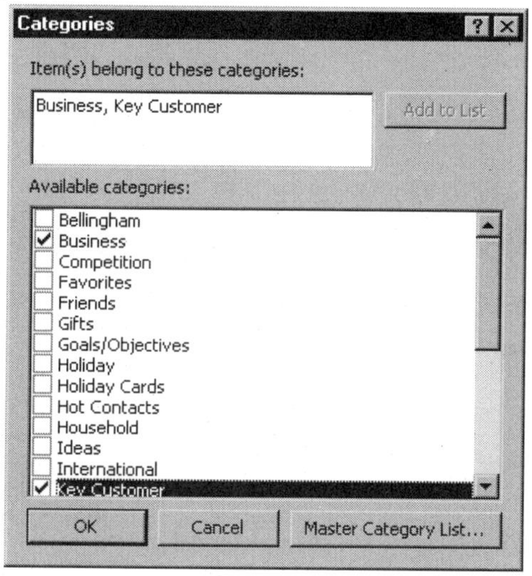


**Figure 5-6** Assigning categories to a contact.

12. **Optionally, make the contact private.**

    If you allow others delegate access to your Contacts folder (using Exchange Server) but you want to hide this contact from your delegates, select the Private check box.

13. **Enter additional details.**

    Click the Details tab to enter additional details about the contact, such as office and department information, the contact's birthday, as well as the location of their Internet Free/Busy information (as discussed in "Skill 6: Managing Your Time"), as shown in Figure 5-7.

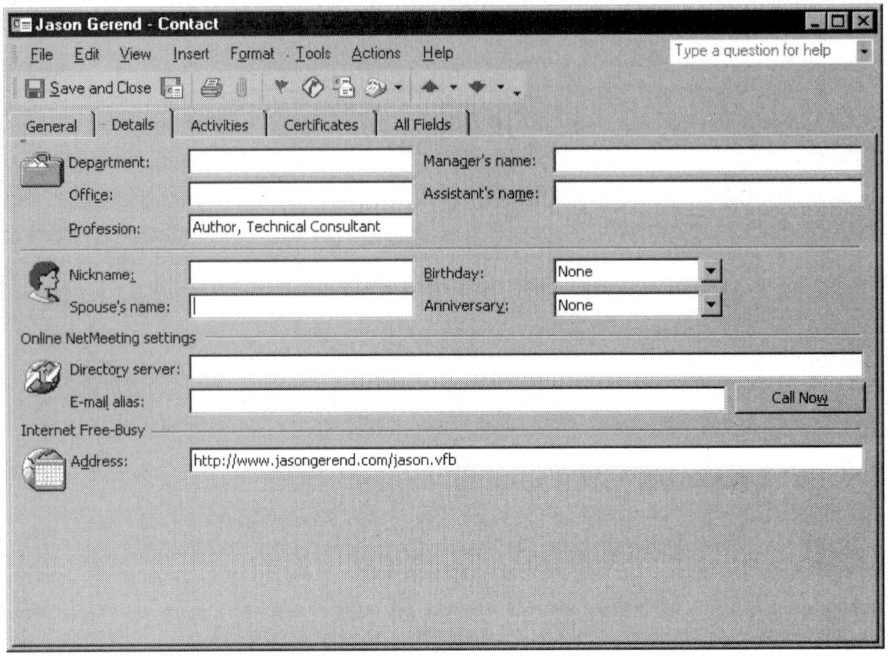


**Figure 5-7** Entering additional details.

**14. Click the Save And Close toolbar button.**

Outlook saves the item and returns you to the Calendar.

TIP *To associate a file with the contact, click the Insert File toolbar button, select the file you want, click the down arrow next to the Insert button and choose Insert As Shortcut from the pop-up menu. (Simply click the Insert button to embed the file in the contact, but remember that this can consume extra room and allow the two copies of the file to get out of sync.)*

# Creating Distribution Lists

If you find yourself frequently sending the same messages to the same group of people, such as coworkers in your department or your golfing friends, consider adding the individual contacts to a distribution list. You can then simply address the message or meeting request to the distribution list and all members will be included.

To create a distribution list, follow these steps:

**1. Create a blank distribution list.**

To do so, click the down arrow next to the New Contact toolbar button and choose Distribution List from the pop-up menu. Alternatively, press Ctrl-Shift-L.

**2. Name the list.**

In the Name box, enter a name for the distribution list, as shown in Figure 5-8.

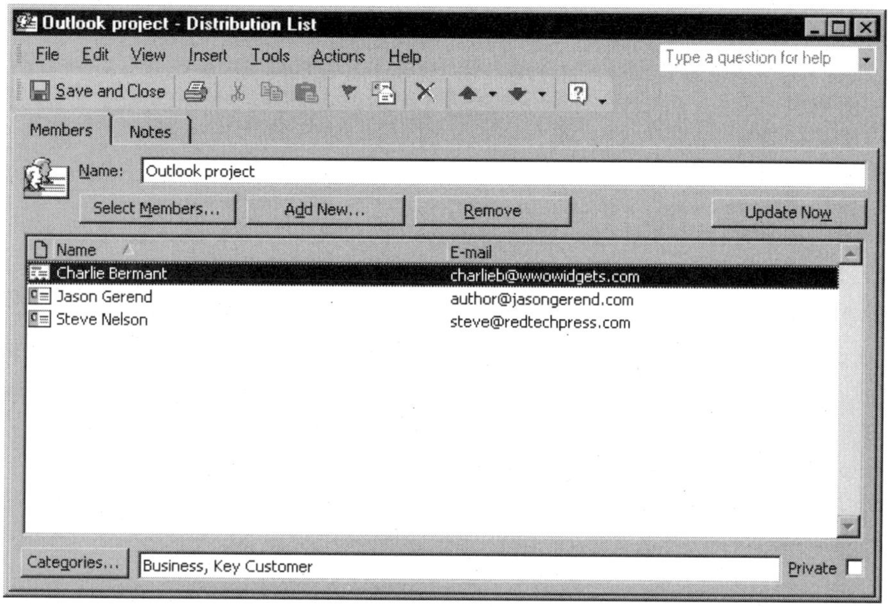


**Figure 5-8** A new distribution list.

**3. Add members.**

Click the Select Members button to add contacts from the Contacts folder or another address book. To add a contact not already in your Contacts folder, click the Add New button and use the Add New Member dialog box to create the contact, which will exist only in this distribution list unless you select the Add To Contacts check box in this dialog box.

**4. Assign the list one or more categories.**

Click the Categories button, and then choose the category or categories to which the distribution list belongs.

**5. Add any notes.**

Click the Notes tab to add any notes about the list.

**6. Click the Save And Close toolbar button.**

Outlook saves the list to your Contacts folder.

TIP *Distribution lists appear in your Contacts folder, Address Book, and Select Names, lists as a contact with an icon showing two people next to it.*

# Finding Contacts

Most of the time you'll access contacts by entering a name in the To field of an e-mail message or by clicking the To button, but sometimes you'll want to look up the full contact information for someone, perhaps to call the contact or look up the contact's address.

You can locate a contact using several different methods, as discussed in the following sections.

## Browsing the Contacts Folder

A basic method of locating a contact is to display the Contacts folder and peruse your Contacts list until you find the name you are looking for.

To do so, click the Contacts shortcut in the Outlook bar to open the Contacts folder, and then use the following techniques to locate a contact:

- Use the scroll bar to scroll to the contact you want.
- Click the lettered buttons along the right side of the Contacts folder to jump to contacts starting with the letter you clicked, as shown in Figure 5-9.

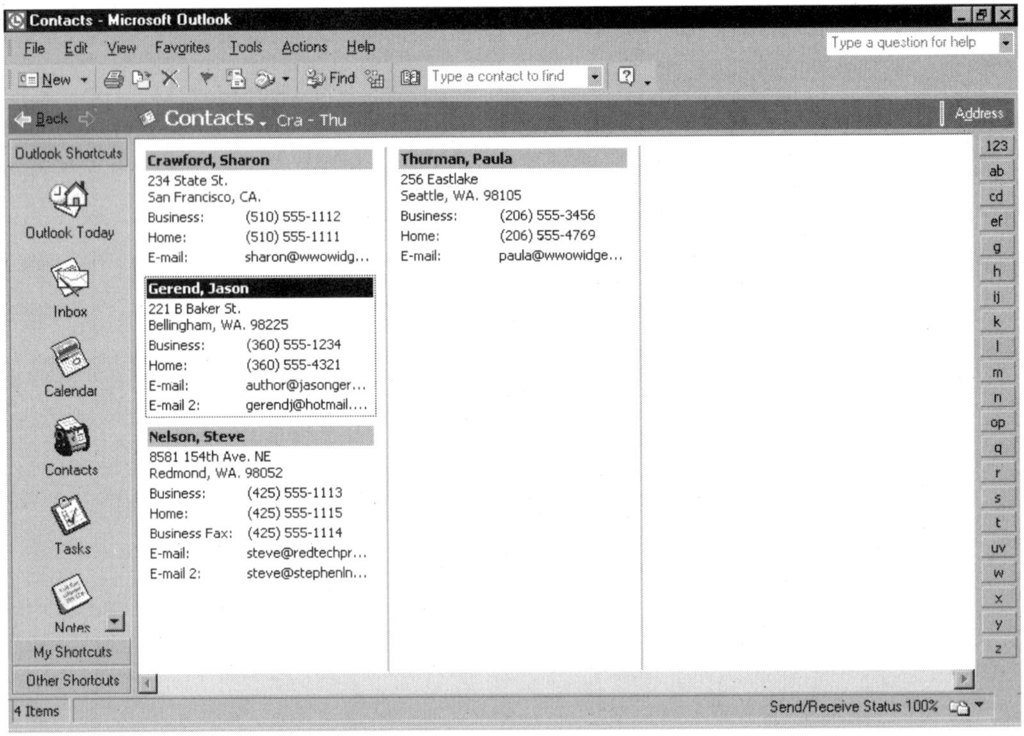


**Figure 5-9** The Contacts folder.

TIP *You can edit contacts without opening them. Simply click in the field you want to edit and enter the new information.*

## Finding Contacts from the Toolbar

Probably the most convenient method of looking up a contact is using the Find A Contact box on the Standard toolbar. Use it in the following ways:

- Enter the name, e-mail address, or title of the contact you're looking for and press Enter, as shown in Figure 5-10.
- If Outlook can't find the correct contact, it displays a list of possible matches. Select the correct contact and click OK.
- To view a list of recently found contacts, click the down arrow next to the box.

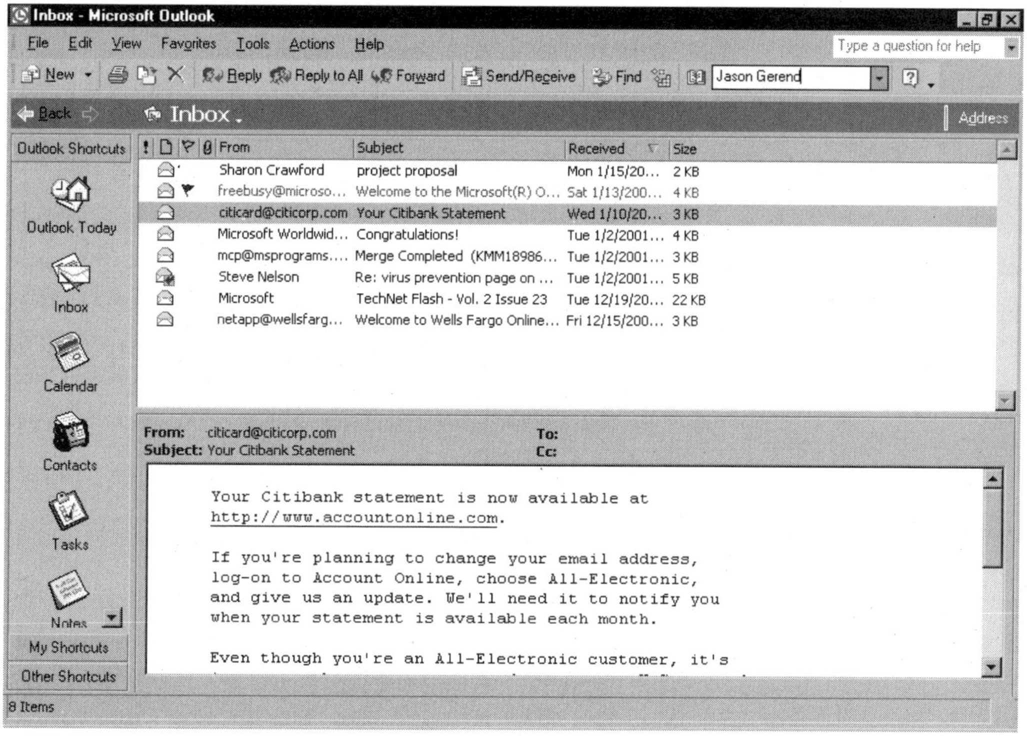

**Figure 5-10** Using the Find A Contact tool.

TIP *You can look up the sender of an e-mail message by right-clicking the sender's name in the From field and then choosing Look Up Contact from the shortcut menu.*

# Searching for a Contact

If you're having trouble locating a contact and you want to perform an actual search for the contact, follow these steps:

1. **Click the Find toolbar button.**

   This displays the Find bar, as shown in Figure 5-11.

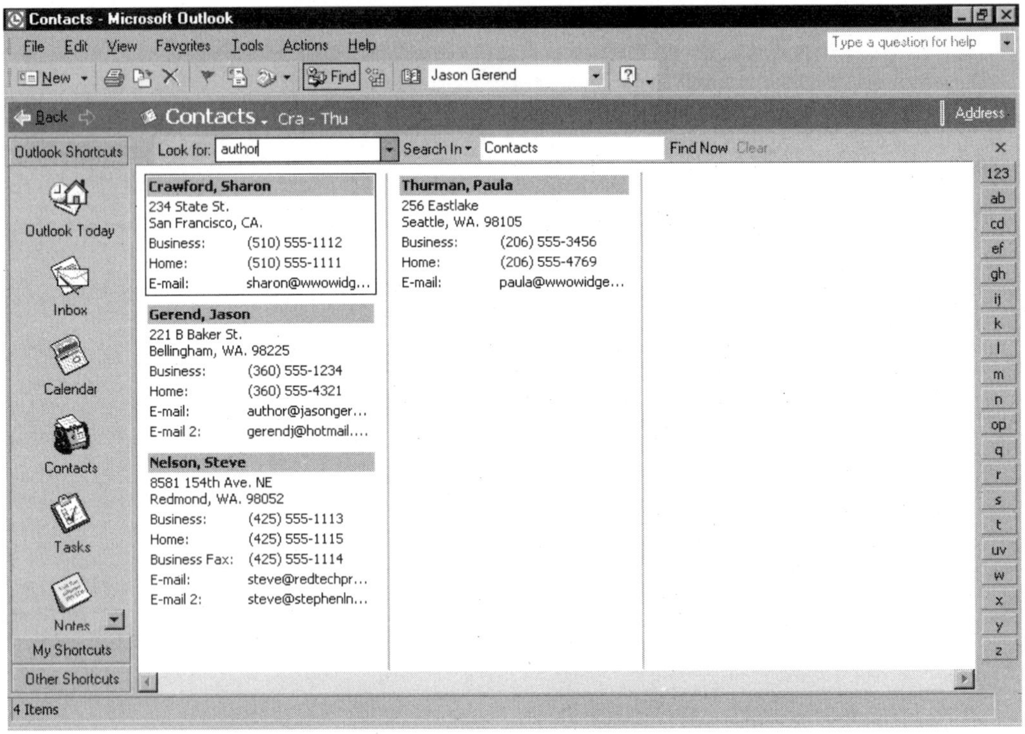


**Figure 5-11** Searching for contacts using the Find bar.

2. **Enter the words for which you want to search.**

   In the Look For box, enter the name, e-mail address, address, or company of the contact for which you're looking. Use the following tips for searching with the Find box:

   - By default, Outlook searches for any contacts with all the words listed.
   - To search for messages with any of the words (the Boolean OR command), separate the search words with commas.
   - To perform a search you previously performed, click the down arrow next to the Look For box to display a list of previous searches.

TIP *If you want to search multiple Contacts folders (presuming you have more than one), click the Search In button, choose the Choose Folders command from the pop-up menu, use the Select Folders dialog box to select the folders you want to search in, and then click OK.*

3. **Click Find Now.**

   Outlook displays the contacts it finds in the current view. Open and work with the contacts normally, but keep in mind that if you switch folders, the search results will disappear. You can also clear the search results by pressing the Clear button.

4. **Close the Find bar.**

   Click the X at the far right end of the Find bar to close it.

TIP *To perform a more advanced search, such as searching for a specific phone number, use the Advanced Find tool. To open this tool, choose the Tools menu's Advanced Find command. For information on how to conduct an advanced search, see "Skill 4: Managing Your E-Mail."*

# Using Contacts

Although the most common use of contacts is for addressing e-mail messages, there is much more that you can do with contacts. For example, you can find a map to a contact's address, view other Outlook items related to a contact, print your Contacts list, or send your contact information to others across the Internet.

## Mapping Contacts

To find a map to a contact's address, follow these steps:

1. **Open the contact.**
2. **Display the address you want to map.**

   To select a different address, click the down arrow under the Address button and then choose Home, Business, or Other from the pop-up menu.

3. **Click the Display Map Of Address toolbar button.**

   Outlook connects to the Internet (if you're not already connected) and searches for the address at Expedia.com. Enter any additional information required, and click the Find A Map link to view the map, as shown in Figure 5-12.

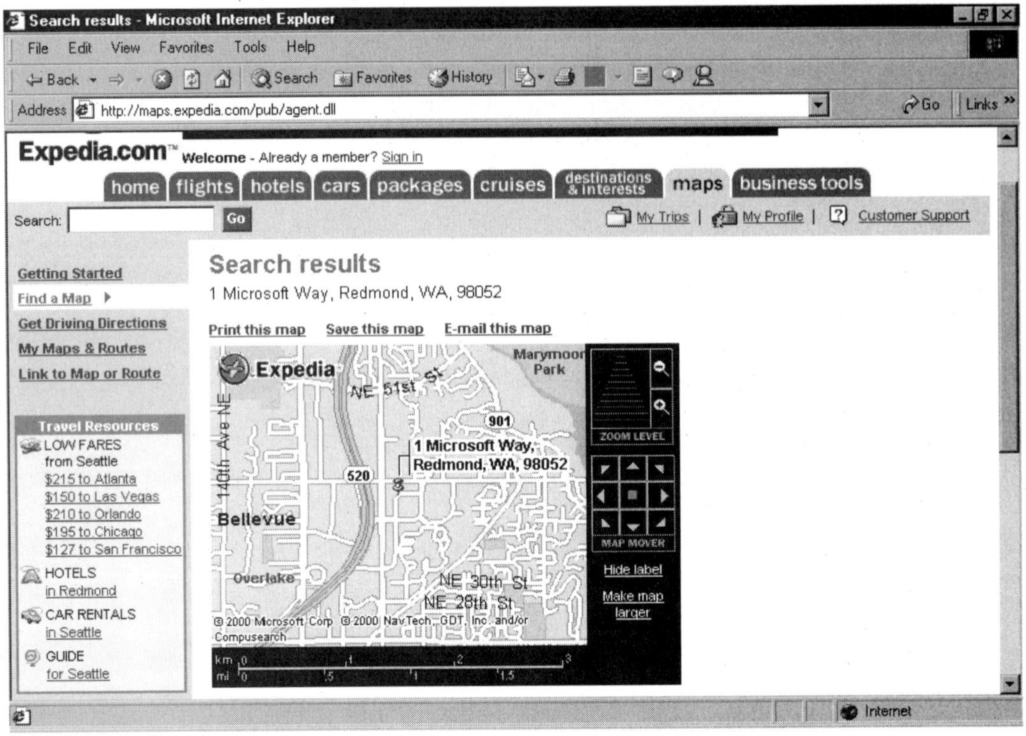


Figure 5-12 A map located using Outlook and Expedia.com.

## Viewing Items Related to a Contact

Outlook contains the useful ability to display all activities related to a contact, including e-mail messages sent to or received from the contact, as well as any meetings, appointments, tasks, or other contacts that you've linked to the contact.

To use the Activities tab of a contact to view this information, follow these steps:

1. **Open the contact.**
2. **Click the Activities tab.**
3. **Select the type of items to look for.**

   In the Show drop-down list box, select the type of Outlook items to look for. Outlook searches for the items and displays them in a list, as shown in Figure 5-13. Double-click an item to open it.

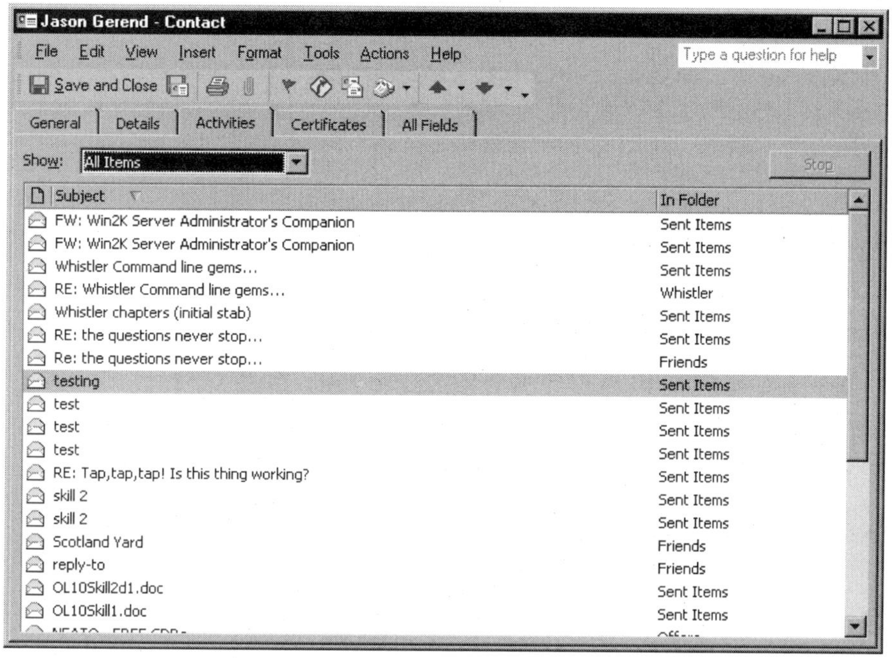


**Figure 5-13** The Activities tab of a contact.

# Printing Contacts

If you have a traditional paper-based day planner, it can be extremely useful to print out your Contacts list for inclusion in your planner. Even if you don't use a day planner, you'll occasionally find the need to print out individual contacts—for example, when you need to meet with someone and you want their address and phone number for reference.

To print out your contacts list or individual contacts, follow these steps:

1. **Select the contact(s) you want to print.**

   In the Contacts folder, select the contacts you want to print. To select individual contacts, hold down the Ctrl key and click each contact.

2. **Choose the File menu's Print command.**

   Alternatively, click the Print toolbar button. (Pushing this button in an open contact's window prints the item immediately using the default settings.)

3. **Specify the printer to use.**

Select the printer from the Name box at the top of the Print dialog box, as shown in Figure 5-14. To modify print options, such as color and resolution, click the Properties button.

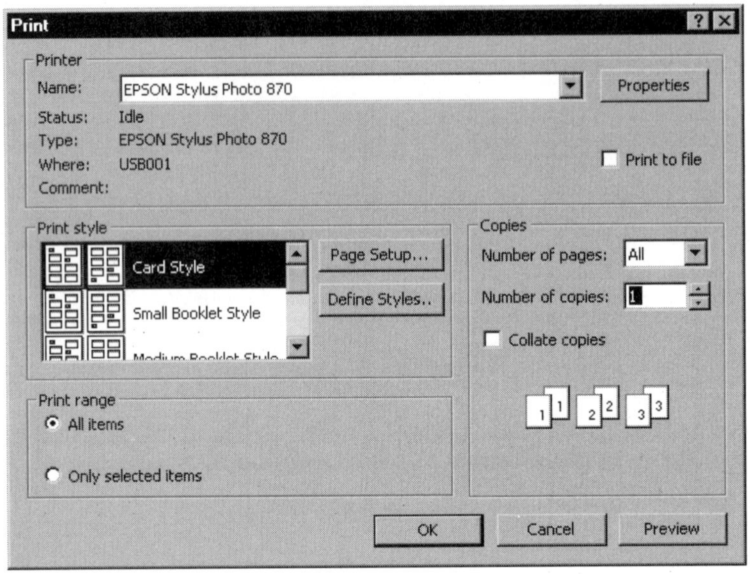


**Figure 5-14** The Print dialog box.

4. **Choose a print style.**

In the Print Style box, select the print style you want to use:

- Card Style prints each contact in an address-card format, almost identical to the default display of the Contacts folder.
- Small Booklet Style/Medium Booklet Style prints contacts in sections so that you can fold up the printouts to make a small or medium-size booklet.
- Memo Style prints details of each contact on a separate page, in a memo style.
- Phone List Style prints only the phone numbers of the contacts, in a list format.

TIP *To control how Outlook formats contacts when printing, click the Page Setup button.*

5. **Choose the appropriate paper size.**

To use a special paper, such as one specifically designed to fit in your day planner, click the Page Setup button, click the Paper tab, and then select a paper size from the Type box.

6. **Specify whether to print all contacts.**

   Click the All Items option button to print your entire Contacts list, or click the Only Selected Items option button to print only those contacts you selected.

7. **Specify the number of pages and copies.**

   Use the Number Of Pages and Number Of Copies drop-down list boxes to specify how many pages to print, as well as the number of copies. Select the Collate Copies check box to print each copy in its entirety before printing the next copy.

8. **Preview the print job.**

   Click the Preview button to display the Print Preview window, as shown in Figure 5-15. Click the Print toolbar button to return to the Print dialog box.

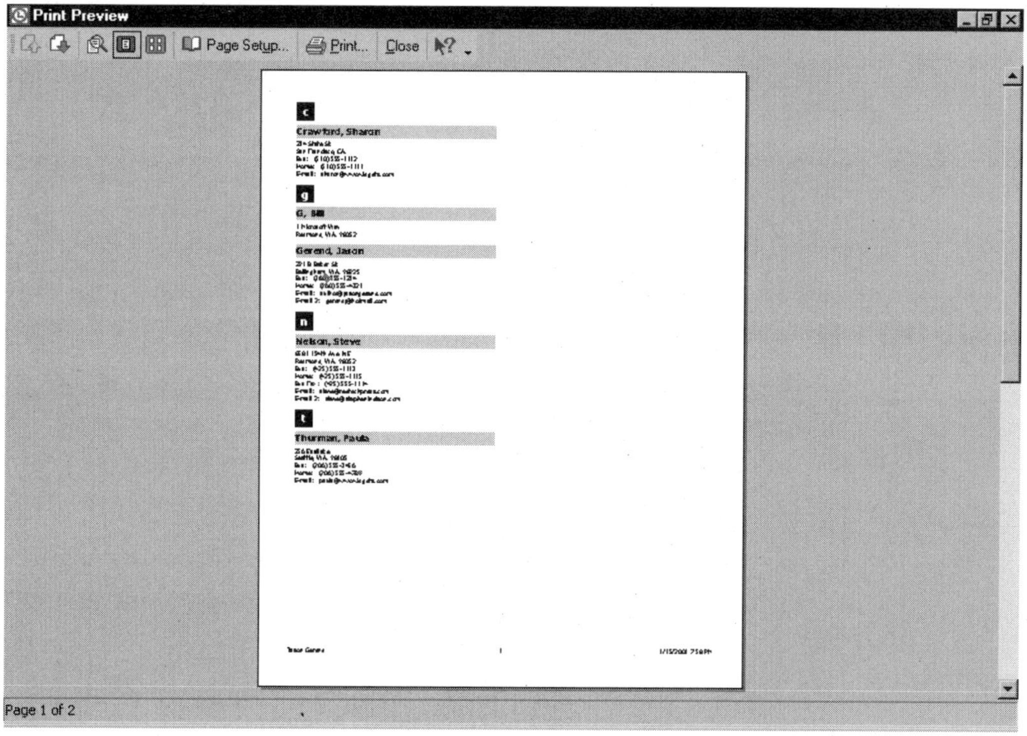


**Figure 5-15** The Print Preview window.

9. **Click OK.**

   Outlook sends the print job to your printer, which then prints the contacts.

## Sending Contact Information Across the Internet

The easiest way to send contact information—either your own or someone else's—is to attach the contact directly to an e-mail message. This allows the recipient to open the attachment and save it directly into their own Contacts folder or address book. This is also the best way to give someone the location where your Internet Free/Busy information is stored, if you use this feature with your own server (instead of Microsoft's).

To forward a contact to someone via e-mail, follow these steps:

1. **Select or open the contact.**
2. **Forward the contact.**

   If you know that the person to whom you're forwarding the contact also uses Outlook, choose the Action menu's Forward command. Otherwise, choose the Action menu's Forward As vCard command to send the contact using the vCard standard (using the .vcs file extension).

3. **Compose and send the message.**

   Outlook attaches the contact or vCard to a blank message, which you can then compose and send normally.

## Calling Contacts and Using the Journal

Outlook can serve as a super speed-dial tool, making it easy to place phone calls. In order to use Outlook to dial phone calls, your computer needs to have a modem installed, and you need to have a telephone plugged into your modem (so that you can talk on the phone after the modem dials the number).

Besides serving as a handy way to dial phone numbers, you can use Outlook's dialing feature in conjunction with its Journal feature to keep track of the time you spend on the phone and take notes—a boon for people who need to bill their hours.

To use Outlook's dialing and journal features, follow these steps:

1. **Select or open the contact.**
2. **Choose the number to dial.**

   Click the AutoDialer toolbar button, and select the number to dial, as shown in Figure 5-16.

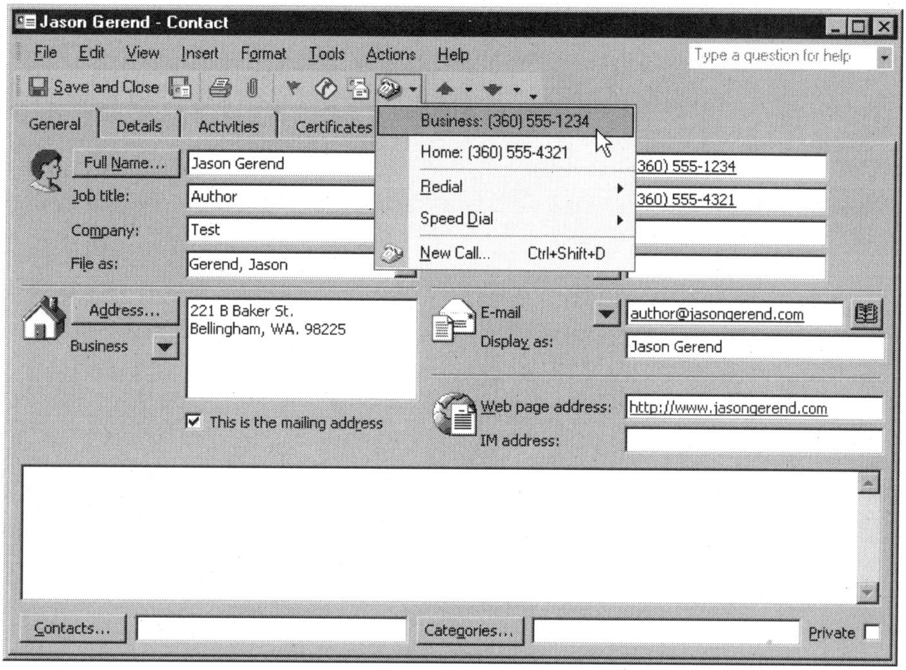


Figure 5-16 Selecting a phone number to dial.

3. **Start the call and create the journal entry.**

   Select the Create New Journal Entry When Starting New Call check box if you want to record details of the phone call, and then click the Start Call button to dial the number, as shown in Figure 5-17.

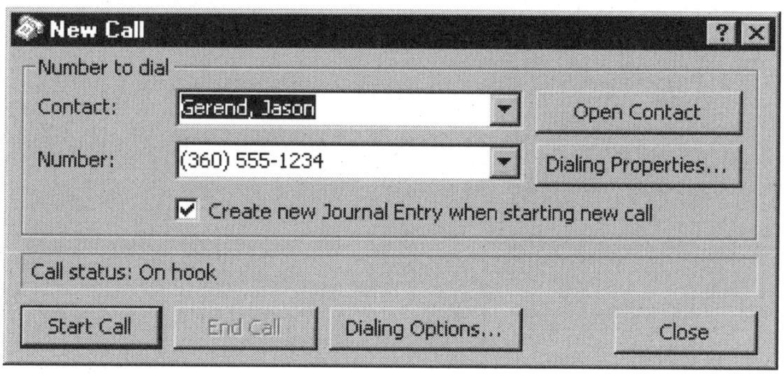


Figure 5-17 Dialing a phone number.

4. **Pick up the phone and talk.**

   Unless your computer has some built-in speakerphone capabilities, you need to pick up your normal phone and start talking.

5. **Take notes in the new journal entry.**

   In the Journal Entry window, as shown in Figure 5-18, enter a subject and start taking notes in the body of the window. We also recommend that you assign a category to the journal entry.

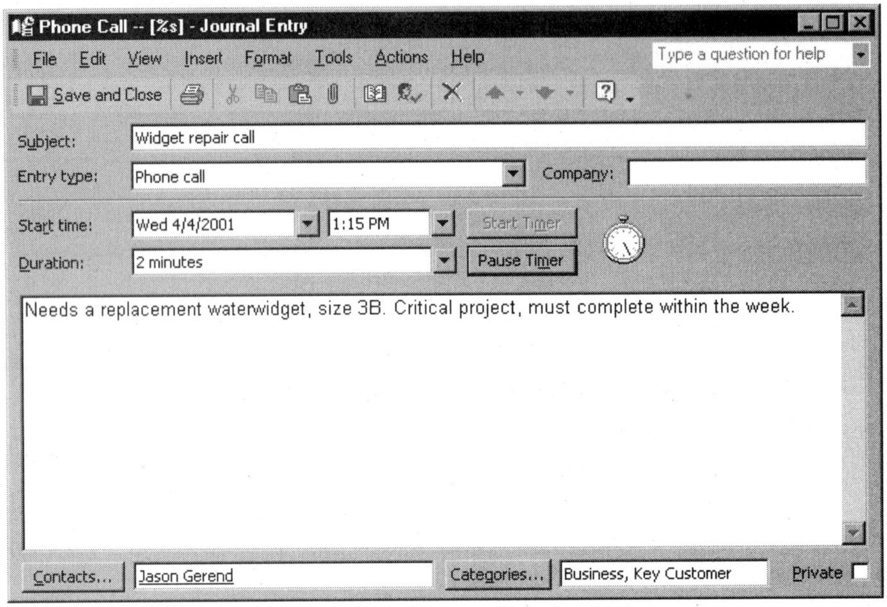


**Figure 5-18** Entering notes in a new journal entry.

6. **Switch to the New Call window to hang up.**

   When you're ready to hang up, switch to the New Call window and press the End Call button. (If the window is hidden, click the New Call item on the Windows taskbar.) Then hang up the phone. (Outlook stops the timer when you press the End Call button, so if you're billing your time, hang up shortly after pressing this button.)

7. **Make any further notes, and then save the journal entry.**

   To save the journal entry, click the Save And Close toolbar button. Outlook saves the entry to the Journal folder.

8. **Open the journal entry later.**

   To locate a journal entry, open the contact that you called, click the Activities tab, and select Journal from the Show drop-down list box. Alternatively, display the Journal folder by clicking the My Shortcuts group in the Outlook bar and then clicking the Journal shortcut. This displays all journal entries you've created.

TIP *You can also create journal entries for other purposes. To do so, select or open the contact with which you want to associate the journal entry and then choose the Action menu's New Journal Entry For Contact command.*

# Managing Address Books

Although many users need only a single Contacts folder and no additional address books, some business users may find themselves with multiple address books and possibly the need for additional Contacts folders.

Use the information in the following two sections to create additional Contacts folders as necessary and to specify which address books and Contacts folders Outlook uses to address messages.

## Creating Multiple Contacts Folders

If you want to keep some contacts completely separate from your other contacts—perhaps to keep your personal contacts separate from your business contacts—you can create multiple contacts folders. To do so, follow these steps:

1. **Create a new folder.**

   Choose the File menu's New command, and then choose Folder from the submenu.

2. **Choose the type of items the folder should store.**

   Select Contact to create a new Contacts folder.

3. **Name the folder.**

   Enter a short but descriptive name for the folder in the Name box.

4. **Specify where to place the folder.**

   Use the Location drop-down list box to select the folder in which you want to store your new folder (for example, your existing Contacts folder). Alternatively, click the folder icon next to the box to visually select a folder.

5. **Click OK.**

   When Outlook asks if you want to create a shortcut to the folder on the Outlook bar, click Yes. Outlook creates the folder and adds a shortcut to the My Shortcuts group on the Outlook bar.

TIP *To add an old Personal Address Book (.pab), choose the Tools menu's E-Mail Accounts command, select the Add A New Directory Or Address Book option, and then click Next. Select Additional Address Books, click Next, select Personal Address Book, and then click Next. Use the Personal Address Book dialog box to specify the location of the existing Personal Address Book.*

## Controlling Message Addressing

If you have multiple address lists (Contacts folders or address books) set up in Outlook, you may want to change how Outlook works with them. To do so, follow these steps:

1. **Click the Address Book toolbar button.**

   Outlook displays the Address Book dialog box.

2. **Choose the Tools menu's Options command**

   Outlook displays the Addressing dialog box, as shown in Figure 5-19.

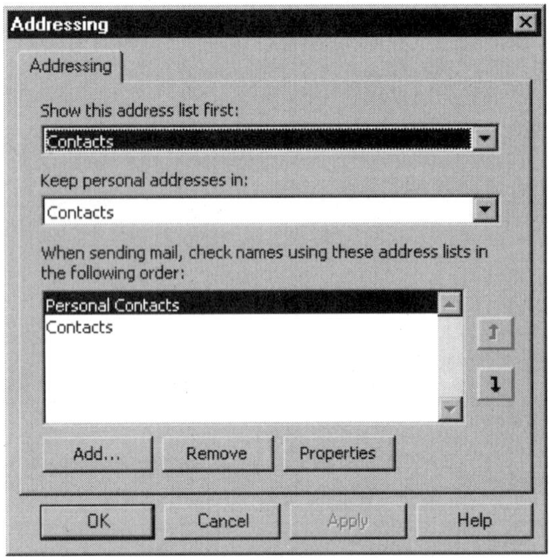


**Figure 5-19** The Addressing dialog box.

3. **Select which address list to display first.**

   Select the address list Outlook should display first in the Select Names and Address Book dialog boxes.

4. **Select where Outlook should store new contacts.**

   In the Keep Personal Addresses In drop-down list box, select the address list that Outlook should create new contacts in by default.

5. **Specify which address lists Outlook should check for names.**

   When you type a name in the To field of an e-mail message, Outlook automatically checks your address lists for a possible match. Use the Add and Remove buttons to add address lists or remove them from this name checking process. Use the up and down arrow buttons to control the order in which Outlook checks the address lists. (We recommend that you use a local address list, such as the Contacts folder, as the first list.)

## Summary

Outlook's Contacts folder is an invaluable tool for storing, retrieving, and managing all sorts of information about your contacts. In this skill we started with an overview of the Contacts folder and the explored the differences between it and the Address Book. We then walked you through creating and editing contacts and distribution lists, as well as locating and putting contacts to use. We finished by showing you how to create and manage multiple Contacts lists.

*Skill 6*

# MANAGING YOUR TIME

## Featuring:

- Basic Terminology
- Viewing Your Calendar
- Finding Calendar Items
- Creating Appointments
- Creating Events
- Editing Calendar Items
- Scheduling Meetings
- Printing from the Calendar
- Working with Tasks
- Using Reminders

Outlook's time management features are easy to use and thoroughly integrated with Outlook's messaging capabilities, making Outlook truly shine as a time-saving business tool.

Outlook provides two main tools for managing your time: the Calendar and Tasks folders. You can use Outlook's Calendar to schedule appointments and events, plan meetings with others on an Exchange Server network or across the Internet, as well as make printouts for inclusion in a traditional paper-based day planner. (You can also synchronize your data with personal digital assistants [PDAs].)

You can use the Tasks folder to keep track of your tasks, assign them to other users as appropriate, and send status reports on tasks that have been assigned to you.

This skill covers how to use both of these tools to effectively manage your time, and also covers using the Reminders window to handle reminders that you set for various Outlook items, such as upcoming meetings, task deadlines, and messages that you need to follow up.

## Basic Terminology

Although Outlook treats all time blocks similarly, it uses three types of Calendar items to differentiate how you schedule your time.

- An appointment is simply a block of time when you have something scheduled—work, lunch, a meeting with a client.
- A meeting in Outlook is an appointment in which you invited other people to attend by using the Outlook application. Even if you truly are going to a meeting, unless you or someone else used Outlook to invite the attendees to the meeting, Outlook simply considers it an appointment.
- An event is any appointment or meeting that lasts 24 hours or longer, such as a conference. Birthdays and anniversaries are also considered events.

In addition to the three types of Calendar items, you can also create tasks, which are activities that you have to do but that don't explicitly occupy time on your calendar. For example, you might create a task for a project proposal or a presentation that you need to create.

You work with tasks using the Tasks folder, or the TaskPad, an interface to the Tasks folder that you can use from within the Calendar folder.

## Viewing Your Calendar

To display the Calendar, as shown in Figure 6-1, click the Calendar shortcut on the Outlook bar.

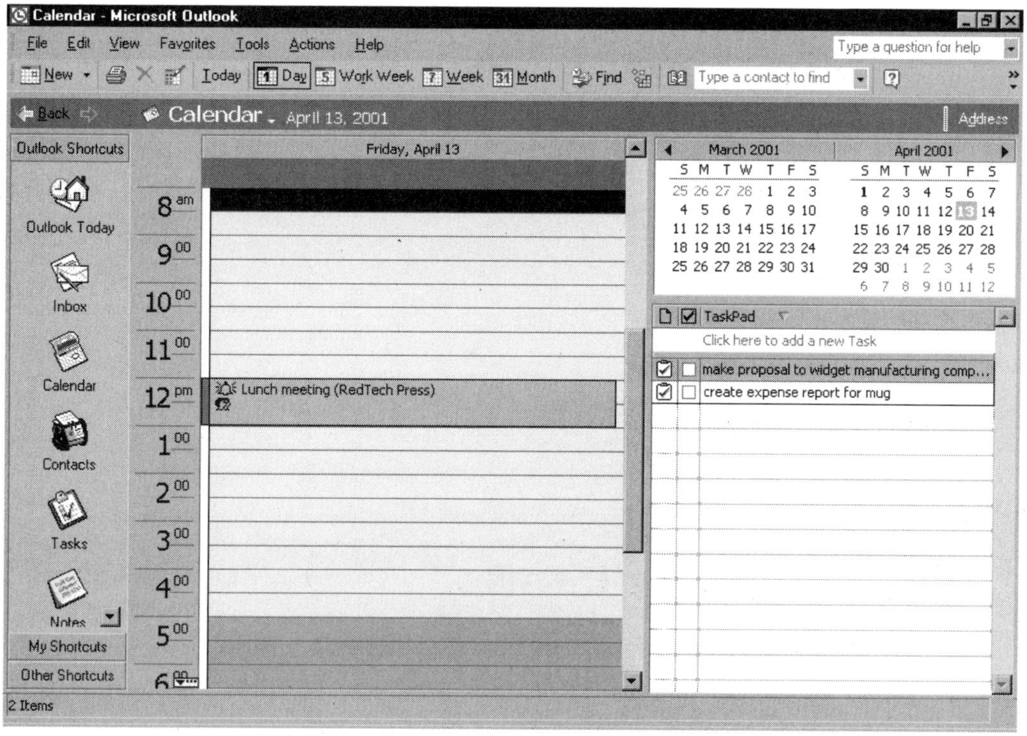


**Figure 6-1** The Calendar, showing the Date Navigator and TaskPad.

Use the following methods to view your calendar in different ways:

- To view different parts of the selected day, use the scroll bar. A small triangle will appear at the bottom or top of the day if you have something scheduled that isn't currently visible.
- To view a different day, click the date you want in the Date Navigator (the small calendar(s) located in the top right part of the Calendar window). Drag across multiple dates to display several days at once. Days in which you have something scheduled will appear in bold.
- To view dates in a different month, either click the triangles on the right and left side of the Date Navigator or click a month in the Date Navigator and choose another month from the pop-up menu.
- To go to a distant date, right-click an empty time slot in the Calendar and choose Go To Date from the shortcut menu. Use the Go To Date dialog box to display the date.
- To return to the current date, click the Today toolbar button.

- To change the number of days Outlook displays at once, click the Day, Work Week, Week, or Month toolbar buttons.
- To open an appointment, meeting, or event, double-click the item (events appear as banners above the day(s) during which they take place).
- To resize the Date Navigator and TaskPad (the tasks list displayed under the Date Navigator), move the mouse over the vertical divider between the Calendar view and the TaskPad until it turns into a dual-headed arrow, and then drag the line to the appropriate size.

TIP *To open a separate window for the Calendar, right-click the Calendar shortcut on the Outlook bar and choose Open In New Window from the shortcut menu.*

## Finding Calendar Items

Locating a specific appointment can be difficult, especially if you have a full calendar. Although you can always display the Calendar and start hunting for a particular appointment, meeting, or event, performing a search for it is oftentimes more efficient. To do so, follow these steps:

1. **Click the Find toolbar button.**

   This displays the Find bar, as shown in Figure 6-2.

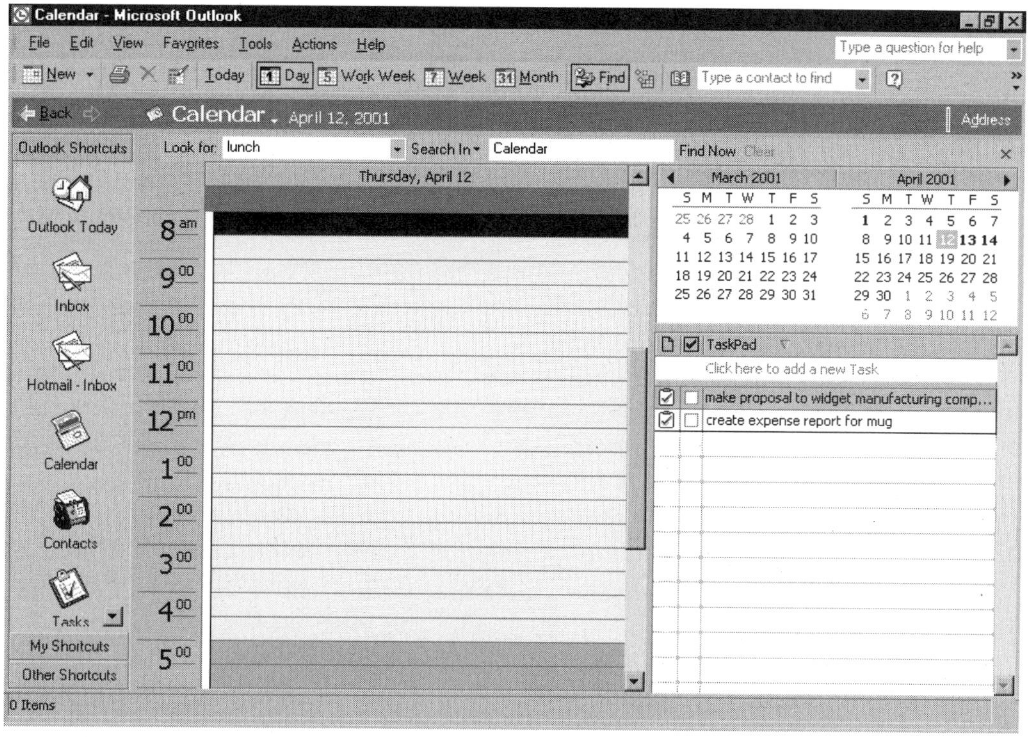

**Figure 6-2** Searching for Calendar items using the Find bar.

TIP *To perform a more advanced search, choose the Tools menu's Advanced Search command. For a detailed discussion of the Advanced Search tool, see "Skill 4: Managing Your E-Mail."*

2. **Enter the words for which you want to search.**

   In the Look For box, enter the words for which you want to search. Below are some tips for searching with the Find box:

   - By default, Outlook searches for any Calendar items with all the words listed.
   - To search for Calendar items with any of the words (the Boolean OR command), separate the search words with commas.
   - To perform a search you previously performed, click the down arrow next to the Look For box to display a list of previous searches.
   - To search for Calendar items in another folder (something you might want to do if you have multiple Calendars), click the Search In button and choose the appropriate folder from the pop-up menu (select Choose Folders for a complete list).

3. **Click Find Now.**

   Outlook displays the messages it finds, as shown in Figure 6-3. Double-click an item to open it, but keep in mind that if you switch folders, the search results will disappear. You can also clear the search results by clicking the Clear button.

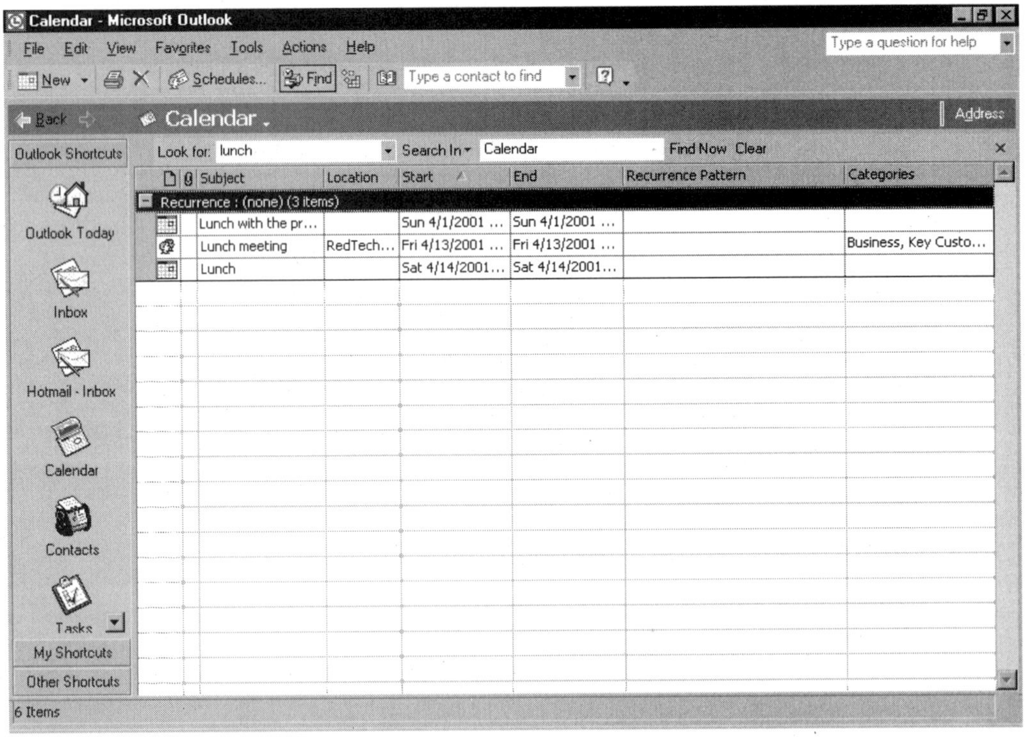


**Figure 6-3** The results of a search.

4. **Close the Find bar.**

   Click the X at the far right end of the Find bar to close it.

TIP *If you find yourself "stuck" in a list view and want to get back to the normal Calendar view, choose the View menu's Current View command and then choose Day/Week/Month from the submenu.*

## Creating Appointments

Creating appointments is a model of simplicity—just use one of the following methods:

- Select a time period in the Calendar by dragging the mouse from the beginning time to the end time, and then enter the title for the appointment (see Figure 6-3).
- Click the New Appointment toolbar button and use the Untitled Appointment window to create your appointment, as discussed in the Editing Appointments section.
- Press Ctrl-Shift-A. This opens a blank appointment that you can edit.
- To create an appointment from another Outlook item, such as a task or e-mail message, drag the item onto the Calendar shortcut on the Outlook bar. This opens an appointment with the contents of the Outlook item inserted in the body of the appointment, as shown in Figure 6-4 (dragging a contact to the Calendar creates a meeting request linked to the contact).

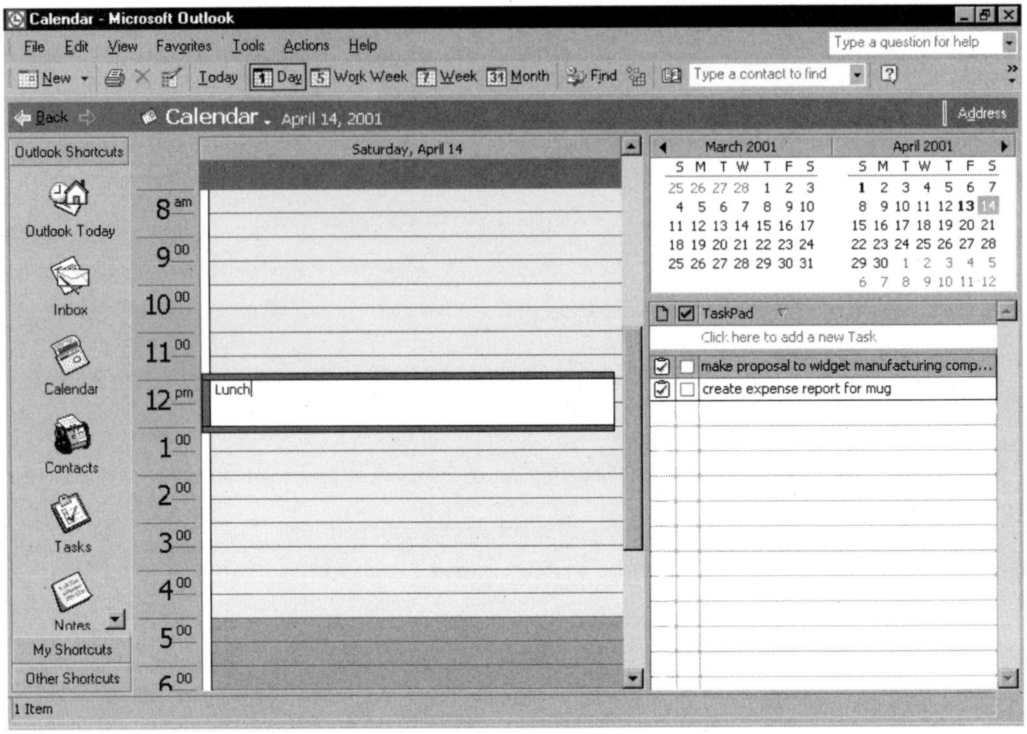

Figure 6-4 Creating a new appointment in the Calendar.

# Creating Events

To create an event (an appointment that lasts 24 hours or longer), use one of the following methods:

- In a daily view, such as Day, Work Week, or Week, click in the blank area below the date listing (but above the actual hours) and enter the title for the event, as shown in Figure 6-5.

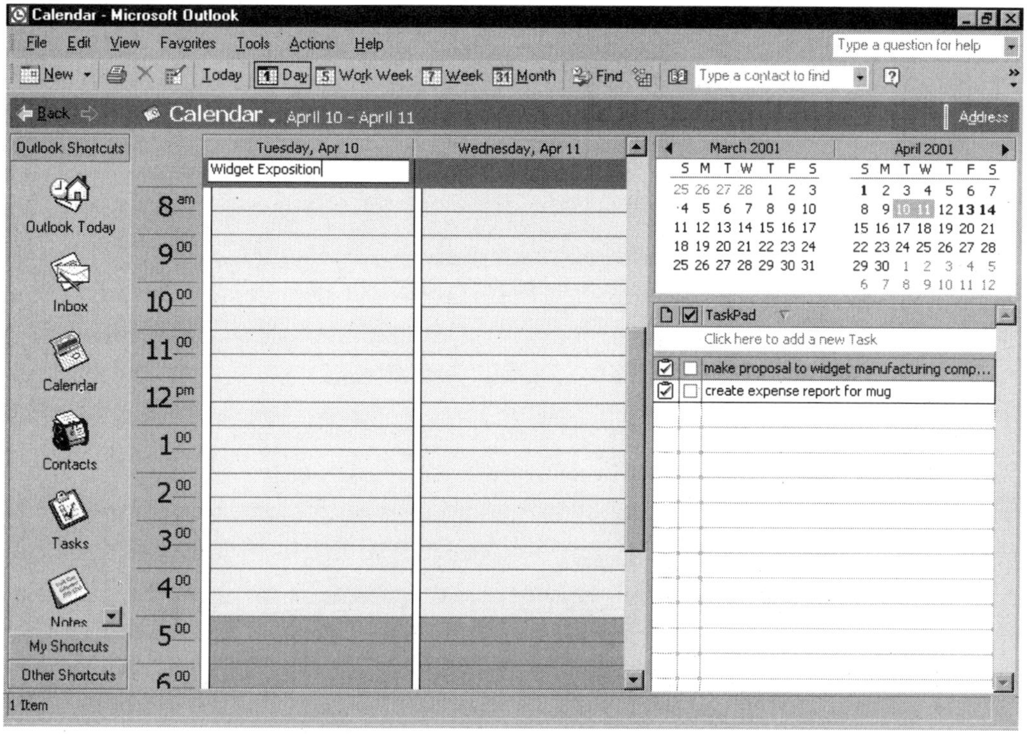


**Figure 6-5** Entering a title for an event.

- To create a multiday event, drag the mouse across the top of the days on which the event takes place (but above the actual hours), and enter the title for the event.
- In the month view, click a date and enter the title for the event.
- Choose the Actions menu's New All Day Event command.
- Open an appointment and set the start time and end time to reflect a duration of 24 hours or more (as described in the following section).

# Editing Calendar Items

You can edit a Calendar item either by directly manipulating it in the Calendar itself or by opening the item and using its Properties box to edit its advanced details.

## Editing Directly in the Calendar

You can easily accomplish many common editing tasks by working directly in the Calendar, as described below:

- To delete an appointment, event, or meeting, select it and then click the Delete toolbar button.
- To move an appointment, event, or meeting to a different date, drag the item to the appropriate timeslot or date in the Calendar. For distant dates, drag the item to the date on the Date Navigator.
- To create an identical appointment, event, or meeting at a different time or date, hold down the Ctrl key and drag the item to the particular time or day. (If the appointment, event, or meeting happens at regular intervals, you may want to use the recur feature, which is discussed in the next section.)
- To change the start or end times of an appointment or meeting, in Day, Work Week, or Week view, move the mouse over the top or bottom of the item until the cursor turns into a sizing handle (a double arrow) and then drag the top or bottom of the item to the specific start or end time, as shown in Figure 6-6.

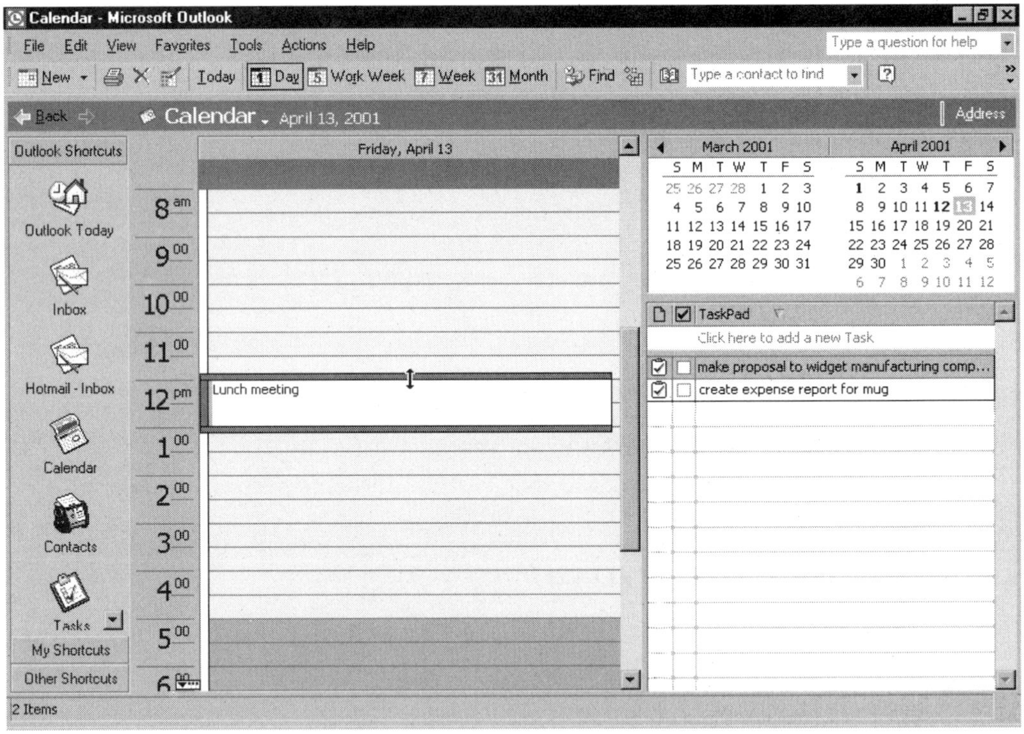


**Figure 6-6** Changing the start time for a meeting.

NOTE *If you change the details for a meeting, Outlook will ask you if you want send updates to the attendees. Of course, click Yes.*

## Editing Advanced Details

To edit the details of an appointment or an event, or to set a reminder, first create the appointment or event and then follow these steps:

1. **Open the appointment or event.**

   Double-click the appointment or event in the Calendar to open it in its own window, as shown in Figure 6-7.

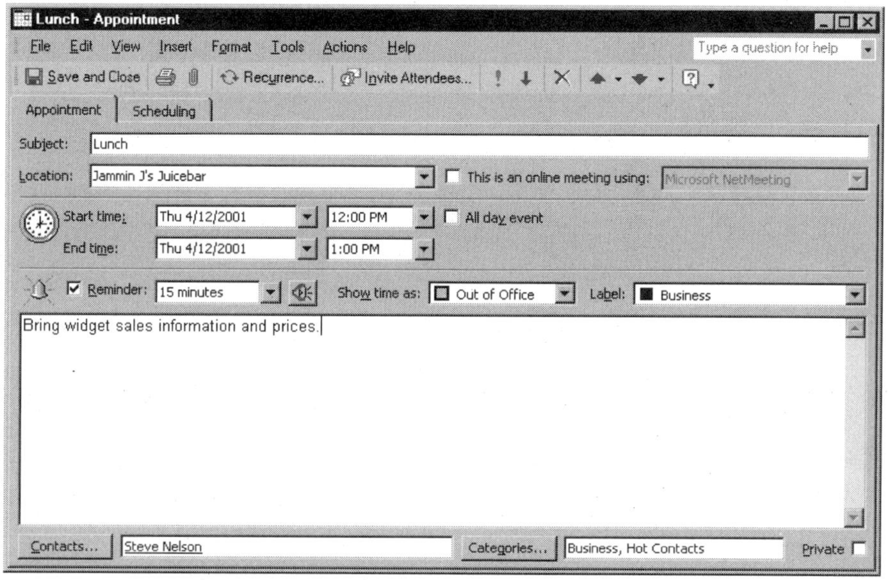


**Figure 6-7** Changing the details of an appointment.

2. **Modify the subject.**

   The subject appears on your Calendar, so make it short and descriptive.

3. **Specify the location.**

   Enter the location of the appointment or event in the Location box, or click the drop-down arrow to display a list of the last ten locations you entered. The location appears in parentheses under the subject.

4. **Enter a start time and end time.**

   In the Start Time and End Time boxes, enter the date and time that the appointment or event begins and ends. Optionally, click the drop-down arrow next to each field to display a list of dates and times from which to choose. Select the All Day Event check box to schedule the appointment to take all day (thereby turning it into an event).

5. **Set a reminder.**

   Select the Reminder check box and enter the number of minutes, hours, days, or weeks before the appointment, meeting, or event that you want to be reminded. (You can also click the drop-down arrow next to the Reminder box to select a time from the list.)

6. **Specify whether you're busy during this time.**

   Use the Show Time As drop-down list box to specify whether you're Free (available for meetings), Tentative, Busy, or Out Of The Office. This is especially important if you use Outlook to schedule meetings with others in your organization. (For more information, see the "Scheduling Meetings" section.)

7. **Optionally, provide a label.**

   In the Label drop-down list box, select the appropriate label for the item, such as Important or Travel Required. Labels color-code your Calendar items, allowing you to distinguish between items at a glance.

8. **Enter any notes about the item.**

   In the main text box, enter any additional information you may have about the item, such as preparation notes, a list of things to bring, or anything else of use to you.

9. **Link the item to any relevant contacts.**

   If the item relates to any contacts, click the Contacts button to select the related contacts (hold down the Ctrl key to select multiple contacts). Double-click a linked contact's name to open the contact.

TIP *Most of Outlook's date fields can recognize a variety of date styles. For example, you could enter 3/2, March 2, Friday, next Friday, or tomorrow and Outlook would then fill in the actual date when you moved to the next box.*

10. **Assign the item to one or more categories.**

    Click the Categories button, and then choose the category or categories to which the item belongs, as shown in Figure 6-8. Linking Calendar items to contacts and categories makes it much easier to locate related items later. (For example, the Calendar item will appear on the Activities tab of the contact, as described in "Skill 5: Using a Contacts List.")

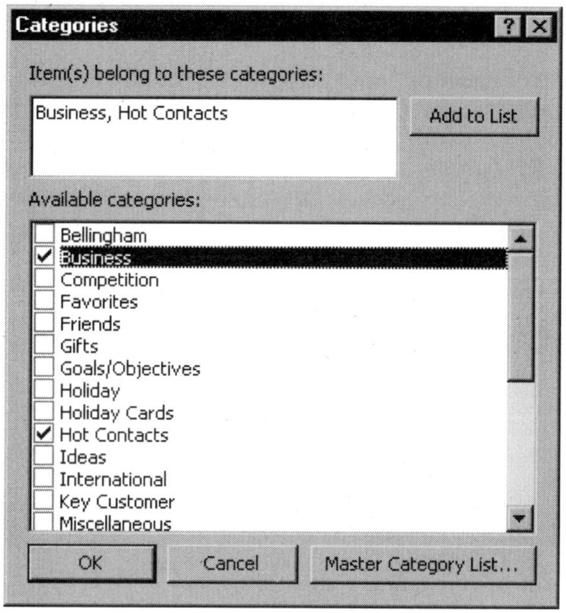


**Figure 6-8** Assigning categories to a Calendar item.

**11. Optionally, make the appointment private.**

If you allow others delegate access to your Calendar (using Exchange Server) and want to hide the details of this appointment from your delegates, select the Private check box.

**12. Click the Save And Close toolbar button.**

Outlook saves the item and returns you to the Calendar.

TIP *To associate a file with the Calendar item, click the Insert File toolbar button, select the file, click the down arrow next to the Insert button, and choose Insert As Shortcut from the pop-up menu. (Simply click the Insert button to embed the file in the Calendar item, but remember that this can consume extra room and allow the two copies of the file to get out of sync.)*

## Making Items Recur

To make an appointment, event, or meeting recur at regular intervals, follow these steps:

1. **Open the appointment, event, or meeting.**

   Double-click the item in the Calendar to open it in its own window.

2. **Click the Recurrence toolbar button.**

   Outlook displays the Appointment Recurrence dialog box, as shown in Figure 6-9.

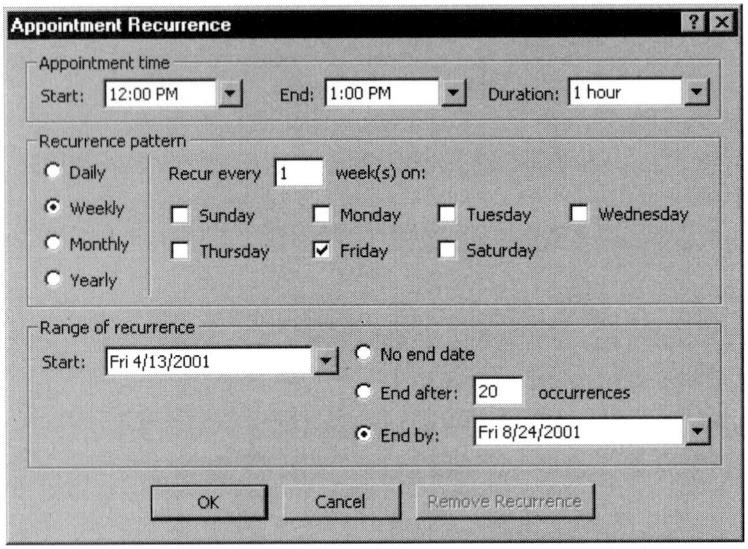


**Figure 6-9** The Appointment Recurrence dialog box.

3. **Enter a start time and an end time.**

   In the Start Time and End Time boxes, enter the time when the appointment, meeting, or event begins and when it ends. Outlook then updates the information in the Duration box.

4. **Specify how often the appointment, meeting, or event takes place.**

   In the Recurrence Pattern section, select how often the appointment, meeting, or event takes place—Daily, Weekly, Monthly, or Yearly. Then use the other boxes to specify the particular days—for example, every week on Thursday.

5. **Specify for how long the recurrence takes place.**

   In the Range Of Recurrence section, specify a start date for the series of appointments, meetings, or events and, optionally, select an end date. For example, if you were scheduling a conference that lasted for five days, select the End After option and enter *5* in the Occurrences text box.

6. **Click OK.**

Outlook removes the Start Time and End Time boxes from the item and replaces them with a summary of the schedule, as shown in Figure 6-10.

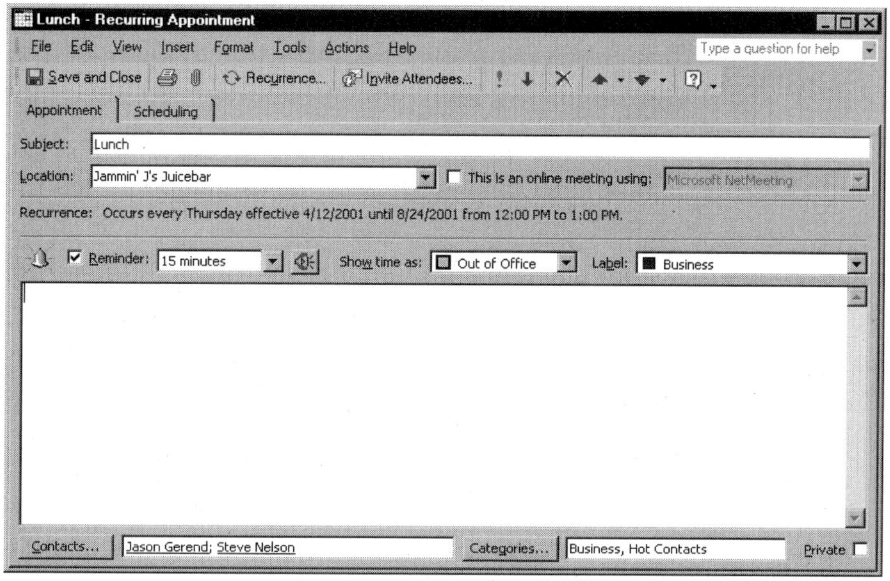


**Figure 6-10** A recurring appointment.

# Scheduling Meetings

To schedule meetings with Outlook, you may want to send meeting requests to others (if you're the one organizing the meeting), respond to meeting requests that you receive, or use Outlook's Scheduling/Plan A Meeting feature to coordinate schedules with others.

The following sections describe how to accomplish these tasks, as well as how to set up Outlook's Internet Free/Busy Information feature, which enables you to coordinate your schedule with others across the Internet. (If your company uses an Exchange Server, you may already be configured.)

## Creating and Sending Meeting Requests

To create a new meeting and send meeting requests, follow these steps:

1. **Create a new meeting.**

To do so, open an appointment or event that you want to turn into a meeting by sending meeting requests, or use one of the following methods:

- Click the down arrow next to the New Appointment toolbar button and choose New Meeting Request from the pop-up menu.
- Press Ctrl-Shift-Q.
- Select a time period in the Calendar by dragging the mouse from the start time to the end time, right-click the time period, and then choose New Meeting Request from the shortcut menu, as shown in Figure 6-11.

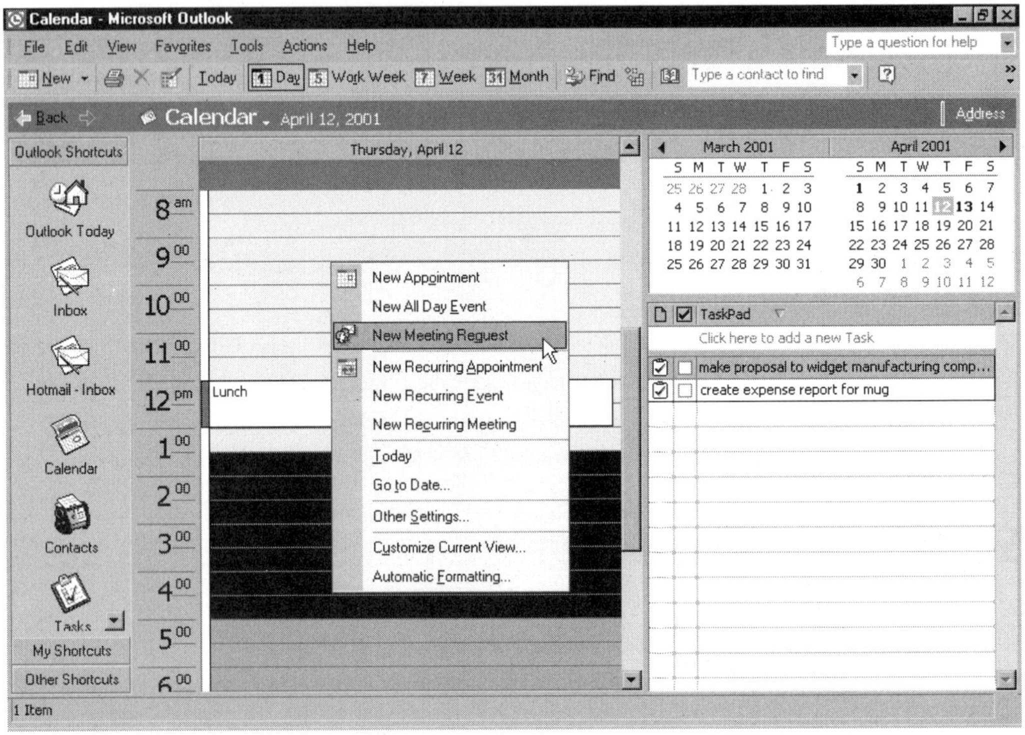


**Figure 6-11** Creating a meeting request.

**2. Enter the meeting information.**

Enter the subject of the meeting, the location, the start and end times, and any other important information about the meeting, as shown in Figure 6-12.

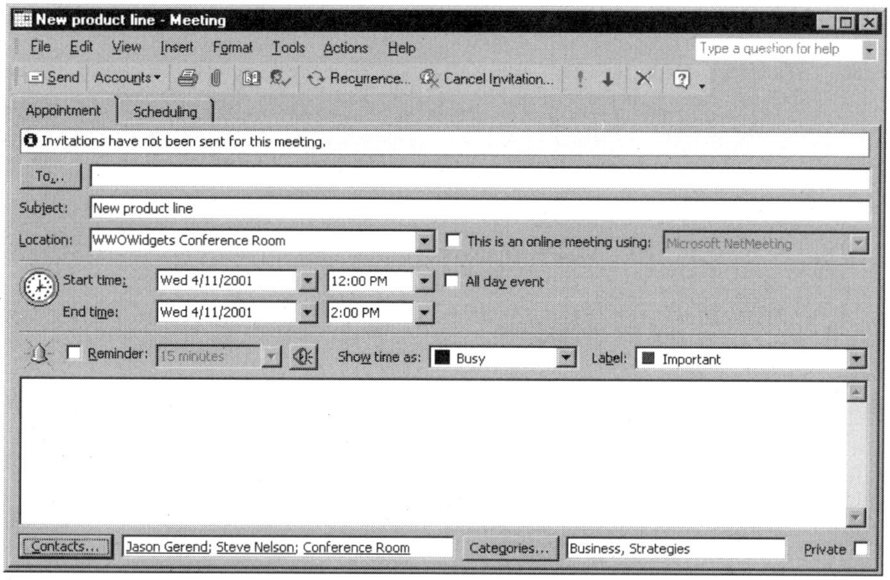

Figure 6-12 Entering meeting information.

3. **Click the To button.**

Outlook displays the Select Attendees And Resources dialog box, as shown in Figure 6-13.

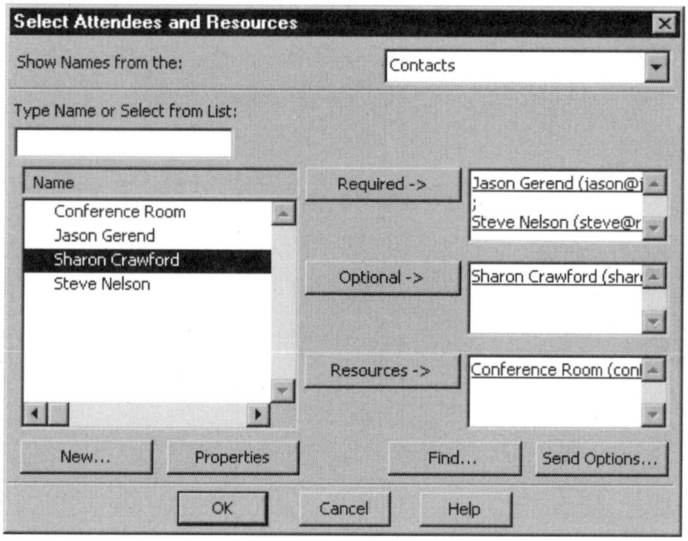

Figure 6-13 The Select Attendees And Resources dialog box.

4. **Select attendees, and then select resources.**

   Select the appropriate address book to search in (most likely the Contacts folder) from the Show Names From The drop-down list box, select the required attendees, and click the Required button. Select optional attendees, and click the Optional button. Select any resources (such as a conference room, projector, etc.) that you need for the meeting, and click the Resources button. Click OK to continue.

5. **Check the schedules of the attendees.**

   If your attendees are set up with Internet Free/Busy information or you're on an Exchange Server network, click the Scheduling tab to select a time for the meeting when everyone can attend. (For more information, see the "Finding Appropriate Times for Meetings" section later in this skill.)

6. **Click the Send toolbar button.**

   Outlook then delivers the meeting request (if you're connected to the Internet) or places the meeting request in the Outbox for delivery the next time you send and receive your mail.

## Sending Updates and Tracking Responses

After you send out meeting requests, you may want to update the time of the meeting or track which attendees have responded to your request. To do so, follow these steps:

1. **Open the meeting.**

   Double-click the meeting in the Calendar to open it.

2. **Click the Tracking tab.**

   This displays the status of each attendee, as shown in Figure 6-14.

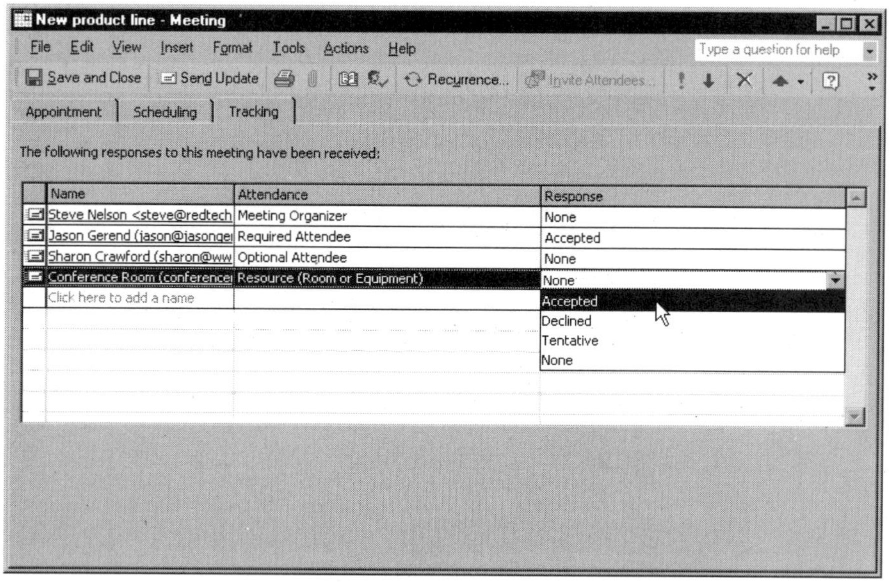


**Figure 6-14** Tracking the responses to a meeting request.

3. **Modify the status of attendees as required.**

   If an attendee responded verbally or by using an e-mail program other than Outlook, update the attendee's status by choosing the appropriate response from the Response column. To change an attendee's attendance requirement (which mainly affects using the Scheduling tab to plan the meeting), select Required Attendee, Optional Attendee, or Resource from the Attendance column.

4. **Update or add details about the meeting.**

   Edit the details of the meeting as necessary.

5. **Click the Send Update toolbar button.**

   Outlook then sends out an e-mail updating all attendees as to the changes in the meeting.

## Responding to Meeting Requests

To respond to a meeting request that someone sent you using Outlook, follow these steps:

1. **Open the meeting request.**

   Double-click the meeting request to open it, or select it to view it in the Preview pane, as shown in Figure 6-15.

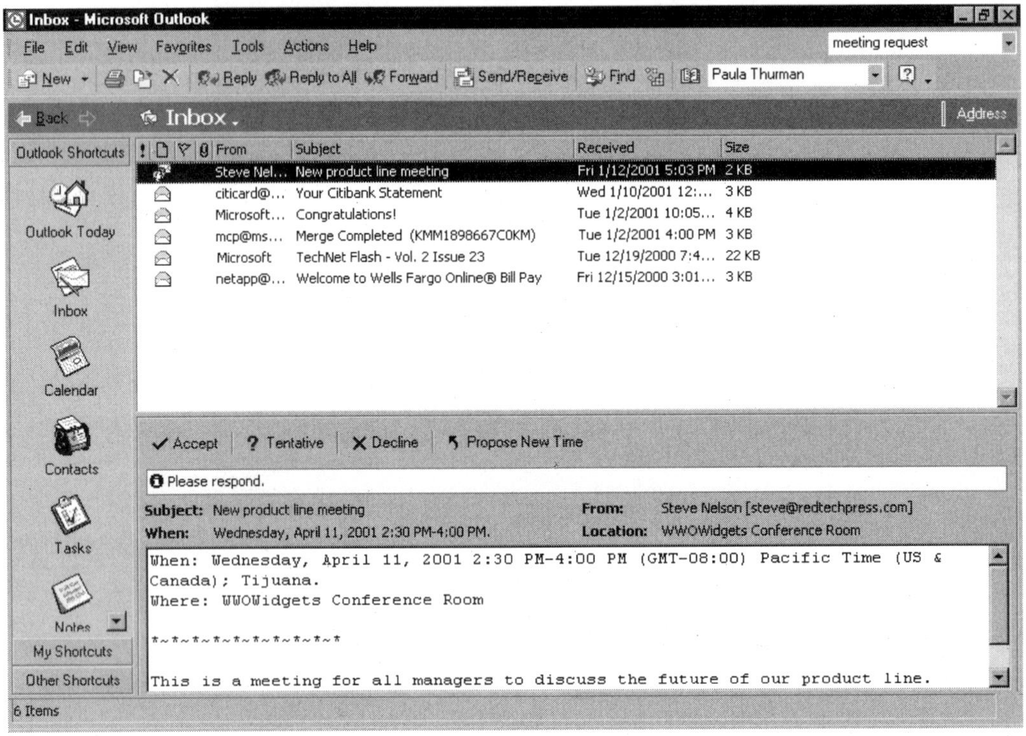


**Figure 6-15** A meeting request in the Preview pane.

2. **View the meeting in your calendar.**

   Click the Calendar toolbar button to open your Calendar in a new window and view the meeting as it would appear if you accepted the meeting request.

3. **Accept or decline the request.**

   Click the Accept or Decline toolbar buttons. Alternatively, click the Tentative toolbar button, or click the Propose New Time toolbar button to open the Propose New Time dialog box, which you can use to find a more suitable time for the meeting. (For more information, see the following section.)

## Finding Appropriate Times for Meetings

Outlook contains a useful Plan A Meeting/Scheduling feature that you can use to find a meeting time that works for all required attendees and resources. In order to use this feature, everybody must either be on the same Exchange Server network or use the Internet Free/Busy Information feature. (To set up this feature, see the following section.)

To find an appropriate time for a meeting, follow these steps:

1. **Create or open the meeting.**

   Double-click an existing meeting in the Calendar to open it, or choose the Action menu's Plan A Meeting command to skip straight to scheduling the meeting (and step 3 below).

2. **Click the Scheduling tab.**

   If you opened an existing meeting, click the Scheduling tab to open the Scheduling/Plan A Meeting window, as shown in Figure 6-16.

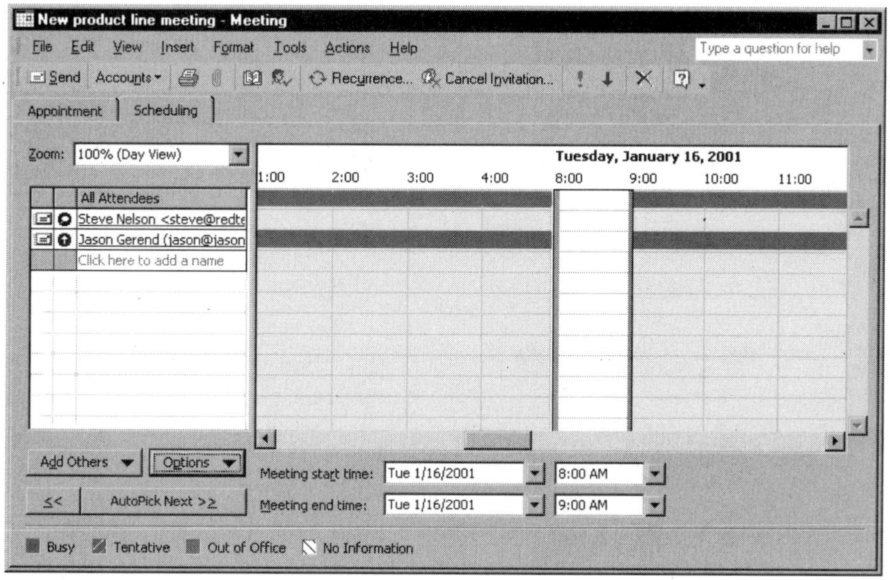


**Figure 6-16** The Scheduling tab of a meeting request.

3. **Add any attendees and/or resources.**

   Click the Add Others button, and select Add From Address Book to display the Select Attendees And Resources dialog box, as shown in Figure 6-17, that you can use to invite additional attendees and resources to the meeting.

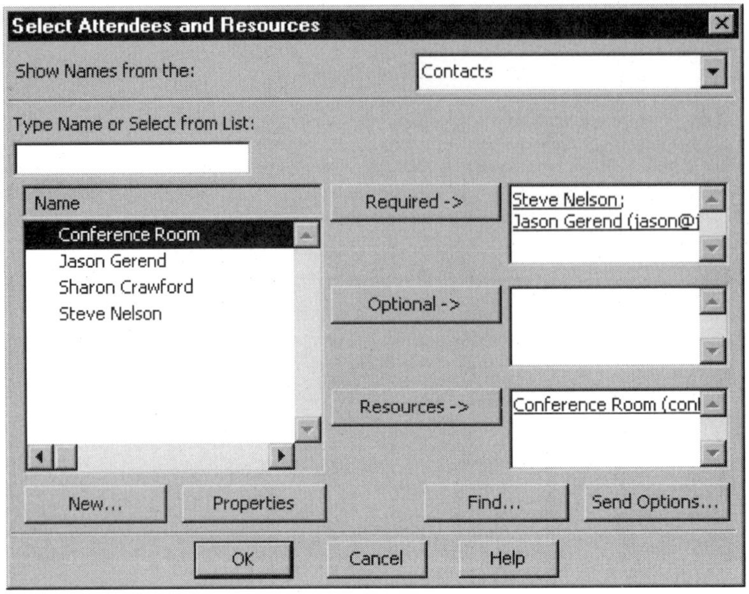


**Figure 6-17** The Select Attendees And Resources dialog box.

**4. Use the AutoPick feature to select the next available meeting time.**

Click the AutoPick Next button to automatically locate the next timeslot of the appropriate duration in which all attendees and one resource are free. To modify these requirements, click the Options button, choose AutoPick from the pop-up menu, and then choose one of the following requirements from the submenu:

- All People And Resources
- All People And One Resource
- Required People
- Required People And One Resource

**5. Send the meeting request.**

If you're using the Plan A Meeting window, click the Make Meeting button to create the meeting request; otherwise, click the Appointment tab to verify your meeting request details are correct and then press the Send toolbar button to send the meeting request.

TIP *To manually select a start and end time, enter the desired date and time in the Meeting Start Time and Meeting End Time boxes, or locate a free time and drag the mouse to select the meeting time. (The start time is indicated by a green vertical line and the end time by a red vertical line.) Use the key at the bottom of the dialog box to discern between times when attendees are Busy, Tentative (possibly busy), Out Of The Office, or times when there is no scheduling information for the contact.*

## Setting Up Internet Free/Busy Information

In order to use the Plan A Meeting tool or the Scheduling tab of a meeting request to find a meeting time when all necessary attendees aren't busy, you need to either be using Exchange Server or the Internet Free/Busy feature.

Although Outlook has had an Internet Free/Busy information feature since Outlook 98, it hasn't worked well (or at all) until Outlook 2002. While this feature is based on the open iCalendar (iCal) standard, interoperability with other programs isn't assured and only Outlook 2002 clients can use Microsoft's Free/Busy servers (the easiest and most convenient way of using the service).

NOTE *Exchange Server users will automatically be able to use Free/Busy information with other Exchange Server users, but in order to plan meetings with Internet users (such as outside consultants or associates from other companies), you'll still need to set up the Internet Free/Busy feature.*

With these caveats aside, the Internet Free/Busy information feature is useful for many businesses, and many users will find that once they get it set up properly, it works very well, particularly when collaborating with other Outlook 2002 users.

### Using the Microsoft Office Internet Free/Busy Service

If all users that you want to share your Free/Busy information with are using Outlook 2002, the easiest way to set up the Internet Free/Busy information is using the Microsoft Office Internet Free/Busy Service. To do so, follow these steps:

1. **Choose the Tools menu's Options command.**

   Outlook displays the Options dialog box.

TIP *Even if you choose to use the Microsoft Office Internet Free/Busy Service to publish and search for Free/Busy information, you may still want to publish your Free/Busy information to your own server for compatibility with other clients. For more information, see the section "Using Your Own Servers."*

2. **Click the Calendar Options button.**

   Outlook displays the Calendar Options dialog box, as shown in Figure 6-18.

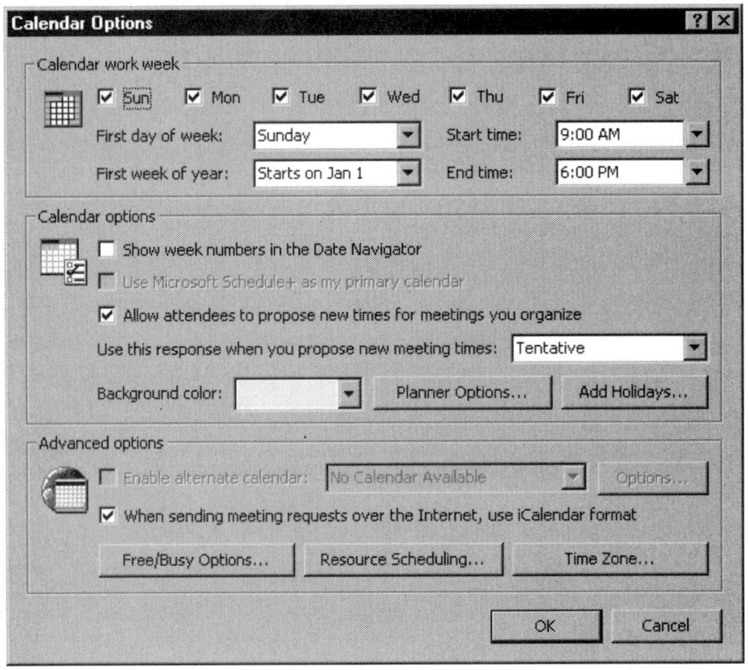


**Figure 6-18** The Calendar Options dialog box.

3. **Click the Free/Busy Options button.**

   Outlook displays the Free/Busy Options dialog box, as shown in Figure 6-19.

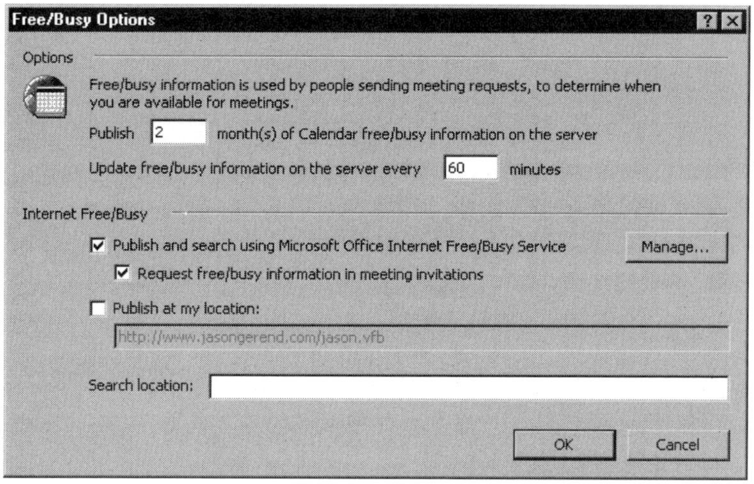


**Figure 6-19** The Free/Busy Options dialog box.

4. **Specify how many months of your schedule to publish.**

   In the first box, enter the number of months of your schedule you want to make available.

5. **Specify how often to update your Free/Busy information.**

   In the second box, enter the frequency with which you want to update your Free/Busy information. Unless you update your Calendar very often, we recommend that you decrease the frequency to minimize network usage. Sixty minutes is a reasonable setting for most users.

6. **Specify where to publish your Free/Busy information.**

   We recommend that you select the Publish And Search Using Microsoft Office Internet Free/Busy Service check box. This is by far the easiest way to share and search for Internet Free/Busy information. For information on configuring your own servers, see the section "Using Your Own Servers."

7. **Click the Manage button.**

   If you're not already logged on using a Microsoft Passport, enter your Microsoft Passport sign-in name and password, as shown in Figure 6-20.

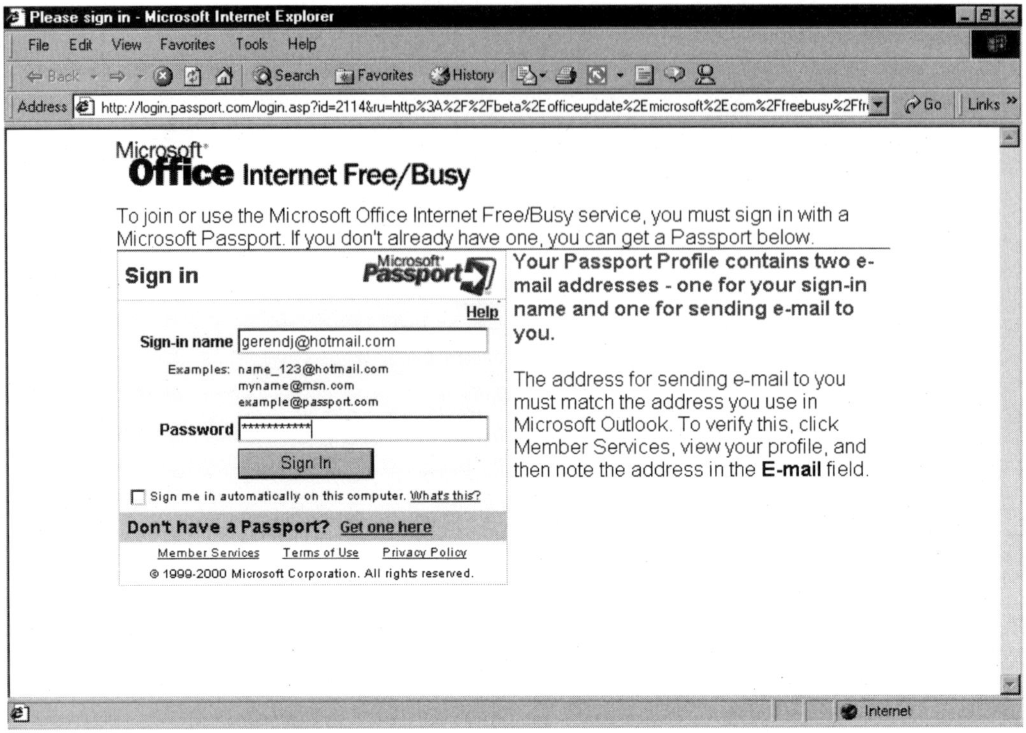


Figure 6-20 Logging on to the Microsoft Office Internet Free/Busy Web site.

NOTE *You need to have your primary e-mail address listed in your Microsoft Passport in order for the Internet Free/Busy feature to work properly. Follow the instructions provided, or locate the Change Profile Settings or similarly named hyperlink at a later time (it may not be immediately available).*

8. **Agree to Microsoft's terms of use.**

   Click the Yes, I Agree hyperlink to use the service.

9. **Click Continue to skip setting up Outlook.**

   Since you already set up Outlook to properly work with the Microsoft Office Internet Free/Busy feature, you don't need to perform any further configuration of Outlook. Click the Continue link, as shown in Figure 6-21, to move on.

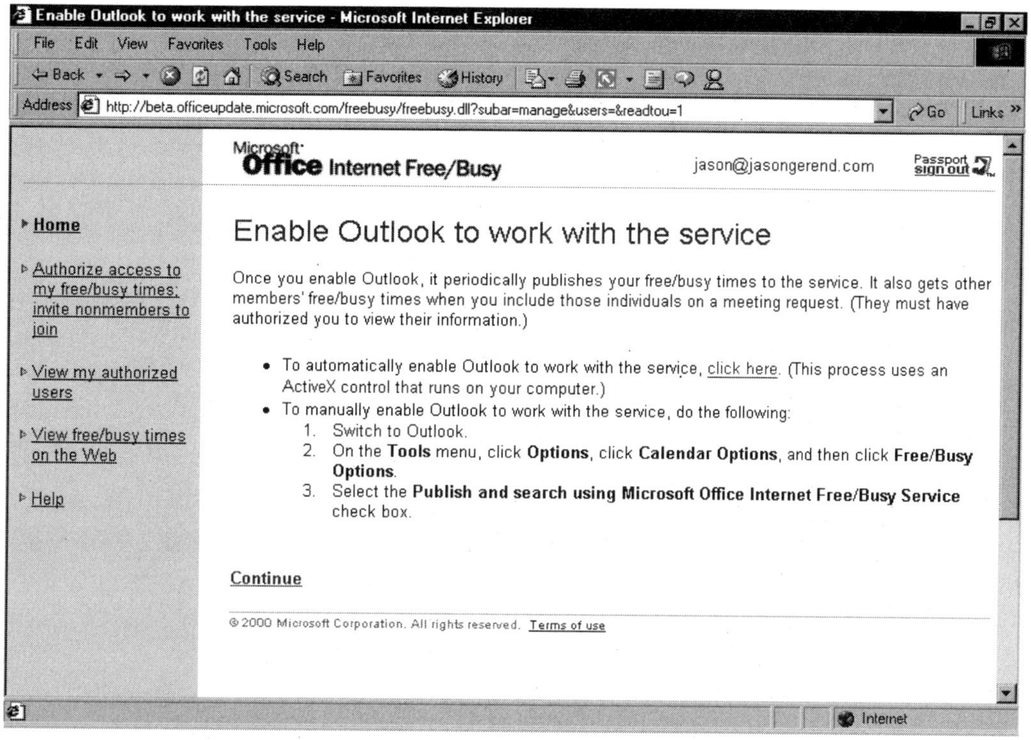


**Figure 6-21** The Enable Outlook To Work With The Service Web page.

**10. Authorize users to view your Free/Busy information.**

In the Authorize Additional Users box, enter the e-mail addresses of all the users you want to be able to access your Free/Busy information, separated by semicolons, as shown in Figure 6-22. Alternatively, to enable anyone to access your Free/Busy information, select the All Microsoft Office Internet Free/Busy Service Members check box.

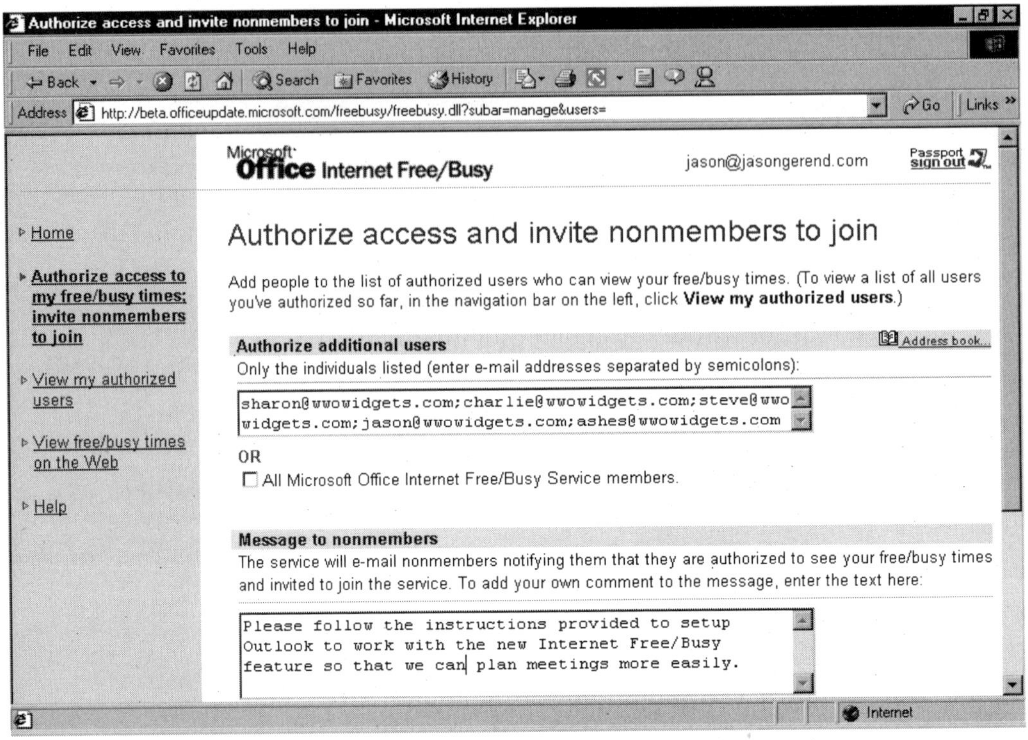


**Figure 6-22** Authorizing users access to your Free/Busy information.

TIP *Click the Address Book link to use select users from your Contacts folder or Exchange Server Global Address List. If Outlook warns you that a program is trying to access your e-mail addresses and that it may be a virus, select the Allow Access check box and click Yes.*

**11. Enter a message for nonmembers.**

E-mail addresses you authorize but that aren't already registered with the service will receive an e-mail with instructions on how to sign up with the service. To add your own comments to this message, enter the comments in the Message To Nonmembers box.

**12. Click OK.**

Your Web browser displays a list of members and nonmembers that are authorized to view your Free/Busy information.

13. **Return to Outlook or view other users' Free/Busy information.**

    You can view other users' Free/Busy information using your Web browser by clicking the View Free/Busy Times On The Web link in the navigation bar on the left side of the Web page. Enter the e-mail addresses for the members whose schedules you want to view, and specify the date and time you want to view, as shown in Figure 6-23.

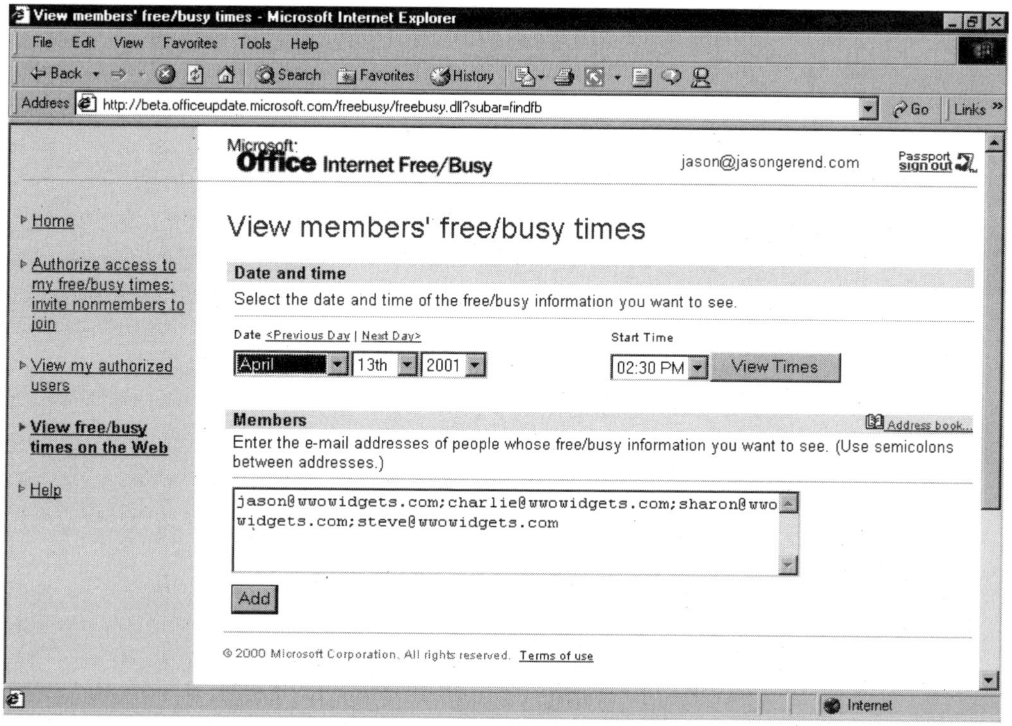


**Figure 6-23** Viewing Free/Busy information on the Web.

## Using Your Own Servers

In order to share Internet Free/Busy information with Outlook 2000 users or users of other scheduling programs that are compatible with the iCalendar format, you need to set up Outlook to work with your own servers. You may also choose to specify your own servers if all the users you want to coordinate your schedules with are on a company network or intranet.

The servers you use can be located on a file server within your network using the file:// protocol, or on an FTP or Web server—either on a company intranet or on the Internet itself.

TIP *You can publish your Free/Busy information to both the Microsoft Office Internet Free/Busy Service and a server of your choice. This brings the most versatility by permitting you to share Free/Busy information easily with Outlook 2002 users, as well as users of other clients.*

To set up Outlook's Internet Free/Busy feature to work with a server of your choice, follow these steps:

1. **Choose the Tools menu's Options command.**

   Outlook displays the Options dialog box.

2. **Click the Calendar Options button.**

   Outlook displays the Calendar Options dialog box.

3. **Click the Free/Busy Options button.**

   Outlook displays the Free/Busy Options dialog box, as shown in Figure 6-24.

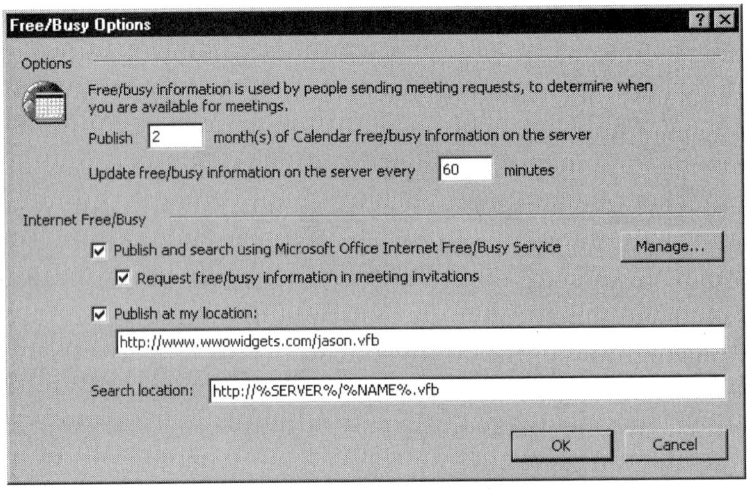


**Figure 6-24** The Free/Busy Options dialog box.

4. **Specify how many months of your schedule to publish.**

   In the first box, enter the number of months of your schedule you want to make available.

5. **Specify how often to update your Free/Busy information.**

   In the second box, enter the frequency with which you want to update your Free/Busy information. Unless you update your Calendar very often, we recommend that you decrease the frequency to minimize network usage. Sixty minutes is a reasonable setting for most users.

6. **Specify where to publish your Free/Busy information.**

   Select the Publish At My Location check box, and enter the full path to your Free/Busy information file—for example, *http://www.wwowidgets.com/jason.vfb*. Use the following guidelines and Table 6-1 to determine how to enter your server information:

   - To share Free/Busy information only with users who have access to your local network, use the file:// protocol to enter the path to a file server on your local network. This is the fastest and most reliable protocol.
   - To share Free/Busy information with users on your intranet or the Internet, use the http:// protocol to specify a server location. You need to be able to publish to this server, and all the users with whom you want to share your Free/Busy information need to be able to read from it.
   - Use the ftp:// protocol for publishing to Internet or intranet servers that don't support the http:// protocol.
   - Use the user name.vfb filename where user name is your e-mail user name. For example, for the e-mail address jason@wwowidgets.com, use the jason.vfb filename.

| PROTOCOL | PATH | FILENAME | EXTENSION |
|---|---|---|---|
| file:// | srv1/schedules/ | jason | .vfb |
| ftp:// | ftp.wwowidgets.com/schedules/ | jason | .vfb |
| http:// | www.wwowidgets.com/schedules/ | jason | .vfb |

**Table 6-1** Sample publishing locations for each protocol.

NOTE *Outlook searches first for the Free/Busy information of contacts at the URL specified in the Search Location box. If it doesn't find the Free/Busy information, it then looks at the Internet Free/Busy Address field located on the Details tab of the person's contact entry.*

7. **Specify where to search for Free/Busy information.**

   Enter the default location Outlook should search for other users' Free/Busy information. We strongly recommend that you use a substitution parameter in the Search Location box. For example, you might want to enter *http://%SERVER%/%NAME%.vfb*. For a contact with the e-mail address jason@jasongerend.com, Outlook would then search at the *http://jasongerend.com/jason.vfb* location.

TIP *If the users with whom you plan to scheduling meetings don't publish to a server with the same name as their e-mail address, don't use the %SERVER% substitution. Instead, enter the actual path to the publishing location, followed by the %NAME%.vfb parameter.*

## Updating Your Free/Busy Information

When connected to the Internet, Outlook automatically updates your Free/Busy according to the frequency you specified when setting up your Internet Free/Busy information. (The default is every 15 minutes for both Exchange Server and Internet users.)

If you make changes to your Calendar and you want to force Outlook to publish the changes to your Free/Busy information, follow these steps:

1. **Display any folder other than Outlook Today.**
2. **Send your Free/Busy information.**

   To do so, choose the Tools menu's Send/Receive command and choose Free/Busy Information from the shortcut menu, as shown in Figure 6-25. If you're asked to provide your user name and password, enter your Microsoft Passport user name and password (if prompted) or the user name and password for the Web, ftp, or file server on which your Free/Busy information is published.

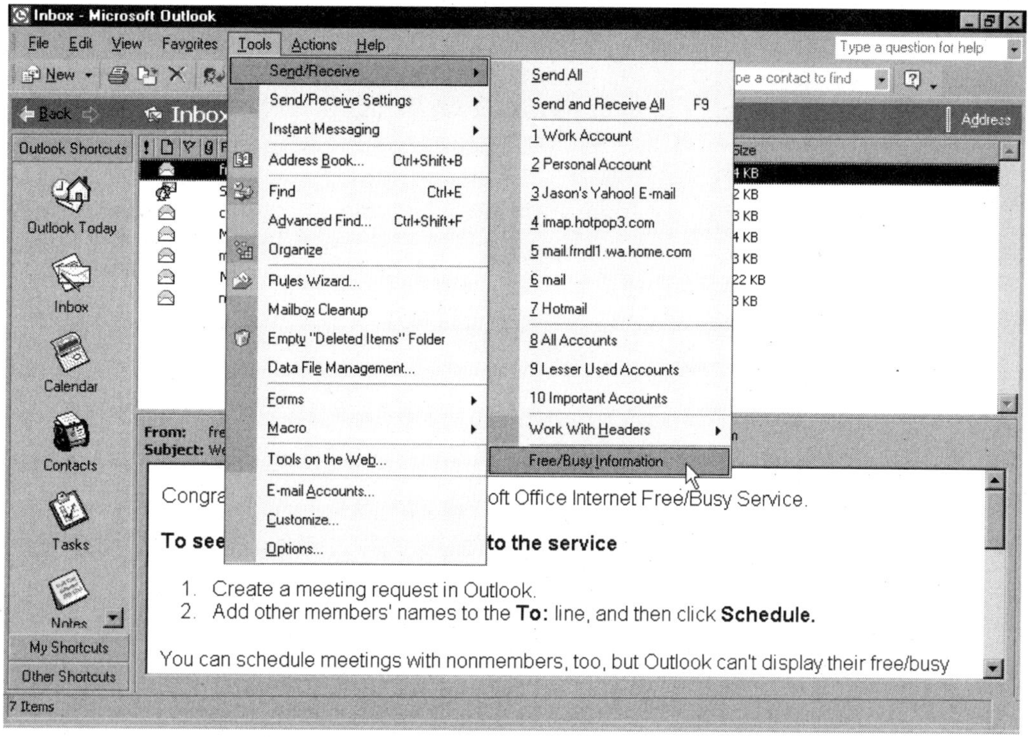

Figure 6-25 Manually updating Free/Busy information.

# Printing from the Calendar

Although Outlook works well with PDAs, many people still find it far superior (and less expensive) to synchronize their Outlook data with their personal organizer the old-fashioned way—by printing it out. Outlook provides a number of different styles you can use to print out your Calendar or selected appointments.

To print your Calendar or appointments, follow these steps:

**1. Select the item(s) you want to print.**

In the Calendar, select the appointments you want to print or display the days you'd like to print in the desired view. (For example, to print your work schedule for this week, click the Work Week toolbar button.)

2. **Choose the File menu's Print command.**

   Alternatively, click the Print toolbar button. (Pushing this button in an open item's window prints the item immediately using the default settings.)

3. **Specify the printer to use.**

   Choose the printer you want from the Name box at the top of the Print dialog box, shown in Figure 6-26. To modify print options such as color and resolution, click the Properties button.

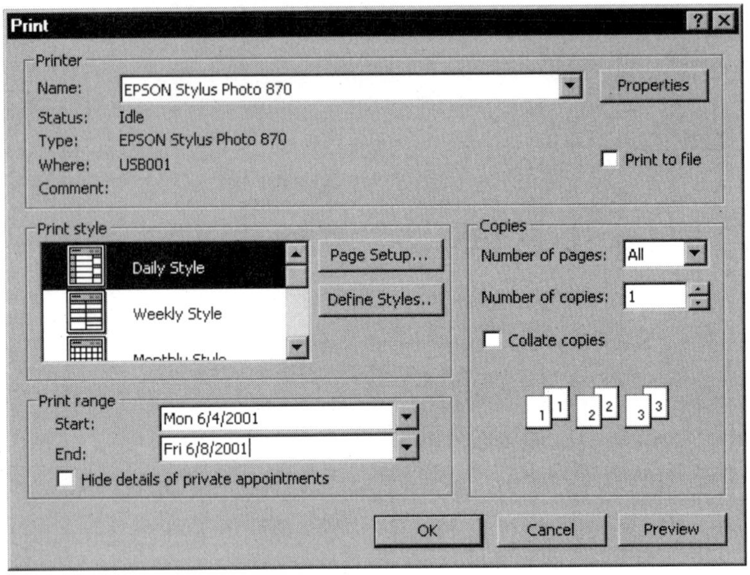


**Figure 6-26** The Print dialog box.

4. **Choose a print style.**

   In the Print Style box, select the print style you want to use:

   - Daily Style prints each day on a separate page with the TaskPad and a region for notes along the right side of the page.
   - Weekly Style prints each week on a separate page, with a box for each day, as in the Week Calendar view.
   - Monthly Style prints each month on a separate page in the classic monthly calendar format.
   - Tri-Fold Style prints a separate page for each day, with three columns on each page: a column for the detailed Daily style, a column for the TaskPad, and a column for the current week, in the Weekly style.

- Calendar Details prints all details of every appointment, meeting, and event in the specified date range in a list.
- Memo Style prints each appointment, meeting, or event in the specified date range in memo style—a separate memo for each item.

TIP *To turn on or off the printing of the TaskPad, notes region, or to control how the Calendar is formatted, click the Page Setup button.*

**5. Choose the appropriate paper size.**

To use a special paper, such as one specifically designed to fit in your day planner, click the Page Setup button, click the Paper tab, and then select a paper size from the Type box, as shown in Figure 6-27.

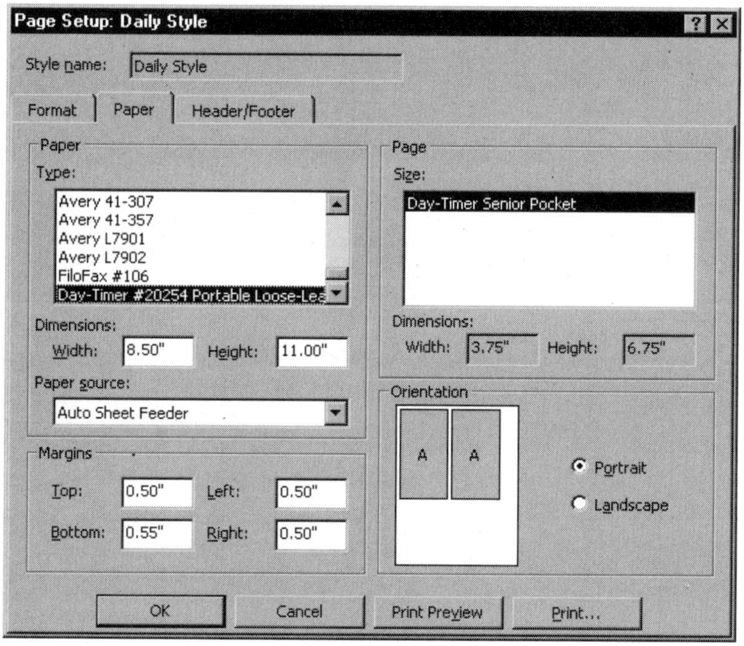


**Figure 6-27** Specifying a special paper size.

**6. Specify the number of pages and copies.**

Use the Number Of Pages and Number Of Copies drop-down list boxes to specify how many pages of the message(s) to print, as well as the number of copies. Select the Collate Copies check box to print each copy in its entirety before printing the next copy.

7. **Preview the print job.**

   Click the Preview button to display the Print Preview window, as shown in Figure 6-28. Click the Print toolbar button to return to the Print dialog box.

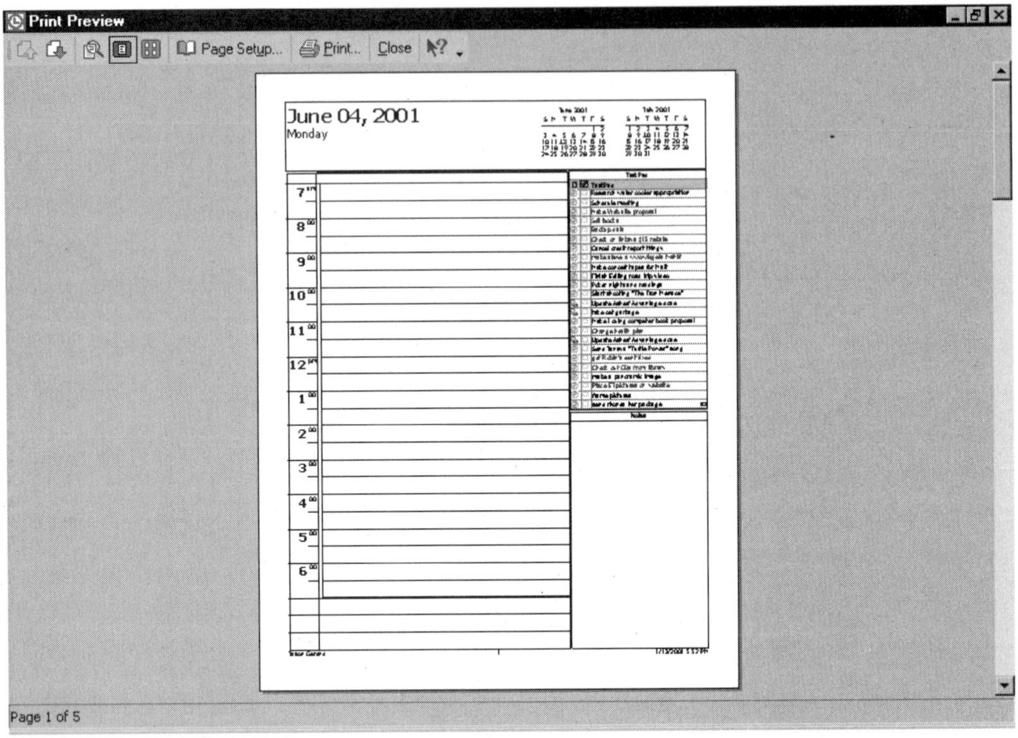


**Figure 6-28** The Print Preview window.

8. **Click OK.**

   Outlook sends the print job to your printer, which then prints the message(s).

# Working with Tasks

Tasks are another useful tool that Outlook provides for managing your time. Tasks are things that you must accomplish that don't have a specific time allocated for them. For example, you might need to create a presentation within a certain timeframe, while you're not busy with other projects. Tasks are also perfect for maintaining a to-do list.

Tasks are well integrated with the rest of Outlook, making them very powerful. You can assign tasks to other users via e-mail, set reminders for tasks, assign categories to your tasks, and track your progress on tasks as you complete them.

## Creating Tasks

To create a new task, follow these steps:

1. **Display the Tasks folder.**

   To do so, click the Tasks shortcut on the Outlook bar.

2. **Enter the subject of the task.**

   At the top of the Tasks list, enter a subject for your new task in the Subject column, as shown in Figure 6-29.

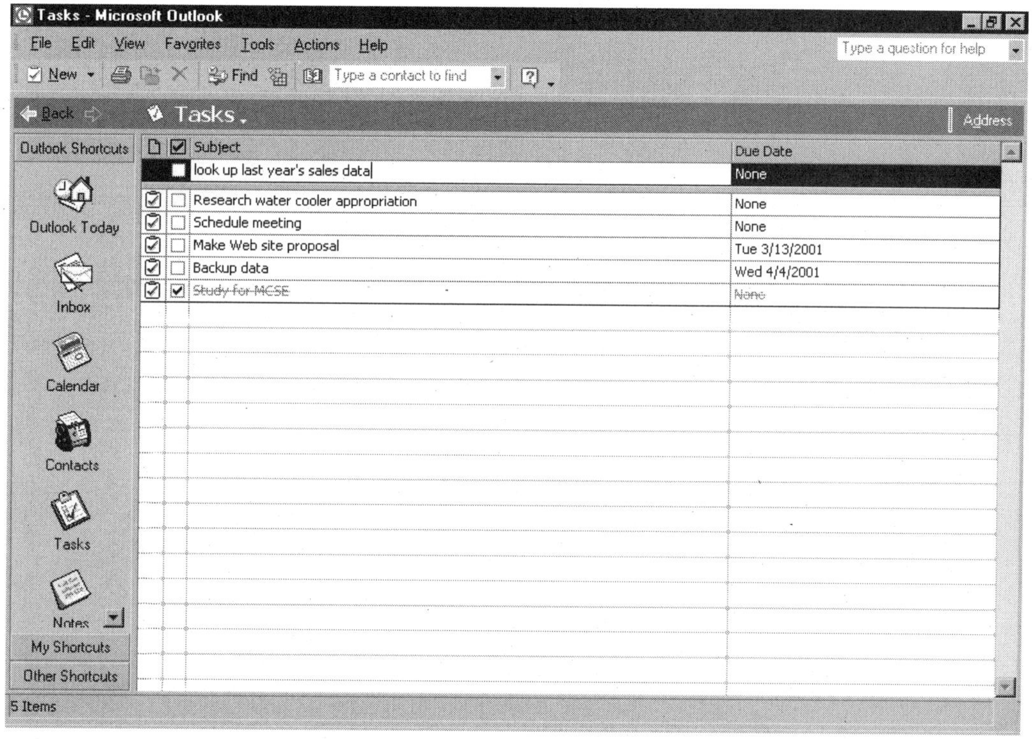


**Figure 6-29** Creating a new task.

TIP *You can also create a new task by clicking the New Task toolbar button or by pressing Ctrl-K. Doing so opens a new task item that you can then edit, as described in the following section.*

3. **Enter a due date.**

   Press the Tab key to move to the Due Date field (or click in the Due Date column), and then enter the due date for the task, if any.

TIP *Create some easy tasks as well as your hard tasks. Marking off easy tasks as completed can help give you the momentum to accomplish the harder tasks.*

TIP *Consider switching your Tasks folder view either to the Detailed List or By Category views, both of which allow you to specify a category when creating new tasks. To do so, choose the View menu's Current View command and then choose the view you want from the submenu.*

## Editing Tasks

To specify a status, set a reminder, assign categories to a task, or edit other details of a task, follow these steps:

**1. Open the task.**

Double-click the task in the Tasks folder to open it in its own window, as shown in Figure 6-30.

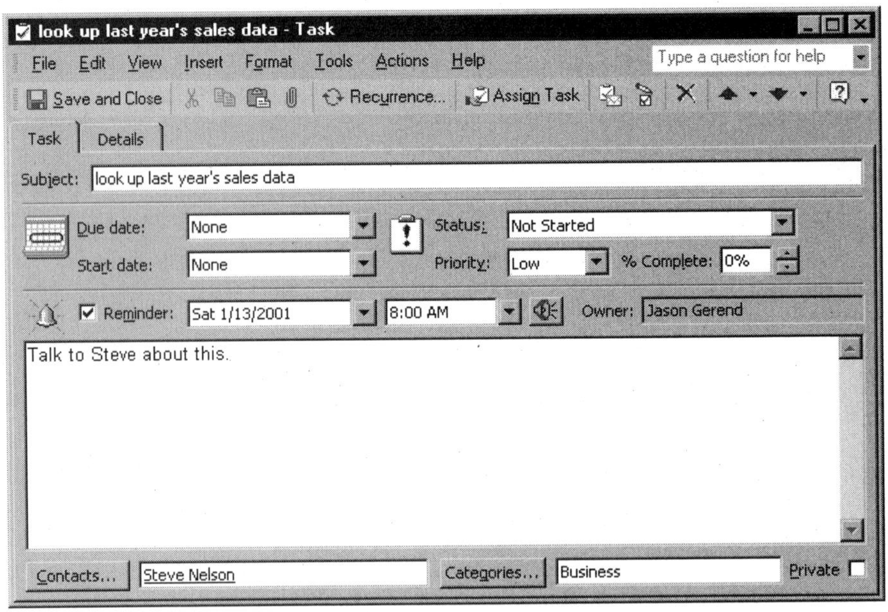


**Figure 6-30** Changing the details of a task.

**2. Modify the subject.**

The subject appears in your Tasks list, on the TaskPad (which behaves identically to the Tasks folder), and in Outlook Today, so keep it short and descriptive.

3. **Enter a due date and start date.**

   In the Due Date box, enter the date the task is due, if it has a due date. (Overdue tasks appear in red on your Tasks list.) Optionally, enter the date you will start the task in the Start Date box. (This enables you to use a Gantt-style timeline to view the amount of time the project takes.)

TIP *Most of Outlook's date fields can recognize a date and time entered in a variety of ways. For example, you could enter 3/2, March 2, Friday, next Friday, or tomorrow. Outlook would then fill in the actual date when you moved to the next box.*

4. **Specify the current status.**

   Choose the current status of the task from the Status drop-down list box, and use the % Complete box to provide further detail about how far you are into the project.

5. **Choose a priority from the Priority drop-down list box.**
6. **Set a reminder.**

   Select the Reminder check box and the date and time when you want Outlook to remind you of the task.

7. **Enter any notes about the task.**

   In the main text box, enter any additional information you may have about the task, such as a strategy for accomplishing it or resources you can use.

8. **Link the task to any relevant contacts.**

   If the task relates to any contacts, click the Contacts button to select the related contacts (hold down the Ctrl key to select multiple contacts), as shown in Figure 6-31. Double-click a linked contact's name to open the contact.

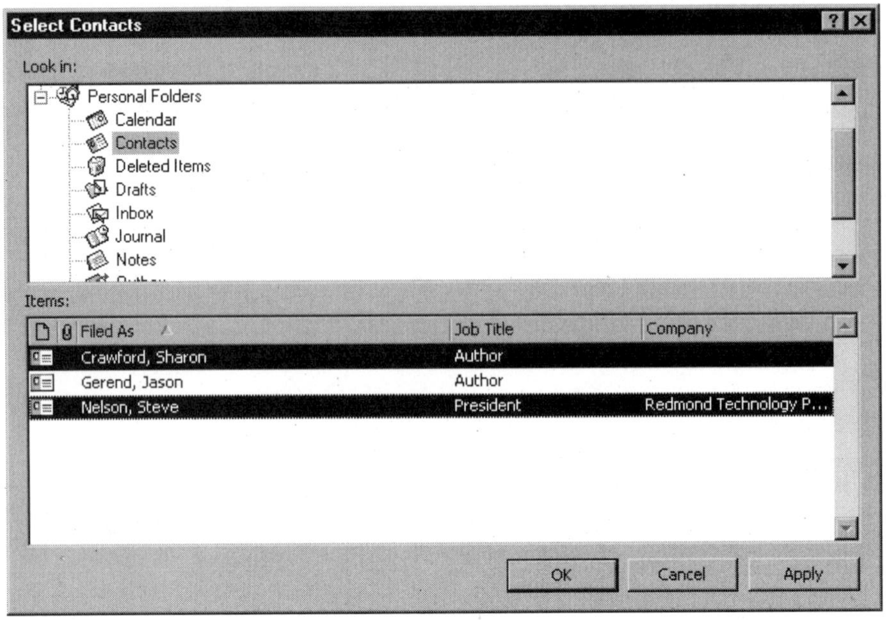


**Figure 6-31** Linking a task to related contacts.

**9. Assign one or more categories to the task.**

Click the Categories button, and then choose the category or categories the item belongs to, as shown in Figure 6-32. Linking tasks to contacts and categories makes it much easier to locate related items later. (For example, the Task item will appear on the Activities tab of the contact, as described in "Skill 5: Using a Contacts List.")

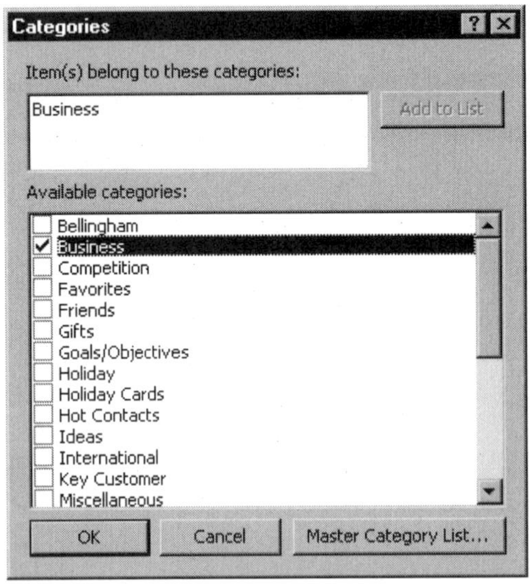


**Figure 6-32** Assigning categories to a task.

10. **Optionally, make the task recur.**

    Click the Recurrence toolbar button to specify that the task should recur at regular intervals. Use the Task Recurrence dialog box, as described earlier in the "Making Items Recur" section (the procedure is identical).

11. **Optionally, make the appointment private.**

    If you allow others delegate access to your Tasks folder (using Exchange Server) and want to hide the details of this appointment from your delegates, select the Private check box.

12. **Click the Save And Close toolbar button.**

    Outlook saves the item and returns you to the Calendar.

TIP *To associate a file with the task, click the Insert File toolbar button, select the file, click the down arrow next to the Insert button and choose Insert As Shortcut from the pop-up menu. (Simply click the Insert button to embed the file in the Calendar item, but remember that this can consume extra room and allow the two copies of the file to get out of sync.)*

## Assigning Tasks to Others

The ability to assign tasks to other people is one of those hidden gems of Outlook. This feature allows you to create a task and assign it to another Outlook user, who can then accept or reject the task.

If the recipient accepts the task, it appears as a task in their Tasks list, but remains "linked" to the original task that you created. This link makes it easy to send status reports, reassign tasks while keeping the original owner up-to-date, and notify the original owner when the task is complete.

NOTE *Task requests may not work as intended when one party is using Outlook with Exchange Server and the other party isn't. Before relying on task requests, it's prudent to test the feature with everyone involved.*

To assign a task to another person, follow these steps:

1. **Open the task.**

   Double-click the task to open it in its own window.

2. **Click the Assign Task toolbar button.**

   Outlook adds several additional fields to the Task window, as shown in Figure 6-33.

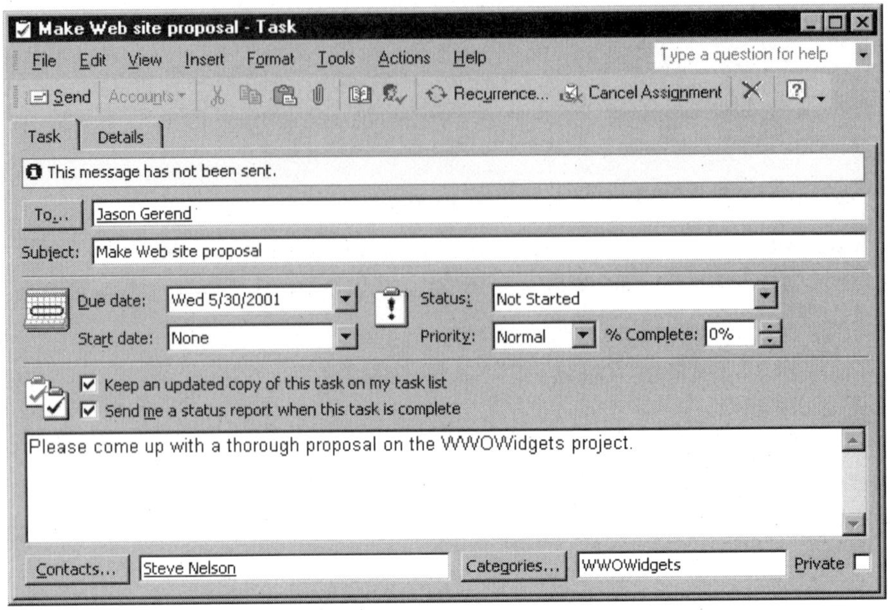


**Figure 6-33** A task request.

3. **Address the task request.**

   Enter the person's name or e-mail address to whom you want to assign the task in the To box. Alternatively, click the To button to select the recipient from your Contacts folder or another address book.

NOTE *Don't assign the same task to multiple people—it prevents task updates from working. Instead, create subtasks and assign those individually.*

4. **Specify whether you want to be updated.**

   To remove the task from your Tasks list after you assign it, clear the Keep An Updated Copy Of This Task On My Task List check box. If you don't want to be notified when the task is completed, clear the Send Me A Status Report When This Task Is Complete check box.

5. **Check for spelling errors.**

   Choose the Tools menu's Spelling command to check for spelling mistakes before sending the task.

6. **Click the Send toolbar button.**

   Outlook then sends the task request as it would a normal e-mail message.

## Receiving Task Requests

Task requests appear in your Inbox. To accept or decline a task request, follow these steps:

1. **Open or display the task request.**

   Select the task request in your Inbox to display it in the Preview pane, as shown in Figure 6-34, or double-click the task request to open it.

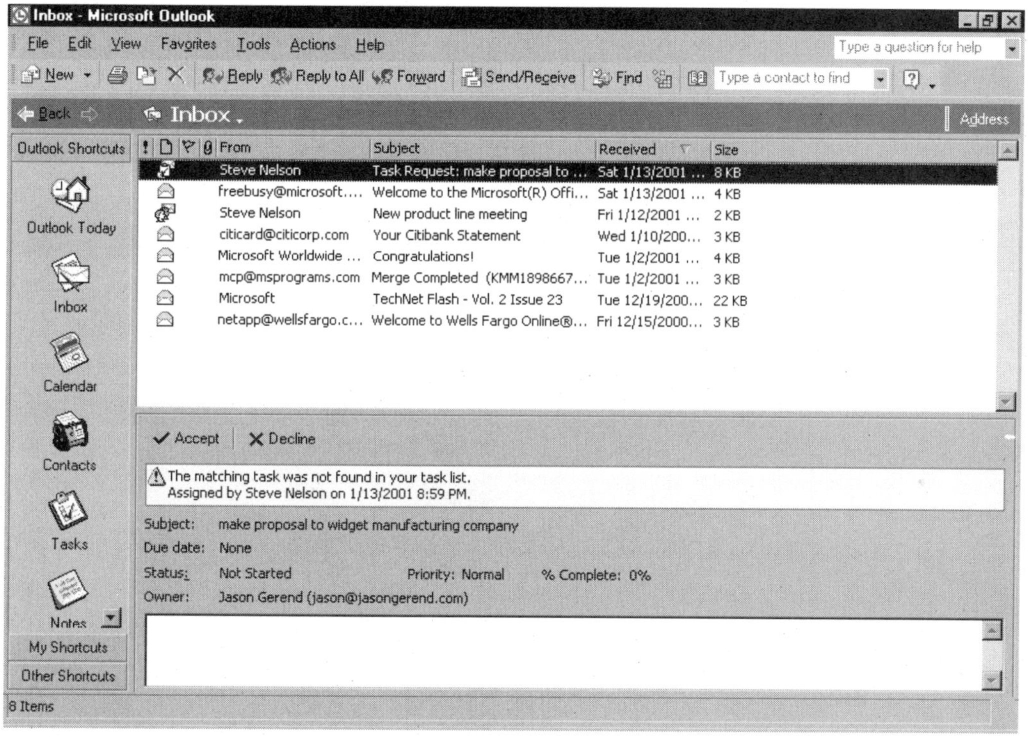


**Figure 6-34** A task request in the Inbox.

2. **Accept or decline the request.**

   Click the Accept button to take ownership of the task, and choose whether to edit the response before sending it (if you have some changes to make) or to send it immediately. Outlook then removes it from the Inbox, adds it to your Tasks folder, and notifies the sender that you accepted the task.

   Click the Decline button to refuse the task request, which deletes the task request and notifies the sender that you declined it.

NOTE *In some instances, there may not be Accept or Reject buttons. To accept the task in this situation, reply to the message stating that you'll accept the task, and then drag the message to your Tasks folder to create a new task based on the message.*

## Updating Tasks

As you work on a task, you'll probably want to update its status—perhaps send a status report or mark the task as complete. To do so, follow these steps:

1. **Open the task.**

   Double-click the task in the Tasks folder to open it in its own window, as shown in Figure 6-35.

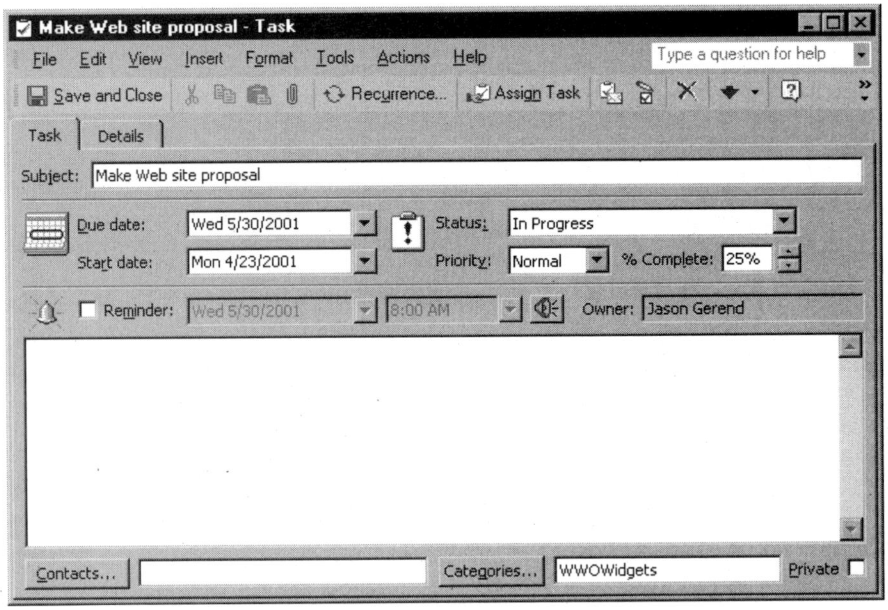


**Figure 6-35** Updating a task.

2. **Update the task.**

   Use the Status, % Complete and notes fields to update the task.

3. **Mark the task complete (if it is).**

   Click the Mark Complete toolbar button if you're finished with the task.

4. **Send a status report.**

   To do so, click the Send Status Report toolbar button and use the Task Status Report window to compose and send the status report e-mail message.

TIP *You can also mark tasks as complete by selecting the check box next to them in the Tasks folder.*

## Changing the Appearance of the Tasks Folder

Although the Tasks folder's default view—Simple List—is great for providing an uncluttered view of your tasks, you may want to switch to a more sophisticated view. Other views provide more information about the tasks, as well as let you view them in different ways.

To choose an alternate view, choose the View menu's Current View command and then choose a view from the submenu, as described below:

- To use a more detailed list format, use the Detailed List view.
- To filter out tasks that are marked as complete, use the Active Tasks view.
- To display only tasks due in the next week, use the Next Seven Days view. Outlook hides all messages that don't have a due date in the next seven days. (It hides overdue tasks as well.)
- To display only overdue tasks, use the Overdue Tasks view.
- To display tasks grouped by category, use the By Category view, as shown in Figure 6-36. This is one of the most useful ways of viewing the Tasks folder, and many people use this view predominately.

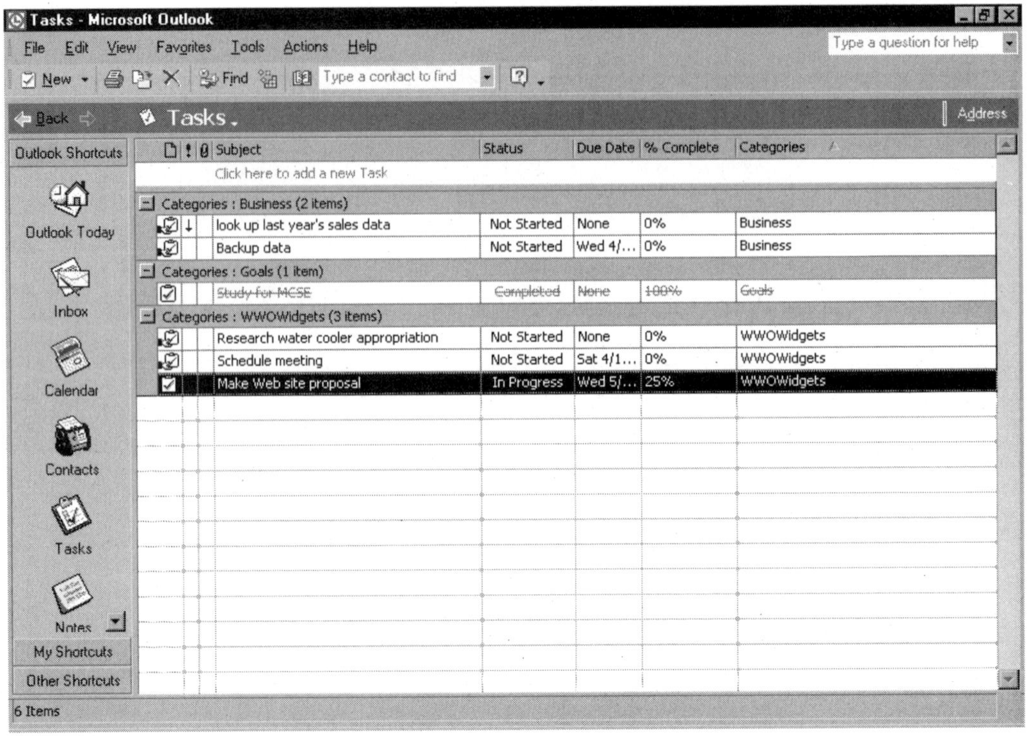

**Figure 6-36** The By Category task view.

NOTE *For some views, Outlook displays (Filter Applied) next to the Tasks folder heading to indicate that it's not displaying all items.*

- To display only overdue tasks, use the Overdue Tasks view.
- To view tasks according to who's responsible for them, use the By Person Responsible view. This view is preferable to the more limited Assignment view.
- To display only completed tasks, use the Completed Tasks view.
- To display tasks in a Gantt-style timeline view, which displays the start and end dates for tasks, use the Task Timeline view, as shown in Figure 6-37.

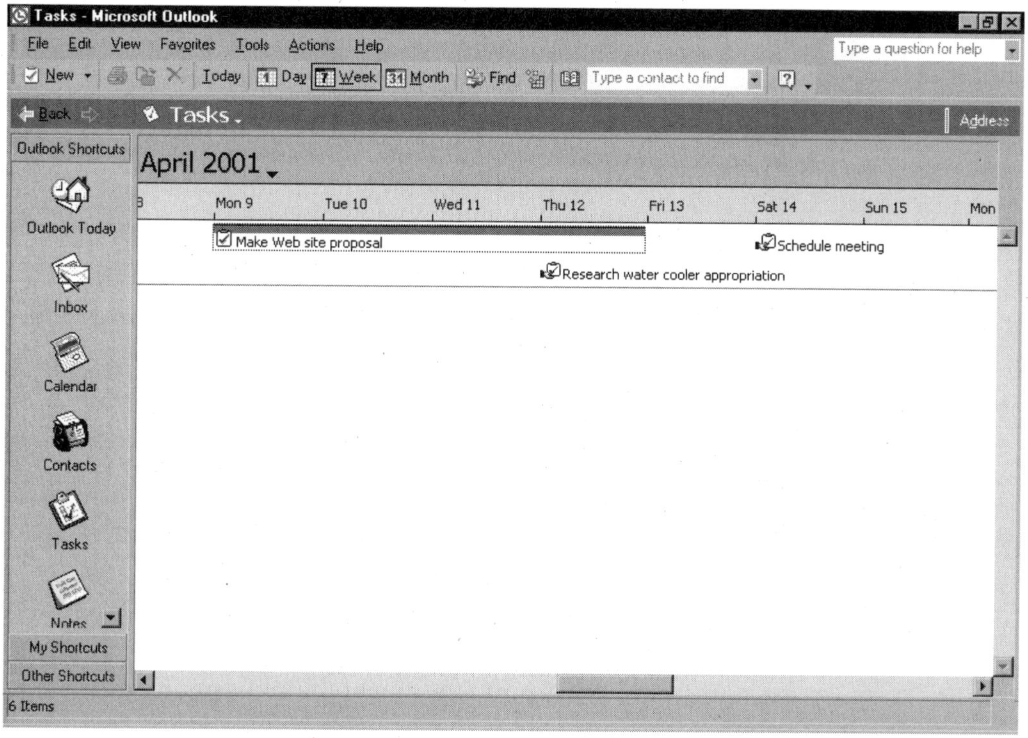


**Figure 6-37** The Task Timeline view.

TIP *You can apply many of these views to other Outlook folders.*

# Using Reminders

You can set reminders for almost any item in Outlook—messages, tasks, calendar items—even contacts. (The only item that you can't set a reminder for is Notes.)

When a reminder comes due, Outlook displays the newly enhanced Reminders window, as shown in Figure 6-38. (If Outlook isn't currently running, it displays this window the next time you open Outlook.)

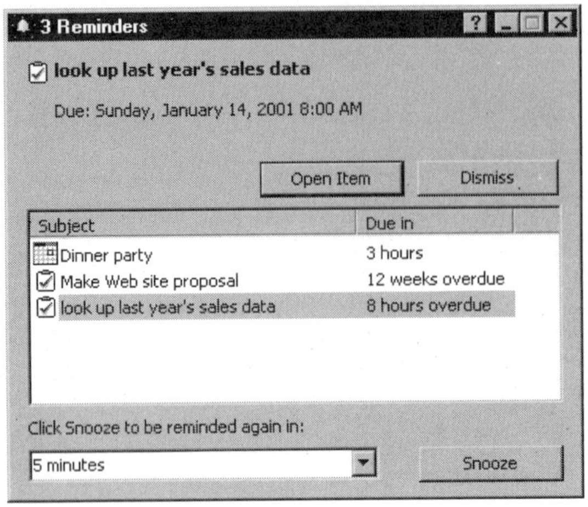


**Figure 6-38** The Reminders window.

To work in the Reminders window, use the following list:

- To open an item, double-click the item or select the item and then click the Open Item button.
- To dismiss a reminder, select the item and click the Dismiss button.
- To be reminded of the item again later, select how long to postpone the reminder from the drop-down list box at the bottom of the window and then click the Snooze button.
- To mark a task as completed from the Reminders window, right-click the task and choose Mark Complete from the shortcut menu.
- To close the Reminders window, click the Close button (marked with an X) in the top right corner of the window.
- To open the Reminders window, choose the View menu's Reminders Window command.

# Summary

In this skill we discussed how to use the Calendar and Tasks folders to effectively manage your time, as well as how to use the Reminders window to handle reminders that you set for appointments, tasks, or other Outlook items. Some of the tasks that we covered include creating appointments and events, planning meetings, creating tasks, and assigning tasks to other Outlook users.

*Skill 7*

# MAINTAINING OUTLOOK

**Featuring:**

- Managing Outlook Data Files
- Managing E-Mail Accounts
- Sharing Data Between Computers
- Backing Up and Restoring Outlook Data
- Customizing Outlook
- Troubleshooting Common Problems

Although Outlook is usually set up well to begin with, you may want to make some changes so that Outlook serves you better and perform some tasks on a regular schedule to increase Outlook's operating efficiency. These tasks include emptying the Deleted Items folder, archiving old items, managing e-mail accounts, and backing up your Outlook data.

In this skill we show you how to accomplish these tasks as well as how to manage your e-mail accounts, back up and restore your Outlook data and settings, and troubleshoot some common problems.

## Managing Outlook Data Files

You may want to perform a few maintenance tasks with Outlook's data files to keep Outlook running optimally. These tasks include cleaning up your folders to reduce hard disk space as well as opening or creating other Outlook data files. You may also need to manage your e-mail accounts.

## Cleaning Up Folders to Improve Performance

All Outlook items are stored in folders such as the Inbox, the Contacts folder, and the Calendar folder. These folders in turn are stored within a single data file called a folder store.

After using Outlook for a while, this folder store can start to get big, especially if you send or receive messages with large attachments. A large folder store causes Outlook to consume more system memory and hard disk space, and makes searching for items slower.

For this reason, Outlook provides the Mailbox Cleanup tool, which you can use to control the size of your Outlook folder store.

WARNING *Don't let your Outlook folder store exceed 2GB (2 million KB) in size. Doing so will render all data stored within it inaccessible. Check the size of your Outlook folder store by choosing the Tools menu's Mailbox Cleanup command and then clicking the first Click Here button.*

### Finding Items to Delete

The Mailbox Cleanup tool makes it easy to find old or large items that you may want to delete. To do so, follow these steps:

1. **Open the Mailbox Cleanup tool.**

   Choose the Tools menu's Mailbox Cleanup command. Outlook displays the Mailbox Cleanup tool, as shown in Figure 7-1.

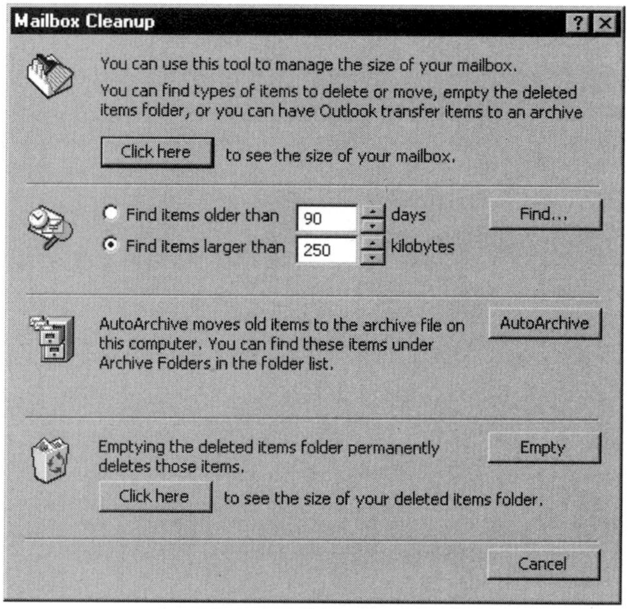


Figure 7-1 The Mailbox Cleanup tool.

2. **Specify a minimum size or age.**

   Select the Find Items Older Than option to search for old items, or leave the Find Items Large Than option selected to search for large items (recommended). Use the box provided to specify a minimum size or age to look for, and then click the Find button.

3. **Delete unneeded items.**

   In the Advanced Find dialog box, as shown in Figure 7-2, select the items you no longer need, and press the Delete key to delete them.

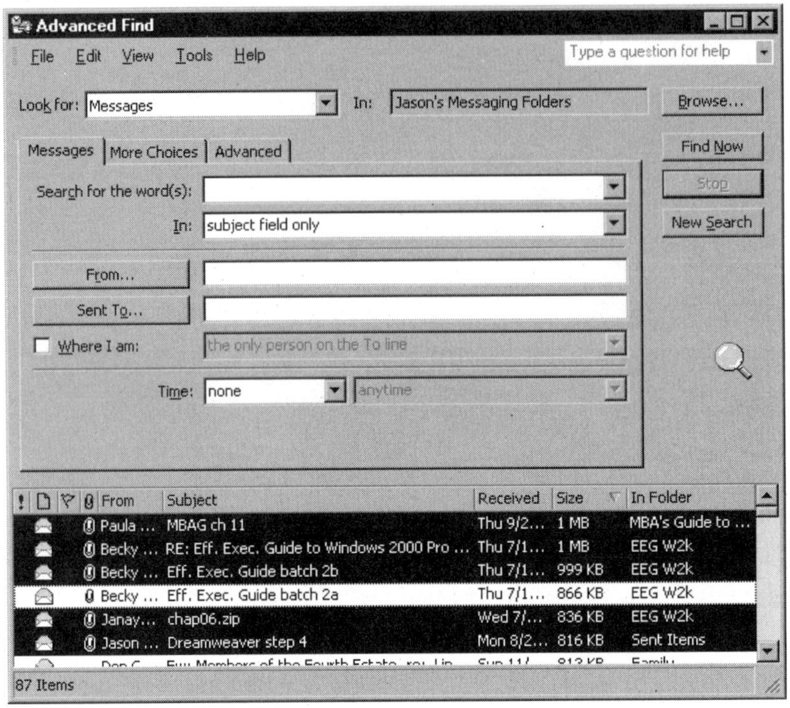


**Figure 7-2** Selecting unneeded items to delete.

## Using AutoArchive

If you want to clean up your Outlook folder store but want to keep a record of old files, we recommend that you archive them using Outlook's AutoArchive feature. This feature takes old items and moves them to a separate folder store that you can access as needed.

AutoArchive is turned on by default and will run automatically every 14 days. To archive items manually, choose the File menu's Archive command and use the Archive dialog box to specify which folders to archive, or to use the default settings.

To modify the default AutoArchive settings, follow these steps:

1. **Open the AutoArchive dialog box.**

   Choose the Tools menu's Options command, click the Other tab, and then click the AutoArchive button.

2. **Specify how often to archive items.**

   In the first box, enter how often Outlook should archive your items, as shown in Figure 7-3. Clear the Prompt Before AutoArchive Runs check box if you want Outlook to do so without prompting you first. (Outlook will be less responsive while it's archiving.)

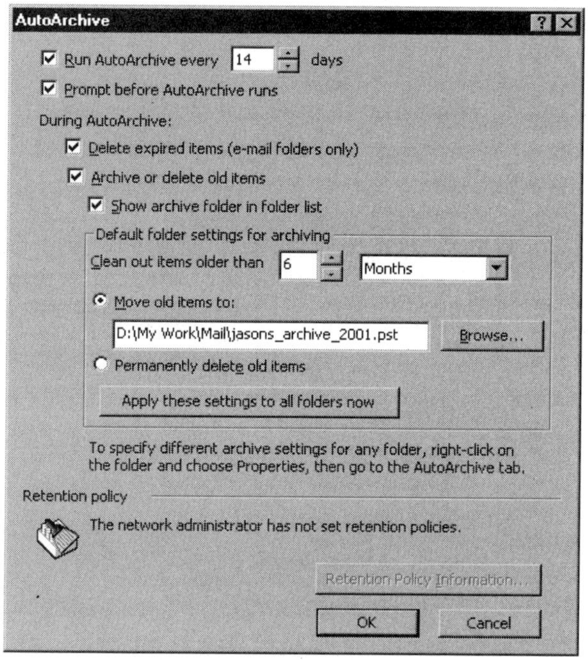


**Figure 7-3** Setting AutoArchive settings.

TIP *To disable AutoArchive, clear the Run AutoArchive Every [ ] Days check box.*

**3. Set a minimum age.**

In the Clean Out Items Older Than box, enter the minimum age of items that you want to archive.

**4. Specify an archive file to use.**

In the Move Old Items To box, use Outlook's default folder, or specify your own. (We recommend specifying a subfolder of your My Documents folder.)

**5. Optionally, apply these settings to all folders.**

If you had previously changed the AutoArchive settings for individual folders, click the Apply These Settings To All Folders Now button to apply the new settings to all folders. Click OK when you're finished.

**6. Optionally, modify the settings for individual folders.**

To change the AutoArchive settings for an individual folder, for example, to prevent Outlook from archiving items in the folder, right-click the appropriate folder either in the Outlook bar or in the Folder List, choose Properties from the shortcut menu, and then click the AutoArchive tab.

## Emptying the Deleted Items Folder

When you delete an item, Outlook moves it to the Deleted Items folder—the "Recycle Bin" of Outlook.

To empty the Deleted Items folder and free up hard drive space, right-click the Deleted Items folder and choose Empty Deleted Items from the shortcut menu. Click Yes when Outlook asks if you want to permanently delete the items.

WARNING *Emptying the Deleted Items folder permanently deletes the files—they don't end up in the Windows Recycle Bin. However, Exchange Server users can occasionally recover deleted items by choosing the Tools menu's Recover Deleted Items command.*

To set up Outlook to automatically empty the Deleted Items folder every time you exit Outlook, follow these steps:

1. **Open the Options dialog box.**

   Choose the Tools menu's Options command, and then click the Other tab, as shown in Figure 7-4.

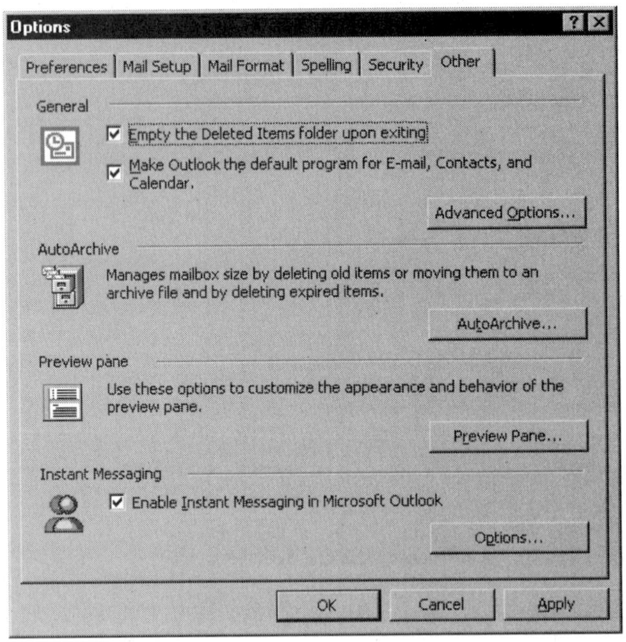


**Figure 7-4** Telling Outlook to automatically empty the Deleted Items folder.

2. **Select the Empty The Deleted Items Folder Upon Exiting check box.**

### Purging Deleted Messages from IMAP Folders

IMAP-based e-mail accounts don't store deleted messages in the Deleted Items folder—they simply mark the messages for deletion and leave them in their original folder.

This can quickly lead to a cluttered Inbox. To deal with this issue, you have two options:

- Hide deleted messages. To do so, choose the View menu's Current View command and then choose Hide Messages Marked For Deletion from the submenu.
- Purge deleted messages. To do this, choose the Edit menu's Purge Deleted Items command. This permanently removes deleted messages from the current IMAP folder.

## Opening Other Outlook Folder Stores

If you have multiple Outlook folder stores, such as your standard folder store (the Personal Folders File or Exchange Server mailbox) and one or more archive folders, at some point you'll probably want to open these other folders. To do so, follow these steps:

1. **Open the Create Or Open Outlook Data File dialog box.**

   Choose the File menu's Open command, and then choose Outlook Data File from the submenu.

2. **Choose the Outlook data file to open.**

   Use the Create Or Open Outlook Data File dialog box to locate and select the folder store you want to open, as shown in Figure 7-5. (Outlook folder stores are saved in the .pst or .ost file format.) Click OK to open the folder store.

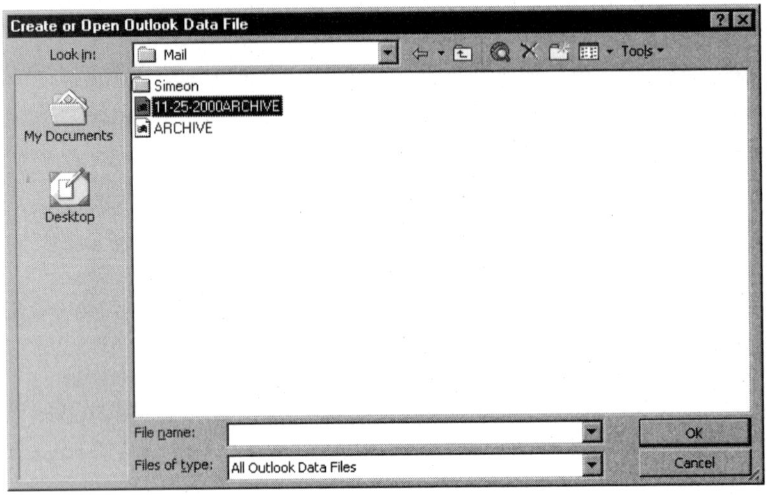


Figure 7-5 Opening an Outlook folder store.

NOTE *You can also manage Outlook folder stores by choosing the Tools menu's Data File Management command.*

3. **Display the folder you want.**

   Outlook initially displays the root of the folder store, which typically is blank. To access the items in the folder store, display the Folder List either by choosing the View menu's Folder List command or clicking the name of the folder store and then clicking the pushpin button in the upper right corner of the Folder List to keep the Folder List open. Use the Folder List to open other folders and work with your Outlook items.

4. **Close the folder store.**

   To close a folder store when you're finished, right-click the name of the folder store and choose Close from the shortcut menu, as shown in Figure 7-6.

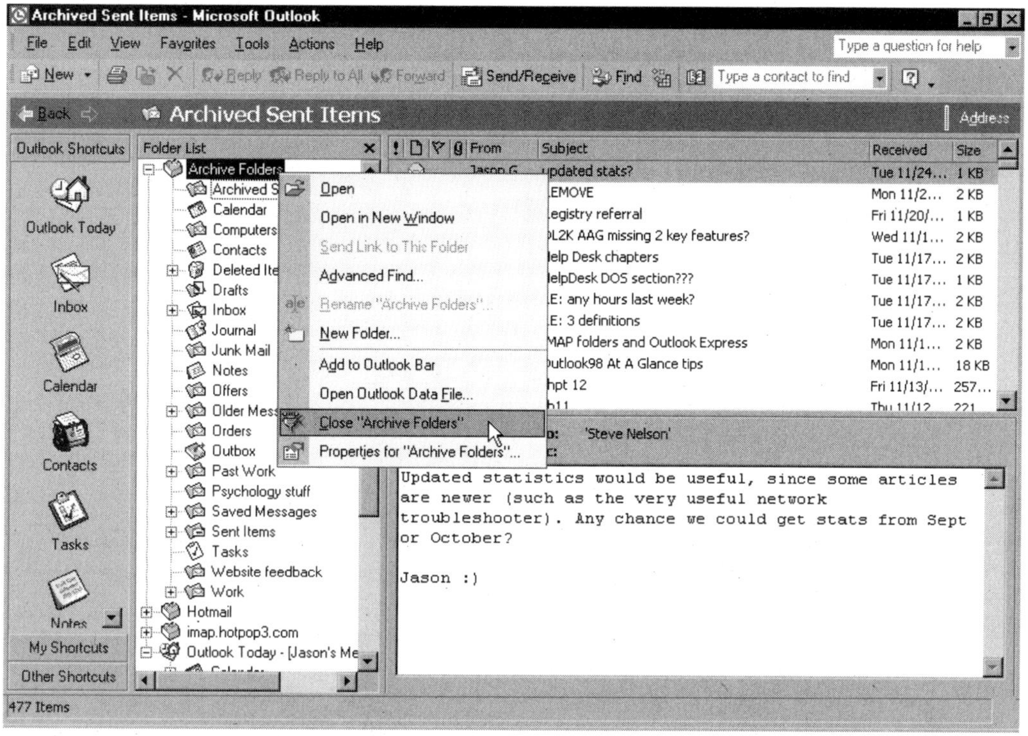


**Figure 7-6** Closing an Outlook folder store.

NOTE *Although accessing another folder store uses additional memory (RAM), Outlook manages this memory usage well, and most users won't find any performance penalty for leaving additional folder stores open.*

## Creating New Folder Stores

Although most business users don't need to create additional folder stores, you may want to for the following reasons:

- Outlook folder stores occasionally become corrupt, so compartmentalizing your data reduces the amount of data you might lose.
- Using multiple folder stores reduces the size of each folder store file, making them easier to back up.
- Outlook folder stores can't exceed 2GB in size without self-destructing. If you want to store more than 2GB of Outlook data, you must create additional folder stores.
- It's often a good idea to archive old archive folder stores. For example, you may want to rename your existing archive folder to something like 2001archive.pst, burn it on a CD-ROM, and start a new archive file.

However, before you get the idea that multiple folder stores are the path to e-mail nirvana, keep in mind that Outlook has some limitations when it comes to dealing with multiple folder stores:

- Reminders don't work in secondary folder stores.
- You can search through only one folder store at a time using Outlook's Find and Advanced Find commands.
- Message rules that move messages to a different folder store will work only if the other folder store is open in Outlook.

With this said, here's how to create new folder stores in Outlook:

1. **Open the Create Or Open Outlook Data File dialog box.**

   Choose the File menu's New command, and then choose Outlook Data File from the submenu. Alternatively, click the down arrow next to the New Message toolbar button and choose Outlook Data File from the pop-up menu.

2. **Specify a filename and location.**

   Select the folder in which you want to create your new folder store (we recommend either the current folder or a subfolder of the My Documents folder), and enter a filename. Click OK.

3. **Name the folder store.**

   Enter a name for the folder store in the Name box of the Create Microsoft Personal Folders dialog box, as shown in Figure 7-7.

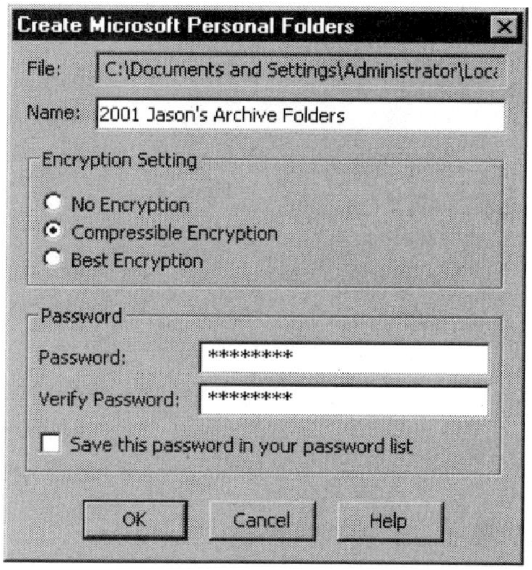


Figure 7-7 Creating an Outlook folder store.

4. **Specify security settings.**

   To encrypt the file for added security, click the Compressible Encryption option button (recommended). Click the Best Encryption option button if your items are particularly sensitive. Then enter a password in the Password boxes, and click OK.

5. **Create folders.**

   Outlook displays the root of your new folder, which is empty. Create folders or move existing folders into the new folder store, as discussed in "Skill 4: Managing Your E-Mail."

## Managing E-Mail Accounts

To manage your e-mail accounts—delete old accounts, change the folder store to which messages are delivered, modify account settings, or switch dial-up accounts—follow these steps:

1. **Open the E-Mail Accounts dialog box.**

   Display the Inbox, choose the Tools menu's E-Mail Accounts command, and then click Next.

2. **Specify the folder store where Outlook should deliver mail.**

   Outlook delivers all messages from your POP3 e-mail accounts to the folder store–that's shown in the list box at the bottom of the E-Mail Accounts dialog box, as shown in Figure 7-8. To specify a different folder store, select the appropriate data file from the drop-down list box.

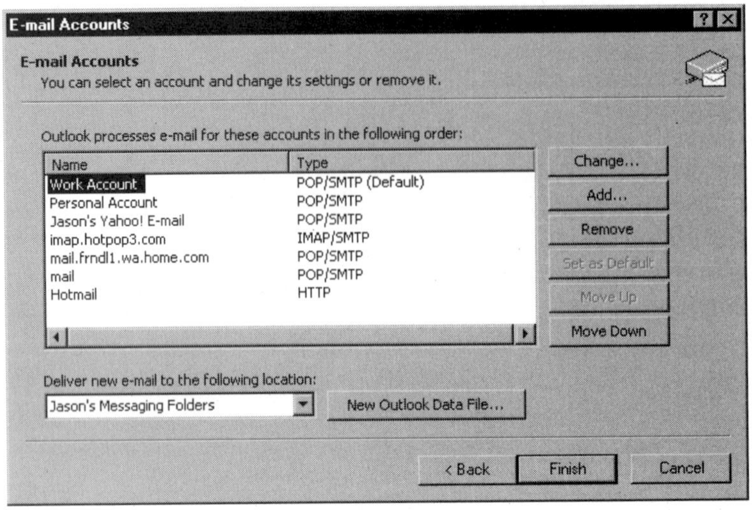


**Figure 7-8** Managing e-mail accounts.

TIP *To set up or modify Send/Receive groups, see "Skill 2: Reading E-Mail."*

3. **Remove unneeded e-mail accounts.**

   Select any obsolete e-mail accounts, and click the Remove button. This speeds up Outlook's Send/Receive process.

4. **Specify the order in which Outlook checks your accounts.**

   Use the Move Up and Move Down buttons to reorder your e-mail accounts so that Outlook checks for new messages on the most important accounts first.

5. **Modify account settings.**

   Select an account you want to modify, and click the Change button to display the account's settings. In the Incoming and Outgoing Mail Server boxes, enter the mail server names provided to you by your network administrator or mail provider. Enter your e-mail user name and password in the User Name and Password boxes. Click the Test Account Settings button (POP accounts only) to test your settings.

6. **Modify advanced settings.**

   From the Internet E-Mail Settings, click the More Settings button. Use the following list to modify advanced e-mail settings:

   - To change the name Outlook uses for the account, enter a descriptive name on the General tab and, optionally, enter your organization's name.
   - To have replies sent to a different e-mail address, enter that address in the Reply E-Mail box on the General tab.

- To force Outlook to log on to your outgoing mail (SMTP) server, use the Outgoing Server tab.
- To change how Outlook connects to the Internet for this mail account, click the Connection tab. If you use a dial-up connection, click the Connect Using Internet Explorer's Or A 3rd Party Dialer option button, as shown in Figure 7-9, to centralize your Internet connection settings.

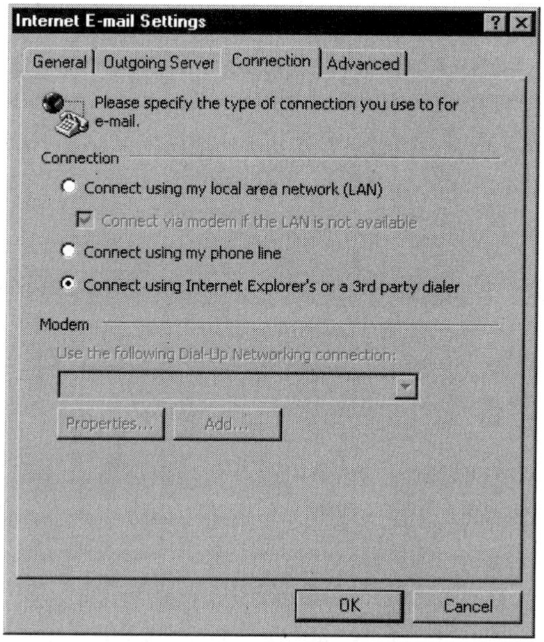


**Figure 7-9** Changing how Outlook connects to the Internet.

- To increase the amount of time Outlook allows before timing out (giving up on) your mail server, or to leave a copy of messages on your mail server, click the Advanced tab.

TIP *To change Microsoft Internet Explorer's connection settings, click the Start button, choose Settings, and then click Control Panel. Double-click the Internet Options icon, and then click the Connections tab.*

## Sharing Data Between Computers

A couple problems are inherent with trying to share messages and other Outlook data with another computer. First, Outlook stores all data in a single file—the Personal Folders File. (IMAP accounts are an exception—they store messages on the mail server but all other Outlook items in the locally stored Personal Folders File.) This file cannot be accessed while it's open, which means that if it's open on one computer, another computer can't access it.

Second, POP3 accounts weren't designed with sharing in mind. Since messages are downloaded and stored locally on your hard drive, you can't access these messages from another location or computer unless you have access to Outlook's Personal Folders File (which is unlikely for most users).

Microsoft briefly experimented with a Personal Folders Synchronization Wizard that would make it easy to synchronize Outlook data between multiple computers, but it apparently abandoned the effort. Until Microsoft releases this tool as a free download (it may never happen), you can work around these limitations in a couple ways, as described in the following sections.

NOTE *Users of Exchange Server accounts are exempt from this discussion—you can easily share a single Exchange Server mailbox with multiple computers using Outlook, and even access your folders from the Internet using a Web browser if your company's Exchange Server is set up with Outlook Web Access.*

## Leaving Messages on the Server

If you want to be able to check for new messages on more than one computer, but want to centralize the storage of all messages in one location (your primary computer), you can set up your secondary computer(s) to leave all messages on the server.

With this configuration, you can download messages on your secondary computer(s) to read, but your primary computer serves as the central repository. Once it downloads the messages, they're no longer available for downloading elsewhere.

Unfortunately, this solution has some drawbacks. Once you download messages on the primary computer, they're no longer available for reading on other computers (unless you configure all computers identically and only expend effort to manage messages on your primary computer). Additionally, you won't be able to read or access messages that you send using one computer from another (which is also the case with other Outlook items).

Despite these drawbacks, setting up Outlook to leave a copy of your messages on the server is the next best alternative to an IMAP-based account (which leaves all messages on the server). To do so, follow these steps:

1. **Open the E-Mail Accounts dialog box.**

   On each computer except your primary computer, display the Inbox, choose the Tools menu's E-Mail Accounts command, and then click Next.

2. **Select your POP3 e-mail account, and click Change.**

3. **Open the account's advanced settings.**

   Click the More Settings button, and then click the Advanced tab in the E-Mail Settings dialog box.

4. **Select the Leave A Copy Of Messages On The Server check box.**

   We recommend that you also select the Remove From Server When Deleted From 'Deleted Items' check box as well, as shown in Figure 7-10.

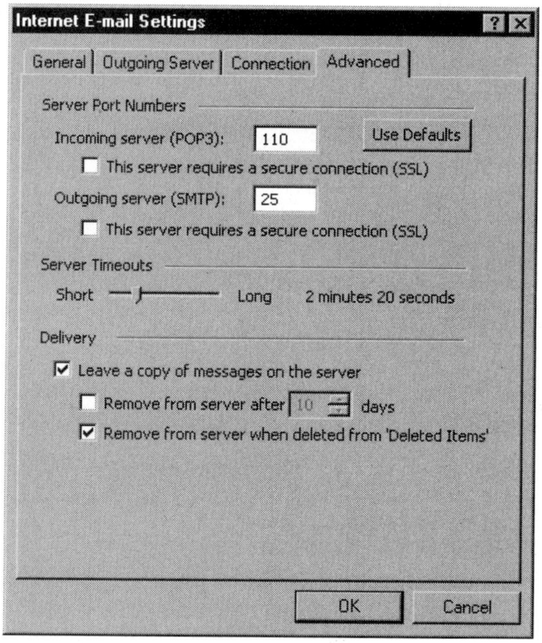


**Figure 7-10** Leaving a copy of messages on the server.

NOTE *Most e-mail accounts have a maximum mailbox size between 3.5MB and 10MB. If your Inbox exceeds this size, you will most likely receive one (or possibly many) warning messages, and then your e-mail provider will delete the oldest messages.*

## Sharing Your Folder Store on a Network

If your computer is on a network, you can share a single Outlook folder store among several computers, as long as you have Outlook open on only one computer at a time. To set this up on all computers you want to access your folder store, follow these steps:

1. **Open the Outlook folder store.**

   Choose the File menu's Open command, choose Outlook Data File from the submenu, and then locate and select the folder store you want to open. (It will need to be stored on a network share that's accessible from all necessary computers.) Click OK to open the folder store.

2. **Specify that Outlook should deliver e-mail to this folder store.**

   Choose the Tools menu's E-Mail Accounts command, click Next, and then select the correct folder store from the Deliver New E-Mail To The Following Location drop-down list box, as shown in Figure 7-11, and then click Finish.

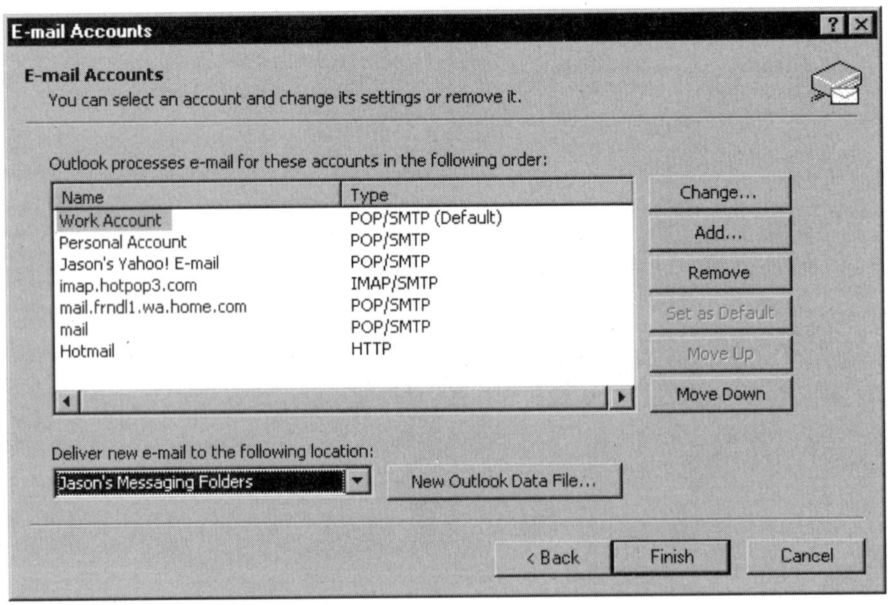


**Figure 7-11** Specifying the delivery location for e-mail.

3. **Restart Outlook.**

   Outlook will ask if it's OK to rebuild the Outlook bar. Click Yes to do so.

4. **Close your old folder store.**

   Although it's not necessary, if you want to close your old folder store, choose the View menu's Folder List command to display the Folder List, right-click the root of the old folder store, and choose Close from the shortcut menu.

## Backing Up and Restoring Outlook Data

As a business user, it's vital that you back up valuable data. This doesn't apply just to Outlook data—it is true for all of your data.

If you're on a corporate network, it's likely that your data is stored on a network server that is automatically backed up on a nightly basis, obviating the need for you to worry about it. If you're in a smaller environment, chances are the backup duty falls on you. In this case, use the next two sections to learn how to back up and restore your Outlook data and settings.

### Backing Up Your Outlook Data and Settings

The proper way to back up your Outlook data is to perform a full system backup of your entire computer—programs, Windows, data, and all. However, if you want to make a special backup of *just* your Outlook data and settings to supplement your full backups, follow these steps:

1. **Write down the names of your Outlook folder stores.**

   Choose the View menu's Folder List command, right-click the folder store you want to back up, and choose Properties from the shortcut menu. Click the Advanced button, and then make a note of the path listed in the Filename box.

NOTE *The Outlook Personal Folders Backup tool, which should be available for download from* http://officeupdate.com, *makes backing up your Outlook folder store much easier. You will still need to use steps 4 through 8 below to back up your message rules and Outlook settings.*

2. **Locate the folder stores.**

   Click the Start button, choose Search, and then click Search For Files And Folders. In the Search Results window, as shown in Figure 7-12, type **.pst* in the Search For Files Or Folders Named box to locate all Personal Folder Files on your local hard drives.

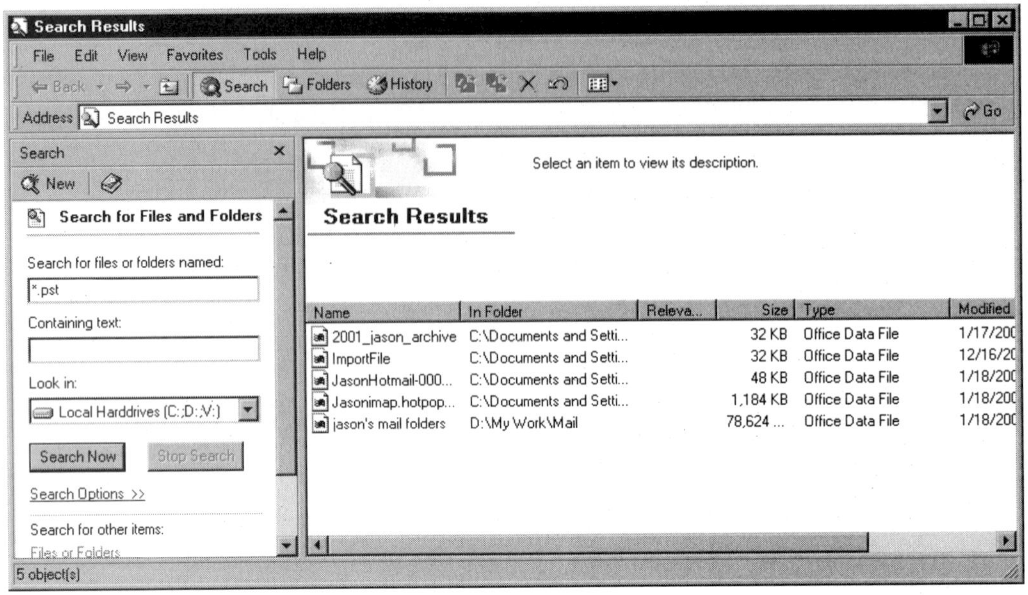


**Figure 7-12** Locating your Outlook folder stores.

3. **Copy or back up the folder stores.**

   To copy the files, open Windows Explorer to the backup location or your choice and then drag your folder stores to this location.

NOTE *You can also use a backup program such as Windows Backup to back up your folder stores. Simply locate the folder stores as described here, and add them to your normal backup operations.*

4. **Open the Save My Settings Wizard.**

   Close all open Microsoft Office programs, and then click the Start button, choose Programs, choose Microsoft Office, and then click Save My Settings Wizard. Click Next to begin the wizard.

5. **Choose to save or restore settings.**

   Click the Save The Settings From This Machine option button, as shown in Figure 7-13, and click Next.

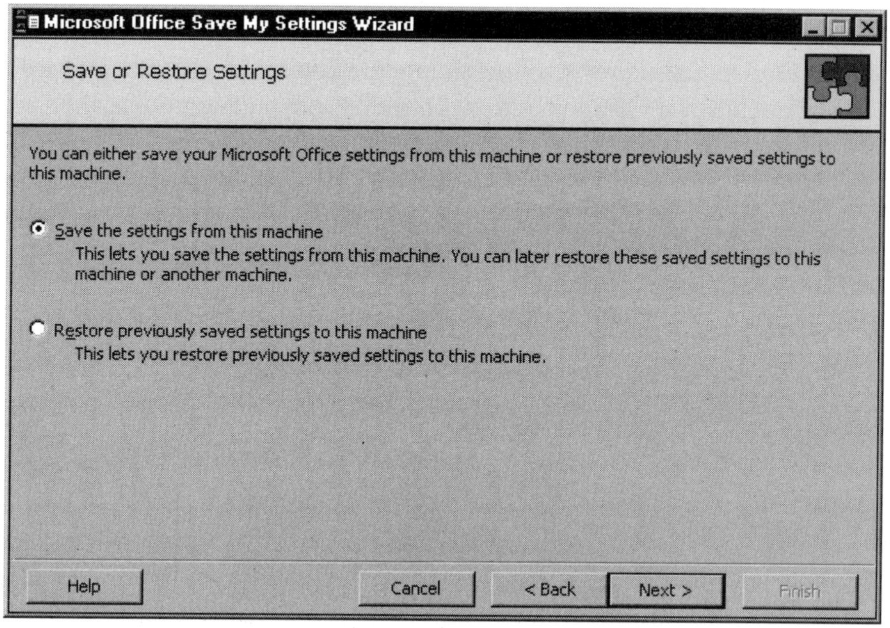


**Figure 7-13** The Save My Settings Wizard.

**6. Choose where to save your settings.**

Click the Save The Settings To The Web option button to save your Office 2002 settings to a secure and private Microsoft Web server. This allows you to retrieve the settings anywhere with an Internet connection. Alternatively, click the Save The Settings To A File option button and specify the location where to save the file, and then click Finish.

NOTE *Unfortunately, there is no easy way to back up your e-mail accounts. You should write down your account settings as a backup.*

**7. Sign in, and specify an e-mail address.**

Click Next, and sign in to Microsoft Passport, if required. In the next screen, enter an e-mail address where you want to be notified when your settings will expire. (Microsoft stores them for three months before you need to update them.) Click Finish to upload your settings to Microsoft's server.

8. **Back up your message rules.**

   Open Outlook, display the Inbox, choose the Tools menu's Rules Wizard command, and then click the Options button. In the Options dialog box, as shown in Figure 7-14, click the Export Rules button, specify a filename and location, and click the Save button.

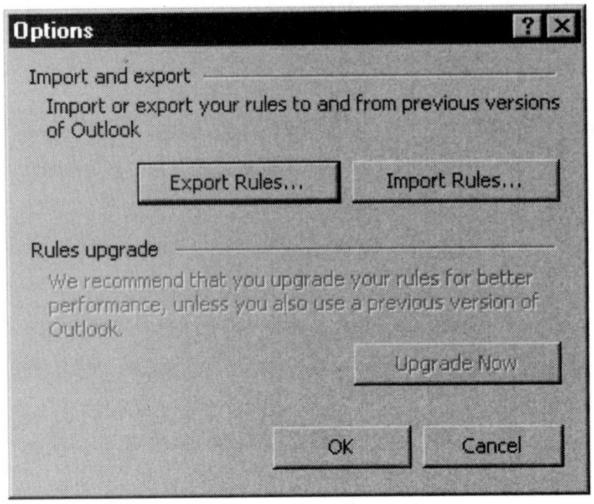


**Figure 7-14** Backing up message rules.

# Restoring from a Backup

To restore your Outlook data and settings or to transfer them to a new computer, follow these steps:

1. **Restore your Outlook settings.**

   Close all open Office programs, and then click the Start button, choose Programs, choose Microsoft Office, and then click Save My Settings Wizard. Click Next, click the Restore Previously Saved Settings To This Machine option button, click Next again, select where to restore your settings from, and then click Finish.

2. **Copy your folder stores to the correct location.**

   Copy (or restore from backup) your Outlook folder stores to their original location, or designate a suitable location on your new computer (we recommend the My Documents folder).

3. **Open the folder stores.**

   In Outlook, choose the File menu's Open command, and then choose Outlook Data File from the submenu. Locate and select the folder store you want to open, and then click OK to open the folder store.

4. **Specify the folder store where Outlook should deliver mail.**

   Display the Inbox, choose the Tools menu's E-Mail Accounts command, and then click Next. Choose the appropriate data file from the drop-down list box, and then click Finish.

5. **Import your message rules.**

   Choose the Tools menu's Rules Wizard command, and then click the Options button. In the Options dialog box (see Figure 7-14), click the Import Rules button, specify the filename and location, and click the Open button.

# Customizing Outlook

Outlook's default setup is a good start, but you may want to change Outlook to better suit your particular needs. For example, you may want to customize the Outlook bar, prevent Outlook from using Microsoft Word as its e-mail editor, or make other changes.

## Customizing the Outlook Bar

The Outlook bar is an extremely useful location to place shortcuts to your most frequently accessed folders. Although the Outlook bar is usually configured optimally when you first begin to use Outlook, as you create additional folders you may want to customize the Outlook bar so that your most important shortcuts are easily reachable.

To customize the Outlook bar, use the following list:

- To change the size of the shortcuts displayed in the Outlook bar, right-click the group's name on the Outlook bar and choose Small Icons or Large Icons from the shortcut menu, as shown in Figure 7-15.

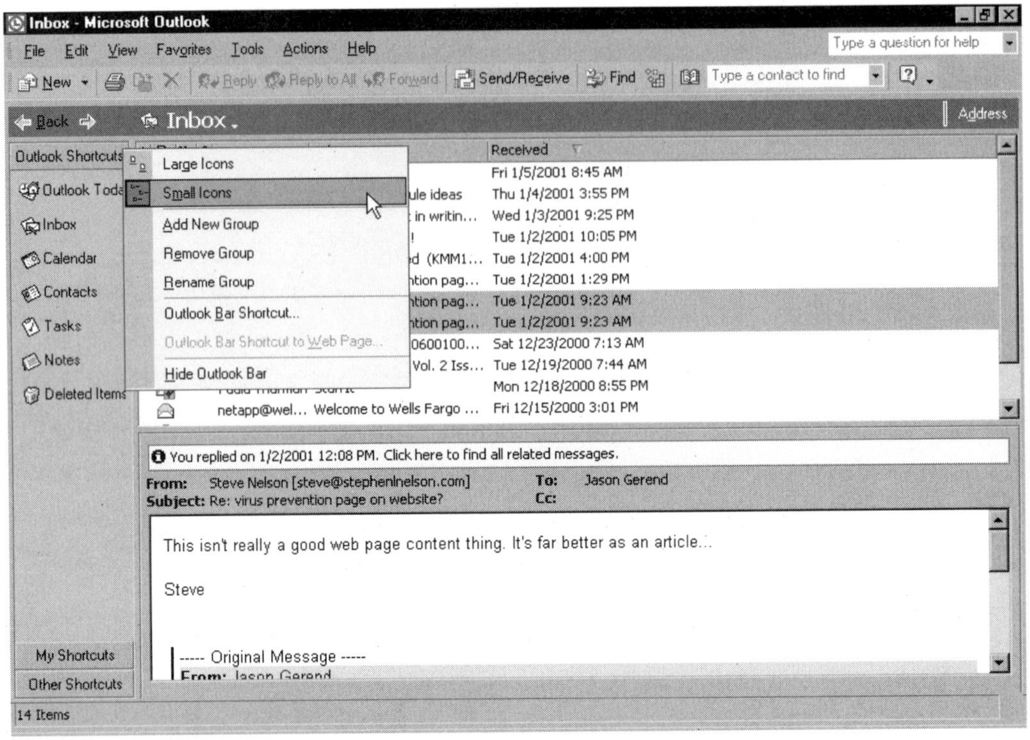


**Figure 7-15** Changing the size of Outlook bar shortcuts.

- To add a shortcut to the Outlook bar, first display the Folder List by clicking the Inbox folder title (next to the Back button) and clicking the pushpin button to lock it open. Then drag the folder you want to create a shortcut to onto the Outlook bar.
- To rename a shortcut, right-click the shortcut and choose Rename Shortcut from the shortcut menu.
- To remove a shortcut from the Outlook bar, right-click the shortcut and choose Remove From Outlook Bar from the shortcut menu.
- To move a shortcut to a new location on the Outlook bar, drag the shortcut to the location of your choice.
- To move the shortcut into a different group, drag the shortcut onto the group's button, such as My Shortcuts, wait until the group opens, and then drag the shortcut to the desired location in the open group.
- To add a new group for shortcuts, right-click a group, choose Add New Group from the shortcut menu, enter a name for the group, and then click elsewhere. (You have a maximum of 12 groups.)

- To add a shortcut to a file or folder on your hard drive or the Internet, open Windows Explorer or Internet Explorer and drag the file or Internet address to the location of your choice on the Outlook bar.
- To hide the Outlook bar, right-click a group and choose Hide Outlook Bar from the shortcut menu. If you hide the Outlook bar, consider displaying the Folder List.

## Disabling Word as Your E-Mail Editor

Using Word as your e-mail editor has a number of advantages, such as better language handling capabilities and enhanced spelling and grammar checking tools and abilities. However, using Word does use more system memory and prevent you from easily adding signatures on a message-by-message basis.

For these reasons, you may opt to use Outlook's built-in e-mail editor, which is quite capable in its own right. To switch your default e-mail editor, follow these steps:

1. **Open the Options dialog box.**

   Choose the Tools menu's Options command, and then click the Mail Format tab, as shown in Figure 7-16.

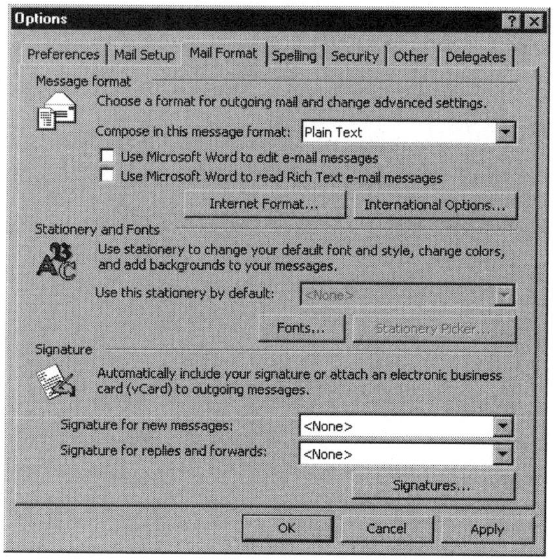


**Figure 7-16** Disabling Word as your e-mail editor.

2. **Clear the Use Microsoft Word To Edit E-Mail Messages check box.**

   Click OK when you're finished.

TIP *If your default editor is Outlook but you want to use Word to create a single e-mail message, display the Inbox, choose the Actions menu's New Mail Message Using command, and then choose Microsoft Word from the shortcut menu.*

# Troubleshooting Common Problems

Although Outlook is a robust application, you'll inevitably run into trouble at some point. The following sections cover a few of the most common issues. For additional help, see the end of "Skill 1: Getting Started with Outlook" for a list of resources.

## Locating Missing IMAP Folders

In general, IMAP folders behave like any other folders in Outlook. However, if you seem to be missing some folders, this might be because you're not "subscribed" to them. To remedy this situation, use the IMAP Folders tool. To use the tool, follow these steps:

1. **Display your IMAP account's Inbox.**

   A shortcut to your IMAP Inbox usually appears beneath the regular Inbox and bears the name of your IMAP server.

2. **Choose the Tools menu's IMAP Folders command.**
3. **Enter the name of the missing folder.**

   If you can remember the name of the missing folder, enter it in the box provided; otherwise, leave it empty.

4. **Click Query.**

   Outlook displays a list of folders in your IMAP account. Double-click a folder to subscribe to it, which adds it to the list of folders that Outlook displays and synchronizes.

## Messages Are Stuck in the Outbox

If messages are stuck in the Outbox and Outlook won't deliver them, follow these steps:

1. **Send messages on all accounts.**

   Choose the Tools menu's Send/Receive command, and then choose Send All from the submenu. This forces Outlook to send messages on all accounts, even those that are excluded from normal Send/Receive operations because of Send/Receive groups (discussed in "Skill 2: Reading E-Mail").

2. **Open the message.**

   Display the Outbox by clicking the My Shortcuts group on the Outlook bar and then clicking the Outbox shortcut. Open any messages stuck here.

3. **Specify a valid account with which to send.**

   Click the Accounts toolbar button, and select the e-mail account you want to send the message with. (If you reply to a message sent to an e-mail account you no longer have, Outlook may try to use this obsolete account.)

4. **Resend the message.**

   Click the Send toolbar button to attempt to resend the message. Sometimes simply opening and resending a message will fix the problem.

## Mail Server Keeps Asking for a Password

Perhaps the most frequent problem that you will face when using Outlook with an Internet e-mail account is an account that doesn't seem to like your user name and password, even though they worked previously.

Unfortunately, this problem usually occurs when your e-mail server is temporarily busy or malfunctioning, or your Internet connection is down.To deal with this situation, follow these steps:

1. **Check your user name and password.**

   You've probably already done this, but double-check that you have the right user name and password.

2. **Check your Internet connection.**

   Open a Web browser and see if your Internet connection is working.

3. **Wait.**

   Chances are good that your mail server is temporarily unavailable. This happens to us on an almost daily basis, so we've gotten used to just clicking the Cancel button and waiting until the server decides to come back to life. This may be as quick as a couple minutes, or it may take all day.

4. **Re-create your mail account.**

   If the server never does come back to life, and you are sure that your user name, password, and mail server settings are correct, your e-mail account may be corrupt. Create a new account and test it. If the new account works, delete the old one. If you still can't get your e-mail working, it's time to call your e-mail provider.

## Repairing Your Outlook Folder Store

Although it doesn't happen often, Outlook's Personal Folders File can become corrupted, preventing you from accessing your items. To fix this problem, use the Inbox Repair tool. To do so, follow these steps:

1. **Open Windows' Search or Find tool.**

   To do so, click the Start button, choose Search, and then click Search For Files And Folders.

2. **Find the Inbox Repair tool.**

   This tool is well hidden—we can never remember where it's located ourselves, so you need to search for it by entering *scanpst.exe* in the box provided, and clicking Search Now. Double-click the scanpst.exe file that Windows locates, as shown in Figure 7-17.

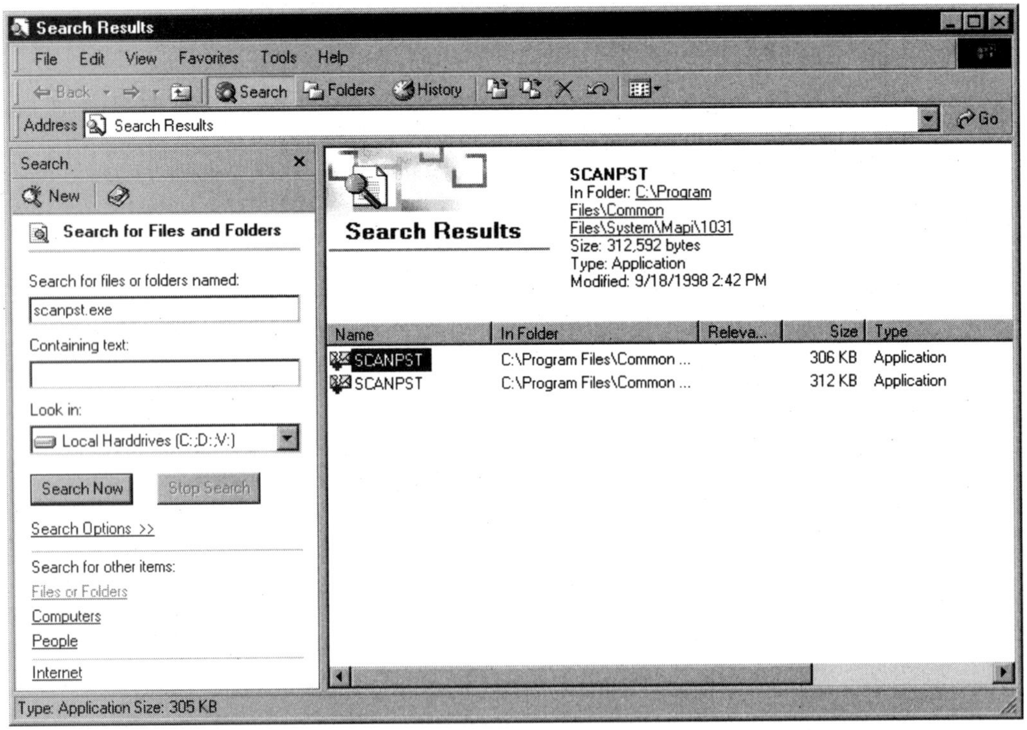


Figure 7-17 Finding the Inbox Repair tool.

3. **Specify the location of your Personal Folders File.**

   Click the Browse button in the Inbox Repair Tool dialog box, as shown in Figure 7-18, to locate your Outlook folder store. (If you have trouble finding it, use the Windows Search tool to perform a search for *.pst.)

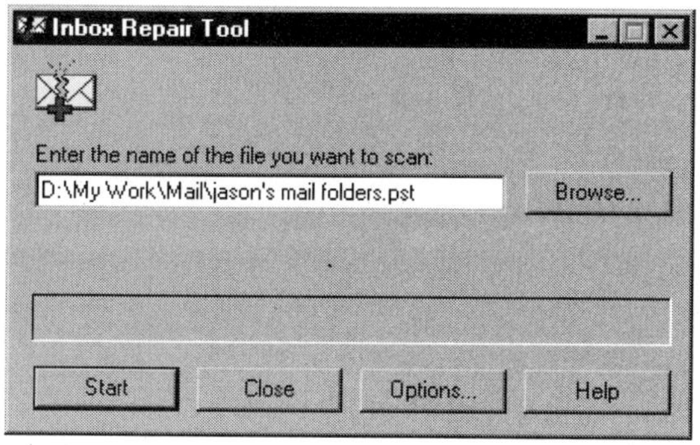


**Figure 7-18** The Inbox Repair tool.

4. **Scan the file.**

   Make sure that Outlook is closed, and then click the Start button to begin scanning your Personal Folders File. Note that Outlook doesn't actually make any repairs at this point.

5. **Repair any errors.**

   The Inbox Repair tool displays a summary of what it found. To repair your Personal Folders File, click the Repair button. (We highly recommend that you allow the tool to create a backup of your file, as it does by default.)

## Summary

In this skill we showed you a number of maintenance tasks that you may want to perform from time to time to keep Outlook running smoothly for you. These tasks included cleaning up your Outlook folders to improve performance, managing e-mail accounts, and backing up your Outlook data. We also showed you how to set up Outlook to check your messages from more than one computer and how to customize various aspects of Outlook.

# *Appendix A*

# USING NOTES

## Featuring:

- Creating Notes
- Working with Notes

Notes are a simple feature of Outlook that don't often get the credit they deserve. The digital equivalent to those sticky yellow pieces of paper that are no doubt adorning your monitor and workspace, Outlook Notes are also small and yellow.

Like sticky notes, Outlook Notes don't do much, but in their simplicity lies their power—they're perfect for jotting down things that don't yet warrant creating a task, document, or message. For example, we often use notes for writing down Web site URLs we want to investigate, issues we want to talk with coworkers about when they come back from lunch, or tips for using a clunky printer in the mail room.

## Creating Notes

To create a note, follow these steps:

1. **Click the Notes shortcut on the Outlook bar.**

   Outlook displays the Notes folder.

2. **Click the New Note toolbar button.**

3. **Jot your note.**

   In the new Note item, as shown in Figure A-1, enter anything that you want. When you're finished, you can leave the window open or close it. Outlook automatically saves your notes to the Notes folder.

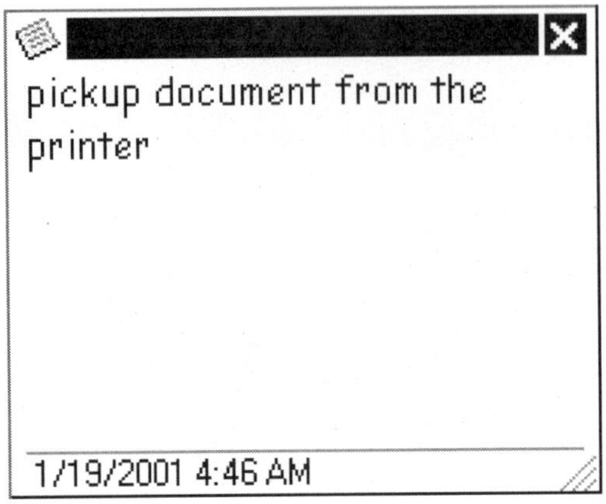


**Figure A-1** A note.

## Working with Notes

Use the following list to work with notes you create:

- To open a note, click the Notes shortcut on the Outlook bar and then double-click the note you want to open.
- To delete a note, select it and click the Delete toolbar button.
- To change the Notes folder view, click the Small Icons or List toolbar buttons.
- To link a note to a contact or category, click the icon in the top left of a note's window and choose Contacts or Categories from the shortcut menu.
- To change a note's color, click the icon in the top left of a note's window, choose Color from the shortcut menu, and choose a color from the submenu.
- To forward a note to another Outlook user, click the icon in the top left of a note's window and choose Forward from the shortcut menu.
- To save a note to the Microsoft Windows desktop, click the icon in the top left of a note's window and then choose Save As from the shortcut menu. Select Message Format from the Save As Type drop-down list box, and click Save.

NOTE *Notes are closed automatically when you close Outlook.*

*Appendix B*

# OUTLOOK AND EXCHANGE

**Featuring:**

- Server-Side Storage Overview
- Using Public Folders
- Using Delegates
- Setting Up Offline Folders
- Using the Out Of Office Assistant

Outlook 2002 functions almost identically whether you use it with or without an Exchange Server. However, Outlook provides some additional features when it's used in conjunction with an Exchange Server. These features include the ability to access public folders on your company or organization's Exchange Server to read and post messages, as well as the ability to set up delegates with access to your Outlook items.

In this appendix we cover these and other features, as well as providing you with an overview of Exchange Server's server-side storage of Outlook folders.

## Server-Side Storage Overview

Outlook items are stored differently when using an Exchange Server—they're stored on the server instead of your local computer.

When using Outlook with Internet mail accounts, you have one (or possibly more) Personal Folders File (folder stores with a .pst file extension) that resides on your hard drive. All Outlook items, including e-mail messages, appointments, and tasks, are stored in this file. (IMAP accounts are an exception—they store their messages on an IMAP server.) Your Contacts folder is also stored in this file.

When using Outlook with an Exchange Server, all Outlook data is stored on the Exchange Server in your Exchange Server mailbox. You also have access to another address book, the Global Address List, which is an address book listing all other users of your Exchange Server.

Although these features are generally transparent, note the following points about server-side storage:

- Message rules (in general) are run on the server, and therefore can continue processing your messages even when Outlook isn't open (or when you're out of the office).
- Accessing your items may take slightly longer because they must be retrieved from across the network.
- You can access your Outlook folders from any computer on the Exchange Server network where you have a user account and Outlook.
- Outlook synchronizes your Exchange Server mailbox with an offline folder file so that you can access your Outlook items while disconnected from the network (if properly set up). This is mostly automatic, although you have some control over this.
- Data is safer because it resides on the server, where it is probably backed up nightly.

# Using Public Folders

Public folders are folders on the Exchange Server where you can post messages for others in your company or organization to read, as well as read messages other Exchange Server users have posted. To use public folders, refer to the following sections.

## Reading Posts

To read posted messages in a public folder, follow these steps:

1. **Display the Folder List.**

   To do so, choose the View menu's Folder List command.

2. **Open the folder of your choice.**

   Click the plus sign next to the Public Folders folder store in the Folder List to view the public folders to which you have access. Select a folder to display the posts stored within it.

3. **Read the post of your choice.**

   Select a post to display the contents of the post in the Preview pane, as shown in Figure B-1. Press the spacebar to quickly scroll through the current message, and use the Up and Down arrow keys to view the next or previous message. To open a post in a separate window, double-click it.

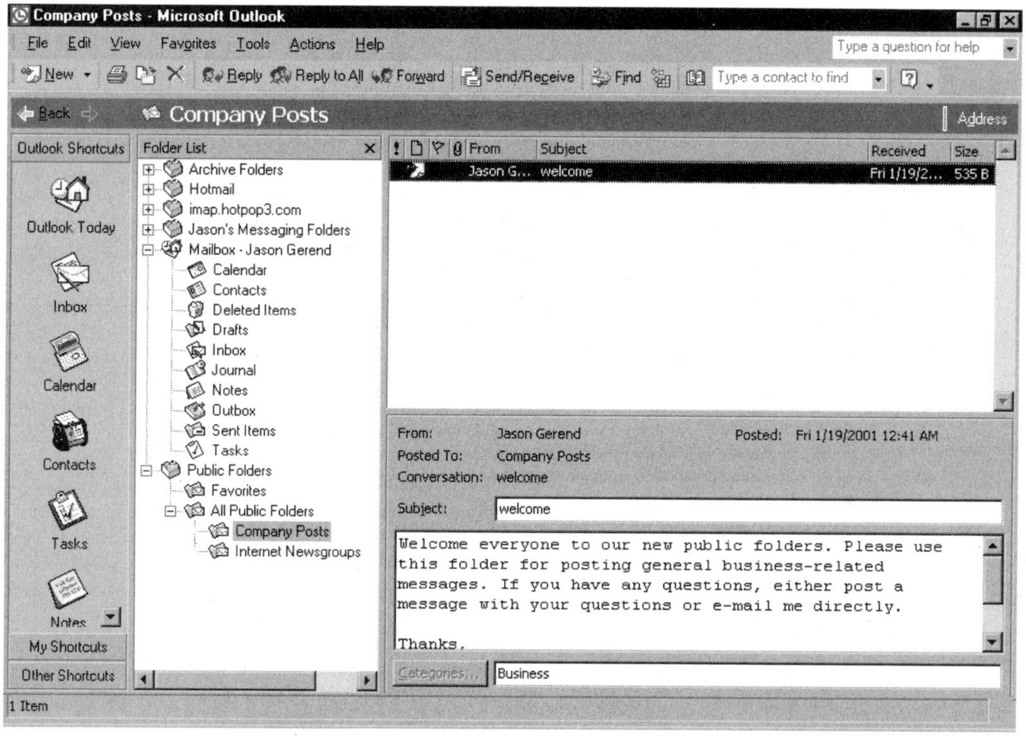


**Figure B-1** Reading a post in a public folder.

TIP *If your company or organization has many public folders, consider adding the ones you use most often to your public folders Favorites folder. To do so, right-click a folder and choose Add To Favorites from the submenu. Name the folder, and click Add.*

## Posting Messages

To post messages to a public folder, follow these steps:

1. **Create a new post.**

   Display the public folder you want, and then use one of the following techniques to create a new message:

   - To create a new blank message, click the New toolbar button or press Ctrl-Shift-S.
   - To reply to a message, select an existing message and click the Reply toolbar button.
   - To reply to all recipients of the selected message, click the Reply To All toolbar button.
   - To forward the selected e-mail to another person, click the Forward toolbar button.

2. **Enter a subject.**

   In the Subject box, enter a subject for the post. Keep the subject short (5 to 10 words or less), and make it easy to identify the contents of the message. Press the Tab key to move the cursor into the main message body.

TIP *Don't change the subject of posts to which you reply to unless you're changing the topic of conversation. Doing so makes it appear as if the post is starting a new conversation.*

3. **Compose the message.**

   Enter your message in the main message body as you would a normal e-mail, as shown in Figure B-2.

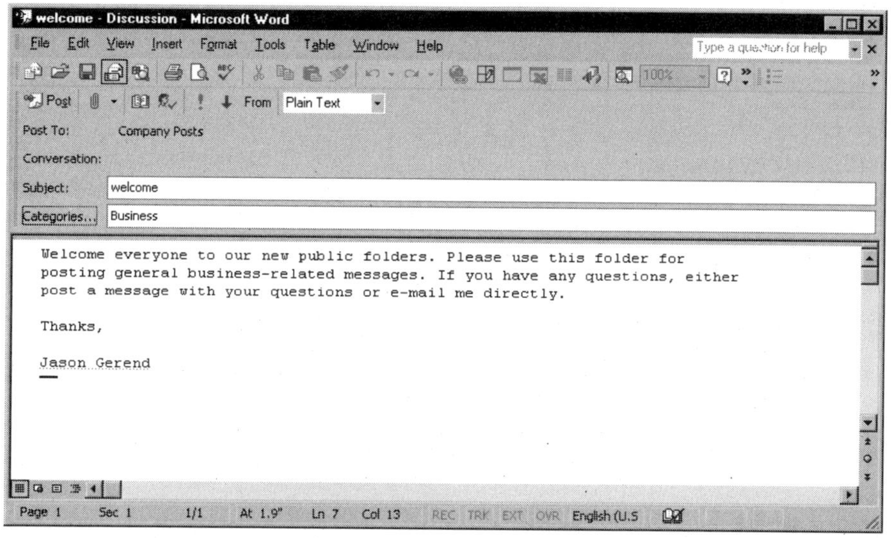


**Figure B-2** Composing a post for a public folder.

4. **Spell check your message.**

   Making spelling errors isn't a very good way to impress your superiors, and a good way of losing the respect of your employees, so check for spelling mistakes before posting any messages. If you have Microsoft Word 2002 installed, Outlook will underline misspelled words as you type, just like in Word. Right-click an underlined word to display a list of alternatives. If you don't have Word 2002, choose the Tools menu's Spelling command.

5. **Click the Post toolbar button.**

   Outlook posts the message to the public folder. If you discover an error after posting a message, edit it. To do so, open the message, make your corrections, and click the Post toolbar button again.

## Creating New Public Folders

If you have sufficient permissions, you can create additional public folders. To do so, follow these steps:

1. **Create a new folder.**

   Select the public folder in which you want to create a new folder, choose the File menu's New command, and then choose Folder from the submenu.

2. **Choose the type of items the folder should store.**

   In general, leave the folder type set to Mail And Post, as shown in Figure B-3. If you want to create a group calendar, choose Calendar.

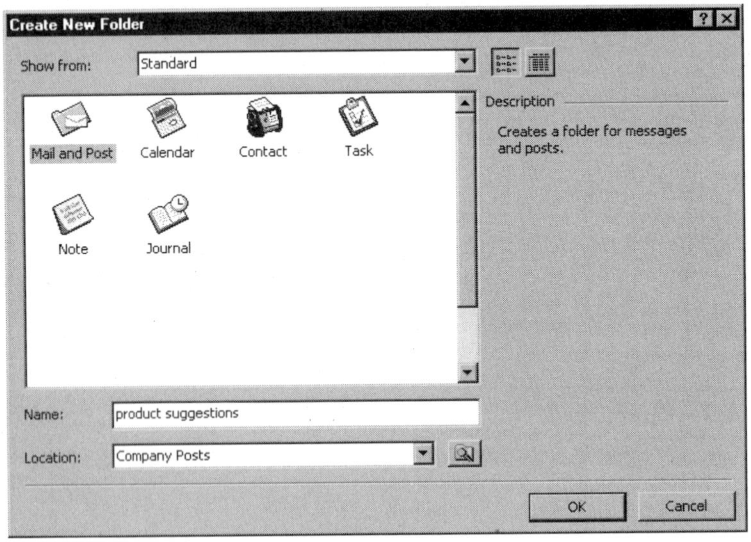


**Figure B-3** Specifying the folder type, name, and location.

3. **Name the folder.**

   Enter a short but descriptive name for the folder in the Name box.

4. **Specify where to place the folder.**

   Use the Location drop-down list box to select the folder in which you want to store your new folder. Alternatively, click the folder icon next to the box to visually select a folder.

5. **Click OK.**

   When Outlook asks if you want to create a shortcut to the folder on the Outlook bar, click Yes. Outlook creates the folder and adds a shortcut to the My Shortcuts group on the Outlook bar.

NOTE *To modify the permissions of the folder, create rules to process the posts or to set up the folder to be moderated, right-click the folder, and choose Properties from the shortcut menu.*

# Using Delegates

If you have an assistant or coworker with whom you collaborate closely, you may want to give them delegate access to your Outlook folders. Doing so allows them to send and receive messages on your behalf, as well as schedule appointments and manage your other Outlook folders.

Use the following sections to grant delegate access to another user, send messages on behalf of someone else, or open another user's Outlook folders to whom you've been granted delegate access.

## Assigning a Delegate

To grant another Exchange Server user delegate access to one or more of your Outlook folders, follow these steps:

1. **Open the Options dialog box at the Delegates tab.**

   Choose the Tools menu's Options command, and then click the Delegates tab.

2. **Click Add to add a delegate.**

3. **Select a delegate.**

   In the Add Users dialog box, select the user you want to grant delegate access to your Exchange mailbox, click Add, and then click OK.

4. **Specify delegate permissions.**

   For each Outlook folder, specify the permissions you want to grant the delegate, as shown in Figure B-4. Optionally, use the check boxes at the bottom of the dialog box to notify the delegate of these permissions or to allow them to see Outlook items you marked as private. Click OK when you're finished.

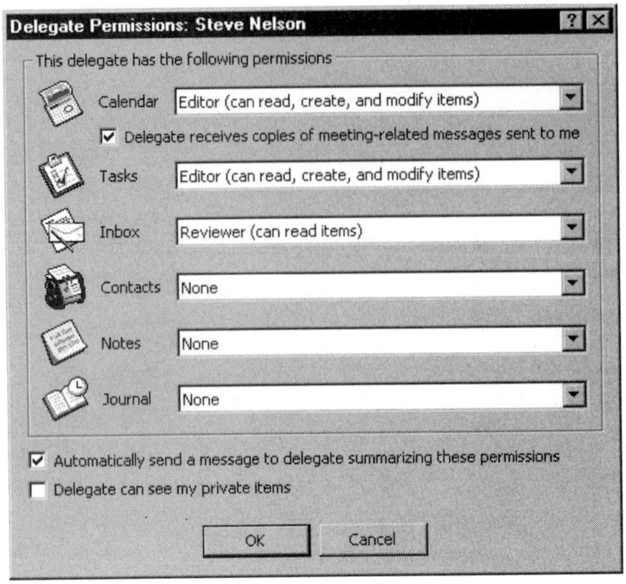


**Figure B-4** Settings permissions for a delegate.

NOTE *If the Delegates tab isn't available, click the Other tab instead, and then click the Advanced Options button. Click the Add-In Manager button in the next dialog box, and make sure the Delegate Access item is selected in the Add-In Manager dialog box.*

## Opening Another User's Folders

If another user has granted you delegate access to their Outlook folders, you can open them and work with them as if they were your own. To do so, follow these steps:

1. **Open the Open Other User's Folder dialog box.**

   Display the Inbox, choose the File menu's Open command, and then choose Other User's Folder from the submenu.

2. **Enter or select the appropriate user's name.**

   Enter the appropriate user's name in the Name box, as shown in Figure B-5. Alternatively, click the Name button, choose Global Address List from the Show Names From The drop-down list box, and then double-click the appropriate user's name.

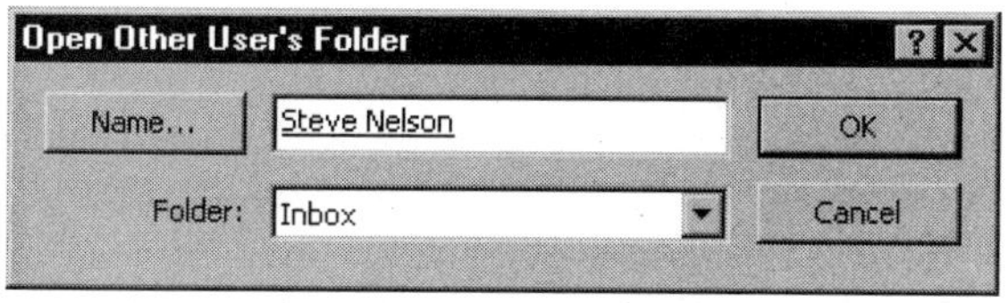


**Figure B-5** Opening another user's folder.

**3. Select the folder to open.**

Choose the folder you want to open from the Folder drop-down list box, and then click OK. Outlook opens a new window with the selected folder.

## Sending Messages on Someone's Behalf

To send a message on behalf of someone who has given you delegate access to their Outlook folders, follow these steps:

**1. Create a new message.**

Display the Outlook Inbox, and click the New toolbar button.

**2. Display the From field.**

Click the down arrow next to the Options toolbar button, and then choose From from the pop-up menu, as shown in Figure B-6.

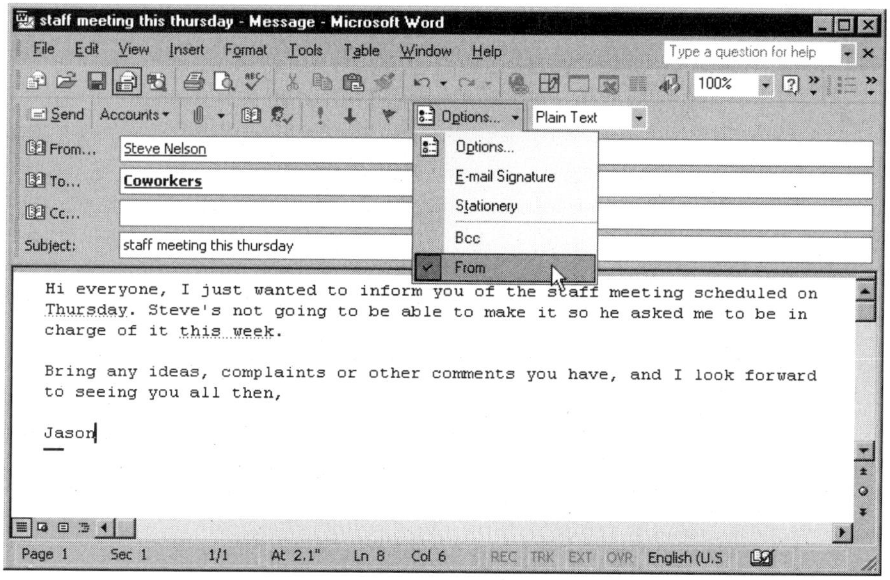


**Figure B-6** Sending a message on someone's behalf.

3. **Select the name of the person on whose behalf you're writing.**

   Click the From button, select Global Address List from the Show Names From The drop-down list box, and then double-click the appropriate user's name.

NOTE *Exchange Server may not recognize your permission to send messages on someone's behalf unless you select the person's name from the Global Address List.*

4. **Compose and send the message.**

   Address and compose the message as you would normally, and click the Send toolbar button to send the message. The message will report it was sent from you on behalf of the person specified in the From field.

## Setting Up Offline Folders

If Outlook is set up properly, it automatically synchronizes your Outlook folders between the Exchange Server and your local computer. This permits you to work offline—an especially handy feature for users of laptop computers. This synchronization process occurs when you open or close Outlook, or when you choose the Send/Receive All command from the Tools menu's Send Receive submenu.

If for some reason offline folder access is disabled, follow these steps to enable it:

1. **Open the Send/Receive Groups dialog box.**

   Display the Inbox, choose the Tools menu's Send/Receive Settings command, and then choose Define Send/Receive Groups from the submenu.

2. **Select the appropriate Send/Receive group.**

   Select the Send/Receive group that contains your Exchange Server account (most likely All Accounts; see "Skill 2: Reading E-Mail" for more information). Click Edit.

3. **Select your Exchange Server account.**

   In the Accounts list on the left side of the Send/Receive Settings dialog box, as shown in Figure B-7, select your Exchange Server account. Optionally, specify which folders Outlook should synchronize while online, and then click the Account Properties button.

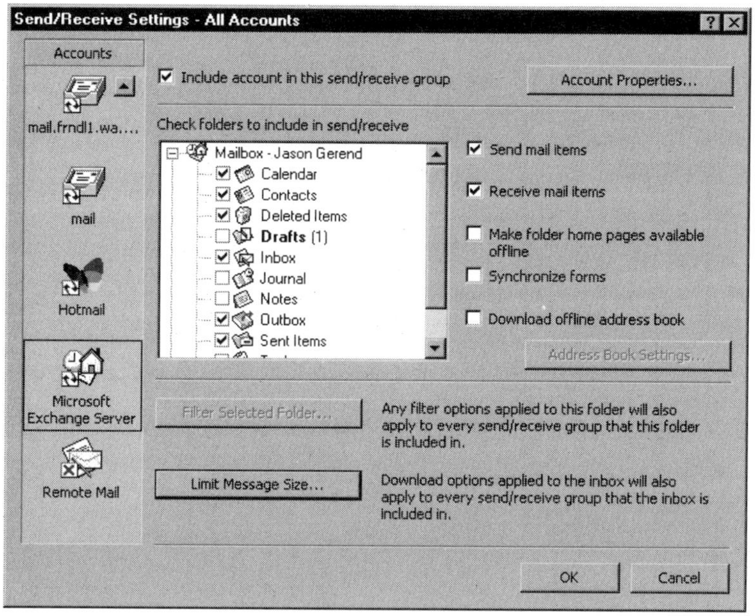


**Figure B-7** The Send/Receive Settings dialog box.

TIP *To prevent large messages from downloading unless you specifically request them, click the Limit Message Size button.*

**4. Enable offline use of your Exchange Server account.**

Click the Advanced tab, and then select the Enable Offline Use check box. Optionally, click Offline Folder File Settings to view or change offline folder file settings. Click OK when you're finished. You may also want to click the General tab and specify whether Outlook should automatically detect whether or not you're connected to the Exchange Server.

TIP *If it takes too much time to synchronize with Exchange Server, you can filter the items Outlook synchronizes on a folder-by-folder basis. To do so, right-click a folder, choose Properties from the shortcut menu, click the Synchronization tab, and then click the Filter button. For information on creating filters, refer to the "Performing Advanced Searches" section of "Skill 4: Managing Your E-Mail."*

# Using the Out Of Office Assistant

If you know that you're going to be away from e-mail for an extended period of time, consider using the Out Of Office Assistant. This useful tool automatically replies to messages you receive using the text you specify.

Although you can accomplish similar functionality with message rules (see "Skill 4: Managing Your E-Mail"), the Out Of Office Assistant has a couple advantages:

- It doesn't require that you leave Outlook running.
- It replies only once to each person who e-mails you, reducing the annoyance factor.

To set up an automatic response to messages you receive notifying the sender that you're out of the office, follow these steps:

1. **Open the Out Of Office Assistant.**

   Display the Inbox, and then choose the Tools menu's Out Of Office Assistant command.

2. **Enter your out-of-office message.**

   Enter your out-of-office message in the box provided, as shown in Figure B-8.

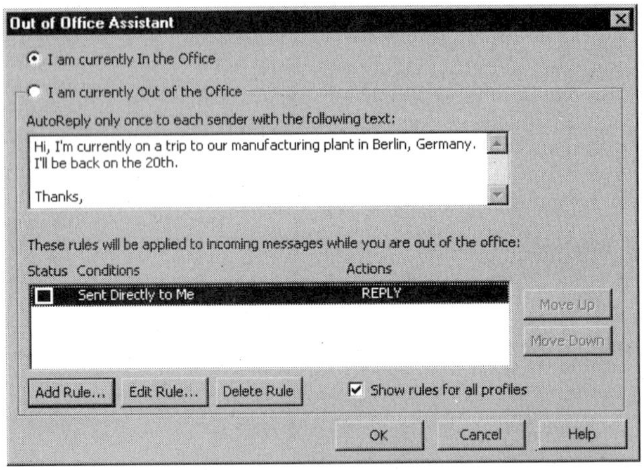


**Figure B-8** The Out Of Office Assistant.

3. **Optionally, add any message-processing rules.**

   Click the Add Rules button to respond to certain messages only, such as messages sent directly to you, or to forward important messages to someone else, such as a coworker. Use the Edit Rule dialog box shown in Figure B-9 to create the rule, and then click OK.

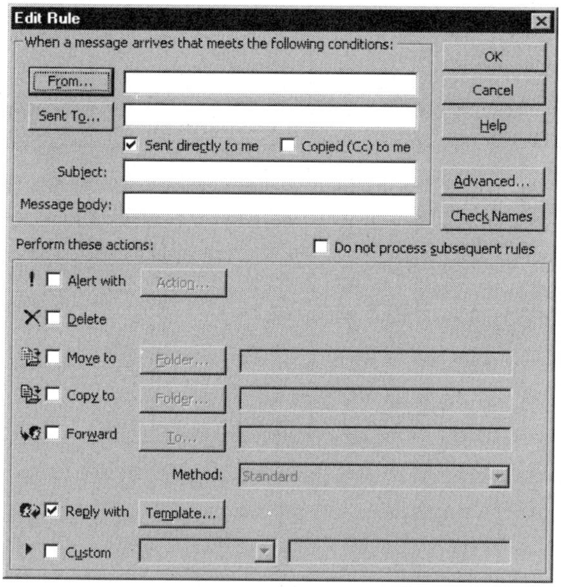


**Figure B-9** Creating an out-of-office rule.

TIP *If you want your rule to reply to the message, select the Reply With check box and click the Template button to compose your reply. Just be sure to leave the To box empty.*

**4. Turn on the Out Of Office Assistant.**

When you're ready to become incommunicado, click the I Am Currently Out Of The Office option button (see Figure B-8). When you return to the office, open the Out Of Office Assistant and click the I Am Currently In The Office option button.

# *Appendix C*

# AUTOMATICALLY PROCESSING FORM DATA

## Featuring:

- Preparing a Form
- Using Outlook to Process Form Data

We live in an instant gratification world, and nowhere is this truer than the Web. If you have a Web site, visitors should be able to easily find what they want on your Web site, but if they can't find what they need, they should be able to receive a prompt reply via e-mail.

The best way to ensure a prompt response is to set up a form on your Web site that sends results to a special e-mail account or alias. You can then set up Outlook to process the received messages and take appropriate action automatically.

For example, depending on the visitor's request, you might create a message rule to forward the message to a different e-mail account, and send a standard e-mail message with a list of frequently asked questions and boilerplate telling the visitor that someone will get back to them in the next 24 hours.

To automatically process form data via e-mail, you need to modify the form's properties in order to e-mail results to the proper e-mail account and then set up Outlook to process the form results.

# Preparing a Form

To use Microsoft FrontPage 2002 to modify a form's properties to properly send its results to your e-mail program, follow these steps (the basic steps are the same for other programs, although the details will differ):

1. **Open the Form Properties dialog box.**

   Right-click the form, and choose Form Properties from the shortcut menu.

NOTE *The form you created must collect the visitor's e-mail address in addition to any other information. You may also want to use a drop-down list box or other multiple-choice field on the form to divide responses into categories, which your mail program can then process differently.*

2. **Click the Options button, and then click the E-Mail Results tab.**

3. **Specify the appropriate e-mail address for the results.**

   Enter the e-mail address where you want to send the form results in the E-Mail Address To Receive Results box. You might want to create a special e-mail account or alias just to handle form results.

4. **Set up the message header.**

   Select the Form Field Name check box next to the Reply-To Line, and enter the field name the form uses to collect a visitor's e-mail address in the box provided, as shown in Figure C-1. Use the Saved Fields tab to see a list of fields for which the form saves results.

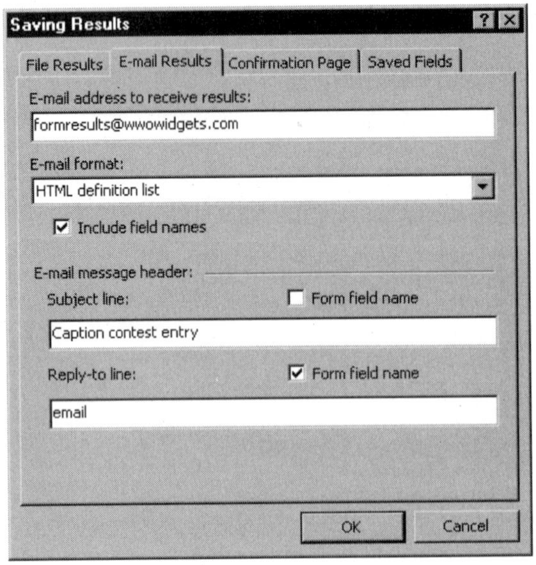


**Figure C-1** Setting up form results for automatic processing via e-mail.

TIP *If you want to automatically reply to information requests with information pertaining to each type of request, set up the subject line with the form field name that collects the type of information request. This information request might be a drop-down list box with options for Troubleshooting, Customer Service, and so forth. By using the field name as the subject line, the visitor's selection becomes the subject of the e-mail, which your mail program can then use to respond with a list of troubleshooting procedures or customer service information.*

## Using Outlook to Process Form Data

After you modify the form to properly e-mail form results to the appropriate e-mail account, create an e-mail message rule to process the form result e-mails. To process the results using Outlook, follow these steps:

1. **Create a new message in Outlook.**

   To do so, click the New Mail Message toolbar button and compose the message you want to automatically send to visitors using your form (but don't address the message).

2. **Save the message as a template.**

   To do so, choose the File menu's Save As command, select Outlook Template from the Save As Type drop-down list box, enter a name for the template in the File Name box, and click Save. (For more information on creating templates, see "Skill 4: Managing Your E-Mail.")

NOTE *If the Outlook template file format isn't available, you need to disable Microsoft Word as your e-mail editor, as described in "Skill 7: Maintaining Outlook."*

3. **Choose the Tools menu's Rules Wizard command.**
4. **Click the New button.**
5. **Select the Start From A Blank Rule option, and click Next.**
6. **Select the conditions to process.**

   Select the With Specific Words In The Subject check box, and select the Through The Specified Account check box, as shown in Figure C-2. Click OK when Outlook warns that this rule won't work with previous versions of Outlook.

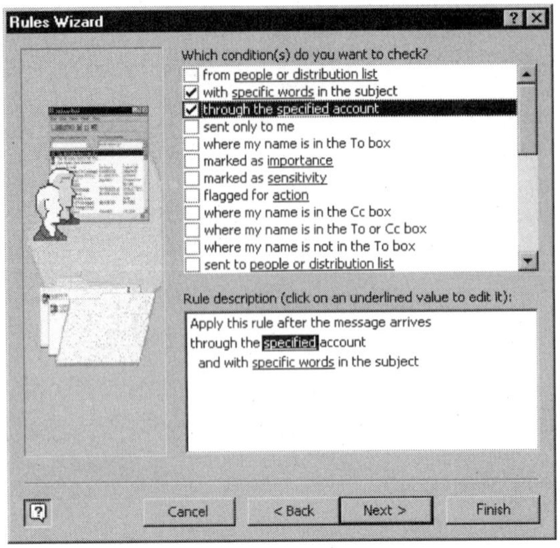


**Figure C-2** Creating a message rule to process form results.

NOTE *If you don't have a separate e-mail account for form results, create an e-mail alias for the results, create a contact in Outlook for this e-mail address, and select the Sent To People Or Distribution List check box instead of the Through The Specified Account check box. Then select the contact you created for the alias. If you don't want to do this, you can set up the form to say "form results" as the subject and use that phrase to identify form results from other e-mail, but this method isn't as powerful or reliable.*

7. **Specify the e-mail account and subject line to process, and then click Next.**

   Click the underlined words at the bottom of the dialog box to specify the e-mail account form results are received with, and to specify the subject line to process. If you want to send different responses based on the subject field, enter only a single term or phrase in the Search Text box. When you're finished creating this rule, create another identical rule, but specify a different subject and in step 8 below, specify a different action to take.

8. **Select the action(s) to take.**

   Specify the actions to take, as shown in Figure C-3. Click Next when you're finished.

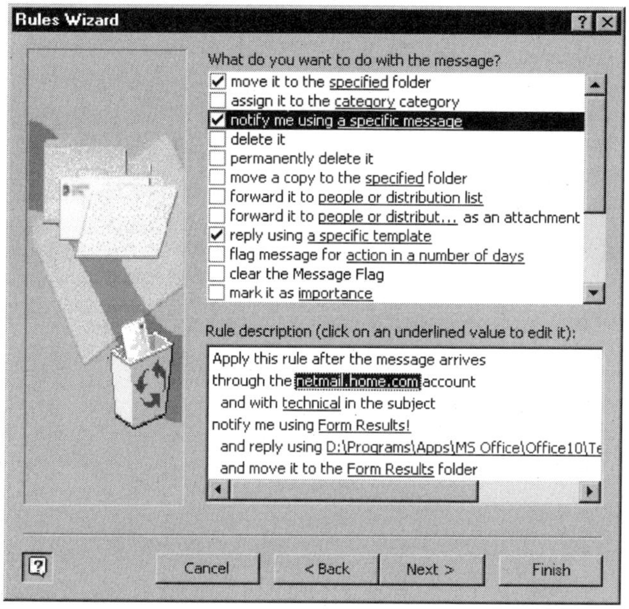


**Figure C-3** Specifying what actions to take with received form results.

Here's a list of actions you might want to perform on the received message:

- To automatically reply to the message, select the Reply Using A Specific Template check box, select User Templates In File System from the Look In drop-down list box, select the appropriate template, and click Open.
- To forward the message to a different e-mail account, select the Forward It To People Or Distribution List check box and click the underlined term to specify the appropriate contact.
- To move the message to a specific folder in Outlook, such as a Form Results folder, select the Move It To The Specified Folder check box and click the underlined term to specify the appropriate folder.
- To display a dialog box informing you that form results have arrived, select the Notify Me Using A Specific Message check box and click the underlined term to enter the text you want to display.

**9. Add any exceptions.**

Select the check boxes corresponding to any exceptions you want to make—perhaps to single out important customers, for example. Click Next to continue.

10. **Name and review the rule.**

    Enter a descriptive name for the rule in the Please Specify A Name For This Rule box, and review the rule description displayed below. To make any changes, click the underlined words or click the Back button. Click Finish to save the rule.

11. **Create additional rules as necessary.**

    Select the rule you created in the list of rules, and click the Copy button to use the previous rule as a start for your new rule (which will probably differ only in the subject words to look for and the e-mail template used to reply to the message).

# GLOSSARY

## Address Book

In Outlook, an interface you can use to access the Contacts folder or other address lists.

## appointment

A generic Outlook calendar item. Appointments can be turned into **meetings** by inviting other people, or **events** by making the appointment last for 24 hours or longer.

## attachment

A file appended to a message that can be opened intact by the recipient.

## bounce back

What happens after sending an incorrectly addressed e-mail message.

## cable modem

A device that allows computers to access the **Internet** using a cable TV connection. The local cable TV company must enable cable modem access to a home or business in order for a cable **modem** to work.

## category

An Outlook field that you can use to assign a category to any Outlook item, thereby allowing you to quickly find items of different types in different **folders** that all pertain to the same category.

## contact

An Outlook item that stores information about a person, such as their e-mail address, physical address, and phone numbers.

## drop-down list box

A field that when clicked displays a list of options that drop down from the box.

## e-mail address

A universal way for people to communicate with e-mail that always includes a name and a domain separated by the @ symbol; for example, lucy@peanuts.com.

## emoticon

Short for emotional icon. An icon or series of characters used to express emotion. Examples include :) a smiley, :( a frowning face, and ;) a wink.

## event

An Outlook **appointment** that lasts 24 hours or longer.

## Exchange Server

An e-mail server and corporate communication server created by Microsoft and used by many businesses and organizations. For more information, see *http://www.microsoft.com/exchange.*

## filter

A way to automatically send specific messages to predetermined **folders.**

## flags

Designations that help you tag important messages for later attention.

## flame

An angry or abusive e-mail message.

## folder

A way to sort messages into different **categories.**

## folder store

An Outlook data file that stores your Outlook **folders.** Typically this is a **Personal Folders File** (with the .pst file extension), but it could also be an **Exchange Server** mailbox or an **Offline Folder File** (with the .ost file extension).

## Free/Busy information

The Outlook Calendar data that you make available to others for the purpose of scheduling **meetings.** Called Free/Busy information because no details are available—only the times that you're free or busy.

## Global Address List

An **Exchange Server** address list that provides the names and mailbox addresses of all users of the Exchange Server.

## HTML

An abbreviation for Hypertext Markup Language. The coding language used to create **Web pages.**

## hyperlink

A piece of text or an image that when clicked takes the visitor to another page, image, or file.

## iCalendar

An **Internet** standard file format for calendar information. Outlook can send **meeting** requests in the iCalendar format (using the .ics file extension), as well as post **Free/Busy information** on the Internet using the iCalendar format (using the .vfb file extension).

## IMAP

Short for Internet Message Access Protocol. A newer e-mail account type that stores all messages on the mail server, allowing users to access their mail from any computer with an IMAP mail client (such as Outlook or Outlook Express).

## Inbox

The **folder** that holds all incoming messages.

## instant messaging

A form of communication that is roughly a cross between **chat** and telephone. Users run an instant messaging program that notifies them when people they know are online. Users can then conduct a text-based "conversation."

## Internet

A worldwide computer network running the TCP/IP protocol suite and consisting of hundreds of millions of computers.

## Internet service provider

Abbreviated ISP. A company that provides access to the **Internet** via dial-up connections, DSL, leased lines, or other connection methods.

## intranet

A private network that uses **Internet** technology—the TCP/IP protocol suite and Web servers.

## IP address

The unique address for a single network card on a network using TCP/IP. All computers (hosts) on the **Internet** or an **intranet** must have an IP address to communicate.

## LDAP

An abbreviation for Lightweight Directory Access Protocol. A means of accessing address lists from across the **Internet** or an **intranet.** It is used to access Internet address lists (such as Bigfoot.com) and Windows 2000 Server address lists (the Active Directory).

## local area network

Abbreviated LAN. A group of computers that are all located within the same local area (typically one building) and that can communicate with each other.

## mailing list

A list to which users can subscribe that allows them to receive **e-mail** messages on a particular topic sent by a company or organization.

## meeting

An Outlook **appointment** that you've invited other people to attend.

## modem

An analog device that allows a computer to communicate with other computers over standard telephone lines. Capable of a maximum of 53Kbps download rate.

## newsgroups

Electronic bulletin boards on the **Internet** where people can post messages, read other users' posts, and reply to them.

## note

A small Outlook item used for jotting small notes. Yellow and small, but not sticky.

## Offline Folders File

The file that stores a copy of your **Exchange Server folders** for use when disconnected from the Exchange Server. Uses the .ost file extension.

## Outlook bar

The bar that runs down the left side of the Outlook window with **shortcuts** to frequently used Outlook **folders.**

## Personal Folders File

The master file that stores all Outlook items. Uses the .pst file extension.

## plain text

E-mail that contains no formatting.

## POP3

Short for Post Office Protocol. The most popular form of e-mail account, POP3 accounts download all messages to your local computer, preventing you from accessing them elsewhere.

## pop-up menu

A menu that pops up (or down) when you click an item, usually a toolbar button. Similar to a **shortcut menu.**

## proxy server

A network server that sits in between the local network and the **Internet,** protecting the local network from attacks as well as caching **Web pages** to improve Web-browsing performance for local clients. A type of firewall.

## public folder

A folder stored on an **Exchange Server** that all users of the Exchange Server can access. Public folders work very similar to **Internet newsgroups.**

## sent mail

A record of all messages sent by a particular user.

## shortcut

An icon that points to another file. You can have many shortcuts pointing to the same file, and deleting a shortcut doesn't affect the file to which it points.

## shortcut menu

The menu that is displayed when you right-click an item on the screen. Also called a context-sensitive menu.

## signature file

Shortened to "sig" file. Text automatically appended to the end of each outgoing message, usually with contact information such as name, address, e-mail address, phone number, and so forth.

## sizing handles

Small squares that appear on the outline of an object. You click a resizing handle to resize the object.

## spam

Unsolicited e-mail. Usually sales oriented.

## status bar

The bar that runs across the bottom of a window displaying the status of the current selection.

## task

An Outlook item that should be accomplished but doesn't have a specific time allocated for it. Perfect for to-do lists.

## template

A message saved in a special template file format (.oft file extension), allowing you to use it as the basis for future messages.

## URL

An abbreviation for Uniform Resource Locator. An address for a file, usually on the **Internet.**

## vCard

An **Internet** standard file format for contact information. Outlook can save contacts in the vCard (.vcs file extension) file format for sharing with other users across the Internet.

## Web browser

A program used to display **Web pages.**

## Web page

A document using the **HTML** file format. A Web page can be stored on the Web, a company **intranet,** or locally on your computer's hard drive or floppy disk.

# Index

## A

access permissions. *See* delegates
accounts. *See* e-mail accounts
address books. *See also* contacts
  vs. Contacts folder, 170, 171
  Global Address List, 171, 295
  glossary definition, 293
  importing, 11–12
  managing, 171, 191–93
  multiple, 191–93
  overview, 171
  Personal Address Book, 171
  selecting names for e-mail messages, 86–87
  which to display first, 193
addresses. *See* address books; contacts; e-mail addresses
Addressing dialog box, 192–93
addressing e-mail messages, 84–88
Advanced Find tool, 134–37
alarms. *See* reminders
alphabetizing. *See* sorting e-mail messages
announcements. *See* post messages
annual events. *See* events, recurring
antivirus programs, 75
applications, Microsoft Office
  disabling Word as e-mail editor, 265–66
  Word as e-mail editor, 115–17
  Word language capabilities, 115–17
appointments. *See also* events; meetings
  adding to Calendar, 201–2
  canceling, 204
  categorizing, 206–7
  changing start or end times, 204
  creating, 201–2
  deleting, 204
  duplicating information, 204
  editing details, 203–7
  vs. events, 196
  finding in Calendar, 198–201
  glossary definition, 293
  linking to contacts, 206
  making private, 207
  moving to different date, 204
  overview, 196
  printing, 227–30
  recurring, 208–9
  rescheduling, 204
  searching for, 198–201
  setting reminders, 206
  ways to create, 201–2
archives. *See* AutoArchive feature
assigning tasks, 235–36
attachments, e-mail
  adding to messages, 102–4
  etiquette aspect, 74, 103
  glossary definition, 293
  opening, 73
  overview, 72–73
  receiving with messages, 73–74
  removing from messages, 74
  saving, 74
  size considerations, 103
  suspicious, 75–76

attachments, e-mail *continued*
tips for sending, 103
vCards as, 188
and viruses, 72, 74, 75–77
AutoArchive feature, 246–47
AutoPick feature, 216
AutoReply feature. *See* Out Of Office Assistant

## B

backing up Outlook data, 259–62
Bcc box, 84, 87, 164–66
blind carbon copies, 84, 87, 164–66
bold text, 97
Boolean operators, 132
bounce back, 293
Brightmail, 167
bulleted lists, 97
business cards, virtual, 188
busy times. *See* Free/Busy information

## C

cable modems, 45, 293
Calendar
adding appointments, 201–2
adding events, 202–3
canceling appointments, 204
categorizing items, 206–7
creating appointments, 201–2
creating events, 202–3
Date Navigator, 197, 198
delegate access permissions, 279–80
deleting appointments, 204
display options, 196–98
editing items, 203–9
finding items, 198–201
linking items to contacts, 206
moving item dates, 204
overview, 195, 196
printing, 227–30
recurring appointments, 208–9
rescheduling appointments, 204
scheduling meetings, 209–27
searching for items, 198–201
setting reminders, 206
terminology, 196
as time-management tool, 195–96
ways to view, 196–98
canceling appointments, 204
carbon copies, 84, 87
categories
for appointments, 206–7
for Calendar items, 206–7
for contacts, 177
for e-mail messages, 58–60
for events, 206–7
glossary definition, 293
for notes, 272
for tasks, 234
Cc box, 84, 87
character sets, 115, 116
Chek.com Web site, 15
cleaning up folders, 244–49
coloring-coding e-mail messages, 143
columns, folder
adding, 52–53
moving, 52
resizing, 51
composing
e-mail messages, 88–117
post messages, 276–77
compression utilities, 103
contacts. *See also* address books
adding to Contacts folder, 172–74
browsing list for names, 180
categorizing, 177
creating entries, 172–74
creating more than one folder, 191–92
distribution lists, 178–79
editing entries, 174–78
finding, 180–83
forwarding information via vCard, 188
glossary definition, 294

importing lists, 11–12
linking appointments to, 206
linking events to, 206
linking tasks to, 233
linking to other contacts, 176
linking to other Outlook items, 177
making entries private, 177
mapping addresses, 183–84
multiple folders for, 191–93
opening, 174
overview, 170–71
printing list, 185–87
saving entries, 178
searching for, 180–83
selecting addresses for e-mail messages, 86–87
viewing related items, 184–85
ways to access data, 170–72
ways to create entries, 172–74
ways to use information, 183–91
courtesy copies, 84, 87
crashes, Outlook, 117–19
Create New Folder dialog box, 16–17, 139
customizing Outlook, 263–66

## D

data compression, 103
Date Navigator, 197, 198
dates
changing in Calendar, 204
for tasks, 233
deferred delivery, 99–101
delegates
assigning access, 279–80
opening another user's folders, 280–81
overview, 279
specifying permissions, 279–80
Deleted Items folder
emptying, 248
and IMAP accounts, 61–62, 249
recovering items from, 61
vs. Recycle Bin, 248
sending deleted items to, 61–62
deleting
e-mail messages, 60–62
items from folders, 244–46
delivering e-mail messages
postponing delivery, 99–101
preventing immediate delivery, 119–21
ways to deliver, 99, 100–101, 119–22
dialing telephone numbers, 188–91
dial-up Internet accounts, 38
directories. *See* folders
distribution lists, 178–79
domain names
perceived images, 15
reasons for obtaining, 3
types of domains, 15
draft e-mail messages, 98–99
Drafts folder, 98–99
drop-down list boxes, 294

## E

editing
appointments, 203–7
contact items, 174–78
events, 203–7
meeting details, 203–4
received e-mail messages, 67
tasks, 232–35
electronic business cards, 188
electronic mail. *See* e-mail
e-mail. *See also* distribution lists; messages, e-mail
adding message flags, 54–57
assigning message priority, 58
attaching files to messages, 102–4
changing displayed font for plain text messages, 68–70
changing message format from HTML to plain text, 91–93
changing message format to HTML for individual messages, 93–94
composing messages using templates, 146–47, 151
creating message rules, 152–58

e-mail. *continued*
creating messages, 82–83
creating message templates, 143–45
deleting messages, 60–62
editing received messages, 67
etiquette, 74, 90, 103
filtering messages, 65, 143
finding messages, 127–37
formatting HTML messages, 95–97
forwarding messages, 110–14
grouping messages, 129–31
junk mail messages, 158–67
keeping messages short, 50–51
leaving messages on server, 256–57
moving messages between folders, 140–41, 142, 155
opening attachments, 73
organizing messages, 137–43
plain text vs. HTML as message formats, 91
printing messages, 70–72
and privacy, 10
reading messages, 47–50
receiving attachments, 73–74
receiving messages, 47–50
recovering deleted messages, 61–62
recovering messages after Outlook crashes, 117–19
replying to messages, 66, 95, 110–14
resending messages, 123–24
sending messages immediately, 84, 119
sending without checking messages, 122
tips for managing messages, 65–66
undeleting messages, 61–62
unwanted messages, 88
ways to deliver messages, 99, 100–101, 119–22
e-mail accounts
additional setups, 21–23
corporate vs. personal, 7–8
for form results, 289
initial setup, 5–7
leaving messages on server, 256–57
managing, 253–55
maximum mailbox size, 257
modifying settings, 254–55
multiple, 4, 7–8, 21–23
personal, 3–4
POP vs. IMAP, 2
removing, 254
sending mail using other than default account, 121–22
setting up to be checked in groups, 38–40
types of servers, 2
using redirection, 4
e-mail addresses
entering in messages, 84–88
glossary definition, 294
guarding, 158
keeping private, 158
multiple, 7
specifying when setting up Outlook, 6
embedding files in Calendar items, 207
emoticons, 294
emptying Deleted Items folder, 248
etiquette, 74, 90, 103
events
adding to Calendar, 202–3
vs. appointments, 196
categorizing, 206–7
creating, 202–3
duplicating information, 204
editing details, 203–7
finding in Calendar, 198–201
glossary definition, 294
linking to contacts, 206
moving to different date, 204
overview, 196, 202
recurring, 208–9
setting reminders, 206
Exchange Server
glossary definition, 294
and offline folders, 282–83
storage overview, 273–74
Expedia, 183–84

## F


files. *See also* attachments, e-mail; folders
- attaching to e-mail messages, 102–4
- compressing, 103
- embedding in Calendar items, 207
- saving e-mail messages as, 64–65

filters. *See also* message rules
- benefits of using, 65
- for e-mail messages, 65, 143
- glossary definition, 294
- for weeding out junk mail, 160–67

filters.txt file, 163

Find A Contact box, 181

Find bar
- using to find Calendar items, 198–99
- using to find contacts, 182–83
- using to find e-mail messages, 131–34

finding
- Calendar items, 198–201
- contacts, 180–83
- e-mail messages, 127–37
- help information, 25–29

flags
- adding to e-mail messages, 54–57
- benefits of using, 66
- clearing, 57
- glossary definition, 294
- marking complete, 57
- vs. priority settings, 58
- ways to use, 58

flames
- avoiding, 90
- dealing with, 90
- glossary definition, 294

Folder List, 10

folders. *See also* Calendar; contacts ; Inbox; Journal; mail folders; notes; tasks
- benefits of using, 65
- cleaning up, 244–49
- column options, 51, 52–53
- creating in Outlook, 16–17, 138–40
- creating shortcuts to, 17
- Deleted Items folder, 61–62, 248
- deleting items, 244–46
- Drafts folder, 98–99
- glossary definition, 295
- moving e-mail messages between, 140–41, 142, 155
- naming, 17, 139
- offline, 282–83
- organizing, 137–43
- saving e-mail messages to, 63
- synchronizing, 282–83

folder stores
- archiving, 246–47
- backing up, 259–62
- closing, 250–51
- controlling size, 244, 246
- creating, 252–53
- glossary definition, 295
- limitations, 244, 252
- maximum size, 244, 252
- multiple, 249–51
- opening, 249–50
- repairing when corrupted, 268–69
- restoring, 262–63
- sharing on networks, 258
- specifying default, 253

fonts, changing display of plain text e-mails, 68–70. *See also* plain text

foreign languages, 115–17

formatting
- HTML in e-mail messages, 95–97
- original message text in e-mail message replies, 110–14

forms, Web site
- creating message for mailing results, 289
- modifying properties, 288–89
- overview, 287
- using Outlook to process data, 289–92

forwarding
- contact information via vCard, 188
- e-mail messages, 110–14
- formatting original message text, 110–14

Free/Busy information, 217–27, 295

free e-mail accounts, 3. *See also* Hotmail

# G


Global Address List, 171, 295. *See also* contacts
grouping e-mail messages, 129–31
groups, adding to Outlook bar, 147–48
group scheduling, 215–16


# H


Help feature, 25–29
Help menu, 26–27
Help system, 25–29
hidden files, 148–49
high-speed Internet connections, 45–47
hoaxes, virus, 76–77
Hotmail
  configuring Outlook to download messages from accounts, 45–47
  as e-mail account, 2, 3, 4
  reading messages in Outlook Inbox, 47
HTML e-mail messages
  changing format to plain text, 91–93
  changing from plain text to HTML for individual messages, 93–94
  formatting, 95–97
  vs. plain text messages, 91
HTML (Hypertext Markup Language), 295
hyperlinks
  creating in e-mail messages, 97
  glossary definition, 295


# I


iCalendar, 217, 223, 295
IMAP (Internet Message Access Protocol)
  configuring Outlook to download messages from accounts, 45–47
  and Deleted Items folder, 61–62, 249
  and e-mail accounts, 2
  glossary definition, 296
  locating missing folders, 266
  reading messages in Outlook Inbox, 47
  verifying server settings, 50
importance, message, 58
Import And Export Wizard, 11–12, 13–14, 17–20
importing
  address lists, 11–12
  e-mail account settings, 5, 13–14
  e-mail messages, 11–12
  from other programs, 16–21
Inbox
  column options, 51, 52–53
  displaying, 47
  forwarding messages, 49
  glossary definition, 296
  listing contents, 48
  opening, 47
  previewing messages, 49
  read vs. unread messages, 53–54
  received messages, 48
  replying to messages, 49
Inbox Assistant. *See* Rules Wizard
Inbox Repair tool, 268–69
Information Viewer, 9
Insert File dialog box, 102–3
instant messaging, 296
Internet, defined, 296
Internet connections
  adjusting Send/Receive settings, 40–43
  high-speed, 45–47
  maximizing, 40–47
  slow, 40–45
  specifying hang-ups, 40–43
Internet Explorer, mapping contacts using Expedia, 183–84
Internet Free/Busy Service, 217–23, 226–27
Internet Message Access Protocol. *See* IMAP (Internet Message Access Protocol)
Internet service providers
  changing, 3
  and e-mail accounts, 2–4
  glossary definition, 296
intranets, 296
IP addresses, 296
ISPs. *See* Internet service providers
italic text, 97

items. *See also* appointments; contacts; events; Journal; meetings; messages, e-mail; notes; tasks
- archiving, 246–47
- deleting, 244–46
- linking to contacts, 177
- organizing in folders, 137–43

## J

Journal
- creating entries, 189, 191
- opening entries, 190
- saving entries, 190
- using with dialing feature, 188–91
- viewing list of entries, 190

junk e-mail
- adding to Junk Senders list, 161–62
- enabling basic message rules, 160–61
- enabling more powerful message rules, 162–67
- filtering out secret messages, 164–66
- overview, 158
- third-party anti-spam solutions, 167
- tips for avoiding, 159

## L

languages, 115–17

LDAP (Lightweight Directory Access Protocol)
- finding e-mail addresses, 87, 171
- glossary definition, 297
- setting up, 23–25

local area networks, 297

## M

Mac users, 103

mail. *See* e-mail; messages, e-mail

Mailbox Cleanup tool, 244–46

mail folders
- configuring for sorting, 51–53
- sorting messages, 129–31

mailing lists, 297. *See also* distribution lists

Mail Snoop, 167

mapping contacts, 183–84

marking e-mail messages, 53–58

McAfee VirusScan, 75

Meeting Planner. *See* meetings

meeting requests, 211–14, 216

meetings
- AutoPick feature, 216
- changing start or end times, 204
- creating in Calendar, 209–12
- duplicating information, 204
- editing details, 203–4
- finding in Calendar, 198–201
- glossary definition, 297
- group scheduling, 215–16
- moving to different date, 204
- overview, 196
- Plan A Meeting feature, 215–16
- recurring, 208–9
- responding to requests, 214
- scheduling, 209–27
- sending requests, 211–12, 216
- tracking responses, 212–13

menu bar, 8–9

message rules
- creating based on existing messages, 142, 152–56
- creating from scratch, 156–58
- enabling filters for junk mail, 160–67
- naming, 155, 158
- vs. Out Of Office Assistant, 284
- overview, 151–52
- for processing form result e-mails, 289–92
- ways to use, 151–52

messages, e-mail. *See also* post messages
- adding hyperlinks, 97
- adding signatures, 107–9
- addressing, 84–88
- assigning priority, 58
- attaching files, 102–4
- automatic processing, 151–67
- bullets in, 97
- categorizing, 58–60

messages, e-mail *continued*
changing displayed font for plain text, 68–70
changing format from HTML to plain text, 91–93
changing format to HTML for individual messages, 93–94
checking, 33–47
checking automatically, 36–37
color-coding, 143
composing, 88–117
composing using templates, 146–47, 151
creating, 82–83
creating rules for, 152–58
creating templates for, 143–45
deferred delivery, 99–101
deleting, 60–62
delivery options, 99–101
disabling Send Immediately feature, 119–21
drafts, 98–99
filtering, 65, 143
finding, 127–37
flagging, 54–57
formatting in HTML, 95–97
formatting original message text in replies, 110–14
for form results, 289–92
forwarding, 110–14
grouping, 129–31
junk mail, 158–67
keeping short, 50–51
leaving on server, 256–57
marking, 53–58
moving between folders, 140–41, 142, 155
opening attachments, 73
organizing, 137–43
plain text vs. HTML formats, 91
postponing, 98–101
postponing delivery, 99–101
preventing immediate delivery, 119–21
previewing, 49
printing, 70–72
reading, 47–50
reading offline, 44–45
read vs. unread, 53–54
received, editing, 67
receiving, 47–50
receiving attachments, 73–74
recovering after deletion, 61–62
recovering after Outlook crashes, 117–19
replying to, 66, 95, 110–14
resending, 123–24
saving, 62–65
sending as delegate, 281–82
sending copies, 84, 87
sending immediately, 84, 119
sending to distribution lists, 178–79
sending without checking, 122
sorting, 129–31
specifying delivery time, 100–101
tips for managing, 65–66
undeleting, 61–62
unwanted, 88
ways to create, 82
ways to deliver, 99, 100–101, 119–22
writing, 50–51
Microsoft Exchange Server. *See* Exchange Server
Microsoft Expedia, 183–84
Microsoft Knowledge Base, 28
Microsoft Office
disabling Word as e-mail editor, 265–66
Word as e-mail editor, 115–17
Word language capabilities, 115–17
Microsoft Office Internet Free/Busy Service, 217–23, 226–27
Microsoft Outlook. *See* Outlook
Microsoft Word
disabling as e-mail editor, 265–66
as e-mail editor, 115–17
language capabilities, 115–17
translating text in, 116–17
modems, 297
moving
Calendar items, 204
e-mail messages between folders, 140–41, 142, 155

## N


names. *See* contacts
naming
  folders, 17, 139
  message rules, 155, 158
Nelson add-on, 66
netiquette, 74, 90, 103
new folders, creating, 16–17, 138–40
Norton AntiVirus, 75
notes
  for Calendar items, 206
  categorizing, 272
  changing folder view, 272
  closing, 272
  coloring, 272
  creating, 271–72
  deleting, 272
  forwarding, 272
  glossary definition, 297
  linking to contacts, 272
  opening, 272
  overview, 271
  saving to desktop, 272
  using, 272
  writing, 272


## O


Office. *See* Microsoft Office
Office Assistant. *See* Out Of Office Assistant
offline folders, 282–83, 297
.oft files, 149
online Help, 25–29
opening
  another user's folders, 280–81
  attachments, 73
  contacts, 174
  folder stores, 249–50
  Inbox, 47
Organize pane, 142–43
organizing
  e-mail messages, 137–43
  items in folders, 137–43
Outbox folder, 122, 266–67
Outlook
  AutoArchive feature, 246–47
  backing up data and settings, 259–62
  customizing, 263–66
  delegate access, 279–82
  Folder List, 10
  handling crashes, 117–19
  importing items and files, 11–12
  Information Viewer, 9
  interface elements, 8–10
  menu bar, 8–9
  Offline mode, 44–45
  online Help, 25–29
  Preview pane, 9, 49
  restoring backed up data and settings, 262–63
  setting up, 4–7
  Standard toolbar, 9
  starting, 5, 31–32
  Startup Wizard, 5–7
  status bar, 10
  troubleshooting, 266–69
  window, 8
Outlook bar
  adding groups to, 147–48
  adding message templates to, 147–51
  adding shortcuts to, 17
  customizing, 263–65
  glossary definition, 298
  overview, 9
Outlook Startup Wizard, 5–7
Outlook Today, 78–79
Out Of Office Assistant
  creating standard response, 284–85
  defined, 284
  vs. message rules, 284
  turning on and off, 285

# P


passwords, needless requests for, 267
permissions, for delegate access, 279–80
Personal Address Book, 171. *See also* contacts
personal e-mail, 3–4
Personal Folders File. *See also* folder stores
  glossary definition, 298
  overview, 255–56
  repairing when corrupted, 268–69
personal items. *See* privacy
phone calls, speed dialing, 188–91
plain text
  changing displayed font for messages, 68–70
  changing message format from HTML to, 91–93
  changing message format to HTML for individual messages, 93–94
  glossary definition, 298
  vs. HTML as message formats, 91
Plan A Meeting feature, 215–16
POP3
  e-mail accounts, 2, 3, 5
  glossary definition, 298
pop-up menus, 298
post messages
  posting to public folders, 276–77
  public folders for, 274–79
  reading, 274–75
  writing, 276–77
postponing e-mail messages
  deferring delivery, 99–101
  disabling Send Immediately feature, 119–21
  preventing immediate delivery, 119–21
  saving drafts, 98–99
  specifying delivery time, 100–101
  waiting to send, 98–101
previewing incoming messages, 49
previewing printing, 71–72
Preview pane, 9, 49
printing
  appointments, 227–30
  calendars, 227–30
  contact list, 185–87
  e-mail messages, 70–72
  previewing first, 71–72
  using Print button vs. Print command, 70
prioritizing e-mail messages, 58
privacy. *See also* security
  and e-mail, 10
  making appointments private, 207
  making contact entries private, 177
  making tasks private, 235
private appointments, 207
private tasks, 235
proxy servers, 298
public folders
  creating, 278–79
  glossary definition, 298
  posting messages, 276–77
  reading posts, 274–75


# Q


Quick Launch toolbar, 32


# R


reading
  e-mail messages, 47–50
  messages offline, 44–45
  posts in public folders, 274–75
receiving
  e-mail attachments, 73–74
  e-mail messages, 47–50
  meeting requests, 214
  task requests, 236–37
recurring items
  adding to Calendar, 208–9
  appointments, 208–9
  events, 208–9
  meetings, 208–9
  tasks, 235
Recycle Bin vs. Deleted Items folder, 248
redirection, e-mail, 4

reminders
  for appointments, 206
  for events, 206
  for meetings, 206
  setting, 241–42
  for tasks, 233
replying to e-mail messages
  finding related messages, 128–29
  formatting original message text in replies, 110–14
  formatting replies, 110–14
  limiting time spent, 66
  ways to use original message, 95
requests
  meeting, 211–14, 216
  task, 235–38
rescheduling appointments, 204
resending e-mail messages, 123–24
restoring Outlook data, 262–63
Rules Wizard
  creating rules based on existing messages, 152–56
  creating rules from scratch, 156–58
  creating rules that filter out junk mail, 163–66

## S

saving
  e-mail attachments, 74
  e-mail messages as drafts, 98–99
  e-mail messages as files, 64–65
  e-mail messages in Inbox, 62
  e-mail messages to Outlook folders, 63
scheduling meetings using Plan A Meeting feature, 215–16
searching
  for Calendar items, 198–201
  for contacts, 180–83
  for e-mail messages, 127–37
  for help information, 25–29
  for message templates, 149–50
security. *See also* privacy
  making appointments private, 207
  making contact entries private, 177
  making tasks private, 235
Select Names dialog box, 170, 171–72
Send All feature, 122
Send Error Report button, 117–18
sending e-mail
  addressing messages, 84–88
  composing messages, 88–117
  disabling Send Immediately feature, 119–21
  overview, 81–84
  postponing delivery, 99–101
  preventing immediate delivery, 119–21
  ways to deliver, 99, 100–101, 119–22
Send/Receive Groups dialog box
  configuring IMAP and Hotmail download information, 45–47
  creating groups, 38–39
  editing account settings, 42–43
  modifying schedules, 39, 41–42
Send/Receive Progress window, 34–35
Sent Items folder
  reviewing messages, 123–24
  viewing as history, 124–25
sent mail
  glossary definition, 298
  reviewing, 123–24
  viewing as history, 124–25
servers, 2, 7, 256–57. *See also* Exchange server
server-side storage, 273–74
sharing folder stores on networks, 258
shortcut menus, 299
shortcuts, 17, 299
signatures
  adding to e-mail messages, 107–9
  creating, 104–7
  for e-mail messages, 104–10
  glossary definition, 299
  inserting individually, 107–8
  keeping simple, 109–10
  setting default, 108–9
sizing handles, 299
sorting e-mail messages
  configuring Outlook for, 51–53
  for finding quickly, 129–31
spam, 158–67, 299. *See also* junk e-mail

Spam Killer, 167
special characters, 116
speed dialing, 188–91
Standard toolbar, 9, 181
starting Outlook, 5, 31–32
Startup folder, 32
Startup Wizard, 5–7
stationery, 97
status bar, 10, 35, 299
StuffIt, 103
suspicious e-mail attachments, 75–76
synchronizing folders, 282–83

## T

TaskPad, 196, 198
tasks
  accepting, 237–38
  adding to Tasks list, 231–32
  assigning to others, 235–36
  categorizing, 234
  creating, 231–32
  creating requests, 235–36
  declining, 237–38
  editing, 232–35
  folder views, 239–41
  glossary definition, 299
  making private, 235
  marking completed, 238, 239
  overview, 230
  receiving requests, 237–38
  recurring, 235
  setting reminders, 233
  start and end dates, 233
  and time-management, 195–96
  updating status, 238–39
telephone numbers, speed dialing, 188–91
templates
  adding to Outlook bar, 147–51
  creating for e-mail messages, 143–45
  for form result messages, 289
  glossary definition, 299
  as hidden files, 148–49
  searching for, 149–50
  using to compose e-mail messages, 146–47, 151
text. *See* plain text
time, managing. *See* Calendar; Tasks folder
to-do lists. *See* tasks
translating text, 116–17
troubleshooting Outlook, 266–69

## U

undeleting e-mail messages, 61–62
unhiding files, 148–49
unread messages, 53–54
unwanted e-mail messages, 88
updating task status, 238–39
URLs, 300

## V

vCards
  attaching to e-mail messages, 188
  glossary definition, 300
virtual business cards, 188
viruses
  defending against, 75–76
  and e-mail messages, 72, 74, 75–77
  spotting hoaxes, 76–77

## W

Web browsers, 300
Web pages
  glossary definition, 300
  for Outlook Help, 27–28
WinZip, 103
wizards
  Import And Export Wizard, 11–14
  Outlook Startup Wizard, 5–7
  Rules Wizard, 152–58
Word. *See* Microsoft Word

World Wide Web, using Microsoft Expedia maps, 183–84
writing
  e-mail messages, 50–51, 88–90
  post messages, 276–77

## Y

Yahoo!Mail, 3

## Z

ZIP files, 103

The manuscript for this book was prepared and submitted to Redmond Technology Press in electronic form. Text files were prepared using Microsoft Word 2000. Pages were composed using PageMaker 6.5 for Windows, with text in Frutiger and Caslon. Composed files were delivered to the printer as electronic prepress files.

*Project Editor*
Paula Thurman

*Layout*

Minh-Tam S. Le

*Indexer*

Julie Kawabata